"When it comes to spiritual teachers, there are those safe, gentle, consoling, soothing, caring; and there are the outlaws, the living terrors, the Rude Boys and Nasty Girls of God realization, the men and women who are in your face, disturbing you terrifying you, until you radically awaken to who and what you really are."

Ken Wilber

"If the book we are reading does not wake us as with a fist hammering on our skull, why then do we read it? A book should serve as an ice-axe to break the frozen sea within us."

Franz Kafka

Deep Recovery – Contemplative Spirituality for Daily Living in Recovery
with 25 Centuries of Wisdom Quotes, annotated by SHARABI

"*This remarkable book is a Ph.D. guidebook course in contemplative spirituality for people in recovery from alcoholism, drug abuse, or any obsessive/compulsive addiction. Drawing on the wisdom in quotations of mystics, poets, theologians, and philosophers from Lao-Tzu (6th century B.C.) to Maya Angelou (late 20th century,) the annotator-author, a recovering alcoholic, adds, "Recovery Reflections." These insightful interpretations relate each quote to A.A. or other spiritual principles useful in personal recovery.*

"*Over an 18-month period, I have read this book twice, often taking two or three pages at a time on my journey to explore spirituality. I visited God with Meister Eckhart, contemplated that God was dead with Nietzsche, came to understand that is was okay—even wise—to not have an understanding of a Higher Power, that the real secret of life—the meaning of recovery—is to be completely engaged in what you are doing, being fully alive and present and doing the next right thing with delight, accepting and loving myself as I am in the present moment, and accepting life as it is with Alan Watts and Thomas Merton, and that, with Emerson, the purpose of life is not to be happy, but to be of service to others which will result in joy.*

"*Sharabi teaches, along with Meister Eckhart and Plato, that a life of Deep Recovery involves a spiritual journey of continuing reflection—an examined life.*

"*This book is my daily companion and guide on this journey.*"

Harvey M.
July 11, 2021

DEEP
RECOVERY

CONTEMPLATIVE SPIRITUALITY
FOR DAILY LIVING IN RECOVERY

with 25 Centuries of Wisdom Quotes

Annotated by

SHARABI

Deep Recovery © 2022 Sharabi

Alpine Lake Publishing
Cleveland, OH.
www.AlpineLakePublishing.com

Library of Congress Control Number: 2018954750

Publishers Cataloging-In-Publication Data

Deep Recovery / Sharabi
    p. cm.
    ISBN 978-0-9816054-1-8

    1. Alcoholics anonymous—recovery 2. Alcoholism—Quotations, maxims, etc.
    3. Alcoholics—Rehabilitation. 4. Twelve step programs.
    5. Spirituality   I. Title

    HV5072.S53 2018
2011937332
    362.29286—dc21   0 412

Discounts on quantity orders available to organizations
involved in recovery, like A.A. Central Offices, bookstores,
A.A. clubs and treatment programs.
        Visit *www.AlpineLakePublishing.com*

A. A.® and Alcoholics Anonymous® are registered trademarks
of A.A. World Services, Inc.

CONTENTS

Dedicated to the memory of my sponsor

Frank Harnichar (1948 - 2020)

who showed me that whatever I thought of something,
there were always other ways to think of the same thing.

*"Buying books would be a good thing if I could also buy the
time to read them in; but as a rule, the purchase of books is
mistaken for the appropriation of their contents."*

Arthur Schopenhauer (1788 - 1860)

1) If you find you have put the book on the shelf and have
stopped using it, please consider giving it to someone else in
recovery who might use it and enjoy it.

2) If you appreciate this book and the work that went into it,
please share it (and the thoughts contained in it) with others.

3) If you obtained a free copy of this book, please consider making a contribution to the A.A. Central Office in your area, or to
some organization involved in recovery.

PREFACE

"It is necessary for the perfection of human society that there should be men who devote their lives to contemplation."

Thomas Aquinas (1224 - 1274)

The recovery Community is inspiring a large segment of today's society into exploring personal spiritual growth as a foundation of life. Although it can accommodate people who come in with their beliefs, this new spirituality is distinct from traditional religious paths. Each individual is free to define any stance towards God and walk on his or her own path. The arrival of Covid-19 into this world has resulted in online meetings burgeoning, and with it, injected a multiplicity of viewpoints and perspectives on spirituality. No longer is A.A. limited to a simple or "traditional-God" based recovery. The number of online meetings representing secular, agnostic, freethinking, and pagan approaches announces a true broadening of the 12-Step approach and is indicative that A.A. is truly "coming of age."

The fellowship contains people of all races and religious backgrounds, people from various professions and different classes, people with little formal education as well as people trained in many subjects and disciplines; in other words, people with varying ideas and convictions—about God and about not-God. Each is attempting to find a spiritual basis for life. Each is thirsty for a spiritual awakening. And they do this respectfully, without gouging out each other's eyes. This book, with its diverse ideas and multiple viewpoints, represents this broadening of perspectives on recovery and spirituality.

So what is spirituality? Spirituality in recovery transcends religion and specific belief systems. Yet, there is a sense of the profound, an awareness of something deep—perhaps even sacred—excitement about the journey, and a commitment to being honest, open, and willing in one's explorations. Sobriety and recovery literature provide a launching pad for spiritual pursuit, self-examination, contemplation, and discovery. Each person is striving to become deeper.

In order to make massive changes like the ones called for in recovery, it becomes necessary to access a sense of awe and reverence and connect with a deep humility. For some, contemplating the idea of God or a Higher Power provides access to awe and wonder. For others, it may be nature, or a sense of how sacred children are, a love of animals, a deep connection with family members, etc. It could also be amazement at consciousness itself and gratitude at this wonderful gift called "existence" or life. Gratitude can fuel this fire of change and transformation, as can connection with a sense of God, a commitment to goodness and love, amazement at the miracle of life—human, animal, or plant. It does not matter what, but this "sense of the deep" is needed to anchor recovery. It is insufficient just to decide to stop drinking because it would be equally easy, at some later point, to decide to drink again. There are no protections against the mind and the decisions it can make in the future. These changes necessary for sustained recovery are too profound and far-reaching to be carried out with mere "self-will" and determination, things that affect only a superficial level of being.

Here, the explorer is being offered a collection of spiritual sayings and writings of great voices from the past and present: sages, poets, writers, philosophers, and mystics spanning a multitude of time periods, countries, perspectives, tonalities, and styles. Some voices are deeply God-based—exoteric or esoteric—and others are skeptical of the notion of God. These quotes provide a rich fountain of ideas guaranteed to trigger insights, thoughts, and simply wonderment. These quotes and reflections are not presented as "truths" but merely as thoughts and phrases to stimulate your own contemplative state. This is meant to be a deeply personal book for you and can become as much your personal journal as something just to read, contemplate, and enjoy.

This book does not present a consistent set of beliefs or a coherent path towards spiritual growth and recovery. With a collection obtained from so many diverse sources from different time periods, there are many conflicting, confusing, and contradictory ideas included here—intentionally chaotic. Some ideas will appeal to you more than others, and you might find yourself violently disagreeing with some. No matter. Wouldn't it be limiting to contemplate only ideas you agreed with, to read only those things that supported your viewpoint? There would be no growth or change on that path. Fortunately, ideas do not need anyone's permission to exist; they wave proudly like a flag in the wind, unconcerned about who agrees and who disagrees. Each quote here expresses a deep truth, and none of them is "wrong" as truth is often paradoxical. Many wisdom traditions contain paradox and exult in a world beyond logic.

The collection points outwards and away in many directions providing a far broader base than "recovery literature" as it exists today. Any single thought or quote can breathe unexpected vitality into your own spiritual explorations and expand you as a person, changing the trajectory of your path in life.

Within are 26 individuals who are the source of these main quotes. Each has been chosen because he or she has a body of work that lends itself to interpretations supportive of the path of recovery as practiced today. Others could easily have been chosen, and I have no explanation of why your favorite author, poet, or sage has not been included. Perhaps you can compile a collection of your own favorite quotes and add them to this compilation. The idea, after all, is to broaden and enrich the wisdom base on which your own recovery is built.

I have tried to relate each quote to ideas useful in recovery: to connect it to sobriety and to the personal journey of the alcoholic and addict. These "Recovery Reflections" are annotations offered after the original quote, and you are—of course—free to ignore these additions. There are also a number of "secondary quotes" interspersed through the book, and a list of these sources has been provided on pages xii to xxii, along with a listing of the pages where they have been referenced. Each of these authors is a tremendous fountain of wisdom in his or her own right, and I would encourage you to check out any who appeal to you in some way. Humanity has a wonderful—almost inexhaustible—store of wise thoughts and profound ideas waiting to be discovered, contemplated, and enjoyed.

This collection takes spirituality beyond common cliches and religious injunctions into the wild and fiery realm of imagination and passion. Some tickle playfully with a feathery touch, while others startle with the electric thrill of a trumpet blast. Powerful insights and beautiful phrases offer an opening to self-acceptance, calm and peace, and a deeper spirituality. They can also disrupt complacency and the smugness of "knowing" or "believing." These quotes cover the relationship of self to the material world, self to others and to oneself, self to God or a Higher Power, and, finally, to a transcendence of self that seems to represent the ultimate freeing. Such ecstatic states have been alluded to in many spiritual traditions: as nirvana, enlightenment, emptiness, Tao, oneness or non-duality, as a state of divine ecstasy, or even as union with God. Whether your personal notion of spirituality includes the possibility of such "awakening" or not, you will still find plenty of rational insights, psychological depth, and beautiful sentiments to brighten your life. You can now seek uplifting in the world of spirit/spirituality—and not in bottled "spirits."

For those wishing to use this book for daily contemplation, a randomized list is printed on the very last page (on page 452) that will direct you to a specific reading for each day of the calendar year. Several blank pages are provided towards the end for you to jot down your own thoughts and insights and as pointers to your favorite pages. An index by item number starts on page 423, and an index by words is provided starting on page 440. These are alternate resources to help you navigate through this book.

This book is my service to the recovery community, and I have grown immensely while compiling it. My hope is that you, too, will enjoy this collection and benefit from it as much as I have.

Sharabi
Cleveland, OHIO.
January 2022

BIOGRAPHIES

ALAN WATTS (1915 - 1973): Born in England, Watts moved to the US in his twenties and pursued training in Zen. Although ordained as an Episcopalian priest, Watt's lifelong interest in Eastern philosophies and ability to explain their ideas in a cogent and lucid manner gained a large following in Berkeley and the San Francisco Bay area in the 1950s and 1960s.

CARL JUNG (1875 - 1961): A Swiss psychiatrist, Jung bridged western psychology and spirituality He had a profound influence on the thinking leading to the founding of A.A. He made place for the role of myth, imagination, and archetypes as having power to move and even dominate the human psyche. Jung valued people's internal experience of a spiritual nature as possessing reality, just as the scientist attributes reality to the outside world.

CICERO (106 B.C. - 46 B.C.): Cicero was one of Rome's most brilliant orators and writers; he was also a philosopher, scholar, lawyer, and politician, the last leading him to be killed by his enemies. He left behind a wealth of writings in Latin, leading one historian to proclaim, "the influence of Cicero upon the history of European literature and ideas greatly exceeds that of any other prose writer in any language."

EMERSON (1803 - 1882): A prolific writer, essayist, and lecturer, Emerson is considered by many to be the center of the transcendental movement in America, which espoused vigorous support for the freedom of the individual over the authority of organized religion. He was an important influence for other writers like Henry Thoreau and Walt Whitman.

EPICTETUS (55 -135 A.D.): Epictetus was born a slave in Turkey and later banished to Greece by the Romans. His stoic philosophy preached calm acceptance of whatever happens. He believed that philosophy should be lived, not merely discussed or expounded. His teachings have found widespread interest in people like the Roman Emperor Marcus Aurelius, to writers like James Joyce, and psychologists like Albert Ellis.

**Pages
257 - 270**

GURDJIEFF (1866 - 1949): Born in Armenia, Gurdjieff traveled extensively in Egypt and Asia and settled in Paris, where he ran "The Institute for the Harmonious Development of Man." He was an influential teacher of modern times who impacted philosophers, thinkers, mystics, artists, writers, and Hollywood celebrities. The story of his travels to achieve enlightenment and inner growth was captured in the movie, "Meetings with Remarkable Men" (1979.) Gurdjieff Societies and groups continue to meet and study his work.

**Pages
49 - 68**

KABIR (1440 - 1518): Kabir lived in India in the 14th-15th centuries. He was a poor, illiterate tailor but also a mystic, poet, and saint. His lyrical poetry straddles Hindu-Muslim-Sufi ideas and is written in vernacular (spoken) dialect. He probably is the most easily understandable of the Indian saints, and his poetry is studied extensively in Indian schools, as well as quoted in Bollywood movies and literary gatherings.

**Pages
362 - 375**

KIERKEGAARD (1813 - 1855): Soren Kierkegaard was one of the first of the existential philosophers. Danish by birth and nationality, he was deeply religious in many of his writings while also displaying a playful humor. A prolific author, he wrote for posterity. His writings were not acknowledged in his lifetime, and he died poor but satisfied, convinced about the importance of his work.

**Pages
83 - 92**

KÜBLER-ROSS. (1926 - 2004): Elisabeth Kübler-Ross was a Swiss-born American psychiatrist, famous for her ground-breaking book, "On Death and Dying," published in 1969. Some of Kubler-Ross's beliefs in spirits and the afterlife sullied her reputation among scientists, but her writings displayed a deep love for life and a wisdom that is perennial.

**Pages
93 - 111**

LAO-TZU (6th CENTURY B.C.): Lao-Tzu is traditionally regarded as the founder of Taoism. There is much debate about facts surrounding his life although his writings embodied in the Tao Te Ching have survived. Lao-Tzu often explained his ideas through paradox and analogy. His exposition of the Tao (the Way) continues to enthrall modern readers and seekers of wisdom.

Pages
271 - 282

MARTIN BUBER (1878 - 1965): Buber was born in Austria, and lived in Poland, Germany, and Israel. He grew up in an Orthodox Jewish family but pursued secular studies, getting interested in the existential philosophers and others. He actually rejected the label of philosopher, claiming he was not interested in ideas but in personal experience. He expressed his notions of relatedness in his famous essay: "I and Thou."

Pages
283 - 298

MAYA ANGELOU (1928 - 2014): Maya Angelou was an American author, poet, activist, feminist, philosopher, professional dancer, actor, and film producer. Her writing embodies a passion for living in a way that transcends race, gender, and class and is dense with earthy wisdom and deep insights.

Pages
22 - 48

MEISTER ECKHART (1268 - 1327): Eckhart, a mystic, theologian, and philosopher, lived in Germany and France in the 13th-14th century. His unusual approach to God, displayed in his sermons, aroused concern in Christian authorities, and he became the only medieval theologian tried as a heretic but died before the sentence was passed. Exonerated since, he is being studied extensively in modern times.

Pages
376 - 389

MERTON (1915 - 1968): Thomas Merton is considered an important 20th-century Catholic mystic; he was also a Trappist monk, writer, and social activist. He promoted interreligious understanding and acceptance and wrote books on Christianity, Buddhism, and Taoism; he was also interested in Hinduism, Jainism, and Sufism. He died in Thailand accidentally, through electrocution, while there to attend a conference.

Pages
171 - 185

MONTAIGNE (1533 - 1592): Montaigne was an influential writer in the French Renaissance movement. His Essays are widely read because they are relevant even today. He mixes deep philosophical discussions with interesting personal anecdotes in an engaging style that was new in those days but which ended up influencing a host of later writers.

**Pages
69 - 82**

NAGARJUNA (c 150 - 240 A.D.): Nagarjuna lived in south India in the 2nd-3rd century and is one of the earliest and greatest of the Buddhist philosophers. He put Mahayana Buddhism on a firm philosophical foundation, developing the concepts of emptiness and personal detachment. He is often depicted in composite form embodying human and naga (cobra) characteristics, the serpent signifying intelligence, knowledge, and transformation. He was also an early practitioner and scribe of Ayurvedic medicine.

**Pages
112 - 135**

NIETZSCHE (1844 - 1900): Friedrich Nietzsche lived in Germany in the 19th century and is considered one of the most creative, influential, and brilliant philosophers of modern times. A social critic as well as a critic of organized religion, dogma, and intellectual elitism, he claimed that man's inherent creativity and will to freedom would triumph. Some of his ideas were distorted and used to support Nazi ideology. His influence on modern psychology, philosophy, and theology is immense.

**Pages
136 - 156**

NISARGADATTA (1897 - 1981): Nisargadatta Maharaj was an Indian spiritual teacher and philosopher of Advaita (nondualism)—the central perspective embodied in the teachings of Adi Shankara, Ramana Maharshi, and other Hindu sages. He had little formal education and lived a simple life as a storekeeper, later entertaining visitors and disciples in his flat in Bombay (Mumbai) until his death in 1981. He expounded a simple, minimalist—but fiery—perspective on awareness and Being, encouraging contemplation of the nature of Self beyond illusion.

**Pages
299 - 322**

OSHO (1931 - 1990): Osho (Rajneesh) was a brilliant modern Indian mystic and spiritual teacher, well-educated and widely read, a former professor of philosophy at an Indian university. The behavior of his "followers" needs to be separated from the purity and depth of his discourses which have beeen recorded and published extensively. His message of creativity, disruptive freedom, and avoidance of belief systems has found an enthusiastic audience all over the world but was also unpopular with the "authorities."

PLATO (424 B.C. - 348 B.C.): Plato is one of the earliest and certainly, one of the most influential philosophers in Western history. His teacher was Socrates, and one of his most famous students was Aristotle. Together with Aristotle, Plato is one of the founders of logic, argument, science, and reasoning. His writings are still being studied in detail today.

RUMI (1207 - 1275): Jalal ad-Din Rumi, a 13th century Persian Sufi mystic, remains one of the world's most revered and popular poets even today. His writings have been translated into almost every language on the planet, and recordings of his poetry have made USA Billboard's Top 20 list. His works continue to be performed by Hollywood artists and quoted in spiritual sermons. Rumi said that no words could adequately explain the experience of mystical union, but his poetry eloquently points to that sacred experience of inner ecstasy and transcends all religious boundaries.

SIMONE WEIL (1909 - 1943): Simone Weil was born in France to agnostic parents, yet she became a Christian mystic and religious philosopher. Dogged in her ideology and committed to sparseness and asceticism in life, she harbored strong political, theological, and historical opinions. Her writings attracted a great deal of attention and discussion; even today, she is the subject of scholarly articles. Although she died at the young age of 34, she wrote copiously, and her fertile mind was capable of bursts of exotic brilliance, attracting from Albert Camus the description as "the only great spirit of our times."

TERTULLIAN (c 160 - 225 A.D.): Tertullian was an intellectual, mystic, and philosopher, a prolific writer who created the first body of Latin Christian literature. An advocate of discipline and austerity, Tertullian went to extremes in his recommendation of asceticism. The brilliance of his writings and the cogency of his thought have survived through the centuries—indeed through millennia.

VIRGINIA SATIR (1916 - 1988): Virginia Satir was an American author, social worker, and psychotherapist widely regarded as the creator of Family Therapy and systems thinking. Her writings unflinchingly honor the growth and blossoming of the individual and have inspired scores of therapists who have gone on to instruct and liberate legions of clients.

VOLTAIRE (1694 - 1779): Voltaire, pseudonym of François-Marie Arouet, was a French historian and philosopher, also a prolific poet, novelist, essayist, and playwright. He used satire to criticize intolerance and religious dogma and was famous for his wit, his tireless crusade against tyranny, bigotry, and cruelty, as well as his advocacy of freedom of religion and free speech.

WITTGENSTEIN (1889 - 1951): Ludwig Wittgenstein is considered one of the most important modern philosophers. Much of his work was concerned with logic and mathematics. He only published one book within his lifetime, claiming that he felt as though he were writing for people who would think in a different way and breathe a different air of life from that of present day men. He is even credited with inventing the emoji. ☺

SECONDARY QUOTES

There are short quotes embedded in the body of the book.
This list provides a brief description of the person behind the thought.

A. A. Milne (78a, 136a, 370a)
*(1882 - 1956) English author, poet, and playwright, most famous for
"Winnie the Pooh."*

Abraham Lincoln (40a, 150b)
*(1809 - 1865), 16th President of the United States, led the US through the
Civil War, assassinated April 15th.*

Abraham Maslow (129a, 247a)
*(1908 - 1970) American psychologist known for creating Maslow's
hierarchy of needs culminating in self-actualization.*

Albert Camus (102a, 102b, 283b, 298a, 334b, 373a, 396b)
(1913 - 1960) French philosopher, author, and journalist.

Albert Einstein (86b, 204b, 210a, 243a, 286b, 298b)
*(1879 - 1955) Celebrated physicist, German emigre to the United States,
famous for his shattering theories about time, space, and energy.*

Aldous Huxley (119b, 149a, 216a, 345a)
*(1894 - 1963) English writer, novelist, and philosopher, author of nearly 50
books, nominated several times for the Nobel Prize in literature.*

Alfred Korzybski (22b, 132a, 151a, 228b, 280b, 353b, 354b, 355b, 375b, 395a)
*(1879 - 1950) Polish-born American scholar, founder of the field of
"General Semantics" that studies language as a representation of reality.*

Alfred Lord Tennyson (8b, 9b, 10a, 85a, 105a, 119a, 141a, 223b, 354b, 355b)
*(1809 - 1892) Poet Laureate of Great Britain and Ireland during much of
Queen Victoria's reign.*

Alice Miller (226b)
*(1923- 2010) Swiss psychologist and psychoanalyst wrote to raise world
consciousness of child abuse passing off as "normal" child-rearing.*

Aesop (25b)
*(c 620 B.C. - 524 B.C.) Storyteller from ancient Greece credited with a
number of fables now collectively known as Aesop's Fables.*

Alexis de Tocqueville (116a, 330a, 410a)
*(1805 - 1859) French diplomat, political scientist, historian and writer, best
known for his work: Democracy in America.*

Anthony de Mello (4a, 47b, 143b, 173b, 187b, 259a)
*(1931 - 1997) Jesuit priest from India, psychotherapist, wrote popular books
on spirituality drawing from various traditions.*

Antoine de Saint-Exupéry (54a, 66b, 88b, 151b, 164b)
*(1900 - 1944) French writer, poet, aristocrat, journalist, and pioneering
aviator, author of "The Little Prince" and other books.*

Anton Chekhov (62a, 251b, 315a, 320a, 320b, 338b, 360a, 391a)
*(1860 - 1904) Russian playwright and short-story writer, considered to be
among the greatest writers of short fiction.*

Apollinaire (236b, 316a, 316b)
*(1880 - 1918) Polish-born French poet, important literary figure responsible
for coining the terms "cubism" and "surrealism."*

Aristotle (229b, 288b)
*(384 -322 B.C.) Ancient Greek philosopher and a student of Plato,
considered by many to be the father of logic, reasoning, and science.*

Arnold Glasow (115a, 205a, 218a, 295b, 298a, 394a, 401a)
*(1905 - 1998) American thinker, published a humor magazine that he
marketed to business firms nationally; often quoted in business journals.*

Arthur Schopenhauer (ii, 50b, 159b, 343a)
(1788 - 1860) German philosopher, became much more famous posthumously influencing various disciplines like literature, art, and science.

Baba Ram Dass (111b, 140b, 175a, 387b)
(1931 - 2019) American spiritual teacher and author of the seminal book "Be Here Now," published in 1971.

Barbara Johnson (20b, 65b, 79b, 237b,367b)
(1927 - 2007) American literary critic, philosopher and translator, Professor of English, Law and Psychiatry at Harvard University.

Benjamin Franklin (73b, 130b, 254a, 257a, 275a)
(1706 - 1790) Inventor, scientist, printer, politician, freemason and diplomat, one of the Founding Fathers of the United States.

Bertrand Russell (128a, 238a)
(1872 - 1970) British philosopher, mathematician, writer, anti-war activist and social critic, won the Noble Prize in Literature, 1950.

Bessel van der Kolk (64a, 252a, 340a)
(born 1943) Psychiatrist, research scientist and author, doing groundbreaking work in the area of healing from trauma. Books include: "The Body Keeps the Score: Brain, Mind, and Body in the Healing of Trauma."

Bhagavad Gita (100b, 190a)
(circa 500 - 200 B.C.) Hindu text, part of the epic Mahabharata, recounting a conversation between Arjuna and Lord Krishna on the battlefield, considered a sacred text of the Hindus.

Bible (31b, 241b, 393b)
The sacred text of the Jews and Christians. The King James version is an English translation written between 1604 and 1611.

Big Book (various)
(Written 1939 by Bill Wilson and others) The basic book of the Alcoholics Anonymous (A.A.) movement, outlining the Twelve Step program for recovery from alcoholism; later adopted for many addictions like narcotics, food, gambling, and sex.

Blaise Pascal (41b, 147b, 148b, 188a, 326b, 400a)
(1623 - 1662) French mathematician, physicist, religious philosopher and writer, regarded as the founder of the theory of probability.

Bob Dylan (195b, 340b, 406b)
(born 1941) American singer-songwriter, author, and artist who has been an influential figure in popular music and culture.

Bob Marley (29a, 61a 92a, 220a, 384a)
(1945 - 1981) Jamaican musician, songwriter, poet; pioneer of reggae.

Brené Brown (166b, 194b, 234a, 282a, 409b)
(born 1965) American professor, lecturer, author, who has spoken/written on the subjects of courage, vulnerability, shame, leadership, and empathy.

Brennan Manning (43b, 107a, 267b, 318b, 378b, 380b)
(1934 -2013) "Brennan" Manning was a Franciscan priest, author and Christian revolutionary preaching aginst "moralistic religiosity."

Brian Swimme (93a, 215b, 351b, 354a)
(born 1950) Mathematician, cosmologist, and writer, drawing together scientific discoveries in astronomy, geology, and biology, with humanistic insights on consciousness and the nature of the universe.

Buckaroo Banzai (408a)
A character in the 1984 movie, "The Adventures of Buckaroo Banzai."

C. S. Lewis (78b, 90b, 126b, 227b, 380a, 389b)
(1898 - 1963) British novelist, poet, and English lecturer at both Oxford and Cambridge Universities.

Calvin Coolidge (81b)
(1891 - 1933) 30th President of the United States of America.

Carl Rogers (349a)
(1902 - 1987) Humanist psychologist, advocated unconditional positive regard for the client.

Carlos Castenada (42b)
(1925 - 1998) Peruvian born American author and anthropologist, famous for a series of books on a Yaqui Indian "man of knowledge" named Don Juan.

Charles Baudelaire (138b, 268a, 288a, 392a)
(1821 - 1867) French poet, essayist and art critic, one of the first poets to make a radical break with the form of verse into prose poetry.

Charles Buchowski (53a, 63b, 213b, 346a, 363a, 390b, 408b)
(1920 - 1994) German-born American poet, author (and philosopher) who wrote about down-and-out people with a ruthless honesty.

Charlie Chaplin (29b, 34a, 163a, 189b)
(1889 - 1977) byname of Sir Charles Spencer Chaplin, British comedian, producer, writer, director, and composer, regarded as the greatest comic artist of movies.

Christopher Hitchens (135a, 142b, 261b, 273a)
(1949 - 2011) British-American journalist, author, essayist, and social critic known for his intellectual and fiery writings against religious beliefs.

Chuang Tzu (142a, 246b, 294a, 300b, 327a)
(370 - 287 B.C.) Chinese philosopher, also known as Zhuang Zhou, or Zhuangzi.

Confucius (77b, 102b, 120a, 254b)
(559 - 459 B.C.) Influential Chinese philosopher, teacher and political figure, prescribed norms for social interaction.

Course in Miracles (34b, 58a, 124a, 150a, 266b, 309a)
(1976) Book containing a curriculum for spiritual transformation., purportedly as a direct revelation from Jesus, popularized further in books by Marianne Williamson, Gerald Jampolsky and others.

Dale Carnegie (27b, 228a)
(1888 - 1955) American writer, lecturer and the developer of courses in self-improvement, effectiveness and interpersonal skills.

Denis Diderot (116a, 118b, 126a, 223a)
(1713 - 1786) French philosopher, art critic, and writer, attacked conventional morality, served as chief editor of the Encyclopédie, one of the principal works of the Age of Enlightenment.

Don Juan see Carlos Castenada.

Dostoevsky (12b, 21a, 74a. 135b, 154a, 158b)
(1821 - 1881) Russian novelist, short story writer, essayist, journalist, and philosopher.

Elbert Hubbard (26a, 32b, 52a, 57b, 117b, 166b, 191a, 308a, 310a, 377a)
(1856 - 1915) American writer, publisher, artist, and philosopher; "grandfather of marketing." Died on the Lusitania, sunk during WWII.

Eleanor Roosevelt (64b, 90a, 108a, 141b, 172a, 261b, 262a, 379b)
(1884 - 1962) American political figure, diplomat and activist, ranked in a Gallup pull among the 10 most admired people of the 20th century.Married to Franklin D. Roosevelt (FDR) 32nd President of the USA.

Elie Wiesel (318a, 385b)
(1928 - 2016) Romanian-born Holocaust survivor, American professor, Jewish writer, political activist, and winner of the Nobel Peace Prize.

Emile Chartier (174b. 269a, 328b, 372a)
(1868 - 1951) French philosopher and writer, teacher of many including Simone Weil, featured in this collection, and Simone de Beauvoir.

Emily Dickinson (11b, 42a, 110a, 297a, 339a)
(1830 - 1886) American poet, lived in Massachusetts in almost total isolation her whole life, wrote prolifically

Emma Goldman (125b, 182b, 272a, 326b, 327b)
(1869 - 1940) Lithuanian born American emigree, key figure in anarchist political philosophy in North America and Europe.

Erich Fromm (49a, 112a, 158a, 177b, 186a, 200a, 235a, 314a)
(1900 - 1980) German Jew who fled the Nazi regime and settled in the US; psychoanalyst, sociologist, and humanistic philosopher.

Ernest Hemingway (187a)
(1899 - 1961) American novelist, short story writer, and journalist, winner of the Nobel Prize in literature.

Eric Hoffer (114b, 130b, 159a, 194a, 200b, 278b, 323b, 377b)
(1898 - 1983) American immigrant, longshoreman, writer, social philosopher and professor.

Erwin Schrödinger (140a, 275b, 280a)
(1887 - 1961) Nobel prize winning Austrian physicist considered one of the philosophical founders of Quantum Mechanics.

Erving Polster (272b)
(born 1922) Gestalt Therapist teacher and writer, lives in San Diego

F. Scott Fitzgerald (14a, 144a, 261a, 268b, 382a)
(1896 - 1940) regarded as one of the greatest twentieth century writers, his works are seen as evocative of the Jazz Age, a term he coined.

Franz Kafka (9b, 155b, 241a, 384b)
(1883 - 1924) German novelist and writer/philosopher, considered a major literary figure and existentialist.

Fritz Perls (84b, 294a, 334a)
(1883 - 1970) German-born psychiatrist and psychotherapist, immigrated to the US; founded Gestalt Therapy with his wife, Laura Perls and others.

G. K. Chesterton (80b, 328a, 401a)
(1874 - 1936) English poet, writer, philosopher, and literary critic, considered by some to be the best writer of the 20th century.

Gabor Maté (92b, 121a, 250a, 354a, 361a, 409b)
(born 1944) Hungarian born Candian physician, has worked with and written about addicts with a great deal of compassion and understanding.

Gabriel García Márquez (201b, 281b)
(1927 - 2014) Nobel Prize (Literature) -winning novelist, short story writer, and journalist from Columbia.

Gaudapada (209b, 305b)
(6th century) Indian Guru, philosopher, and teacher of Vedantic Hinduism, and a major influence on future generations.

George Bernard Shaw (121b, 200b, 215a, 258b, 327a, 343b, 356a, 366b)
(1856 - 1950) Irish playwright, critic, political activist and a great wit.

Gerald May (350b)
(1940 - 2005) American theologian, psychiatrist, and writer; senior fellow at the Shalem Institute for Spiritual Formation in Bethesda, Maryland.

Giordano Bruno (55a, 181b)
(1548 - 1600) Italian Dominican friar, philosopher, mathematician, poet, early cosmologist and freethinker, burnt at the stake by the Church.

Goethe *(76b, 93a, 189a, 279b, 283a, 307a)*
(1749 - 1832) German writer, poet, dramatist, literary critic and statesman.

H. L. Mencken *(123a, 130b, 197a, 218b, 250b, 402b)*
(1880 - 1956) American journalist, essayist, satirist, cultural critic and scholar, outspoken opponent of organized religion and populism.

Hazrat Inayat Khan *(xxiv, 6a, 31b, 58b, 67a, 72b, 119b, 139a, 139b, 166a)*
(1882 - 1927) Musician and mystic, born in India, moved to London and founded the Sufi Order of the West.

Hegel *(401b)*
(1770 - 1831) Georg Hegel, German philosopher, and idealist, influenced Karl Marx, Nietzsche, and others.

Heinrich Zimmer *(131a, 271a, 351a)*
(1890 - 1943) German-born scholar of Sanskrit and Indian mythology, friend of Jung and Joseph Campbell who edited and published his works.

Henry Miller *(24b, 75a, 77a, 85b, 122a, 158a, 148a, 221a, 271a)*
(1891 - 1980) American writer, lived in Paris, created a new genre of fictionalized autobiography; books were banned in the US until the 1960s.

Heraclitus *(117b, 215b, 393b, 399b)*
(circa 500 B.C.) Heraclitus of Ephesus was a pre-Socratic Greek philosopher, went beyond physical theory into metaphysical foundations.

Hermann Hesse *(1b, 103a, 155a, 176b, 177a, 267a, 283a, 286b, 293b, 296b)*
(1877 - 1962) German-Swiss novelist and poet, awarded Nobel Prize for Literature in 1946.

Heschel *(35b, 39a, 39b, 132b, 368a)*
(1907 - 1972) Abraham Joshua Heschel, Polish-born American rabbi, leading Jewish theologian and philosopher of the 20th century.

Hildegard of Bingen *(23b)*
(1098 - 1179) Benedictine abbess, writer, composer, philosopher, Christian mystic, visionary, founded the scientific study of natural organisms.

Honore de Balzac *(86a, 235b)*
(1799 - 1850) French novelist and playwright, a keen observer of life and society in post-Napoleonic Paris.

Imanuel Kant *(6b, 53b, 91b, 93b, 198b)*
(1724 - 1804) Prussian German philosopher, considered by many to be the central figure in modern philosophy.

James Hillman *(97a, 217a, 256b, 257b)*
(1926 - 2011) American psychologist, Jungian Analyst, writer, and lecturer, re-visioned psychology, stressing archetypal forces in the psyche.

James Hollis *(290b, 329b, 335a)*
(born 1940) Psycholigist, Jungian analyst, author, and lecturer.

Jane Austen *(168a)*
(1775 - 1817) English novelist, author of six major novels.

Jean-Paul Sartre *(79b, 103a, 178b, 185a, 265a, 315b)*
(1905 - 1980) French philosopher, writer, literary critic, one of the key ˙ figures in existentialism, phenomenology, and Marxism.

John Keats *(20a, 59b, 61b, 186b, 246a)*
(1795 - 1821) English Romantic poet, struck down early by tuberculosis.

John of the Cross *(14b, 319a)*
(1542 - 1591) Spanish mystic, writer, friend of Terese of Avila and major figure in the Counter-Reformation; canonized as a Saint in 1726.

John Milton *(88b, 95a, 105b, 143a, 199b, 364b)*
(1608 - 1674) English poet, best known for his epic poem "Paradise Lost," revered by many later poets.

John Ruskin *(75b, 91a, 98b, 145a)*
(1819 - 1900) Gifted painter, art critic and essayist of the Victorian era.

John Wooden *(21b, 76a, 333a, 404b)*
(1910 - 2010) Revered basketball player and coach, known his for short and simple inspirational messages covering sports and also all of life.

Jonathan Swift *(160b, 184b, 287a, 298b, 326a)*
(1667 - 1745) Anglo-Irish essayist, politcal commentator and one of the English language's foremost satirists.

Jorge Luis Borges *(264a, 295b)*
(1899 - 1986) Argentinian writer, essayist, poet, considered to be the creator of a genre called "magical realism."

Jose Ortega y Gasset *(70b, 98a, 331a, 379a, 386a)*
(1883 - 1955) Spanish philosopher, university teacher, and essayist; moved from Spain to Argentina, then back to Portugal and Spain.

Joseph Campbell *(26b, 60b, 94b, 242a, 242b, 245a, 255b)*
(1904 - 1987) American lecturer, writer, best known for his studies of mythology and comparative religion.

Juan Gabriel Vásquez *(101b)*
(born 1973) Columbian writer, essayist and newspaper columnist.

Kahlil Gibran *(7a, 123b, 192b, 203b, 206b, 246a, 13a, 332a, 332b)*
(1883 - 1931) Lebanese born writer, philosopher, and poet, emigrated to the US, most famous for his 1923 book, "The Prophet."

Kalidasa *(168b, 304b)*
(5th century) Indian philosopher, dramatist, and poet, considered the greatest writer in the Sanskrit language.

Ken Wilber *(Front page, 144b, 216b, 263b)*
(born 1949) American writer and philosopher, created Integral Theory, synthesizing a transpersonal theory of human consciousness.

Kris Kristofferson *(38a, 273a, 324b, 336a)*
(born 1936) American singer, songwriter and actor.

Krishnamurti *(1b, 24b, 94a, 107b, 167b, 229b, 233a, 324a, 381a)*
(1895 - 1986) Indian-born philosopher, writer, and teacher, chosen by the Theosophical Society as a new World Teacher, he later rejected that role.

Lal Ded/Lalleshwari *(3b, 17a, 17b, 66a, 306a, 400b)*
(1320 - 1392) Lal Ded (Lalleshwari): sufi poet and mystic from Kashmir. She was the creator of a style of ecstatic musings called "Vakh."

Leo Tolstoy *(36a, 57a)*
(1828 - 1910) Russian novelist and philosopher, with pioneering social, philosophical and religious views.

Leonard Jacobson *(45b)*
(born 1944) Spiritual teacher, retreat leader, and writer, founder of the Conscious Living Foundation teaching awakening through Presence.

Leonardo da Vinci *(111a, 113a, 124a, 180a, 211a)*
(1452 - 1519) A symbol of renaissance, Leonardo da Vinci left a significant legacy not only in the realm of art but in science as well.

Mahatma Gandhi *(185b, 211b, 221b, 222b, 337b, 408a)*
(1869 - 1948) A leader of the Indian Independence movement and preacher of non-violent resistance, assassinated in 1948.

Marcel Proust *(71b, 137b, 161b, 207a, 225a, 243b)*
(1871 - 1922) French writer most famous for his monumental work: "Remembrance of Things Past," later issued as "In Search of Lost Time."

Marcus Aurelius *(76b, 87a, 97b, 130b, 136b, 140b, 162a, 169b, 192a, 208b, 231a, 360b, 381b, 383b, 403b)*
(121 - 180 A.D.) Emperor of Rome, stoic philosopher. His book "Meditations" has "exquisite accent and infinite tenderness."

Margaret Fuller (118a, 314b, 347b, 392b)
(1810 - 1850) American journalist, editor, literary critic and advocate for women's rights and women's education.

Marianne Williamson (285a)
(born 1952) American spiritual teacher, author, and lecturer, Presidential candidate, 2019.

Mark Twain (287b, 329a, 339b)
(1835 - 1910) Pen name of American writer, humorist, essayist, authored Adventures of Tom Sawyer and Adventures of Huckleberry Finn.

Martin Luther King, Jr. (205b, 231b, 382b)
(1929 - 1968) American Baptist minister and civil rights activist, awarded Nobel Peace Prize in 1964, assassinated in 1968.

Mary Oliver (198b, 336b, 365b, 370b)
(1935 - 2019) Best-selling American poet, winner of Pulitzer Prize and National Book Award.

Mary Shelley (127b, 281a, 310b)
(1797 - 1851) English novelist, short story writer, dramatist and essayist, wrote "Frankenstein," purportedly on a dare from her husband, the poet Percy Bysshe Shelley, and Lord Byron.

Maurice Merleau-Ponty (128b, 147b, 157b, 408b)
(1908 - 1961) French philospher, Head of Philosophy at the Sorbonne, existentialist, wrote about phenomenology and the nature of perception.

Max Muller (1a, 149b, 225b, 345b, 406a)
(1823 - 1900) German-born professor at Oxford, studied religions, Sanskrit, became the leading western intellectual commentator on and admirer of the culture of India; translated the Upanishads.

May Sarton (36b, 195a, 219a, 369b)
(1912 - 1995) Belgian-born American poet, and novelist, famous as a writer of revealing and sensitive memoirs and journals.

Michel Focault (63a, 96a, 178b)
(1924 - 1986) French historian, philosopher and social commentator.

Mihaly Csikszentmihalyi (115b, 145b, 150b, 351b, 356b, 362a)
(born 1934) Hungarian-American psychologist. recognised and named the concept of "flow," a highly focused mental state conducive to productivity.

Mirabai (13b, 19a)
(1498 - 1546) a Hindu mystic poet from Rajasthan, India, and devotee of Krishna. Many legends and myths are associated with her, and she has been the subject of folk tales and movies.

Mother Teresa (74b, 356b)
(1910 - 1997) Mother Teresa, known in the Catholic Church as Saint Teresa of Calcutta, was an Albanian-Indian Roman Catholic nun and missionary doing charity work with the poor in the streets of Calcutta.

Nachman (48b, 51b, 162b, 376b)
(1772 - 1810) founder of the Breslov Hasidic movement gained prominence translating the esoteric teachings of the Kabbalah into practical advice.

Nelson Mandela (211a)
(1918 - 2013) South African anti-apartheid revolutionary, political leader, and philanthropist. first black President of South Africa.

Neil deGrasse Tyson (201b, 209a, 259a, 285b)
(born 1958) American astrophysicist, author, and science communicator.

Oscar Wilde (95b, 239a, 289b, 357a)
(1854 - 1900) Irish poet, playwright, and wit, wrote many social comedies and a famous novel, "The Picture of Dorian Gray."

Ovid *(79a, 375a)*
(43 B.C. - 17A.D.) Roman poet who lived during the reign of Augustus, considered one of the three canonical poets of Latin literature.

Pablo Picasso *(68b, 109b, 121b, 162b, 193b, 381a)*
(1881 - 1973) Universally renowned as one of the most influential and celebrated artists of the twentieth century.

Parmahansa Yogananda *(41b, 108b, 154b, 213a, 232a)*
(1893 - 1952) Indian monk, yogi and guru who lived in the US in later life and introduced millions to meditation and yoga through his book "Autobiography of a Yogi."

Paul Tillich *(226a, 249b, 315b)*
(1886 - 1965) German-born American writer-philosopher, considered by many to be the most influential Christian theologian of the 20th century.

Pema Chödrön *(32b, 115a, 123b, 183a, 197a, 269b, 302b, 387b)*
(born 1936) American Tibetan Buddhist teacher and author.

Peter Drucker *(7b, 169b, 189b, 215a, 257b, 290a, 295b, 308b, 339a, 370a)*
(1909 - 2005) Austrian-born American management philosopher, educator, and author.

Pierre Teilhard de Chardin *(112b, 202b, 293a, 296a, 322b, 388a)*
(1881 - 1955) French idealist philosopher and Jesuit priest who trained as a paleontologist and geologist.

Quentin Crisp *(34b, 160a, 256a)*
(1908 - 1999) English writer, humorist and actor., identified as a gay man for most of his life; just before his death, wrote that he was transgender.

R. D. Laing *(84a, 174a, 306b, 402b)*
(1927 - 1989) Scottish psychiatrist and humanitarian noted for his pioneering approach to the treatment of schizophrenia.

Rabindranath Tagore *(28a, 32a, 96b, 154a, 219b, 312b, 346b)*
(1861 - 1941) Bengali (Indian) lyrical poet and song-writer, first non-European to be awarded the Nobel Prize in Literature.

Ramana Maharshi *(22a, 40b, 295a, 348b, 374b)*
(1879 - 1950) Hindu sage, teacher of inquiry into the nature of Self, the foremost modern proponent of Advaita philosophy (non-duality.) In Sanskrit, "Maha" = "Great"; "Rshi" = enlightened person, a sage;

Ramayana *(156a)*
Ancient Indian epic poem, attributed to the sage Valmiki and probably written around 300 B.C.

Rainer Maria Rilke *(4b, 30a, 114b, 171b, 274b, 300a, 352b, 387a)*
(1875 - 1926) One of the most lyrical of modern German-language poets, even regarded as a mystic by his large set of followers and admirers.

Richard Bach *(55b, 114a, 157a, 270a, 292b, 366b, 388b)*
(born 1936) American author of 1970's best-sellers, "Jonathan Livingston Seagull" and "Illusions: Adventures of a Reluctant Messiah.

Richard Bandler *(6a, 103b, 192b, 229a, 254b))*
(born 1950) American author and trainer, co-founder of NLP (Neuro-Linguistic Programming.)

Richard Dawkins *(110a, 117a, 164a, 325a)*
(born 1941) English scientist and author, famous for his popular science books on biology and evolution.

Richard Rohr *(5a, 18a, 155b, 230a, 348a)*
(born 1943) Franciscan friar ordained to the priesthood in the Roman Catholic Church, author, spiritual writer, voice for modernization.

Robert Bly *(8a, 204a, 208b)*
(1926) - 2021) American poet, essayist, and developer of a modern male movement involving myth, poetry, and rituals.

Robert Frost *(2a, 80a, 179b, 180a, 227a, 305b)*
(1874 - 1963) American poet, received four Pulitzer Prizes and the Congressional Gold Medal for poetry.

Robert Louis Stevenson *(25b, 109b, 164b, 173b, 205b, 248b, 341b, 410a)*
(1850 - 1894) Scottish novelist, poet and travel writer.

Robert M. Pirsig *(52b, 157b, 184a)*
(1928 - 2017) An American philosopher and writer, author of "Zen and the Art of Motorcycle Maintenance:" and other novels.

Rollo May *(83b, 99a, 182b, 222a)*
(1909 - 1994) American writer, philosopher, and existential psychologist.

Rudolf Steiner *(12a, 38a, 212a, 232a)*
(1861 - 1925) Austrian philosopher and social reformer, founder of an esoteric spiritual movement: anthroposophy.

Sadhguru *(4a, 156b, 277a, 287b, 301a, 308b, 333b, 370a)*
(born 1957) Modern Indian yogi, guru and mystic; environmentalist and social reformer through a foundation of volunteers.

Saint Augustine *(27a, 37b, 38b, 205a, 404a)*
(354 - 430 A.D.) Roman African, early Christian theologian/philosopher, influenced Western Christianity and Western philosophy.

Saint Francis of Assisi *(xxiv, 70a, 165b, 178a, 252b, 274a)*
(1181 - 1226) Italian Catholic friar, deacon and preacher, founder of the Franciscan Order, patron saint of animals and the natural environment.

Samuel Johnson *(46a, 175b, 210a, 256a, 265b)*
(1709 - 1784) English writer, poet, essayist, moralist, literary critic, biographer, editor and lexicographer.

Sappho *(50b, 214b, 253b)*
(620 B.C. - 550 B.C.) Lyric Greek poet and songstress, she lived on the island of Lesbos and is a symbol of love and desire between women.

Seneca *(183b)*
(4 B.C. to 65A.D.) Roman philosopher, statesman, dramatist, prominent member of the Stoic school which includes Epictetus.

Shakespeare *(106a, 160a, 383a, 391b)*
(1564 - 1616) English playwright, poet and actor, known as the Bard of Avon, considered to be the greatest writer in the English language.

Sigmund Freud *(179b, 199a, 208a, 224a, 276b, 376b)*
(1856 - 1939) Austrian neurologist, founder of psychanalysis, proposed a radically new conceptual and therapeutic basis for human psychology.

Simone de Beauvoir *(14a, 198a, 323b, 324b)*
(1908 - 1986) French writer, philosopher, Her 1949 book, "The Second Sex" laid the foundation of the modern feminist movement.

Sitting Bull *(125a)*
(1831 - 1890) Native American of Lakota tribe, leader, and wise man; led his people in resistance against the United States government after many failed treaties, killed by government agent during his arrest.

Socrates *(104a, 287a)*
(470 - 399 B.C.) Classical Greek philosopher considered one of the fathers of Western philosophy, made famous through the writings of his pupils, one of whom was Plato.

Somerset Maugham *(9a, 358b)*
(1874 -1965) British novelist, playwright, and short-story writer. Many of his novels have been made into successful movies.

Sonia Nevis *(244a)*
(1927 - 2017) Psychotherapist and educator, trained in Gestalt Psychology, helped found two training centers in Cleveland, OH, and Wellfleet, MA.

Sophocles (55b, 202a, 291a, 291a)
(496 B.C.- 406 B.C.) Celebrated writer of tragedy plays in ancient Greece; also a philosopher. Only seven of his 123 plays have survived after a mob reportedly burned down the library at Alexandria in 48 B.C.

Spinoza (248b, 365a)
(1632 - 1677) called the "prince" of modern philosophy, lived a simple life, turning down honors and rewards, and gained the ire of both Jewish and Christian religious establishments.

Sri Chinmoy (337a, 317b)
(1931 - 2007) Indian spiritual teacher who moved to New York and set up a number of meditation centers. Many famous musicians were among his followers.

Sri Ramakrishna (5a, 25a, 46a, 49b, 233b, 237a)
(1836 - 1886) Indian mystic, sage, and teacher, promoted harmony between religions of Hinduism, Islam, and Christianity

Stephan Hoeller (8b, 18a, 27b, 63b, 243b, 350b)
(born 1931) Hungarian born author, scholar of Gnosticism and esoteric traditions, and Jungian psychology; speaker for the Theosophical Society in America.

Stephen Hawking (134b, 180b)
(1942 - 2018) English physicist, cosmologist, and author, suffered from a rare neurological disorder that progressively paralyzed him over the decades.

Sun Tzu (104b)
(544 - 496 B.C.) Chinese General and philosopher, wrote "The Art of War" which is still being read today and has influenced military strategy and both Eastern and Western philosophy.

Swami Vivekananda (58b, 310b)
(1863 - 1902) Hindu monk, orator, and disciple of Sri Ramakrishna, a key figure in introducing Yoga and Vedantic Hinduism to America and the Western world through lectures in the US.

T. S. Eliot (263a, 301b)
(1888 - 1965) British poet, essayist, playwright; moved to the US, later renounced US citizenship. Nobel Prize winner in Literature, 1948.

Teresa of Avila (167a, 196b, 299b)
(1515 - 1582) Spanish mystic, Carmelite nun, tender of the sick and writer, canonized as a Saint in 1622.

Theodore (Teddy) Roosevelt (15b, 89a, 109b, 299a, 344a)
(1858 - 1919) 26th President of the United States.

Thich Nhat Hanh (129b, 296b, 347a)
(born 1926) Vietnamese Buddhist monk, currently living in France, writer/ educator providing retreats and seminars on Buddhist principles.

Thomas Aquinas (iii, 15a, 72a, 106b, 110c, 147b, 161a, 191b, 196b, 209b, 264b)
(1224 - 1274) Italian Dominican friar, Catholic priest, and Doctor of the Church; an immensely influential philosopher and theologian.

Thomas Paine (31a, 253a)
(1737 - 1809) English-born American activist, philosopher, and reformer, one of the Founding Fathers of the United States.

Thoreau (37a, 81a, 113b, 114a, 183b, 193a, 238b, 293b, 389a)
(1817 - 1862) American writer, philosopher, naturalist, tax resister, abolitionist and historian; student and friend of Emerson.

Tilopa (152b)
(988 - 1069) Indian spiritual master, considered the originator of the lineage that led to Tibetan Buddhism.

Toni Morrison (3a, 20a, 89b, 322a, 368b, 369b)
   (1931-2019) American novelist, essayist, and teacher, winner of the Nobel Prize in Literature in 1993.

Upanishads (45a, 137a, 207b)
   Ancient Hindu texts, probably dating back to 6th century B.C. or earlier.

Viktor Frankl (108b, 240b, 244b, 314a)
   (1905 - 1997) Austrian neurologist, psychiatrist and existentialist; Holocaust survivor and author of "In Search of Meaning."

Virginia Woolf (16a, 45a, 201a, 217a, 276a, 292a, 306b, 371b)
   (1882 - 1941) Important modernist 20th century English writer, a pioneer in the use of stream of consciousness.

W. H. Auden (5b, 41b, 82a, 133b, 206a, 224b, 297b, 330b, 349b)
   (1907 - 1973) English-American poet noted for his engagement with politics, morals, love, and religion.

Wallace Stevens (15b, 364b, 397a, 399a)
   (1879 - 1955) Modern American poet, eminent abstractionist and a provocative thinker.

Walt Whitman (65a, 158b, 172b, 367b)
   (1819 - 1892) American poet, essayist, and journalist, often called the father of free verse, most famous for Leaves of Grass."

Wayne Dyer (124b, 146a, 170b, 203a, 329b, 335a)
   (1940 - 2015) American self-help and spiritual author, and motivational speaker. His book "Your Erroneous Zones" sold over 100 million copies.

Werner Erhard (59b, 65b, 94a, 103b, 136b, 248a, 373b)
   (born 1935) American author, lecturer, and teacher, most famous for founding EST training, a seminar for personal transformation.

Werner Heisenberg (35a, 222b, 353a, 355a, 380a, 382b)
   (1901-1976) German physicist and philosopher, key pioneer of quantum mechanics and the notion that nature and "reality" are "unknowable."

Will Durant (288b, 405b)
   (1885 - 1991) American historian, writer, philosopher and teacher, author of "The Story of Philosophy,: and co-author of "The Story of Civilization.'

William Blake (19b, 45b, 153a, 304a)
   (1757 - 1827) English poet and painter received much recognition and praise only after his death.

William Carlos Williams (47a, 234b)
   (1883 - 1963) American poet, also a practicing physician.

William James (133a, 190b, 219b, 232b, 288a)
   (1842 - 1910) American physician, philosopher, and psychologist, wrote "Varieties of Religious Experience." He was the first educator to create and teach a psychology course in the United States.

William Paley (212b, 358b)
   (1743 - 1805) English clergyman and philosopher. His comment on "contempt prior to investigation," has been incorrectly attributed to Herbert Spencer.

Winston Churchill (2b, 127a, 176a, 333b, 385a, 403a)
   (1874 - 1965) British statesman, philosopher and writer, served as Prime Minister during the Second World War.

Yogi Berra (73a, 179a, 321b, 361b, 362b, 372b)
   (1925 - 2015) American baseball catcher, manager and coach. Known for his pithy and odd sayings which came to be called "Yogi-isms."

Zig Ziglar (2a, 184a, 219a, 279b, 329a, 340b)
   (1926 - 2012) American author, salesman, and motivational speaker.

How to use this book.

You can read the original quote only, not bothering with the annotation: "Reflection for Deep Recovery." The book can be used this way by all, not just by recovering alcoholics and addicts. Or you can read and contemplate both. Don't agree or disagree; just sit with it and let it simmer. Peel the thought, so its texture opens up for you; let it carry you into uncharted territory, transport you into a contemplative space.

(1) You can open the book to a random page and engage with the thought or quote that has opened up to you.

(2) You can use this book for daily contemplation. A table at the very end (page 452) directs you to a specific page for each day of the year. There are morning and evening quotes (a and b) but if you wish for only one quote each day, use the upper quote for the first year and the lower quote for the second year. Then, you can make this book last two years. But by then you will have forgotten the first quote, and so, perhaps, you can go on repeating the process.

(3) Not all the quotes are listed in the quote-by-calendar-day table, but a list is provided of quotes that are not accessible this way. You can explore them as additional items when the daily selection seems insufficient or when you are looking for more inspiration.

(4) You can also choose one particular section and read the quotes sequentially, together as a body to get a sense of the thinking and writing of that particular sage, poet, philosopher or mystic. We must be grateful to those translators who have studied and rendered non-English writings into English. Consider purchasing and studying the original writings when a particular set of quotes calls to you.

(5) You can examine the detailed table of contents starting on page 426 and go to the idea that catches your attention.

(6) You can search by keyword for a quote or quotes relating to a specific topic by going to page 441 and consulting that index.

I have not carried out detailed research to settle the matter of origin and correctness of each quote. I am more interested in the idea itself than in its origin. Also, I apologize if I have not included your favorite author/guru/guide in this collection. There is a surfeit of richness available when it comes to contemplative spirituality, profundity, wisdom, and beauty. My wish is only to enlarge the spirituality of recovery to include sources beyond traditional A.A. literature.

A final note: I use the pronoun "we" in many of the annotations, but it must not be mistaken for the author trying to speak for all the people in recovery. At best, it reflects a viewpoint possibly shared by some. Reject any ideas you cannot use... and move on!

Enjoy!

"I asked for strength,
and God gave me difficulties to make me strong.
I asked for wisdom,
and God gave me problems to learn to solve.
I asked for prosperity,
and God gave me a brain and brawn to work.
I asked for courage,
and God gave me dangers to overcome.
I asked for love,
and God gave me people to help.
I asked for favors,
and God gave me opportunities.

I received nothing I wanted.
I received everything I needed."

Hazrat Inayat Khan

"Lord, make me an instrument of your peace:
where there is hatred, let me sow love;
where there is injury, pardon;
where there is doubt, faith;
where there is despair, hope;
where there is darkness, light;
where there is sadness, joy.

O divine Master, grant that I may not so much seek
to be consoled as to console,
to be understood as to understand,
to be loved as to love.
For it is in giving that we receive,
it is in pardoning that we are pardoned,
and it is in dying that we are born to eternal life."

St. Francis of Assisi

Rumi
1207 - 1273

a) Quote for Morning Contemplation

"Christian, Jew, Muslim, Shaman, Zoroastrian,
Stone, ground, mountain, river,
Each has a secret way of being with the mystery,
Unique and not to be judged." (Rumi)

Reflection for Deep Recovery (Sharabi)

We each seek the Divine in our own way. The "God of my understanding" is unique to me and not to be judged by you, or by your God, or by your understanding of God—or by any "authority." This is why recovery is a form of free spiritual anarchy and not an organized religion. Here, I am responsible for my relationship with God; I cannot abrogate that responsibility to the theologians and religious "leaders," or even to my sponsor.

"The person who knows only one religion does not know any religion."

Max Muller (1823 - 1900)

---

b) Quote for Evening Contemplation

"Set your life on fire.
Seek those who fan your flames." (Rumi)

Reflection for Deep Recovery (Sharabi)

I must leave no stone unturned; I must surrender fully. I cannot just wander around the periphery of recovery, being a "spectator" at meetings and muttering meek "hello"s to people who greet me, hoping no one asks me to do anything. I must not just dip my toe in the water; I need to jump in and give myself completely to this program. I will seek a sponsor or a spiritual guide who will set my heart aflame, and I will hang around people who will fan the flames and ignite a transformation in me.

"The bourgeois prefers comfort to pleasure, convenience to liberty, and a pleasant temperature to the deathly inner-consuming fire."

Hermann Hesse (1877 - 1962)

"You must understand the whole of life, not just one little part of it. That is why you must read, that is why you must look at the skies, that is why you must sing and dance, and write poems and suffer and understand, for all that is life."

Krishnamurti (1895 - 1986)

Rumi
1207 - 1273

a) Quote for Morning Contemplation

"Come, come, whoever you are. Wanderer, worshiper, lover of leaving. It doesn't matter. Ours is not a caravan of despair. Come, even if you have broken your vows a thousand times. Come, yet again, come... come..." (Rumi)

Reflection for Deep Recovery (Sharabi)

Come, we tell you, come even if you have fallen off the wagon a thousand times. Don't stay away from shame; you're always welcome here. Your intelligence and willpower are not going to conquer this. But we have a way, a solution. Come, this is home.

"You don't drown by falling into water. You only drown if you stay there."
Zig Ziglar (1926 - 2012)

"Home is the place where, when you have to go there, they have to take you in."
Robert Frost (1874 - 1963)

---

b) Quote for Evening Contemplation

"Sit, be still, and listen,
  Because you're drunk,
  And we're at the edge of the roof." (Rumi)

Reflection for Deep Recovery (Sharabi)

You may not get another chance. You are drunk, and we are at the very edge. "Sit still," we say, "and listen. Don't move, don't make it worse. Just listen to what we are saying here, for it can make the difference between life and death." Beginning to question this path of sobriety—even if you are not drinking right now—means you are on the edge of the roof. It is the beginning of relapse. Relapse does not start with the taking of a drink; it ends with the taking of a drink. Relapse does not happen suddenly; it is a process. When you notice the process beginning: that is when you must listen to the voices of sanity you hear in these rooms.

"Courage is what it takes to stand up and speak. Courage is also what it takes to sit down and listen."
Winston Churchill (1874 - 1965)

Rumi
1207 - 1273

a) Quote for Morning Contemplation

**"I have lived on the lip
of insanity, wanting to know reasons,
knocking on a door. It opens.
I've been knocking from the inside." (Rumi)**

Reflection for Deep Recovery (Sharabi)

I kept looking for explanations and reasons, wondering "why?"
I have lived hard, trying to push against my misery, my despair,
and my rage at the unfairness of life. Now I can see that the chaos
and insanity of my life arose out of my disease. If I can accept that
and surrender to it, I can let it enter and take the house. I am not
fighting it now. I am no longer interested in protecting the house
that I have built. I am opening the door and going outside to be
under the open sky.

"If you surrendered to the air, you could ride it."

Toni Morrison (1931-2019)

---

b) Quote for Evening Contemplation

**"I know you're tired but come,
this is the way." (Rumi)**

Reflection for Deep Recovery (Sharabi)

You have come through these doors and into these rooms—tired.
You have finally found us, and we have welcomed you. We are
really glad to see you here, and we say, "Yes: this is the way. This
is a path out of the problems that drinking has brought to you."
We also show you a way to deal with life, with the world and its
myriad demands, with people. We say: "Yes, life can be hard but
come, we are all traveling it together." We say to you: "Trust this
process," and you say to us, "I am willing."

*"Bitter can be sweet, and sweet, poison; it is a question of what your
tongue wants. It is hard work to tell what it wants, but keep going...
The city that you are dreaming of is at the end of this road."*

Lal Ded/Lalleshwari (1320 - 1392)

Rumi
1207 - 1273

a) Quote for Morning Contemplation

**"Yesterday I was clever, so I wanted to change the world.
Today I am wise, so I am changing myself." (Rumi)**

Reflection for Deep Recovery (Sharabi)

When I change myself, everything outside is transformed. When things seem intolerable, when people seem impossible: I can change my attitudes, my expectations and demands, and my "shoulds" for others. God grant me the courage to change the things I can, and the wisdom to know that it's me, not others.

"If it is peace you want, change yourself, not other people. It is easier to protect your feet with slippers than to carpet the whole earth."

Anthony de Mello (1931 - 1997)

"If you want to make yourself miserable, you have endless opportunities because someone will always do something you don't like."

Sadhguru (born 1957)

---

b) Quote for Evening Contemplation

**"This being human is a guest house; every morning is a new arrival.
A joy, a depression, a meanness,
Some momentary awareness comes as an unexpected visitor...
Welcome and entertain them all.
Treat each guest honorably, the dark thought, the shame, the malice;
meet them at the door laughing, and invite them in.
Be grateful for whoever comes,
Because each has been sent as a guide from beyond." (Rumi)**

Reflection for Deep Recovery (Sharabi)

I welcome each sensation, not just the ones I like. I accept all of my feelings; they have been sent here to teach, providing information about my insides. I will learn from them. It is these unexpected visitors that awaken me to the glory of life, show me the largeness of life, and the complexity that is "me."

*"Let everything happen to you, beauty and terror.
Just keep going; no feeling is final."*

Rainer Maria Rilke (1875 - 1926)

Rumi
1207 - 1273

a) Quote for Morning Contemplation

"There are a hundred ways to kneel and kiss the ground." (Rumi)

Reflection for Deep Recovery (Sharabi)

... a hundred ways to conceive of a Higher Power... a hundred ways to let God in... a hundred ways to pursue growth... a hundred ways to love... a hundred ways to stay sober... but one way to end up drunk.

"More are the names of God and infinite are the forms through which He may be approached. In whatever name and form you worship Him, through them you will realize Him."

Sri Ramakrishna (1836 - 1886)

"If our love of God does not directly influence, and even change, how we engage in the issues of our time on this earth, I wonder what good religion is."

Richard Rohr (born 1943)

---

b) Quote for Evening Contemplation

**"When you do things from your soul,
you feel a river moving in you, a joy." (Rumi)**

Reflection for Deep Recovery (Sharabi)

I am not settling for half-measures; I will not offer just 50% or even 95%. I give myself completely to this program of recovery. Yes, I feel a river moving in me, a joy; I see what you people have been talking about, and the sense of freedom that comes when I do things from my soul.

"In times of joy, all of us wished we possessed a tail we could wag."

W. H. Auden (1907 - 1973)

Rumi
1207 - 1273

a) Quote for Morning Contemplation

**"There is a candle in your heart, ready to be kindled.
There is a void in your soul, ready to be filled.
You feel it, don't you?" (Rumi)**

Reflection for Deep Recovery (Sharabi)

Yes, you feel it now, don't you? You have long known that
something was missing; you have known that void in your
soul all along. You kept pouring alcohol into it—into that
black hole—hoping to fill it... hoping to fill it... hoping to fill it.
Momentarily you were able to forget about it, but next evening it
was back. Here, you and I have found a different way to fill it.

"God breaks the heart again and again and again until it stays open."
Hazrat Inayat Khan (1882 - 1927)

---

b) Quote for Evening Contemplation

**"You were born with wings;
why prefer to crawl through life?" (Rumi)**

Reflection for Deep Recovery (Sharabi)

You had resigned yourself to crawling through life—and even that,
you were not doing well. Then you found this fellowship. But I am
wondering now: why are you trying to crawl through this program
like a worm when you could be soaring like an eagle? You need to
examine what is keeping you from fully embracing this path. What
are you protecting that you fear losing? What is it you think you
cannot do without—that is dominating you? What is it that you are
not willing to give up? You must discover this or you will find the
world constantly stepping on you.

*"If man makes himself a worm he must not complain when he is trodden
on."*

Immanuel Kant (1724 - 1804)

*"You are born with only two fears: fear of falling and fear of loud noise.
All the rest is learned. And it's a lot of work!"*

Richard Bandler (born 1950)

Rumi
1207 - 1273

a) Quote for Morning Contemplation

"What you seek is seeking you." (Rumi)

Reflection for Deep Recovery (Sharabi)

Alcohol was seeking you, and you were seeking alcohol. But sobriety was seeking you too. Sobriety wants you now; you can tell because it keeps knocking on the door. The question is: will you let it in? Do you understand that for sobriety to come in, you need to chase out those other guests, pretty and interesting as they are? Are you beginning to understand, also, that God is seeking you just as you are seeking God? You just have to go halfway and meet Him. Are you willing?

"Your pain is the breaking of the shell that encloses your understanding... Much of your pain is self-chosen. It is the bitter potion by which the physician within you heals your sick self."

Kahlil Gibran (1883 - 1931)

b) Quote for Evening Contemplation

**"Don't grieve.
Anything you lose comes round in another form." (Rumi)**

Reflection for Deep Recovery (Sharabi)

If you believe that you have lost something in giving up drinking—certain friends, a type of social life and party scene, etc.—you might feel grief. But everything that you were seeking in drink is here in recovery, perhaps in a different form... and more. Understand that when one door closes, another will open. Yes, the hallway may be long, though, but that is okay, isn't it? There is plenty of time. And in time, you will reach a far better place than you can possibly imagine right now. The things you consider important today may appear to you—one day—as trivialities, for you will be setting your sights on things that really matter.

"There is surely nothing quite so useless as doing with great efficiency what should not be done at all."

Peter Drucker (1909 - 2005)

Rumi
1207 - 1273

a) Quote for Morning Contemplation

**"The wound is the place where
the Light enters you." (Rumi)**

Reflection for Deep Recovery (Sharabi)

Just as the chisel of the sculptor reveals the form in the stone, it is my wounds that allow the Light, now, to enter my dark depths and reveal me. Had I not been fractured by alcohol, I might not have found these rooms; I might not have seen the Light; I might not have found myself.

"Where a man's wound is, that is where his genius will be."

Robert Bly (1926 - 2021)

"...and out of the darkness came the hands that reach thro' nature, molding men...

Alfred Lord Tennyson (1809 - 1892)

---

b) Quote for Evening Contemplation

**"If you are irritated by every rub,
how will your mirror be polished?" (Rumi)**

Reflection for Deep Recovery (Sharabi)

Each time I was irritated—set off by something—I would rush into action, or rather, into my reaction. Now, I am learning to sit still and pause. I ask myself, "What can my reaction teach me about myself? How is this experience polishing me? Can I learn from this, and how can I apply my learning?" Each abrasive event in my life and each irritating setback is the universe polishing me and getting me ready to shine.

"A pearl is a beautiful thing that is produced by an injured life. It is the tear [that results] from the injury of the oyster. The treasure of our being in this world is also produced by an injured life. If we had not been wounded, if we had not been injured, then we will not produce the pearl."

Stephan Hoeller (born 1931)

"In the end, it is a moral question whether a man applies what he has learned or not."

Carl Jung (1875 - 1961)

Rumi
1207 - 1273

a) Quote for Morning Contemplation

"Why should I seek?
I am the same as He,
His essence speaks through me.
I have been looking for myself!" (Rumi)

Reflection for Deep Recovery (Sharabi)

Why do I seek God out there? Has God not always been here with me—right here, within me? Is not God the very essence of Being? Why am I trying to make up stories about Him that appeal to me, or seeking others for their stories? Was I seeking God with my drunkenness? Why do I even need to seek God? He is already here.

"Some of us look for the Way in opium and some in God, some of us in whiskey and some in love. It is all the same Way, and it leads nowhither."

Somerset Maugham (1874 -1965)

---

b) Quote for Evening Contemplation

"I died as a mineral and became a plant,
I died as plant and rose to animal,
I died as animal and I was Man.
Why should I fear?
When was I less by dying?" (Rumi)

Reflection for Deep Recovery (Sharabi)

Death signals an end and also a new beginning. We must die to be reborn. Do I have the courage to die as a drinking alcoholic? The courage to allow myself to be resurrected as something new, shiny, and glowing, something undefined, uncertain, and exciting? Something I may not be able to visualize clearly yet? Can I let go, jump in and let the river of recovery carry me into the unknown?

"... my purpose holds
To sail beyond the sunset and the baths
Of all the Western stars until I die."

Alfred Lord Tennyson (1809 - 1892)

"A first sign of the beginning of understanding is the wish to die."

Franz Kafka (1883 - 1924)

Rumi
1207 - 1273

a) Quote for Morning Contemplation

**"Why do you stay in
when the door is so wide open?" (Rumi)**

Reflection for Deep Recovery (Sharabi)

Yes, why did you stay in that prison of drunkenness for so
long—for so many years? And now that you have stopped
drinking, how long are you going to stay in that prison of
uncertainty, wondering whether or not to be fully in the program,
wondering whether or not to surrender? The door to freedom is
wide open, but freedom may be unfamiliar to you. You have only
known prison, and your instinct is to stay with the familiar. You
must let go; you must not worry; put your bags down and start
walking towards where recovery is calling you.

"Come, friends, it is not too late to seek a newer world."
Alfred Lord Tennyson (1809 - 1892)

---

b) Quote for Evening Contemplation

**"This drunkenness began in some other tavern. When I get back
around to that place, I'll be completely sober. Meanwhile, I'm
like a bird from another continent, sitting in this aviary... who is
it now in my ears who hears my voice? Who says words with my
mouth? Who looks out with my eyes? What is the soul? I cannot
stop asking. If I could taste one sip of an answer, I could break out
of this prison for drunks." (Rumi)**

Reflection for Deep Recovery (Sharabi)

Ah, those hours spent at the tavern trying to figure out, "Who am
I? Who is it that is looking out of my eyes, having the thoughts
I am having? Why do I like alcohol so much?" I thought I had to
figure this out to stop drinking. Now I am sitting in these meetings
still trying to figure out who I am, still feeling like a bird from
another continent. If I could figure this out—figure out who I
am—maybe I could stop coming to meetings, I could go back to
the bars and start drinking again. "Stop!" you say, "It is here that
you will finally find answers." Or maybe I will simply stop asking
those stupid questions that have no answers, like: "Who am I?
What is the soul? Why did I drink so much? Why does recovery
work?"

Rumi
1207 - 1273

a) Quote for Morning Contemplation

**"I reach out,
wanting you to tear me open... " (Rumi)**

Reflection for Deep Recovery (Sharabi)

You can have all of me.
Tear me, open me up, Lord, do with me as you wish.
I am surrendering my will and my life over to you.
And now that I have no will of my own, I am totally free;
It is all You.

"Prayer is a silent surrendering of everything to God."
Kierkegaard (1813 - 1855)

---

b) Quote for Evening Contemplation

**"There is a community of the spirit,
Join it, and feel the delight
of walking in the noisy street,
and being the noise." (Rumi)**

Reflection for Deep Recovery (Sharabi)

Come and have some coffee,
Join the noise and celebration of recovery.
Come in... come along and walk with us, delight with us!
And rather than ending the meeting with a moment of
somber silence,
Let us make raucous noise, throw our hats in the air,
Let us celebrate this community of the spirit,
This fellowship, this anonymity, this new madness.
Let us be the madness of recovery!

"I am nobody! Who are you? Are you a nobody, too?"
Emily Dickinson (1830 - 1886)

Rumi
1207 - 1273

a) Quote for Morning Contemplation

**"All people on the planet
are children, except for a very few.
No one is grown up except those free of desire." (Rumi)**

Reflection for Deep Recovery (Sharabi)

As long as I think I am missing something—missing out on something—I am still a child; I will always want more. No matter what life gives me: power, success, love—even sobriety—after a while, I will become dissatisfied and want more. All desires are a form of childish self-centeredness. But if I pray only for knowledge of His will and the power to carry it out, when I am looking for ways to be decent and useful, to help others, to contribute to humanity—then I am no longer a child. I have grown up.

"Abundant as are the gifts (nature) has bestowed upon us, still more abundant are our desires. We seem born to be dissatisfied."

Rudolf Steiner (1861 - 1925)

---

b) Quote for Evening Contemplation

**"The wine we really drink is our own blood.
Our bodies ferment in these barrels.
We give everything for a glass of this.
We give our minds for a sip." (Rumi)**

Reflection for Deep Recovery (Sharabi)

When I drank, I was drinking my own blood; I was destroying myself. My body and my soul were fermenting inside this bag of skin. I was prepared to give everything for a glass of this, a sip of that.

(Even in the 13th century of Rumi, they understood the power of alcohol. "Al-kol" is an Arabic word. Even though wine and beer had been around, distilled spirits did not exist until the Arabs invented distillation. Yet, the very land that invented it has banned it and made it a crime to drink alcohol. Does that say something?)

"My soul bleeds, and the blood, steadily, silently, disturbingly, slowly, swallows me whole."

Dostoevsky (1821 - 1881)

Rumi
1207 - 1273

a) Quote for Morning Contemplation

"Listen, O drop, give yourself up without regret, and in exchange, gain the Ocean. Listen, O drop, bestow upon yourself this honor, and in the arms of the Sea be secure. Who indeed should be so fortunate? An Ocean wooing a drop!" (Rumi)

Reflection for Deep Recovery (Sharabi)

As a drunk, I was a mere drop trying to survive—maintaining and protecting my individuality. But I let go of my separateness; I surrendered my ego and stopped insisting that I was unique and different from all other drops. Then, I was able to merge into the sea of anonymous recovering alcoholics in this great worldwide fellowship. The "I" of the drop had melted into the "We" of the river, now all heading towards the Ocean.

---

b) Quote for Evening Contemplation

**"Soul drunk, body ruined, these two
sit helpless in a wrecked wagon.
Neither knows how to fix it." (Rumi)**

Reflection for Deep Recovery (Sharabi)

Alcoholism is a disease of the body and of the soul. The two sit helplessly in a wrecked vehicle—axles broken, radiator fluid all around, glass and metal pieces strewn about—with no idea how to get on in life. But today, we have a cure; we know how to fix it. How fortunate that you and I have been born in an age where the fellowship exists! But first, I must accept the fact of my addiction, not ignore it or deny it. It is only remembering my darkest nights that allows me to accept powerlessness and enter this temple.

"The heat of midnight tears will bring you to God."

Mirabai (1498 - 1546)

Rumi
1207 - 1273

a) Quote for Morning Contemplation

**"And my heart, I'd say it was more
like a donkey sunk in a mudhole,
struggling and getting mired deeper." (Rumi)**

Reflection for Deep Recovery (Sharabi)

The drunk struggling with his fatal obsession, getting mired
deeper with every spasmodic effort to break free—that was me.
Each night I would take a drink, and then a second... and then...
and then... why keep count? I'll figure out tomorrow how to
explain tonight.

*"Change your life today. Don't gamble on the future; act now without
delay."*

Simone de Beauvoir (1908 - 1986)

---

b) Quote for Evening Contemplation

**"It's the old rule that drunks have to argue
and get into fights.
The lover is just as bad; he falls into a hole.
But down in that hole, he finds something shining,
worth more than any amount of money or power." (Rumi)**

Reflection for Deep Recovery (Sharabi)

I fell into the hole of drunkenness. The hole was empty and
bleak. I kept struggling to get out, but I was helpless. But in
that hole of drunken depravity and despair, I found something
shining, something worth more than any amount of money
or power. I found powerlessness. Helplessness was a prison,
but powerlessness liberated me. With powerlessness I found
surrender. I found freedom. I found God.

"In the dark night of the soul, bright flows the river of God."

John of the Cross (1542 - 1591)

Rumi
1207 - 1273

a) Quote for Morning Contemplation

"Be silent now.
Say fewer and fewer praise poems.
Let yourself become living poetry." (Rumi)

Reflection for Deep Recovery (Sharabi)

You must be silent now. It may be time to stop proclaiming your gratitude and devotion loudly at meetings. Who are you trying to convince? Instead, let your actions and your being quietly declare your gratitude and devotion elegantly as living poetry.

"Poets and philosophers are alike in being big with wonder."

Thomas Aquinas (1224 - 1274)

b) Quote for Evening Contemplation

"Excuse my wandering.
How can one be orderly with this?
It's like counting leaves in a garden,
along with the sing-song notes of partridges,
and crows." (Rumi)

Reflection for Deep Recovery (Sharabi)

I was drunk—a seeker, a wanderer—beset with a thirst for wholeness. Now I quench my thirst in these recovery rooms, and it feels chaotic. I have so many character defects, so much confusion, so many amends to make, so many insights coming at me, so many good ideas and advice, so many things to take care of. How can I be orderly and organized? Life is messy unless I retreat to the mountains and become a hermit. And recovery is about tangling with the messiness of life, of people, of relationships. Sober, I enter the fray.

"A violent order is a disorder, and a great disorder is an order.
These two things are one."

Wallace Stevens (1879 - 1955)

Rumi
1207 - 1273

a) Quote for Morning Contemplation

**"I've made up so many love stories.
Now I feel fictional." (Rumi)**

Reflection for Deep Recovery (Sharabi)

I lied so much: people called me "Lord of the Lies." I would say whatever you wanted me to say, be whatever I thought you wanted me to be. I came here to these rooms of recovery, not knowing who I really was. I even made up a story that I was in love with recovery. But I was disgruntled; I had complaints and resentments that I kept hidden—and then I relapsed. I suddenly felt fictional, not knowing what was true. Recovery calls for ruthless honesty with myself. I don't have to become wise; I merely have to admit my stupidity. That is a start.

"If you do not tell the truth about yourself you cannot tell it about other people."

Virginia Woolf (1882 - 1941)

---

b) Quote for Evening Contemplation

**"At night, I open the window and ask the moon to come
and press its face against mine.
Breathe into me.
Close the language-door and open the love-window.
The moon won't use the door, only the window." (Rumi)**

Reflection for Deep Recovery (Sharabi)

Every A.A. meeting contains words... and it contains silence. If I attend to the words only, I soon forget. But the silence is what touches my soul. It is in silence that the moon shows itself, where love is offered and received, where recovery enters the heart. Sitting in a roomful of recovering alcoholics—even in silence—is a sacred experience to be savored. Rather than barraging the newcomer with words and solutions, let me offer a sense of the love that is available in these rooms. Let me be the moon to the newcomer, not the searing sun.

"People don't care how much you know until they know how much you care."

Theodore Roosevelt (1858 - 1919)

Rumi
1207 - 1273

a) Quote for Morning Contemplation

**"Light dawns, and any talk of proof
resembles a blind man's cane at sunrise." (Rumi)**

Reflection for Deep Recovery (Sharabi)

I used to ask for proof of God—for my rational, intellectual, skeptical mind. I was the blind man trying to discover sunlight with his cane. You could not help me except to ask me to put down my cane and turn my face towards the warmth. And God dawned on me as the light dawns on land at sunrise.

*"My mind-horse straddles the sky, crossing thousands of miles
In a blink
It takes wisdom to harness that horse,
He can break the wheels of the chariot."*

Lal Ded/Lalleshwari (1320 - 1392)

b) Quote for Evening Contemplation

**"In your light I learn how to love
In your beauty, how to make poems.
You dance inside my chest,
where no one sees you,
but sometimes I do,
and that light becomes this art." (Rumi)**

Reflection for Deep Recovery (Sharabi)

*"Wrapped up in Yourself, You hid from me.
All-day I looked for You
and when I found You hiding inside me,
I ran wild, playing now me, now You."*

Lal Ded/Lalleshwari (1320 - 1392)

Rumi
1207 - 1273

a) Quote for Morning Contemplation

"Gaze into what is not ashamed or afraid of the truth." (Rumi)

Reflection for Deep Recovery (Sharabi)

Only after the Third Step—turning my will and my life over to
the care of God as I understood Him—do I become capable of
performing a searching and fearless moral inventory. Today I am
not ashamed or afraid of the truth; it is what it is. If truth is going
to destroy my self-image or my ego, then they deserve to die.

"If it can be destroyed by the truth, it deserves to die. "
Anonymous, often misattributed to Carl Sagan

"Gnostics (and Buddhists) have often been labeled pessimists and world
haters because of their willingness to look the dark face of the world in
the eye. Yet, both of these traditions affirm that there is a way out of
suffering and ignorance, and that this way out involves an essential,
salvific change in consciousness."
Stephan Hoeller (born 1931)

---

b) Quote for Evening Contemplation

"A wealth you cannot imagine flows through you." (Rumi)

Reflection for Deep Recovery (Sharabi)

"We are going to know a new freedom and a new happiness."
recovery offers the riches of a spiritual, self-aware existence.
A solitary walk through the woods or a stroll around the
lake —perhaps a moment spent with the full moon—can provide
an intense experience that is far more opulent than the thrills
that money can buy or that the fulfillment of desires can provide.
Many of us are trying to be productive, get someone's approval,
be successful; we are trying so intently to accomplish and to
achieve—to get somewhere—that we overlook the pure joy of
just being present. Lolling in this sober consciousness is itself
an immense and luxurious wealth, one that is available at any
moment we choose to become conscious of it. These days are
bonus days.

"All great spirituality teaches about letting go... At that place, you will
have nothing to prove to anybody and nothing to protect. That place is
called freedom."
Richard Rohr (born 1943)

Rumi
1207 - 1273

a) Quote for Morning Contemplation

**"Wherever you are, and whatever you do,
be in love." (Rumi)**

Reflection for Deep Recovery (Sharabi)

I don't need to wait for something or someone to be in love with.
I can be in love with everything and everybody just as it is, just
as they are—the beauty of a simple flower, the breeze on my
face, the pitter-patter of raindrops, the grass on my bare feet.
I can be madly in love with life, with everything and everyone
in life, and with existence itself. Love is the ultimate answer to
opinion, judgment, worry, complaint, resentment, and the need to
dominate and control. Love is the essence of Being; all I need to do
is come out of hiding, expose my innermost self to existence.

*"Don't forget love; it will bring all the madness you need
to unfurl yourself across the universe."*

Mirabai (1498 - 1546)

b) Quote for Evening Contemplation

**"No more camel's milk.
I want silent water to drink,
and the majesty of a clear waking." (Rumi)**

Reflection for Deep Recovery (Sharabi)

No more gulps from the bottle for me... no more exotic drinks
like camel's milk, or Irish Coffee, or Long Island Iced Tea. How
delicious is simple and silent water... and the majesty of a clear
waking the next morning! Then I can see things as they are, not
the distortions that my needs and shame project onto the world.
Seeing the world as it is, with clarity and presence, shows me the
infinity that is available every moment, the forgiveness and love
that the universe softly cushions me in.

*"The tree which moves some to tears of joy is in the eyes of others only a
green thing that stands in the way."*

William Blake (1757 - 1827)

Rumi
1207 - 1273

a) Quote for Morning Contemplation

**"On a day
when the wind is perfect,
the sail just needs to open, and the world is full of beauty.
Today is such a day." (Rumi)**

Reflection for Deep Recovery (Sharabi)

It is such a beautiful day... Let me open my sail and get to a meeting!

"At some point in life, the world's beauty becomes enough. You don't need to photograph, paint or even remember it. It is enough."

Toni Morrison (1931-2019)

"A thing of beauty is a joy forever: its loveliness increases; it will never pass into nothingness."

John Keats (1795 - 1821)

---

b) Quote for Evening Contemplation

**"Put your thoughts to sleep,
do not let them cast a shadow
over the moon of your heart.
Let go of thinking." (Rumi)**

Reflection for Deep Recovery (Sharabi)

I need to distract myself from my thoughts; it is necessary, sometimes. Many of my thoughts are there just to complain about the world, criticize myself, judge others, and generate regret and anxiety. All they do is cast a shadow and bring me down. Love and Joy are not thoughts. I must surrender to that mad and wondrous excitement in my heart that recovery has brought me. I am going to let go of thinking—even if it is just for moments—and I am going to savor the moon of my heart.

"Regret will not prevent tomorrow's sorrows; it will only rob today of its strength."

Barbara Johnson (1927 - 2007)

Rumi
1207 - 1273

a) Quote for Morning Contemplation

"What hurts you, blesses you.
Darkness is your candle." (Rumi)

Reflection for Deep Recovery (Sharabi)

I have learned to think of pain as a messenger sent to get my attention, to wake me up. Given what the pain of my alcoholism delivered for me, I do not—any longer—need to shrink in anticipation of pain. I can even look upon pain as a blessing; so complete is my belief in this process of recovery, of coming to knowing, of coming to God.

"The darker the night, the brighter the stars,
The deeper the grief, the closer is God."

Dostoevsky (1821 - 1881)

b) Quote for Evening Contemplation

"When someone beats a rug,
the blows are not against the rug,
but against the dust in it." (Rumi)

Reflection for Deep Recovery (Sharabi)

When life buffets me about, I consider that these blows are aimed at false notions that I am still carrying: notions of how life ought to be, presumptuous ideas of how people ought to behave, arrogant conclusions about who I am and what I deserve, and grandiose thoughts on how God must direct my world. Only when I completely let go of my ideas and just accept what is—accept everything as God's will—will I experience that the blows have ceased.

"Talent is God-given. Be humble. Fame is man-given. Be grateful. Conceit is self-given. Be careful."

John Wooden (1910 - 2010)

Meister Eckhart
1260 - 1328

a) Quote for Morning Contemplation

"The eye with which I see God is the very eye with which God sees me; my eye and God's eye are one eye, one seeing, one knowing, one love." (Meister Eckhart)

Reflection for Deep Recovery (Sharabi)

One interpretation is that we are in a sea of love without subject or object; our love of God is the same love that God has for us. But rather than trying to "make sense" of the idea, if we become simply present to it in a diffuse and a-rational manner, we might experience a profound and subtle illumination. Meister Eckhart's vision embodies cosmic oneness and Unity beyond the subject-object relationship of "I" and "God." It is reminiscent of the non-dualistic (Advaita) perspectives of Eastern philosophies.

"The worshipper, the worshipped and the prayer itself, are one and the same thing; all are God."

Ramana Maharshi (1879 - 1950)

---

b) Quote for Evening Contemplation

"Though I put more faith in the scriptures than in myself, it is easier and better for you to learn by means of arguments that can be verified." (Meister Eckhart)

Reflection for Deep Recovery (Sharabi)

I do not expect to take the message of recovery on blind faith just because it has been written down somewhere in print. I have had sufficient experience with alcohol that verifies the arguments for powerlessness. If I need more data, I can obtain it from thousands of people who have gone along the same path as I. Some of them have stayed on the path longer than I did. They can tell me and show me what lies ahead if I continue drinking. But this I understand: it is preferable to learn from other people's bad experiences rather than going through the pain myself. Everyone in this community is my research assistant, helping me discover the truth about what is effective with alcohol and alcoholism.

"There are two ways to slice easily through life; to believe everything or to doubt everything. Both ways save us from thinking."

Alfred Korzybski (1879 - 1950)

Meister Eckhart
1260 - 1328

a) Quote for Morning Contemplation

"Man's best chance of finding God is to look in the place where he left Him." (Meister Eckhart)

Reflection for Deep Recovery (Sharabi)

If God is not present in our life, who left? If we left God, can we remember when? Where? Can we go back there? Some healing may be called for. And it is possible that our relationship with God is based, not on God, but on some story we heard about God, a story that we have rejected. To reject God, we must first define God, and then we can only reject the God we ourselves have defined. So we can ask: who are we to define God? We stop defining God and focus, instead, just on the sense of God, on the presence we feel, and on our inherent sense of the deep, on humility and awe, on compassion and love. God is home; it is we who have left.

"We search for Him here and there while looking right at Him. Sitting at His side we ask, 'O Beloved, where is the Beloved?' "

Rumi (1207 - 1273)

b) Quote for Evening Contemplation

"Do you think you do not have God simply because you have no devotion? If you suffer from this, then just this will be your devotion." (Meister Eckhart)

Reflection for Deep Recovery (Sharabi)

If it bothers me—even slightly—that I do not have a sense of God, that I do not have a relationship with God, then this itself is my prayer. My passionate arguments against God are just my protestations against a concept of God that does not fit me, one that others are trying to push on me. The mind may reject God, but the heart and gut have a sense of something missing. Even the mind will feel an emptiness, the absence of a backbone or purpose to life, and this suffering of the mind itself can be my entry point to my true God.

"Like billowing clouds, like the incessant gurgle of the brook, the longing of the spirit can never be stilled."

Hildegard of Bingen (1098 - 1179)

Meister Eckhart
1260 - 1328

a) Quote for Morning Contemplation

"To know the truth, one has to dwell in unity and be the unity. Be one, that thou mayest find God." (Meister Eckhart)

Reflection for Deep Recovery (Sharabi)

All contradictions are creations of the human mind. If I rise beyond my ideas, thoughts, feelings, and concepts—for a moment—I might catch a glimpse of the "is-ness," the Unity that is God. Even a single conscious moment in that Unity is a breakthrough, for I will have been one with God and I will always know it.

"Once you have known pure being, without being this or that, you will discern it among experiences.."

Nisargadatta (1897 - 1981)

---

b) Quote for Evening Contemplation

"If I spent enough time with the tiniest creature—even a caterpillar—I would never have to prepare a sermon, So full of God is every creature." (Meister Eckhart)

Reflection for Deep Recovery (Sharabi)

To see God in every creature, every bird, every insect, every flower, every tree, all I need is to gaze at it with wonder-filled eyes. Every creature existing today represents an unbroken evolutionary line from the beginning of life on earth. The detail present in nature can evoke awe and wake me to the vastness that is God. Every new person who walks in through these doors is full of God. Becoming just really present to this person will open my eyes and dissipate the sermon on alcohol and recovery that I was preparing to give.

"The moment one gives close attention to any thing, even a blade of grass, it becomes a mysterious, awesome, indescribably magnificent world in itself."

Henry Miller (1891 - 1980)

"When one loses the deep, intimate relationship with nature, then temples, mosques, and churches become important."

Krishnamurti (1895 - 1986)

Meister Eckhart
1260 - 1328

a) Quote for Morning Contemplation

"Man goes far away or near, but God never goes far off. He is always standing close at hand, and even if he cannot stay within, he goes no further than the door." (Meister Eckhart)

Reflection for Deep Recovery (Sharabi)

God is available. Even if I cannot find God within me, I must understand that God is nearby—no further than the door. I can invite God back in. I do not have to be concerned with what the neighbors will think of this visitor who is entering my home, for God will manage their judgments and concerns. Also, I do not need to make sure my house is clean before God enters; I offer myself as I am.

"A man is truly free, even here in this embodied state, if he knows that God is the true agent and he by himself is powerless to do anything."

Sri Ramakrishna (1836 - 1886)

---

b) Quote for Evening Contemplation

"If the only prayer you ever say in your entire life is thank you, it will be enough." (Meister Eckhart)

Reflection for Deep Recovery (Sharabi)

Gratitude is sufficient prayer; nothing more is needed. And without gratitude, no prayer is sufficient. Gratitude is the foundation of any spiritual life.

"Gratitude turns what we have into enough."

Aesop (c 620 B.C. - 524 B.C.)

"Keep your eyes open to your mercies. The man who forgets to be thankful has fallen asleep in life.

Robert Louis Stevenson (1850 - 1894)

Meister Eckhart
1260 - 1328

a) Quote for Morning Contemplation

"The price of inaction is far greater than the cost of making a mistake." (Meister Eckhart)

Reflection for Deep Recovery (Sharabi)

Better to do a poor Fourth and Fifth Step now—as best as I can—than postponing it, claiming it is not yet right or complete. If I am struggling with the Fourth Step inventory, they say it often works to make a Fifth Step appointment now and to keep that appointment when the day comes, carrying with me my Fourth Step in whatever state of completeness it exists.

"The greatest mistake you can make in life is continually fearing that you'll make one."

Elbert Hubbard (1856 - 1915)

---

b) Quote for Evening Contemplation

"There exists only the present instant... a Now which always and without end is itself new. There is no yesterday nor any tomorrow, but only Now, as it was a thousand years ago and as it will be a thousand years hence." (Meister Eckhart)

Reflection for Deep Recovery (Sharabi)

Eternity is not made up of many moments. Eternity is a single moment, and I am in it right now. "Right now" is where I will ever be; it is all that the ancients ever had. There is no such thing as "change" because all that is real is right now; all I have is the possibility of taking the next right action. There is no need for regret; inventory is not about what I did but what I am right now. In fact, recovery is not about recovering anything from the past; it is about creating anew, of recovering myself in the present. It is about doing the next right thing, living on the cusp of existence, forever falling into the moment about to be. How exciting!

"This fact gives life its poignancy, and you should concentrate your attention on what you are experiencing now."

Joseph Campbell (1904 - 1987)

Meister Eckhart
1260 - 1328

a) Quote for Morning Contemplation

**"To be full of things is to be empty of God.
To be empty of things is to be full of God." (Meister Eckhart)**

Reflection for Deep Recovery (Sharabi)

To let God in, I must empty myself of the other things that occupy me and worry me. Of course, I still have to fill out tax forms, pay bills, take the garbage out, etc., but those things I have been seeking, like comfort, success, fame, prestige, respect—and the symbols that stand for these—will not be the focus of my consciousness and effort. Their importance will fade away gently as God comes into focus, illuminated by the glow of my spiritual seeking.

"Thou must be emptied of that wherewith thou art full, that thou mayest be filled with that whereof thou art empty."

Saint Augustine (354 - 430 A.D.)

---

b) Quote for Evening Contemplation

"One person who has mastered life is better than a thousand persons who have mastered only the contents of books." (Meister Eckhart)

Reflection for Deep Recovery (Sharabi)

People can end up drunk or act like sober idiots even after memorizing every line in the Big Book. Sure, formulas and cliches can help in the beginning, but in the long run, "knowledge" will not keep me sober. Repeating the same old cliches at every meeting will not keep me sober. I must seek something more: to master living through action, through awakening. What this "mastery of life" means—what spiritual awakening means—is the subject of Deep Recovery.

"Monotony is poverty, whether in speech or in life."

Dale Carnegie (1888 - 1955)

"Long as a person will not raise his or her consciousness beyond the physical world to higher, spiritual realities, the soul's enslavement in darkness - whether darkness in the outer, physical world or in."

Stephan Hoeller (born 1931)

Meister Eckhart
1260 - 1328

a) Quote for Morning Contemplation

**"Only the hand that erases can write the true thing."
(Meister Eckhart)**

Reflection for Deep Recovery (Sharabi)

In recovery, I began to realize: what I knew or thought I knew may not really be so. I had learned wrong things throughout my life, made incorrect assumptions, believed false explanations, and used ineffective strategies. Now I have an opportunity to identify the previously unknown errors I have lived by—and to erase them one by one. These errors manifest as character defects often developed to cover my wounds. But recovery tells me that I cannot heal my own wounds; only God can. I can, however, keep them clean and prevent them from getting infected with resentment, righteous anger, self-pity, outrage, and hate.

HEALING PRAYER: "God, please heal my wounds, so I don't have to use my character defects to hold me up."

from DEEP RECOVERY

---

b) Quote for Evening Contemplation

"What we plant in the soil of contemplation, we shall reap in the harvest of action." (Meister Eckhart)

Reflection for Deep Recovery (Sharabi)

In recovery, I try to live an examined life. That is why the Tenth, Eleventh, and Twelfth Steps are daily Steps. Such consistent examination and contemplation—not just of my wrongs but of my wounds—will lead me to the larger questions of living and of spiritual growth. Wounds initially harden us, but later, they soften us. Contemplation of our wounds leads us to sensitiveness for others, and this will naturally lead to proper action in the world. As I focus on the inward work of healing, the outward work will happen. Recovery requires discipline: contemplation, consistency, and repetition. We do what we commit to daily, never postponing it just because "we don't feel like it." We adopt the attitude that contemplation of recovery reveals it to be truthful and correct and, in the end, beautiful.

"Beauty is truth's smile when she beholds her own face in a perfect mirror."

Rabindranath Tagore (1861 - 1941)

Meister Eckhart
1260 - 1328

a) Quote for Morning Contemplation

"The more we have, the less we own." (Meister Eckhart)

Reflection for Deep Recovery (Sharabi)

Wealth in recovery is not measured in financial or material terms or even in how people see me. Great reputations can be destroyed in an instant. The more I covet, the poorer I am. The less I desire, the richer I am. In sobriety, I am learning to be joyful about simple things—or even joyful about nothing. I realize that I own nothing. People and possessions: they are all merely being loaned to me, and they will be gone one day. This knowledge allows me to appreciate and enjoy what I have today and not be destroyed when they are gone. I need to treasure every moment with every person I encounter, for who knows how long I will have them?

"Don't gain the world and lose your soul; wisdom is better than silver or gold."

Bob Marley (1845 - 1981)

---

b) Quote for Evening Contemplation

"We know so many things, but we don't know ourselves! Why, thirty or forty skins or hides, as thick and hard as an ox's or bear's, cover the soul. Go into your own ground and learn to know yourself there." (Meister Eckhart)

Reflection for Deep Recovery (Sharabi)

In recovery, "... the capacity to be honest with myself," will propel me on this exciting journey of self-discovery. It is a slow process, like peeling onions or cleaning an animal covered with forty layers of skin, but it is my central job in recovery. It was Socrates who famously said, "Know thyself!" Here, I seek to know myself not just by my likes and dislikes nor by my wants and feelings; not just by the things that bother me or trigger me, not just by my opinions on subjects or my judgments and my reactions; I will get to know myself spiritually. I will get to know myself beyond any particular description of myself. This is real work, not the mindless memorization of books—slogans and cliches.

"Remember, you can always stoop and pick up nothing."

Charlie Chaplin (1889 - 1977)

Meister Eckhart
1260 - 1328

a) Quote for Morning Contemplation

**"Be willing to be a beginner every single morning."
(Meister Eckhart)**

Reflection for Deep Recovery (Sharabi)

We are all beginners here; every day, we try to learn how to be sober that day. We re-learn each day—and we get to practice—how to be kind, generous, patient, authentic, interested, dependable, happy, joyous, and free. We do this not merely from memory and habit; we do not just focus on the reactions and judgments that arise spontaneously within us, but we develop a conscious attitude and action that we re-generate newly in the moment. Being a beginner means forgetting all we know—or think we know. We approach each person and each day fresh, not from memory. This is the way of the truly awakened being.

"... asking each morning in meditation that our Creator show us the way of patience, tolerance, kindliness, and love."

BIG BOOK, Ch. 6.

b) Quote for Evening Contemplation

"Spirituality is not to be learned by flight from the world, or by running away from things, or by turning solitary and going apart from the world. Rather, we must learn an inner solitude wherever or with whomsoever we may be. We must learn to penetrate things and find God there." (Meister Eckhart)

Reflection for Deep Recovery (Sharabi)

Recovery does not involve becoming a hermit and retreating into the mountains. We continue living in the world, dealing with people, work, money, taxes, traffic tickets, politicians, stand-up comics... At the same time, we are in touch with a deep and satisfying inner solitude, even at a meeting where lots of words are being spoken. This inner solitude is the place in which God dwells and the place where we go to increase our conscious contact with God.

"I could give you no advice but this: to go into yourself and to explore the depths where your life wells forth."

Rainer Maria Rilke (1875 - 1926)

Meister Eckhart
1260 - 1328

a) Quote for Morning Contemplation

"And suddenly you know: it is time to start something new and trust the magic of beginnings." (Meister Eckhart)

Reflection for Deep Recovery (Sharabi)

The moment of surrender contains the magic of new beginnings; it is the doorway to a sober life. That magical feeling that was present at the beginning of this new life is also available today. Each time I act, not from habit or pattern, but based on the requirement of that unique moment is a moment of magic, for it represents a beginning. It is a fresh step into a new and exciting unknown.

"We have it in our power to build the world over again."

Thomas Paine (1737 - 1809)

---

b) Quote for Evening Contemplation

"Nothing in all creation is so like God as stillness." (Meister Eckhart)

Reflection for Deep Recovery (Sharabi)

Become still and contemplate the above statement. The deepest way to improve conscious contact with God is through the stillness available in a meditative attitude: through the quieting of the mind. The constant chatter in our head distracts us from awareness of the Divine, but when we calm it down, even for a moment, God appears in the silence. An emptiness is needed for God to appear, and the best way to prepare for receiving God is to clear the mind. And we clear the mind, not by wrestling the mind to the ground and "conquering" it, but by focusing on something around me, present—like a flower, a tree, sunlight, the sky, God— something outside the mind and thoughts.

"My heart is tuned to the quietness that the stillness of nature inspires."

Hazrat Inayat Khan (1882 - 1927)

"Be still, and know that I am God."

Psalm 46:10, King James Version of the Bible

Meister Eckhart
1260 - 1328

a) Quote for Morning Contemplation

"Wisdom consists in doing the next thing you have to do, doing it with your whole heart, and finding delight in doing it."
(Meister Eckhart)

Reflection for Deep Recovery (Sharabi)

Life in Deep Recovery is simple: do the next right thing and do it with heart; do it with delight, do it right. Every little thing you do is sacred, a privilege; every little thing you are able to do is its own reward. We can take delight in our recovery service work. We can take delight in each of the chores we must complete for life itself.

"I slept and dreamt that life was joy.
I awoke and saw that life was service.
I acted and behold: service was joy."

Rabindranath Tagore (1861 - 1941)

---

b) Quote for Evening Contemplation

"Some people want to see God with their eyes as they see a cow, and to love Him as they love a cow—for the milk and cheese and profit it brings them. This is how it is with people who love God for the sake of outward wealth or inward comfort. They do not rightly love God when they love Him for their own advantage."
(Meister Eckhart)

Reflection for Deep Recovery (Sharabi)

Do I think, if I turn my will and my life over to the care of God, He or She might let me win the lottery? Bring me romance? Bring peace to my heart? If so, I am loving God for reasons—for reward. When I turn myself over to God, I must have no thought of any ensuing reward. Sobriety is not merely a reward for turning my life over to God; sobriety is the vehicle for turning myself over to God.

"Theism is a deep-seated conviction that there's some hand to hold: if we just do the right things, someone will appreciate us and take care of us."

Pema Chödrön (born 1936)
"The highest reward that God gives us for good work is the ability to do better work."

Elbert Hubbard (1856 - 1915)

Meister Eckhart
1260 - 1328

a) Quote for Morning Contemplation

"One must not always think so much about what one should do, but rather what one should be. Our works do not ennoble us, but we must ennoble our works." (Meister Eckhart)

Reflection for Deep Recovery (Sharabi)

I must be conscious of where I am coming from, what my attitude is, what my motives are: who I am Being rather than what I am doing. If I focus on my Being, noble actions will naturally come out. When I reach out from a place of unconditional love, acceptance, and reverence, I can transform my experience of anyone and everyone. I transform my experience of the circumstances I am in, and I transform my experience of life itself. The rest of my life begins when I accept where I am—and how it is—right now. Otherwise, I am lost in hypothetical "how it should be" and "what is wrong" instead of just being with what is.

---

b) Quote for Evening Contemplation

"Some people prefer solitude. They say their peace of mind depends on this. Others say they would be better off in church. If you do well, you do well wherever you are. If you fail, you fail wherever you are. Your surroundings don't matter. God is with you everywhere—in the marketplace as well as in seclusion or in the church. If you look for nothing but God, nothing or no one can disturb you." (Meister Eckhart)

Reflection for Deep Recovery (Sharabi)

The noise of the party next door to the meeting room does not have to distance me from God. I can include it as just another aspect of God. Things in my life that are not to my liking do not distance me from God. Nothing needs to be in any particular way for God to be present to me; for me to be present to God. It is what it is. Nothing is wrong. Everything is perfect—perfectly what it is—already. God is already here and my focus must be on Him, not on the petty things occupying my judgmental mind. My mind wants to make editorial comments on everything around me: people, places and happenings. It is generating the noise in my life distracting me from God.

Meister Eckhart
1260 - 1328

a) Quote for Morning Contemplation

"My Lord told me a joke. And seeing Him laugh has done more for me than any scripture I will ever read." (Meister Eckhart)

Reflection for Deep Recovery (Sharabi)

My Lord told me: "If you think I don't have a sense of humor, just look at how I made you!" We alcoholics know to laugh at ourselves. Laughter is sacred, and humor is a necessary part of a spiritual life. Humor is the antidote to religiousness; in fact, religion + humor = spirituality. Many of us truly experience the "lightness of Being" in recovery, but some take ourselves—and life—way too seriously, trying too hard to be "normal" and "humble" and "eternally vigilant." The following is good advice: "Take your sobriety seriously... but not life!"

"All my pictures are built around the idea of getting in trouble and so giving me the chance to be desperately serious in my attempt to appear as a normal little gentleman."

Charlie Chaplin (1889 - 1977)

b) Quote for Evening Contemplation

"God is not good, or else he could do better." (Meister Eckhart)

Reflection for Deep Recovery (Sharabi)

God is all things. God is not this or that. God is beyond being judged by humans as "good." Haven't there been times when we have all wanted to write to God telling Him what to do and showing how He (or She) could run the world better? Every appeal and every prayer for an outcome are against the Third Step. Accepting God's will means that we no longer have to offer God suggestions. What "is" is God's will; it is neither good nor bad; it cannot be better or worse because all that exists is only what is.

"The only meaningful prayer is for forgiveness because those who have been forgiven have everything."

Course in Miracles (1976)

"I am unable to believe in a God susceptible to prayer. I simply haven't the nerve to imagine a being, a force, a cause which keeps the planets revolving in their orbits, and then suddenly stops in order to give me a bicycle with three speeds."

Quentin Crisp (1908 - 1999)

Meister Eckhart
1260 - 1328

a) Quote for Morning Contemplation

"Theologians may quarrel, but the mystics of the world speak the same language." (Meister Eckhart)

Reflection for Deep Recovery (Sharabi)

We do not need to argue about the interpretation of the Big Book; each interpretation is true for the person who interprets it that way and is using it to stay sober. Every opinion, disagreement, and argument between two people represents a failed attempt on the part of both to be with the mystery. For the true mystic is in a state that is trans-rational: no questions, no interpretations, no disagreement, no agreement. That is the true spiritual awakening: beyond ideas, concepts and words.

"Every word or concept, clear as it may seem to be, has only a limited range of applicability. Not only is the Universe stranger than we think, it is stranger than we can think. The reality we can put into words is never reality itself."

Werner Heisenberg (1901-1976)

---

b) Quote for Evening Contemplation

"Now, you might say: 'How can this be? I cannot feel his presence in any way.' Listen to this. Sensing His presence is not in your power but in his. He will show himself when it suits Him to do so, and He can also remain hidden if that is His wish." (Meister Eckhart)

Reflection for Deep Recovery (Sharabi)

I must not dismiss God merely because I have an inability to feel His presence. If I could decide whether God exists or not based on sensing His presence, then His existence would be in my hands; it would be up to me. I would be God's Creator and Master—the one who brings Him into being. I must understand that even the space in which I am asking the question about His existence is owned by God. My very consciousness is owned by God; I am in God's house, whether I sense God or not. And God need not be the God that I reject; perhaps God is just not where I looked for Him and not how I have pictured Him.

"God is not a hypothesis derived from logical assumptions.... something to be sought in the darkness with the light of reason. He is the light.

Heschel (1907 - 1972)

Meister Eckhart
1260 - 1328

a) Quote for Morning Contemplation

**"Whatever God does, the first outburst is always compassion."
(Meister Eckhart)**

Reflection for Deep Recovery (Sharabi)

I must remember this compassion even in those moments when I am rushing to judge and condemn. Instead of raging first and then gradually calming myself into compassion, I must learn to burst into compassion first. Compassion is simply caring about the feelings and experience of others. But this change in my default reaction has to happen, slowly and naturally through meditation, contemplation, and prayer. One cannot legislate compassion—one cannot force oneself or others into becoming compassionate.

"If once we admit, be it for a single hour or in a single instance, that there can be anything more important than compassion for a fellow human being, then there is no crime against man that we cannot commit with an easy conscience."

Leo Tolstoy (1828 - 1910)

---

b) Quote for Evening Contemplation

**"Whoever possesses God in their being has Him in a divine manner, and He shines out to them in all things; for them, all things taste of God, and in all things, it is God's image that they see."
(Meister Eckhart)**

Reflection for Deep Recovery (Sharabi)

God does not reside just in church or temple or mosque; God does not sit alone on a mountaintop. God is not there just in the blessings He or She creates. God is in everything—even in the small things. The ones who truly possess God in their being can see God, feel God, and taste God in everything. After coming into the presence of God, I am never lonely, and even when I am alone, I am with God. The Eleventh Step is a trumpet call taking me to that place.

"Loneliness is the poverty of self; solitude is the richness of self."

May Sarton (1912 - 1995)

Meister Eckhart
1260 - 1328

a) Quote for Morning Contemplation

"I tell you the truth, any object you have in your mind, however good, will be a barrier between you and the inmost Truth." (Meister Eckhart)

Reflection for Deep Recovery (Sharabi)

Sobriety is the inmost truth for any alcoholic. Whatever I place before sobriety becomes a barrier between me and my inmost truth. Whatever I place before sobriety, I will lose, along with my sobriety. Nothing must come between me and sobriety.

"Rather than love, than money, than fame, give me truth."

Thoreau (1817 - 1862)

---

b) Quote for Evening Contemplation

"God is greater than God." (Meister Eckhart)

Reflection for Deep Recovery (Sharabi)

Infinity is greater than infinity. God, if he "exists," must exist in something, and if so, this something must be larger than God. This is not possible, for nothing can be greater than God. Therefore, God must be beyond any form the human mind can conceive, for all conceptions are finite. Conceiving of God requires us also to conceive the boundary of God. But there is no boundary. There is nothing which is not God.

"God is best known in not knowing him."

Saint Augustine (354 - 430 A.D.)

Meister Eckhart
1260 - 1328

a) Quote for Morning Contemplation

**"We must come into a transformed knowing, an unknowing which comes not from ignorance but from knowledge."
(Meister Eckhart)**

Reflection for Deep Recovery (Sharabi)

My Higher Power is a "God of my beyond understanding." When I see that I cannot understand God, I have come to God from knowledge, not from fear or ignorance, not from a "need" to believe. I can know God without understanding God, just like I can know a mountain without understanding the mountain; just like I can know love and be moved by love without understanding love, defining love, or being able to explain love.

"The capacities by which we can gain insights into higher worlds lie dormant within each one of us."

Rudolf Steiner (1861 - 1925)

---

b) Quote for Evening Contemplation

"Whenever I have taken leave of my own will... and no longer will anything for myself, then God must will on my behalf. And so in all things in which I do not will for myself, God wills on my behalf." (Meister Eckhart)

Reflection for Deep Recovery (Sharabi)

When I stop compulsively lusting after things and willing things for myself, God steps in and wills for me everything I need. Once I have turned my will and my life over to the care of God, I no longer need to talk about "my will" versus God's will. I am no longer in opposition to God and will flow along carried by God's will. Praying for things and outcomes is a cheapened form of religion. Praying for acceptance and strength is spirituality

"Pray as though everything depended on God. Work as though everything depended on you."

Saint Augustine (354 - 430 A.D.)

"You don't paddle against the current, you paddle with it. And if you get good at it, you throw away the oars."

Kris Kristofferson (born 1936)

Meister Eckhart
1260 - 1328

a) Quote for Morning Contemplation

"God flows inside creatures, yet He remains untouched by all of them, He has no need of them whatsoever." (Meister Eckhart)

Reflection for Deep Recovery (Sharabi)

God has no need for my prayer. I do. I pray not to change God but to change myself, to inspire myself, to move myself, to see new sights. God does not need me, but I need God to light up my way.

"Worship is a way of seeing the world in the light of God."

Heschel (1907 - 1972)

b) Quote for Evening Contemplation

"In the very best kind of prayer that we can pray there should be no 'give me this particular virtue or way of devotion' or 'yes, Lord, give me yourself or eternal life,' or rather 'Lord, give me only what you will and do, Lord, only what you will and in the way that you will.' This kind of prayer is as far above the former as heaven is above earth." (Meister Eckhart)

Reflection for Deep Recovery (Sharabi)

After the Third Step, we stop praying for things; our only prayer is: "God, do with me and with my life whatever you will." But some consider it acceptable to pray for others, not for oneself. In any case, we must give up our ideas on how life has to turn out, and the notion of "success" or result becomes meaningless. Wilfulness and forcefulness drop away; my behavior becomes spontaneous, intuitive, not a matter of will, but of effort. Will is often contaminated; effort is always pure. I make the effort; God produces the result. Underneath it all is total acceptance of how life is going to turn out.

"The issue of prayer is not prayer; the issue of prayer is God."

Heschel (1907 - 1972)

Meister Eckhart
1260 - 1328

a) Quote for Morning Contemplation

**"The most important hour is always the present.
The most significant person is precisely the one sitting across
from you; the most necessary work is always love."
(Meister Eckhart)**

Reflection for Deep Recovery (Sharabi)

It is not even One Day at a Time; it is sometimes One Hour at a
Time. The most important hour for staying sober is the present
hour. The most significant alcoholic is the one sitting across from
me or next to me. And the most necessary work in recovery is
to love this fellow alcoholic. I offer the newcomer my kindness,
acceptance, and love, not my thoughts, not my advice. Loving him
or her means confidence in his ability to do what is needed, with
my help and support.

"No man is so tall as when he stoops to help a child."

Abraham Lincoln (1809 - 1865)

---

b) Quote for Evening Contemplation

**"If someone were to renounce a kingdom or the whole world while
still holding onto themselves, then they would have renounced
nothing at all. And indeed, if someone renounces themselves,
then whatever they might keep, whether the kingdom or honor
or whatever it may be, they will still have renounced all things."
(Meister Eckhart)**

Reflection for Deep Recovery (Sharabi)

There is a freedom and bliss, a wholeness beyond contradiction,
that is known only to those who have surrendered ego completely.
But as long as I hang on to self-will, all renunciation is a show.
Without surrender to a Higher Power, my renunciation of alcohol
will be but a willful act of the ego. It can last a few weeks or
months, or even some years, but it cannot be sustained.

*(He)... only who gives himself up entirely, who abandons his ego forever...
Such a man is taken care of wherever he may be. He need not pray. God
looks after him unasked.*

Ramana Maharshi (1879 - 1950)

Meister Eckhart
1260 - 1328

a) Quote for Morning Contemplation

"For whoever does not truly have God within themselves, but must constantly receive him in one external thing after another, seeking God in diverse ways, whether by particular works, people or places, such a person does not possess God." (Meister Eckhart)

Reflection for Deep Recovery (Sharabi)

Recovery spirituality does not require that I attend church, temple or mosque. Once I possess God in my soul, I no longer need to seek God anywhere: in any company, in any place, or in any manner of action. Once I possess God, the action will come naturally. And only when my own faith is weak, will I argue about God and be aroused to anger by others disagreeing with me.

"Faith is different from proof. The latter is human; the former is a gift from God."

Blaise Pascal (1623 - 1662)

b) Quote for Evening Contemplation

"This real possession of God is to be found in the heart, in an inner motion of the spirit towards him and striving for him, and not just in thinking about him always and in the same way. We should not content ourselves with the God of thoughts for, when the thoughts come to an end, so too shall God. Rather, we should have a living God who is beyond the thoughts of all people and all creatures. That kind of God will not leave us." (Meister Eckhart)

Reflection for Deep Recovery (Sharabi)

God is not a concept to be understood—accepted or rejected. God is not so insecure or flimsy that He needs me—or anyone—to "believe." God is not a concept I create with thoughts, nor does He leave when my thoughts cease for He is beyond all thought. I must seek God not in thoughts or ideas, but in my heart.

"A God who is both self-sufficient and content to remain so could not interest us enough to raise the question of His existence."

W. H. Auden (1907 - 1973)

"God does not mind your imperfections; He minds your indifference."

Parmahansa Yogananda (1893 - 1952)

Meister Eckhart
1260 - 1328

a) Quote for Morning Contemplation

"We too should consciously look out for our Lord in all things. This demands much effort and must cost us all that our senses and faculties are capable of. But this is the right thing for us to do, so that we grasp God in the same way in all things and find him equally everywhere." (Meister Eckhart)

Reflection for Deep Recovery (Sharabi)

I can stop attaching my petty labels of "good" and "bad" to things that I encounter, for they are all God. When I am able to see God everywhere, I shall be free of the "shoulds" and "shouldn't" that burden my capacity for joy and ecstasy. Total acceptance is the landing pad I prepare for God's helicopter.

"Find ecstasy in life; the mere sense of living is joy enough."

Emily Dickinson (1830 - 1886)

---

b) Quote for Evening Contemplation

"Not all people are called to follow the same path to God. If you find then that the shortest way for you does not lie in many outward works, great endurance and privation—if you do not find these things right for you—then be at peace and have little to do with them." (Meister Eckhart)

Reflection for Deep Recovery (Sharabi)

I am at peace if even my path to God does not mirror that of others, for I follow my heart.

"Any path is only a path, and there is no affront, to oneself or to others, in dropping it if that is what your heart tells you to do. Look at every path closely and deliberately. Try it as many times as you think necessary and ask yourself only one question: does this path have a heart? If it does, the path is good; if it doesn't, it is of no use."

Carlos Castenada (1925 - 1998) quoting Don Juan.

Meister Eckhart
1260 - 1328

a) Quote for Morning Contemplation

"To the quiet mind, all things are possible. What is a quiet mind? A quiet mind is one which nothing weighs on, nothing worries, which, free from ties and from all self-seeking, is wholly merged into the will of God and dead to its own." (Meister Eckhart)

Reflection for Deep Recovery (Sharabi)

Until self-seeking slips away, the mind is chattering away. Only a quiet mind can merge into the will of God. And rather than forcing the mind into quietness, I can ponder: how am I causing all this noise? The object of meditation is to quiet the mind, to get to the empty mind. No effort is needed; the awakening will happen.

"Only the inner silence is yours. No-one gave it to you. You were born with it, and you will die with it. Thoughts have been given to you. You have been conditioned by them."

Osho (1931 - 1990)

---

b) Quote for Evening Contemplation

"In no way do our works serve to make God give us anything or do anything for us. Our Lord wishes his friends to be freed from such an attitude, and thus he removes their support from them so that they must henceforth find their support only in Him." (Meister Eckhart)

Reflection for Deep Recovery (Sharabi)

Do what is called for and do not expect or await rewards from God. My drinking prayers were: "Lord, get me out of this jam, and I'll do whatever you want. I'll live my life henceforth with devotion to you." Now I realize: there are no "rewards" in life. There is no bartering with God, no exchanging good behavior for good health, no trading attendance at meetings for brownie points. My sobriety is not a reward for my goodness or obedience, nor is it a prize for working the Steps, for praying daily, or for setting up chairs at the meeting. My sobriety is simply my way of reaching out to God.

"Our huffing and puffing to impress God, our scrambling for brownie points, our thrashing about trying to fix ourselves while hiding our pettiness and wallowing in guilt are nauseating to God and are a flat out denial of the gospel of grace."

Brennan Manning (1934 -2013)

Meister Eckhart
1260 - 1328

a) Quote for Morning Contemplation

"There are people who savor God in one way but not in another, and they want to possess God according to one manner of devotion and not another. I can tolerate this, but it is quite wrong. If we are to take God correctly, then we must take him equally in all things: in tribulation as in prosperity, in tears as in joy. He should always be the same for you." (Meister Eckhart)

Reflection for Deep Recovery (Sharabi)

I cannot savor God when the sun is shining and be unhappy with Him or Her when it is cloudy or when it snows. God is not present in only those things that I represent to myself as "good" things; I do not lose faith because of difficulties. God is always God, unaffected and unchanging. This world is not a sport or a game, and I am not a sports critic judging and reporting on God's performance.

b) Quote for Evening Contemplation

"Whoever wants to receive the body of our Lord does not need to scrutinize what they are feeling at the time or how great their piety or devotion is, but rather they should note the state of their will and attitude of mind. You should not place too much weight on your feelings but emphasize, rather, the object of your love and striving." (Meister Eckhart)

Reflection for Deep Recovery (Sharabi)

I must not try to impress others with my proclamations of God's greatness or with statements hinting at the depth of my humility, gratitude, and piety. I must not take pride in how devoted I am—to God or to this program. The focus must be not on what I feel about God but on God. The focus must not be on my feelings about recovery but on the principles of recovery. I must beware of the 30-day wonders who are all excited and enthusiastic about sobriety, ostentatiously praising the fellowship for a few weeks at every meeting... and then disappear. I must not expect that continually declaring my love of—and gratitude for—the program will take me to sobriety.

Meister Eckhart
1260 - 1328

a) Quote for Morning Contemplation

**"For you to ask me: Who is God? What is God?
I reply: Is-ness. Is-ness is God." (Meister Eckhart)**

Reflection for Deep Recovery (Sharabi)

God is not just an abstract creation of the human mind. God is the very essence of Being, that very sense of is-ness that we all possess. It is not that I have conscious contact with God; God is consciousness itself. God is not just present—God is Presence itself. What distracts me from God is words; what brings me to Him is stillness.

Tat Tvam Asi "Thou art that which is."
Upanishads (recorded 6th century B.C. or earlier)

"My own brain is to me the most unaccountable of machinery - always buzzing, humming, soaring roaring diving, and then buried in mud. And why? What's this passion for?"
Virginia Woolf (1882 - 1941)

b) Quote for Evening Contemplation

"God's characteristic is being. For in being, mere being, lies all that is at all. Being is the first name. Defect means lack of being. Our whole life ought to be being." (Meister Eckhart)

Reflection for Deep Recovery (Sharabi)

"You are so fully present that you exist in this moment, and only in this moment. You are awake in the eternal now. At the very deepest level of awakened Presence, the past and future have disappeared, and only the present moment is available to you."
Leonard Jacobson (born 1944)

And in that awakened Presence—in pure Being—there is total freedom: the freedom to drink and the freedom not to drink. My past history does not matter and how I used to behave in the past is irrelevant., There is no such thing as "who I really am," or "what kind of person I am;" no "I am this," or "I am that." I just am—total freedom unencumbered by ideas and concepts.

"If the doors of perception were cleansed, everything would appear to man as it is, infinite."
William Blake (1757 - 1827)

45

Meister Eckhart
1260 - 1328

a) Quote for Morning Contemplation

"He who would be serene and pure needs but one thing: detachment... The aim of man is beyond the temporal—in the serene region of the everlasting Present." (Meister Eckhart)

Reflection for Deep Recovery (Sharabi)

Serenity can be attained through first removing attachment to worldly things and attachment to planned outcomes. As long as I am attached to an outcome, the fear of failure will prevent serenity. Serenity is not an emotional state based on external conditions; these will constantly be changing. My ultimate aim in sobriety must lie beyond the temporal realm, in something timeless and beyond circumstances. My aim is to be in the emptiness of this present moment—which itself is timeless and eternal.

"Pray to God that your attachment to such transitory things as wealth, name, and creature comforts may become less and less every day."

Sri Ramakrishna (1836 - 1886)

b) Quote for Evening Contemplation

"It is not enough for us to perform the works of virtue, exercising obedience, accepting poverty or disgrace or practicing humility or detachment in some other way; rather we should strive ceaselessly until we attain the essence and ground of virtue, practicing virtue without the ulterior motive even of a great and good cause, so that the virtuous acts, in fact, happen spontaneously on account of love of virtue. " (Meister Eckhart)

Reflection for Deep Recovery (Sharabi)

What's the use of "trying" to be humble? I can only "try" to be what I am not. Humility is simply being natural; no need to "try." If I am humble, I wouldn't know it, no one would notice it, and I wouldn't be concerned about being humble or virtuous. There is no "doing" humble; it happens by itself. And when it happens, we will have acquired a deep awe of and respect for people, wherever they are. This is the essence and ground of virtue; we no longer have to "do" virtue, for it occurs spontaneously.

"Almost every man wastes part of his life attempting to display qualities that he does not possess."

Samuel Johnson (1709 - 1784)

Meister Eckhart
1260 - 1328

a) Quote for Morning Contemplation

"... those who cling to their own egos in their penances and external devotions, which such people regard as being of great importance... God have mercy on them, for they know little of the divine truth! These people are called holy because of what they are seen to do, but inside they are asses, for they do not know the real meaning of divine truth. They are greatly esteemed by people who know no better." (Meister Eckhart)

Reflection for Deep Recovery (Sharabi)

There are self-appointed deacons in recovery, pious and pretentious, portraying themselves as holier than others, claiming that they truly understand recovery, and thinking their job is to run around to keep the flock from straying.

"I see a number of angry dwarfs running around trying to grill a whale"
William Carlos Williams (1883 - 1963)

---

b) Quote for Evening Contemplation

"Be silent, therefore, and do not chatter about God, for by chattering about him, you tell lies and commit a sin. If you wish to be perfect and without sin, then do not prattle about God. Also, you should not wish to understand anything about God, for God is beyond all understanding. A master says: If I had a God that I could understand, I would not regard him as God. If you understand anything about him, then he is not in it." (Meister Eckhart)

Reflection for Deep Recovery (Sharabi)

There is no "understanding" God; if I understand anything about Him or Her, I can be sure that is not God. God must be larger and more mysterious than anything the human mind can conceive. The existence of the universe is a mystery. Claiming "God" created the universe does not take away the mystery but merely kicks the can down the street; it gets me no closer to any understanding. A "God of my understanding"—even the word "God,"—is not God, but only a placeholder for God, a pointer to God.

"The final barrier to attaining God was the word and concept, 'God.' "
Anthony de Mello (1931 - 1997)

Meister Eckhart
1260 - 1328

a) Quote for Morning Contemplation

"How then should I love God?' You should love God non-mentally;
that is to say, the soul should become non-mental and stripped
of her mental images. For as long as your soul is mental, she
will possess images. As long as she has images, she will possess
intermediaries, and as long as she has intermediaries, she will not
have unity or simplicity." (Meister Eckhart)

Reflection for Deep Recovery (Sharabi)

We do not hang God's picture in recovery rooms. For recovery,
I need contact with God—a direct connection with a sense of
God—not a story about God, and not a mental concept of God. An
image or concept of God is not God but a creation of the human
mind: an intermediary; I must love God directly, not through an
intermediary. I must let the people I sponsor come to love God in
their own way, not in my way.

---

b) Quote for Evening Contemplation

"Is it not better that we should do something in order to drive
away the darkness and dereliction? Should we not pray or read or
listen to a sermon or do something else that is virtuous in order
to help ourselves? No, certainly not! The very best thing you can
do is to remain still for as long as possible. You should know that
God must pour himself into you and act upon you where he finds
you prepared just as the sun must pour itself forth and cannot
hold itself back when the air is pure and clean." (Meister Eckhart)

Reflection for Deep Recovery (Sharabi)

I cannot try to "do something" to take away my desire for alcohol.
The best I can do is surrender and become still: empty myself and
just become willing to receive. The spirit of God will enter and
remove my compulsion, for this compulsion is not present in total
stillness and silence and in surrender.

*"While praying, listen to the words very carefully. When your heart is
attentive, your entire being enters your prayer without your having to
force it."*

Nachman (1772 - 1810)

Kabir
1440 - 1518

a) Quote for Morning Contemplation

"Kabir says:
Student, tell me, what is God?
He is the breath inside the breath." (Kabir)

Reflection for Deep Recovery (Sharabi)

God is in every breath—no, even more—God is the very essence
of breath. God is the very essence of everything, intimately
intertwined and inseparable. God is the innermost essence of
existence, of Being. To experience God, just deeply experience your
breath—no need for words, no need to explain.

"Man is the only animal for whom his own existence is a problem which
he has to solve."

Erich Fromm (1900 - 1980)

b) Quote for Evening Contemplation

"Are you looking for me?
I am in the next seat. My shoulder is against yours.
You will not find me in the stupas, not in Indian shrine rooms, nor
in synagogues, nor in cathedrals...
When you really look for me, you will see me instantly —
You will find me in the tiniest house of time." (Kabir)

Reflection for Deep Recovery (Sharabi)

I do not have to go looking for God in Holy Places, in grand
shrines or sacred spaces, in cathedrals or temples, synagogues or
mosques, for God is everywhere. Not only is God everywhere, He
is present in every tiny moment. God is right here in this meeting,
sitting next to me, rubbing shoulders with me. I never have to wait
for I can find God even in the smallest moment of time, even in the
space between the words of my prayer.

"Travel in all the four quarters of the earth, yet you will find nothing
anywhere. Whatever there is, is only here."

Sri Ramakrishna (1836 - 1886)

Kabir
1440 - 1518

a) Quote for Morning Contemplation

"But if a mirror ever makes you sad, you should know that it does not know you." (Kabir)

Reflection for Deep Recovery (Sharabi)

It can only be a profound ignorance of Self that leads to "self-hate." It is sheer ignorance to look in the mirror and not like the "me" that I see. Being sad, angry, or angry at myself, beating myself up, comes from not knowing the sacred and divine me. This sense of shame and self-deprecation also leads to alcoholism and addictions. Where did I learn this; who taught me? So, when I encounter a newcomer bathed in his or her own negativity, I see a blessed child who has been misled, a person viewing himself in a distorting mirror, like they have at carnivals. I have compassion, and my job is to help them see themselves kindly. For if I—and others—refuse to engage with the negative newcomers, where will they go to heal?

---

b) Quote for Evening Contemplation

"Many have died; you also will die.
The drum of death is being beaten.
The world has fallen in love with a dream.
Only sayings of the wise will remain." (Kabir)

Reflection for Deep Recovery (Sharabi)

Many have died pursuing something that is not there, died pursuing futile dreams. For dreams are but romantic visions and fantasies, delusions taking us away from being fully in the now, from facing life on life's terms. People have died using drink to numb their fear of death. You as a sober person will die too—yes—but the wisdom of recovery will remain, the goodness will remain. We have become part of something larger—a wisdom tradition that will continue to help thousands and millions in these rooms and this fellowship long after you and I are gone.

"After your death, you will be what you were before your birth."
Arthur Schopenhauer (1788 - 18 60)

"Beauty endures only for as long as it can be seen; goodness, beautiful today, will remain so tomorrow."
Sappho (620 B.C. - 550 B.C.)

Kabir
1440 - 1518

a) Quote for Morning Contemplation

"All know that the drop merges into the ocean, but few know that the ocean merges into the drop." (Kabir)

Reflection for Deep Recovery (Sharabi)

Yes, I realize I am in recovery, but I should also know: recovery is now in me, it is part of me. I am recovery; recovery is me. To the newcomer and to the world, my Being and my behavior represent recovery. I accept the responsibility; I am not bashful or nervous because it is not just me dealing with everything alone. The ocean is in me now.

---

b) Quote for Evening Contemplation

"If you want the truth,
I'll tell you the truth:
Listen to the secret sound,
the real sound,
which is inside you." (Kabir)

Reflection for Deep Recovery (Sharabi)

I look deep inside myself for that secret sound, that real sound, that Higher Power, that Deeper Truth. That deeper conversation with God is wordless. There are no words that can describe the connection with God; words are too limited, frozen, too shallow. Only sound... the primordial vibration of Om... the background radiation of the universe... the reverberation of pure Being... the sound of silence — these represent the Truth.

"The secret conversation is thus entirely spiritual; it is a direct encounter between God and the soul, abstracted from all material constraints."
Nachman (1772 - 1810)

Kabir
1440 - 1518

a) Quote for Morning Contemplation

**"If one wants to be 'loved' one must first know how to give love."
(Kabir)**

Reflection for Deep Recovery (Sharabi)

Cats know how to receive love, but dogs know also how to give love. Humans, on the other hand, are often too cautious to do either. They seek love and go to the bar hoping to find love—by accident. In recovery, rather than seeking love, we must seek to give love. Only by loving do we become beloved. Only by giving it away do we receive it. If we desire sobriety, we must help a fellow alcoholic stay sober; this is the great secret discovered by the founders but known in essence to all the wisdom traditions for centuries and for millennia.

"Love grows by giving. The love we give away is the only love we keep. The only way to retain love is to give it away.

Elbert Hubbard (1856 - 1915)

---

b) Quote for Evening Contemplation

"I burst out laughing when I hear that the fish in the water is thirsty. You don't grasp the fact that what you are looking for, what is most alive, is inside your own house. Yet, you walk from forest to forest, from one holy city to the next, with a confused look!" (Kabir)

Reflection for Deep Recovery (Sharabi)

Recovery is just the act of returning home. I used to go from bar to bar, from girlfriend to girlfriend, from boyfriend to boyfriend, trying to find myself, thirsting for something that would fulfill me, relieve my pain. Now I might be going from meeting to meeting trying to find the "right" holy meeting, trying to find the right, wise, old-timer. But what I really want—what I have been seeking through drinking and now, through sobriety—has been inside me all along. There is no special place to "get" to. It is only at home—where I have been all along—that I will find peace with my deepest self.

"It's a puzzling thing. The truth knocks on the door, and you say, 'Go away, I'm looking for the truth.' And so it goes away. Puzzling."

Robert M. Pirsig (1928 - 2017)

Kabir
1440 - 1518

a) Quote for Morning Contemplation

"Wherever you are is the entry point." (Kabir)

Reflection for Deep Recovery (Sharabi)

Recovery begins where you are right now. Spiritual awakening can begin where I am right now. My meeting begins when I get to the meeting; transformation begins right now. I can let God in right this moment; no preparation is needed to turn my will and my life over to the care of God. No preparation is needed to enter recovery: you do not need to finish that drink.

"A spark can set a whole forest on fire. Just a spark. Save it."
Charles Buchowski (1920 - 1994)

b) Quote for Evening Contemplation

**"I hear bells ringing that no one has shaken;
inside 'love' there is more joy than we know of." (Kabir)**

Reflection for Deep Recovery (Sharabi)

I have acquired the ability to be happy for no reason at all, to hear bells that no one has shaken and that the scientific instruments cannot pick up, to hear music that no one is playing. I am more deeply joyous than I ever knew possible, and even I cannot figure out why. I have seen and felt it. I have been touched by love—not love of or love from—but just love. Perhaps love is just another name for a palpable feel of God; perhaps our love is how we get to touch God. We cannot pray for happiness because it is not God's job to bring it to us.

"Morality is not the doctrine of how we may make ourselves happy, but how we may make ourselves worthy of happiness."
Immanuel Kant (1724 - 1804)

Kabir
1440 - 1518

a) Quote for Morning Contemplation

**"Those who hope to be reasonable about it fail.
The arrogance of reason has separated us from that love.
With the word "reason," you already feel miles away." (Kabir)**

Reflection for Deep Recovery (Sharabi)

All reasons to stop drinking failed to keep me sober; people's reasonable advice that I should cut down on my drinking was useless. All my rational attempts at sobriety failed. I must long for sobriety not for any particular reason but with passion and madness: that is the love-craziness needed. Then the clouds lift; everything opens up.

"If you want to build a ship, don't drum up people to collect wood and don't assign them tasks and work, but rather teach them to long for the endless immensity of the sea."

Antoine de Saint-Exupéry (1900 - 1944)

---

b) Quote for Evening Contemplation

**"Some worship the formless God
Some worship his various forms
In what way He is beyond these attributes
Only the Knower knows
That music cannot be written
How can then be the notes?
Says Kabir, awareness alone will overcome illusion." (Kabir)**

Reflection for Deep Recovery (Sharabi)

Any God will do in the early days—God without form or God in any one of His many forms. Our idea of God can give us access to a certain place, but ultimately, we must see that God is beyond anything that can be said or written, or sung. Recovery is much deeper and more mysterious than the words and stories in its literature. We must not mistake the printed sheet with ledger lines, staffs and clefs for the music, for the sacred music itself lies far beyond any attempts to describe it, to contain it. We cannot explain the waking state to someone who is in a dream. We can explain sobriety to you but we cannot understand it for you.

Kabir
1440 - 1518

a) Quote for Morning Contemplation

**"What is seen is not the Truth
What is cannot be said." (Kabir)**

Reflection for Deep Recovery (Sharabi)

The great Truth cannot be expressed. If it can be expressed in words, it must be less than the Truth, for Ultimate Truth is always larger than what I or anyone can say about it. If someone says to me: "This is exactly what you need to do to stay sober," then I do it, but I understand: it is not enough. I must look beyond, do more, be more. The Truth of sobriety cannot be said, but it can be found; come along!

"The intellectual power is never at rest; it is never satisfied with any comprehended truth, but ever proceeds on and on towards that truth which is not comprehended."

Giordano Bruno (1548 - 1600)

b) Quote for Evening Contemplation

"The truth is you turned away yourself, and decided to go into the dark alone. Now you are tangled up in others and have forgotten what you once knew... and that's why everything you do has some weird sense of failure in it." (Kabir)

Reflection for Deep Recovery (Sharabi)

When I went on that path of drinking and drugs, I turned away and went into the dark alone. I got tangled up and forgot my essence: something I used to know as a child. I reached a place where everything seemed futile and had some weird sense of failure in it. I knew things were wrong, but I did not know what to set right. You folks told me that I could turn back anytime and start returning to my original self. Come in, you said; we are open all the time—anytime, 24 hours a day; we are your real family.

"The bond that links your true family is not one of blood, but of respect and joy in each other's life. Rarely do members of one family grow up under the same roof."

Richard Bach (born 1936)

"I have been a stranger here in my own land: All my life"
Sophocles (496 B.C.- 406 B.C.)

Kabir
1440 - 1518

a) Quote for Morning Contemplation

**"As long as a human being worries about when he will die,
and what he has that is his, all of his works are zero.
When affection for the I-creature and what it owns is dead,
then the work of the Teacher is over." (Kabir)**

Reflection for Deep Recovery (Sharabi)

The sponsor's most challenging job is to work with the petty, self-centered concerns of the ego. Once the ego and the narcissistic outlook is transcended, the sponsor disappears and becomes just a companion. My picture of "my" universe was that there was "me," at the center with all the things I possessed, and there was the rest of the world with the other people and things in it. Today I see clearly that there is just this large and complex world that will continue without a shudder when I am gone. My death is not going to be a major event in the history of the universe, and yet, my life—and every moment in it—is precious.

---

b) Quote for Evening Contemplation

"That state is very strange. I cannot explain it. It has no village or resting place. That state is without qualities. What name can one give it? In that state there is no air or water, and no creation or creator; There is no bud or flower, and no fetus or semen; There is no education or Vedas, and no word or taste; There is no body or settlement, and no earth, air or space; There is no guru or disciple, and no easy or difficult path." (Kabir)

Reflection for Deep Recovery (Sharabi)

Kabir is referring to the Enlightened State, the ultimate state in the evolution of consciousness, that spiritual awakening—that union with God—that every alcoholic, indeed every human being, secretly desires. That state transcends description; it has no qualities, it contains nothing, and there are no easy or difficult paths to it. There are no sponsors or guides, no knowledge either, no feeling or ideas associated with being there. It is a very strange place. You know it... don't you? No, no, don't look there, that's not where it is. It is all around you, NOW! It is consciousness without content; it is non-conceptual awareness; it is pure existence, unfettered being. It is "enlightenment,"—but it only happens in the moment. You cannot hang on to it, but you can return anytime.

Kabir
1440 - 1518

a) Quote for Morning Contemplation

"Look at you, you madman! Screaming you are thirsty and dying in a desert when all around you there is nothing but water." (Kabir)

Reflection for Deep Recovery (Sharabi)

I have everything in sobriety to live with satisfaction and joy, and yet I am mad. I am screaming for things I don't have, complaining about some little annoyance or the other, upset that people are getting away with things. All I need is already here, already mine. I need to become still and look... take it in. In sobriety, I have an obligation and a responsibility to be joyful for what I have and to show up in my gratitude, not wallow in some morose swamp claiming to myself that I am being real when I describe my misery.

"Happy families are all alike. Each unhappy family is unhappy in its own unique way."

Leo Tolstoy (1828 - 1910)   (Anna Karenina opening)

---

b) Quote for Evening Contemplation

"The river that flows in you also flows in me." (Kabir)

Reflection for Deep Recovery (Sharabi)

We are all the same. We are all alcoholics trying to stay sober today. We have a commonness no matter if we are the newcomer who is still drinking or we have forty years of uninterrupted sobriety. The same river flows in each of us. I am the same as you. I am you. You are me.

"We awaken in others the same attitude of mind we hold toward them."

Elbert Hubbard (1856 - 1915)

Kabir
1440 - 1518

a) Quote for Morning Contemplation

"... the divine law of love that speaks so clearly with compassion's elegant tongue, saying, eternally saying: 'all are forgiven – moreover, dears, no one has ever been guilty.'" (Kabir)

Reflection for Deep Recovery (Sharabi)

Forgiveness happens when I see that no wrong was done. Things just happened; no one is guilty or needs to be condemned and then shown mercy; no one needs punishment. That is the divine law of love and compassion. So I forgive others and forgive myself. I forgive my parents, it was not personal; it was merely parents being people. I can give up the notion—right now—that anyone has wronged me or that I have wronged anyone. If I never condemned, I would not need to forgive. Here, compassion is the only right, and there is no wrong.

"Forgiveness is the healing of the perception of separation."

Course in Miracles (1976)

---

b) Quote for Evening Contemplation

"As long as I talked unceasingly about the Lord, the Lord stayed away, kept at a distance. But when I silenced my mouth, sat very still and fixed my mind at the doorway of the Lord, I was linked to the music of the Word, and all my talking came to an end." (Kabir)

Reflection for Deep Recovery (Sharabi)

As long as I am talking, I am focused on the words, on my thoughts, on ideas and meanings, on desires and entreaties—not on God. The presence of God can be sensed only when my words subside into music, into a melody, into silence. Then there is no talk—only God.

"The seeker's silence is the loudest form of prayer."

Swami Vivekananda (1863 - 1902)

"What science cannot declare, art can suggest; what art suggests silently, poetry speaks aloud; but what poetry fails to explain in words, music can express. Whoever knows the mystery of vibrations indeed knows all things."

Hazrat Inayat Khan (1882 - 1927)

Kabir
1440 - 1518

a) Quote for Morning Contemplation

"Look! Here am I right within you.
Not in a temple, nor in a mosque,
Not in Kaaba nor Kailas,
But here, right within you am I." (Kabir)

Reflection for Deep Recovery (Sharabi)

You and I have a sense of mystery, the ability to experience awe and wonderment, a sense of something which is just beyond. And the seed of this mystery, the source of this sense, is not within the mosque nor on the mountaintop where the Gods are supposed to dwell. It is right within you, within me. And those moments when I get it, the distinction between my deepest Self and God disappears. I understand now why Kabir says "I," sometimes, when he is speaking of God. He is lost in the mystical trance of a fully realized and conscious being; it is all "I," no subject or object, all One.

b) Quote for Evening Contemplation

"Admire the diamond that can bear the hits of a hammer." (Kabir)

Reflection for Deep Recovery (Sharabi)

When I have found my Truth, I can resist the onslaught of everyone telling me how to be and what to do. If criticized, I can stay and face it, examine it, see if I want to do something about it. Earlier, I would run immediately if criticized, or I would get mad at them. Today, I can even resist the advice of others while appreciating their desire to help. I do not need to succumb to their pressure to be like them. I can practice, "to thine own self be true."

"Pay no attention to critics. No one ever erected a statue to a critic."
Werner Erhard (born 1935)

"Praise or blame has but a momentary effect on the man whose love of beauty in the abstract makes him a severe critic on his own works.."
John Keats (1795 - 1821)

Kabir
1440 - 1518

a) Quote for Morning Contemplation

**"It is needless to ask of a saint the caste
To which he belongs;
For the priest, the warrior, the tradesman,
And all the thirty-six castes
Alike are seeking for God." (Kabir)**

Reflection for Deep Recovery (Sharabi)

It is needless to ask of an alcoholic what he or she does for a living, what his ethnicity is, and what religion he follows; whether he is a Republican or a Democrat, whether he is a Socialist or a Marxist, a Baptist or a Buddhist. For here, we are all the same; we are all seeking the same.

"I refuse to allow any man-made differences to separate me from any other human beings."

Maya Angelou (1928 - 2014)

---

b) Quote for Evening Contemplation

**"It is the Spirit of the quest which helps;
I am the slave of this Spirit of the quest." (Kabir)**

Reflection for Deep Recovery (Sharabi)

We are all seekers here, seekers of sobriety, seekers of serenity, seekers of humility, seekers of God. Whatever it is that I am seeking: that thing is my Master, and I become its slave. We are enslaved here by our desire to live a life of integrity, authenticity, generosity, and kindness, grounded in spiritual principles. We are all slaves of this spirit of the quest; we have gladly surrendered to the process. We are seeking, but we are now seeking, not in bars, not in alcohol, not in drugs, but in a different plane.

"What is it we are questing for? It is the fulfillment of that which is potential in each of us. Questing for it is not an ego trip; it is an adventure to bring into fulfillment your gift to the world, which is yourself."

Joseph Campbell (1904 - 1987)

"The afternoon of life is just as full of meaning as the morning; only, its meaning and purpose are different..."

Carl Jung (1875 - 1961)

Kabir
1440 - 1518

a) Quote for Morning Contemplation

**"The guest is inside you, and also inside me;
You know the sprout is hidden inside the seed.
We are all struggling; none of us has gone far.
Let your arrogance go, and look around inside." (Kabir)**

Reflection for Deep Recovery (Sharabi)

The seed of recovery and spiritual awakening is hidden inside me
and you—inside each of us. We just need to nurture it, water it,
let it sprout. But my arrogance and my unwillingness to listen,
my unwillingness to "turn it over" and surrender completely to
this path, keeps me struggling. I have stopped drinking, yes, but I
haven't gone far. I should look inside for that sense, let go of my
arrogance and feel that spirit. I want to experience the world just
as it is, and not through my concepts, desires, and distortions.

"Some people feel the rain. Others just get wet."

Bob Marley (1845 - 1981)

---

b) Quote for Evening Contemplation

**"When I give up passion, I see that anger remains;
And when I renounce anger, greed is with me still;
And when greed is vanquished, pride and vainglory remain,
... listen to me, dear seeker!
The true path is rarely found." (Kabir)**

Reflection for Deep Recovery (Sharabi)

Sobriety is merely the gate through which I have entered. I
continue to observe passion, anger, greed, selfishness, and vanity.
Just repressing is not enough. I must discover the underlying
structures that result in these reactions. Recovery is a path, not a
solution, and walking the true path of Deep Recovery requires me
to transcend my reactiveness, my opinions, and my judgments.
This path can take me and each of us an immense distance, but
not many of us find it. Many are merely content with not drinking,
going to meetings, having judgments, complaining, and taking
sides: expressing opinions. I hope I shall seek more.

*"The only means of strengthening one's intellect is to make up one's mind
about nothing, to let the mind be a thoroughfare for all thoughts."*

John Keats (1795 - 1821)

61

Kabir
1440 - 1518

a) Quote for Morning Contemplation

**"Work has no other aim than the getting of knowledge;
When that comes, then work is put away." (Kabir)**

Reflection for Deep Recovery (Sharabi)

The knowledge I acquire in recovery is not merely logical or
conceptual knowledge. It is a deeper knowing. It comes through
working the Steps, contemplating God, becoming active in service,
praying, and meditating. And once that knowledge is acquired,
the books can be put away. Once these spiritual principles have
become part of me, the words, the Steps, and the Promises can
all be put away, for they have already become absorbed into my
bones.

*"We shall find peace. We shall hear angels, we shall see the sky sparkling
with diamonds."*

Anton Chekhov (1860 - 1904)

---

b) Quote for Evening Contemplation

**"He wove the sheet so fine, so fine,
He wove the sheet so fine...
Saints and humans wrap themselves in His sheet
But the wrapping soils the sheet, so fine, so fine...
His servant Kabir wraps himself in the sheet
with effort and care,
he keeps it spotlessly clean
This sheet, so fine, so fine." (Kabir)**

Reflection for Deep Recovery (Sharabi)

Saints and humans may try to grab God's gift, but only the servant
of God knows how to treasure the gift. I must be gentle in how
I handle the gift of sobriety... so fine, so fine. I preserve it with
effort and with care; I strive to keep it spotlessly clean.

Kabir
1440 - 1518

a) Quote for Morning Contemplation

**"I do not quote from the scriptures;
I simply see what I see." (Kabir)**

Reflection for Deep Recovery (Sharabi)

I must beware: quoting from the Big Book will not keep me sober.
I must learn to look and see, and I must trust what I see; that
becomes my truth. Even an "authoritative" book just becomes the
starting point for further discussion and personal exploration.

*"The book is not simply the object that one holds in one's hands... it
indicates itself, constructs itself, only on the basis of a complex field of
discourse."*

Michel Foucault (1924 - 1986)

---

b) Quote for Evening Contemplation

**"When the bride is one
with her lover,
who cares about
the wedding party?" (Kabir)**

Reflection for Deep Recovery (Sharabi)

We come to meetings seeking to be one with our bride and lover;
we come to embrace recovery. Who cares that there may be some
noisy people at the meeting? Or even a party next door? Life is
noisy, and once I access the quiet joy inside my heart, the noise
coexists peacefully with the silence in me.

*"Stop insisting on clearing your head—clear your ****ing heart instead."*
Charles Buchowski (1920 - 1994)

*"Human beings are not on earth to be citizens, or taxpayers, or socially
engineered pawns of other human beings; rather, they are here in order
to grow, to transform, to become their authentic selves."*
Stephan Hoeller (born 1931)

Kabir
1440 - 1518

a) Quote for Morning Contemplation

"Be strong then, and enter into your own body; there you have a solid place for your feet. Think about it carefully! Don't go off somewhere else." (Kabir)

Reflection for Deep Recovery (Sharabi)

My buttock is on the chair, my feet on the floor. I feel the breath going down into my chest and out again. I am learning to inhabit my own body as an embodied self, not just as a bobblehead who agrees with things, has opinions, and makes comments. My drinking urge was a body sensation. It has to be healed at body level, not just mind.

"Traumatized people chronically feel unsafe inside their bodies: the past is alive in the form of gnawing interior discomfort... they become expert at... numbing what is... inside. They learn to hide from their selves."

Bessel van der Kolk (born 1943)

---

b) Quote for Evening Contemplation

"There is nothing but water in the holy pools. I know, I have been swimming there. All the gods sculpted of wood or ivory can't say a word. I know, I have been crying out to them. The Sacred Books of the East are nothing but words. I looked through their covers one day sideways. What Kabir talks of is only what he has lived through. If you have not lived through something, it is not true." (Kabir)

Reflection for Deep Recovery (Sharabi)

We alcoholics can only talk of the truth we have lived through, not philosophies, not the knowledge of books, nor the theories of professionals. I speak my story, speak my experience, speak from my heart. The newcomer will connect because I have lived through what he or she is going through. We do not offer pills to cure them, nor holy water to sanctify them, nor do we suggest abiding by religious laws or paying money to the priests. We offer the truth about alcohol, and we meet them with our heart.

"To handle yourself, use your head; to handle others, use your heart."

Eleanor Roosevelt (1884 - 1962)

Kabir
1440 - 1518

a) Quote for Morning Contemplation

**"If you make love with the divine now,
in the next life you will have the face of satisfied desire." (Kabir)**

Reflection for Deep Recovery (Sharabi)

Sobriety is built on love: love of truth, love of God, love of the present—as is. I must love and accept everything as it is right now, everyone as they are right now, for the "now" is divine. I surrender to love of this divine now. Next moment is another life, and hopefully, my face will show serenity... wait! There is no next moment! This is it. It is all one moment!

"Happiness, not in another place but this place... not for another hour, but this hour."

Walt Whitman (1819 - 1892)

"To love somebody, you have to choose for them to be the way they are. Exactly."

Werner Erhard (born 1935)

b) Quote for Evening Contemplation

**"I am looking at you,
You at him,
Kabir asks, how to solve
This puzzle—
You, he, and I." (Kabir)**

Reflection for Deep Recovery (Sharabi)

Two alcoholics gathered together in the presence of God: You, God and I. You are looking at me and I at God; this is a puzzle. But what is the question? Hanging in there are the three of us, suspended in the moment—you, He and I. There is no puzzle, no question, nothing to be solved. This is it. I get it now.

"Never let a problem to be solved become more important than a person to be loved."

Barbara Johnson (1927 - 2007)

Kabir
1440 - 1518

a) Quote for Morning Contemplation

**"I said to my longing heart,
What is this river you want to cross?
There are no travelers before you; there is no road.
Do you see anyone moving or resting on that bank?"** (Kabir)

Reflection for Deep Recovery (Sharabi)

Oh, the restlessness, the unfulfilled fantasies, the unattainable dreams, the imagined places, the impossible experiences... ! But I came here, and they told me: there is no one on that other bank who is happy, nothing there that will bring you any joy. All that you want is available on this side of the river. "Stay here!" they said. And I stayed and realized: this is my home.

*"I was passionate, filled with longing. I searched far and wide,
But the day that the Truthful One found me,
I was at home."*

Lal Ded/Lalleshwari (1320 - 1392)

---

b) Quote for Evening Contemplation

**"Listen to me brother!
Bring the vision of
the Beloved in your heart."** (Kabir)

Reflection for Deep Recovery (Sharabi)

God is a concept for the theologians, an authority for the religious administrators, and an idea for the philosophers; but for me, the alcoholic, I must relate to God as the vision of goodness and the pure love in my heart, the relatedness I feel with the human race, the connection and compassion I feel towards my fellow alcoholics, and the gratitude I feel for having found this place.

"And now here is my secret, a very simple secret; it is only with the heart that one can see rightly; what is essential is invisible to the eye."

Antoine de Saint-Exupéry (1900 - 1944)

Kabir
1440 - 1518

a) Quote for Morning Contemplation

"Do you believe there is some place that will make the soul less thirsty?
In that great absence, you will find nothing." (Kabir)

Reflection for Deep Recovery (Sharabi)

I must not repress the thirst of my soul; not try to find a place where the thirst will be less. I will end up empty. Instead of asking God to remove the thirst, I point that thirst towards God, towards honesty, towards goodness, towards right living, towards a spiritual awakening.

"So long as one has a longing to obtain any particular object, one cannot go further than that object."

Hazrat Inayat Khan (1882 - 1927)

b) Quote for Evening Contemplation

"There is no river at all, and no boat, and no boatman.
There is not even a rope to tow the boat, and no one to pull it.
There is no earth, no sky, no time, no thing, no shore, no ford."
(Kabir)

Reflection for Deep Recovery (Sharabi)

There is no river to cross, no change to work for, no inspiring words to seek, no one to help me reach the other side. I simply return to the nothingness of Being. There is no such thing as a sober life. There is life, and there is life with drink; a sober life is just "life." If drinking is a "thing," then not drinking—sobriety itself—is a "not thing." It is a "not-thing" that allows me to linger in the pure freedom of emptiness.

"If you really want to be, you will have to drop all concepts of your being. You will have to disappear, by and by. You will have to melt into nothingness."

Osho (1931 - 1990)

Kabir
1440 - 1518

a) Quote for Morning Contemplation

**"Man, here is your worth,
Your meat is of no use!
Your bones cannot be sold
For making ornaments,
And your skin cannot be played
On an instrument." (Kabir)**

Reflection for Deep Recovery (Sharabi)

My profession is not important here, my skills are not important, nor my smooth skin nor bulging muscles nor strong bones nor perfect teeth nor the money I have accumulated. My name is not important either; that is why we are the anonymous. My competence is not important, nor my beauty nor my cleverness. So: what is important? Of course, not drinking is important, but there must be more. I must contemplate this, for I need to come up with my own answer.

b) Quote for Evening Contemplation

"The blue sky opens out farther and farther, the daily sense of failure goes away, the damage I have done to myself fades, a million suns come forward with light when I sit firmly in that world." (Kabir)

Reflection for Deep Recovery (Sharabi)

"That world," that I "sit firmly in," where is it? What is it? It is a world where I am free under the open sky, not fettered with the illusions and false appetites I had surrounded myself with. "That world" is a world where I have returned to my true self, not running around madly pleasing people, somehow believing that my survival depended on approval and praise. "That world" in the quote above refers to a world where I have found that true connection with my Spirit, and I am illuminated by a million suns. I entered that world when I came into the fellowship, and now I sit firmly in my chair. As I let my eyes adjust to the brightness, I begin to see. My job here is to begin discerning what I am seeing.

"If I paint a wild horse, you might not see the horse... but surely you will see the wildness!"

Pablo Picasso (1881 - 1973)

Nagarjuna
c.150 - c.250 AD

a) Quote for Morning Contemplation

"All philosophies are mental fabrications. There has never been a single doctrine by which one could enter the true essence of things." (Nagarjuna)

Reflection for Deep Recovery (Sharabi)

Recovery is not a philosophy; it is not doctrine; it is not therapy, nor is it a call for willpower or mental strength. The intellect cannot understand the true essence of recovery; intellectual attempts to explain recovery are inadequate. The essence is the practice of a spiritual way of life—not philosophies about sobriety, not theories of how to stay sober. A doctrine can become frozen and lifeless, but a tradition persists through time, breathing and staying alive, pulsing and changing continually, staying relevant to the people who keep coming in.

---

b) Quote for Evening Contemplation

"There is nothing to be denied and nothing to be affirmed. See the real correctly, for he who sees the real correctly is released." (Nagarjuna)

Reflection for Deep Recovery (Sharabi)

The real can be perceived correctly without agreeing or disagreeing with anything. Seeing the real (Truth) will set me free from the bondage of alcohol, from the oppression of ideas, and from the prison created by opinions and beliefs. The real can be seen and experienced—directly—but it is not something that can be put into words and concepts. It exists in a plane different from language, opinions, beliefs, judgments, perspectives, models, ideas, and convictions. This is an essential difference between Eastern and Western approaches to "Reality."

"The Tao that can be told of is not the eternal Tao"

Lao-Tzu (6th century B.C.)

Nagarjuna
c.150 - c.250 AD

a) Quote for Morning Contemplation

"Since all is empty, all is possible." (Nagarjuna)

Reflection for Deep Recovery (Sharabi)

Standing in that space of emptiness, I suddenly see possibility—
that sobriety is possible; that sane and satisfying living is possible.
That emptiness—or "nothingness"—is in the now, devoid of past
and future. It contains no memories, hopes, or expectations, no
ideas, no thoughts, no concepts of "good" or "bad." It requires me
to wipe clean the slate of the mind and thoughts and to enter the
pure existence of the moment, that state of consciousness without
content. True, I cannot "function" from such a permanent state of
bliss, but I can learn to access it any time I choose. And, standing
in that emptiness that is now, sobriety becomes available to me as
possibility for the next moment, and from there, for my entire life.

*"Start by doing what's necessary; then do what's possible, and suddenly
you are doing the impossible."*

Saint Francis of Assisi (1181 - 1226)

b) Quote for Evening Contemplation

**"A person is not earth, not water,
Not fire, not wind, not space,
Not consciousness, and not all of them.
What person is there other than these?" (Nagarjuna)**

Reflection for Deep Recovery (Sharabi)

Who is this entity—this illusion—that I have defined as "the real
me"? I am not my thoughts, I am not my feelings, and I am not my
opinions or beliefs; I am not just my body or my brain. I am not
defined by my likes and dislikes or by the things I get triggered by.
Any attempt to describe myself as "who I really am," has already
started off on the wrong path. It serves only to constrain me into
an artificial consistency with my past and, therefore, I do not
attempt to define myself in such rigid, unchanging terms. It is the
non-constancy of the continuously emerging self that represents
freedom, allows for change.

"To be free means to be lacking in constitutive identity."

Jose Ortega y Gasset (1883 - 1955)

Nagarjuna
c.150 - c.250 AD

a) Quote for Morning Contemplation

**"The victorious ones have said
That emptiness is the relinquishing of all views.
For whomever emptiness is a view,
That one has achieved nothing." (Nagarjuna)**

Reflection for Deep Recovery (Sharabi)

Recovery is measured by how gentle and flexible I have become,
how few things offend me, how few people bother me. In
the process of acceptance, I must even give up the idea that
acceptance is something to achieve or a view to cultivate. Consider
that acceptance includes accepting non-acceptance—in myself and
others. Acceptance involves approaching life with total emptiness,
with no point of view. It will happen if I just get my ego out of
the way, for it is the ego that is non-accepting. Acceptance is the
natural state of being, so empty that it does not even need to be
defined.

b) Quote for Evening Contemplation

**"There is pleasure when a sore is scratched, but to be without
sores is more pleasurable still. Just so, there are pleasures in
worldly desires, but to be without desires is more pleasurable
still." (Nagarjuna)**

Reflection for Deep Recovery (Sharabi)

When I am thirsty, "a beer would feel so good!" But unfortunately
for us alcoholics, one beer is too many, and ten beers isn't enough.
Instead, when I lose that thirst, even greater pleasures open up. So
it is also with the desire for worldly pleasures and material riches.
True, the lack of money can bring distress; every alcoholic has had
money problems—even severe at times. But recovery improves
the money situation, slowly, steadily. Money brings comfort, but
I can become its prisoner if my desire exceeds modest needs.
When I transcend worldly desires and stop the mindless pursuit of
"pleasure," a supreme joy awaits me. This will happen naturally,
just as my desire for alcohol evaporated—naturally.

*"We do not succeed in changing things according to our desire, but
gradually our desire changes."*

Marcel Proust (1871 - 1922)

Nagarjuna
c.150 - c.250 AD

a) Quote for Morning Contemplation

"Ultimate serenity is the coming to rest of all ways of taking things, the repose of named things; no truth has been taught by a Buddha for anyone, anywhere." (Nagarjuna)

Reflection for Deep Recovery (Sharabi)

Serenity is the letting go of definitions and notions—even that of serenity. It is the lack of any perspective, or investment in a point of view, the absence of desire to preach or to convert others. Serenity is simply the absence of disturbance, characterized by the lack of attachment, even to "truth," for all attachment leads to disturbance. Truth—in the higher sense, as opposed to "facts"—is not a concept that can be put into words or taught to someone. We cannot function in the world in such a state of permanent serenity, but we can have access to that state at all times.

"Rarely affirm, seldom deny, always distinguish."

Thomas Aquinas (1224 - 1274)

---

b) Quote for Evening Contemplation

"Just as the grammarian makes one study grammar, a Buddha teaches according to the tolerance of his students; some he urges to refrain from sins, others to do good, some to rely on dualism, other on non-dualism; and to some he teaches the profound, the terrifying, the practice of enlightenment, whose essence is emptiness that is compassion." (Nagarjuna)

Reflection for Deep Recovery (Sharabi)

The sponsor tells some of his students to think, others to pray; some to immerse in service, others to contemplate powerlessness. But the most profound teaching A.A. offers is enlightened compassion ("karuna") for the suffering alcoholic. It comes from a deep acknowledgment of the autonomy of the individual and of our own helplessness. It has no desire, no forcing, no attempt at control—only love. This spiritual awakening (enlightenment,) whose essence is emptiness, shows up as a deep compassion.

"Tolerance does not come by learning but by insight; by understanding that each one should be allowed to travel along the path which is suited to their temperament."

Hazrat Inayat Khan (1882 - 1927)

Nagarjuna
c.150 - c.250 AD

a) Quote for Morning Contemplation

**"He who knows the precepts by heart,
But fails to practice them
Is like one who lights a lamp
And then shuts his eyes." (Nagarjuna)**

Reflection for Deep Recovery (Sharabi)

It is no use just memorizing the Steps; they need to be practiced, lived. I have seen the light after coming to these rooms; now I must not shut my eyes. I must practice these principles in all my affairs, especially with the people I have difficulties with. It is easier in these rooms, but to live and behave by these principles outside—with family, work colleagues and with drivers on the road—that is recovery. Spiritual life is a practice, not a theory.

"In theory, there is no difference between theory and practice. In practice, there is."

Yogi Berra (1925 - 2015)

---

b) Quote for Evening Contemplation

**"Those who speak ill of the spiritual life,
Although they come and go by day,
Are like the smith's bellows:
They take breath but are not alive." (Nagarjuna)**

Reflection for Deep Recovery (Sharabi)

Recovery is more than mental and psychological; it is spirituality that breathes life into recovery. Otherwise, recovery merely feels like the giving up of things, a resignation to a life of abstinence, a rational-cognitive attempt to be less unsuccessful in life, a practical attempt to improve relationships. The ones who deny the notion of a spiritual life: they may be sober, and they may be breathing, and their lives may have improved, but they are not alive; they are not in a joyful embrace of life. Am I one of them, or do I truly feel the powerful aliveness of recovery?

"Some people die at 25 and aren't buried until 75."

Benjamin Franklin (1706 - 1790)

Nagarjuna
c.150 - c.250 AD

a) Quote for Morning Contemplation

"Although a cloth be washed a hundred times, how can it be rendered clean and pure if it be washed in water which is dirty? " (Nagarjuna)

Reflection for Deep Recovery (Sharabi)

What is the point of going to a hundred meetings if my soul and my heart have not been cleansed by the Four Essentials of Authenticity, Integrity, Kindness, and Generosity? If I have not surrendered to living my life by these principles? What is the point of singing God's praises or claiming sobriety if I have not become totally honest with myself and compassionate towards my fellows?

"There are things which a man is afraid to tell even to himself, and every decent man has a number of such things stored away in his mind."

Dostoevsky (1821 - 1881)

b) Quote for Evening Contemplation

**"Any man who strives to do his best
Whether his work be great or small
Is considered to be doing the work of a lion." (Nagarjuna)**

Reflection for Deep Recovery (Sharabi)

Spending time with one alcoholic is no less important than giving a speech to a hundred alcoholics or writing a book for a thousand alcoholics. Helping one person get back on his or her feet is a significant and tremendously important mission. The impact I have made on that one life could suffice to justify my whole life in recovery. If I have done my best with one alcoholic, I consider that I have done the work of a lion.

"In this life, we cannot do great things. We can only do small things with great love."

Mother Teresa (1910 - 1997)

Nagarjuna
c.150 - c.250 AD

a) Quote for Morning Contemplation

"The knowledge which teaches arts and handicrafts is merely knowledge for the gaining of a living; but the knowledge which teaches deliverance from worldly existence, is not that the true knowledge?" (Nagarjuna)

Reflection for Deep Recovery (Sharabi)

Many education courses teach a trade or a profession: how to be "successful" in the world, how to make a living, and how to prosper. These are important, but in recovery, I am after bigger riches; I am marching to a higher calling. I am learning to be in this world but not of it. Is this not an education for a higher plane? Is this not true knowledge?

"What does it matter how one comes by the truth so long as one pounces upon it and lives by it?"

Henry Miller (1891 - 1980)

---

b) Quote for Evening Contemplation

"A highly learned man has two sources of happiness: either he abandons all earthly interests or else he possesses much which could be abandoned." (Nagarjuna)

Reflection for Deep Recovery (Sharabi)

The abandonment of earthly interests for the prize of sobriety is the action of a highly learned man or woman. That surrender to this new way of life, and the removal of attachment—to material things and even to outcomes—will lead to a new freedom and a new happiness. Even if I possess much, the very knowledge that all of it could be abandoned is freeing. Because whatever I desire and covet holds me prisoner. It is only when I abandon desires and turn my will and my life over—to God, to a Higher Power, to the Universe—that I am free.

"No human being, however great, or powerful, was ever so free as a fish."

John Ruskin (1819 - 1900)

Nagarjuna
c.150 - c.250 AD

a) Quote for Morning Contemplation

"If you are truly persevering in virtue, what is the place of a haughty attitude? The cow which has no milk will not be purchased, even equipped with a pleasant-sounding bell." (Nagarjuna)

Reflection for Deep Recovery (Sharabi)

The pleasant and profound things people say at meetings could be empty words—not backed by attitude, actions, or character. I must not be drawn merely to the sound of the bell but seek, instead, those who have no haughtiness, no arrogance, no pomp, no bells: I must seek those who have the milk to nourish me in recovery.

"Be more concerned with your character than your reputation, because your character is what you really are, while your reputation is merely what others think you are."

John Wooden (1910 - 2010)

b) Quote for Evening Contemplation

"Who is blind, dumb and deaf will live a peaceful life of a hundred years." (Nagarjuna)

Reflection for Deep Recovery (Sharabi)

One thought that comes from this is that the simple man who does not engage with the outer world, has no opinions, no desires, no "shoulds" and "shouldn't," will live peacefully for a hundred years. Another thought could be: what is the use of seeking peace at such cost? Both of these perspectives are valid and worthy of contemplation. Contemplative spirituality calls for the ability to sit peacefully amidst the tension of opposites. Only a fool will hastily resolve it into a single rigid opinion. We will grow by contemplating the opposite of every opinion.

"What we agree with leaves us inactive, but contradiction makes us productive."

Goethe (1749 - 1832)

"You always own the option of having no opinion. There is never any need to get worked up or to trouble your soul about things you can't control. These things are not asking to be judged by you. Leave them alone."

Marcus Aurelius (121 - 180 A.D.)

Nagarjuna
c.150 - c.250 AD

a) Quote for Morning Contemplation

"After happiness comes suffering. After suffering arises happiness. For beings, happiness and suffering revolve like a wheel." (Nagarjuna)

Reflection for Deep Recovery (Sharabi)

No matter if I am feeling joy or despair, fulfillment or frustration, irritation or peace, I remember: "This too shall pass." Knowing that life is a succession of feelings makes me sturdy and resilient; accepting this makes me deep. If sunshine, then shadow. "Life on life's terms" means that emotional ups and downs are just part of being human. Even when I am satisfied, it can only be temporary. Sometimes I focus on trivia and forget just how content I am! There is an abiding joy that I am sober, that I exist, that I am.

"Life is constantly providing us with new funds, new resources, even when we are reduced to immobility. In life's ledger, there (are)... no frozen assets."

Henry Miller (1891 - 1980)

b) Quote for Evening Contemplation

**"Although you may spend your life killing,
You will not exhaust all your foes.
But if you quell your own anger,
your real enemy will be slain." (Nagarjuna)**

Reflection for Deep Recovery (Sharabi)

The real enemy in sobriety is the anger and resentment that is inside me—not that person or thing out there. No matter how much I execute revenge and dole out punishment to those "jerks" and "idiots" out there, I will never exhaust all my foes. Shall I resent the mountain for being as tall as it is and obstructing my view of the sea? Or shall I accept it? I get angry when I cannot get my way: when I am helpless and when I feel wounded. If I understand this, then my real enemy is slain. It is that simple. To conquer resentment, I just need to give up the notion that others should behave the way I want them to, and be how I think they should be. In fact: everyone I resent, I owe an amend to—for having hung on to this resentment so long.

"To be wronged is nothing unless you continue to remember it."

Confucius (559 - 459 B.C.)

Nagarjuna
c.150 - c.250 AD

a) Quote for Morning Contemplation

**"The logs of wood which move down the river together
Are driven apart by every wave.
Such inevitable parting should not be the cause of misery."
(Nagarjuna)**

Reflection for Deep Recovery (Sharabi)

Separation and loss are inevitable. That is the nature of change—ever-present in the flow of life. I can honor the death of friends and loved ones—soulfully, reverentially—but there is no need to become miserable. I can accept parting and separation as inevitable along the river of life. Everyone in my life is present temporarily. Awareness of this will allow me to treasure and revere their presence, to be grateful for them when they remain and even when they are gone.

"How lucky I am to have something that makes saying goodbye so hard."
Winnie the Pooh, A. A. Milne (1882 - 1956)

b) Quote for Evening Contemplation

**"As long as you watch the way,
As long as your steps are steady,
As long as your wisdom is unimpaired,
So long will you reap profit." (Nagarjuna)**

Reflection for Deep Recovery (Sharabi)

In recovery, it is not important how fast I am moving. As long as I am walking in the right direction—making steady progress and working the Steps thoughtfully—I will reap profit. It is comforting to understand that I do not have to change everything at once.

"We all want progress, but if you're on the wrong road, progress means doing an about-turn and walking back to the right road; in that case, the man who turns back soonest is the most progressive."
C. S. Lewis (1898 - 1963)

Nagarjuna
c.150 - c.250 AD

a) Quote for Morning Contemplation

"An anthill increases by accumulation.
Medicine is absorbed by distribution.
That which is feared lessens by segmentation.
This is the thing to understand." (Nagarjuna)

Reflection for Deep Recovery (Sharabi)

The prospect of a lifetime of sobriety can be intimidating but such a lifetime of sobriety is accumulated one day at a time, just as an anthill is built, grain by grain. The cure of sobriety is not concentrated but spread out, absorbed in small doses, just like medicine. Sobriety did not happen instantaneously on the day I stopped drinking. Segmenting sobriety into days, months, or years makes the idea less fearsome. This is the thing to understand.

"There is only one day left, always starting over: it is given to us at dawn and taken away from us at dusk."

Jean-Paul Sartre (1905 - 1980)

---

b) Quote for Evening Contemplation

"Although you may remain somewhere for a long time,
It is certain that you will have to leave.
Whatever may be the manner of parting,
The actual going cannot be avoided." (Nagarjuna)

Reflection for Deep Recovery (Sharabi)

My desire to avoid change kept me drinking much longer than I needed to. Now I understand that change is inevitable, and I am acquiring the flexibility to accept change—and parting—with grace. "Missing" things is inevitable in life. That's okay; I am learning not to fear. I realize that every time I pick a path, I will miss all the things on the paths I did not take. Every time I make a change, I am parting with a path, and I have had to leave many paths and change direction many times to get to this point in life. This realization can help me let go of the fear of change. I trust that I will find my way through change with the help of the fellowship, the principles of recovery, God, and the Universe.

"No one likes change but babies in diapers."

Barbara Johnson (1927 - 2007)

79

Nagarjuna
c.150 - c.250 AD

a) Quote for Morning Contemplation

**"He who does not try a remedy
For the disease of going to hell
What will he do when he reaches that place
Where there is no cure to be found?" (Nagarjuna)**

Reflection for Deep Recovery (Sharabi)

Beware of postponing the remedy recovery has to offer for the illness that is taking you towards hell. The longer you wait, the harder it is to turn around. And if you are still drinking, you may be getting close to the point of no return from that voyage of drunkenness. But notice: it is your decision and your right to reject the cure or to accept it.

"I hold it to be the inalienable right of anybody to go to hell in his own way."

Robert Frost (1874 - 1963)

---

b) Quote for Evening Contemplation

**"When young, rejoice in the tranquility of the old.
However great your glory grows, be forbearing in your manner.
Boast not of what you know, even when learned.
However high you may rise, be not proud." (Nagarjuna)**

Reflection for Deep Recovery (Sharabi)

Humility is simplicity. I cannot be proud of myself, no matter how many years of sobriety I have accumulated, how much knowledge I have acquired, how many people I have sponsored, and how many people love me or respect me or look up to me. Wherever I am, I remain simple.

*"If I had only one sermon to preach, it would be a sermon against pride...
One sees great things from the valley; only small things from the peak."*

G. K. Chesterton (1874 - 1936)

Nagarjuna
c.150 - c.250 AD

a) Quote for Morning Contemplation

**"One's desire to be attractive and happy
And to enjoy the pleasures of wealth,
Is like the foolishness of a drunken person
Who, though healthy, must be carried." (Nagarjuna)**

Reflection for Deep Recovery (Sharabi)

The desire to have wealth, beauty, and power, to be admired by everyone—even my concern with being happy—distracts me from the pursuit of the truly important things in life. As a drunk, I may have been admired as the life of the party, but I needed help walking to the bathroom safely. Happiness, attractiveness, popularity, fame—are temporary. I must go after deeper things if I am to achieve a meaningful contentment and serenity.

"Wealth is the ability to fully experience life."

Thoreau (1817 - 1862)

---

b) Quote for Evening Contemplation

**"If you desire ease, forsake learning.
If you desire learning, forsake ease.
How can a man at ease acquire knowledge?
And how can an earnest student enjoy ease?" (Nagarjuna)**

Reflection for Deep Recovery (Sharabi)

If I just want to be lazy, I can find a sponsor—a slack one at that—and take it easy. Hopefully, I will exist without drinking, but I will never become that earnest student of recovery. However, if I am serious about growth and spiritual awakening, I must prepare to work for recovery. Acquiring what Deep Recovery offers calls for perseverance, determination, and industriousness, but the reward is profound.

"Nothing in this world can take the place of persistence. Talent will not; nothing is more common than unsuccessful men with talent. Genius will not; unrewarded genius is almost a proverb. Education will not; the world is full of educated derelicts. Persistence and determination alone are omnipotent.

Calvin Coolidge. (1891 - 1933)

Nagarjuna
c.150 - c.250 AD

a) Quote for Morning Contemplation

"Things derive their being and nature by mutual dependence and are nothing in themselves." (Nagarjuna)

Reflection for Deep Recovery (Sharabi)

I exist in recovery, not as an isolated individual, but as a web of interconnections with other alcoholics. I derive my being through mutual dependence; I am nothing in and of myself. That is why some identify themselves as an alcoholic, first, and only then give their name. I obtain my identity from the people who know me and from the way they know me. My name is not important. What is primary is the fellowship to which I belong and the diversity of individuals who are united. Sobriety is a team sport; we win as a sober community.

"Civilizations should be measured by the degree of diversity attained and the degree of unity retained."

W. H. Auden (1907 - 1973)

---

b) Quote for Evening Contemplation

"The Buddha's teaching of the Dharma is based on two truths: a truth of worldly convention, and ultimate Truth. Those who do not understand the distinction drawn between these two truths do not understand the Buddha's profound Truth." (Nagarjuna)

Reflection for Deep Recovery (Sharabi)

The truth of worldly convention is based on factual matters in the realm of physical existence, of scientific truth. It includes the effort to be honest with oneself and helpful to others. This leads to abstinence, attendance at recovery meetings, and practice of the principles of recovery. But there is another truth, an ultimate truth, enunciated in Buddhism and hinted at in the Big Book: that there is no entity as self—only selflessness, only emptiness. In the world of consciousness, the notion of self is a mere construct, a story created by ego and rooted in social interaction. Therefore, anonymity—manifesting as loss of self—is considered to be the spiritual foundation of sobriety. In recovery, it is reached when we have succeeded in turning our will and our life entirely over to God. Then, there is no ego and no self. This is the profound truth which coexists with the other kind of truth of worldly convention.

Kübler-Ross
1926 - 2004

a) Quote for Morning Contemplation

"Learn to get in touch with the silence within yourself, and know that everything in life has purpose. There are no mistakes, no coincidences; all events are blessings given to us to learn from." (Kübler-Ross)

Reflection for Deep Recovery (Sharabi)

The goal of meditation is to become present to the luxurious stillness within each of us. In that silence, events and happenings, and even desires, appear totally open and without demands—and they seem willing to accept any labels we put on them. We must distinguish the events themselves from our reactions and feelings towards them. We can label the events as mistakes or as coincidences, or we can label them as opportunities and blessings—lessons with meaning and purpose. Then we actively engage in the question: what can we learn from this happening? In recovery, we manage ourselves, not events or happenings—or even desires and cravings—for they are not entirely within our control.

---

b) Quote for Evening Contemplation

"It is not the end of the physical body that should worry us. Rather, our concern must be to live while we're alive—to release our inner selves from the spiritual death that comes with living behind a facade designed to conform to external definitions of who and what we are." (Kübler-Ross)

Reflection for Deep Recovery (Sharabi)

In the beginning of recovery, I made an effort to do and to be what the recovery community expected of me. This was better than following the wild whims—the "brain-storms" generated by my brain—and this safe approach slowly brought some sanity to my life. But as I proceed now in Deep Recovery, I must become true to my authentic self, not hide behind a persona designed to please or impress others. I must examine: how much do I contort myself, trying to please others? I must stop seeking the approval of society or even of the people in recovery—stop trying to conform to external definitions of who I should be. This is the path of the courageous.

"The opposite of courage in our society is not cowardice; it is conformity."
Rollo May (1909 - 1994)

Kübler-Ross
1926 - 2004

a) Quote for Morning Contemplation

"We're put here on Earth to learn our own lessons. No one can tell you what your lessons are; it is part of your personal journey to discover them. On these journeys, we may be given a lot, or just a little bit, of the things we must grapple with, but never more than we can handle." (Kübler-Ross)

Reflection for Deep Recovery (Sharabi)

I got into trouble in my life because I refused to learn what I was supposed to learn. Much pain was caused by my unwillingness to change. Now, in recovery, I am going full-steam ahead, learning life's lessons as part of a fellowship and community. I share my learning with others, and we compare notes. In the end, learning is change; if no change is occurring, then no learning has registered.

"There is a great deal of pain in life, and perhaps the only pain that can be avoided is the pain that comes from trying to avoid pain."

R. D. Laing (1927 - 1989)

---

b) Quote for Evening Contemplation

"The ultimate lesson all of us have to learn is unconditional love, which includes not only others but ourselves as well." (Kübler-Ross)

Reflection for Deep Recovery (Sharabi)

Unconditional love means being a loving presence, free of judgments, and devoid of "shoulds." Love is about where I am coming from: a state of openness and welcome, of joy overflowing from the heart. I "am" love as opposed to "doing" love. I am not doling out my love as a reward for behavior that I approve of. My love is not dependent on the conditions of myself or others or on circumstances. No one is judged as "deserving" love or "not deserving" love, not even myself. I have no demands for anyone or anything to be different, no complaints about the way things and people are. This is acceptance; this is serenity. And it all begins with self-acceptance. There is no love without acceptance.

"I do my thing, and you do your thing. I am not in this world to live up to your expectations, and you are not in this world to live up to mine. You are you, and I am I, and if by chance we find each other, it's beautiful. If not, it can't be helped."

Fritz Perls, (1883 - 1970) "Gestalt Prayer."

Kübler-Ross
1926 - 2004

a) Quote for Morning Contemplation

"The truth does not need to be defended." (Kübler-Ross)

Reflection for Deep Recovery (Sharabi)

It is one thing to defend myself in a court of law, but when I catch myself trying to make arguments within myself to justify my attitude or behavior, I realize I have begun lying. For the truth never needs justification or arguments to defend it; it is merely what is. We alcoholics have been notorious for lying to ourselves, for justifying our follies, for rationalizing our mistakes, for minimizing the seriousness of our transgressions. The capacity to see through my own lies and arguments is the gift from working the Steps, and the willingness to let go of my rationalizations and justifications—not just about alcohol—is the most courageous action called for in recovery.

"A lie which is half a truth is ever the blackest of lies."

Alfred Lord Tennyson (1809 - 1892)

---

b) Quote for Evening Contemplation

"Learning lessons is a little like reaching maturity. You're not suddenly more happy, wealthy, or powerful, but you understand the world around you better, and you're at peace with yourself. Learning life's lessons is not about making your life perfect, but about seeing life as it was meant to be." (Kübler-Ross)

Reflection for Deep Recovery (Sharabi)

When I drop my protests about life—that it should be some other way and not the way it is—but learn to deal with life as it is, I have learned a significant lesson. Serenity is about seeing the world as it is and accepting it—as it is. I may not always like it, and I may have reactions and feelings about it, but at a deep level, I understand: it is what it is, and I am okay with that. Serenity is not when my struggles end but when I accept my struggles. If my serenity has to be carefully protected, it may not be the deep and abiding serenity promised at the end of the spiritual journey.

"The world is not to be put in order; the world is order, incarnate. It is for us to harmonize with this order."

Henry Miller (1891 - 1980)

Kübler-Ross
1926 - 2004

a) Quote for Morning Contemplation

"I've told my children that when I die, to release balloons in the sky to celebrate that I graduated. For me, death is a graduation." (Kübler-Ross)

Reflection for Deep Recovery (Sharabi)

For the alcoholic, graduation occurs when he or she dies without having taken a drink. That is success; he or she has now graduated from recovery college. But the point of entering recovery college is not to graduate from it but to immerse myself in it: to enjoy the learning and the course-work that is available on a daily basis and offered for free. It is called "life." And the more difficult the problems are on the take-home exam, the deeper the learning and the more profound the freedom and liberation that comes from the learning.

"Men die in despair while spirits die in ecstasy."

Honore de Balzac (1799 - 1850)

---

b) Quote for Evening Contemplation

"It's only when we truly know and understand that we have a limited time on earth and that we have no way of knowing when our time is up, that we will then begin to live each day to the fullest as if it was the only one we had." (Kübler-Ross)

Reflection for Deep Recovery (Sharabi)

I can try to live each day as if it is my last day. I complete unfinished business without postponing, make amends wherever possible, admit my wrongs promptly and declare my love frequently and generously to the ones close to me. I can also live each day as if I will live forever. I can linger to smell the roses and to greet each person that I meet—even kneel down to buddy up to dogs on a walk with their owner—for I am in no hurry. I treat each day as a bonus day, an extra day, for I should have been dead a long time ago were it not for an act of grace that got me sober and is keeping me alive. And since each day is a bonus day, I try to live it to the fullest, not waste it complaining about the way things are.

"Life is a preparation for the future, and the best preparation for the future is to live as if there were none."

Albert Einstein (1879 - 1955)

Kübler-Ross
1926 - 2004

a) Quote for Morning Contemplation

"I always say that death can be one of the greatest experiences ever. If you live each day of your life right, then you have nothing to fear." (Kübler-Ross)

Reflection for Deep Recovery (Sharabi)

Truly absorbing the idea: "One day at a time," frees me from terror of the "idea of death." I find it unnecessary to seek comfort in some beliefs about life after death or in reassurances about the future. What is important is my present experience and who I show up as in life today. My responsibility is to live life; I do not have to live death. Nor do I have to live in fear of death.

"It is not death that a man should fear, but he should fear never beginning to live."

Marcus Aurelius (121 - 180 A.D.)

---

b) Quote for Evening Contemplation

"As far as service goes, it can take the form of a million things. To do service, you don't have to be a doctor working in the slums for free or become a social worker. Your position in life and what you do doesn't matter as much as how you do what you do." (Kübler-Ross)

Reflection for Deep Recovery (Sharabi)

Service in recovery can take a million forms too, from setting up chairs at the meeting to making coffee, greeting people at the door and giving rides; from organizing picnics to going to recovery conferences. But the deepest ways to serve involve working with the new person, one-on-one: asking someone, "How are you?" and merely listening. It calls for patience, compassion, generosity, and benevolence. I must extend myself for others the same way people extended themselves for me; this is what keeps recovery going and keeps us all growing.

"If you want happiness for an hour, take a nap; for a day, go fishing; for a month, get married; for a year, inherit a fortune; for a lifetime, help someone else."

Chinese Proverb

Kübler-Ross
1926 - 2004

a) Quote for Morning Contemplation

"I believe that we are solely responsible for our choices, and we have to accept the consequences of every deed, word, and thought throughout our lifetime." (Kübler-Ross)

Reflection for Deep Recovery (Sharabi)

I can no longer blame circumstances and bad luck entirely for my plight. Yes, things happen, but how I react to them is up to me. It is my choices that land me where I end up, and for these, I must accept responsibility. I might not have chosen my alcoholism, but continuing to drink in the face of overwhelming evidence that I was alcoholic and needed recovery—that is a choice that cannot be blamed on anyone else. Once a path to recovery has been shown to me, I have an obligation to choose it, to agree to work on sobriety on a daily basis.

"You become responsible for what you have tamed."
Antoine de Saint-Exupéry (1900 - 1944)

---

b) Quote for Evening Contemplation

"It is important to feel the anger without judging it, without attempting to find meaning in it. It may take many forms: anger at the health-care system, at life, at your loved one for leaving. Life is unfair. Death is unfair. Anger is a natural reaction to the unfairness of loss." (Kübler-Ross)

Reflection for Deep Recovery (Sharabi)

I had to deal with anger that I could not drink anymore, anger at the police for arresting me, anger at my boss for firing me, anger at my husband (or wife) for deserting me, anger at the death of a loved one. I cannot pour fuel on my anger by finding justification for it, feeling sorry for myself, or plotting revenge. Anger is always a distorted recognition of helplessness. I must not get attached to it or justify it; I must simply endure it. Anger not justified will dissipate soon, normally; it is merely a temporary chemical that gets reabsorbed. But anger shored up with justification fossilizes into deadly resentment.

"He that studieth revenge keepeth his own wounds green, which otherwise would heal and do well."
John Milton (1608 - 1674)

Kübler-Ross
1926 - 2004

a) Quote for Morning Contemplation

"The most beautiful people we have known are those who have known defeat, known suffering, known struggle, known loss, and have found their way out of those depths." (Kübler-Ross)

Reflection for Deep Recovery (Sharabi)

Nowhere does this statement apply as thoroughly as it does to a group of recovering alcoholics. We are the ones who have known defeat, suffering and struggle, known loss, known loneliness, and have found our way out of those depths. We have penetrated deeply into life, and we are mature souls who have lived—and are living—a life with texture. We have an understanding of what you have been through, and we have a solution. We are all interested in crowd-funding your sobriety.

"I have never in my life envied a human being who led an easy life. I have envied a great many people who led difficult lives and led them well."

Theodore Roosevelt (1858 - 1919)

---

b) Quote for Evening Contemplation

"The opinion which other people have of you is their problem, not yours." (Kübler-Ross)

Reflection for Deep Recovery (Sharabi)

This refers to negative opinions of me as well as positive opinions. A person who knows himself and is accepting of himself or herself is not too swayed by praise or by condemnation. At the same time, he or she must examine the opinion to see whether some correction is worthy of consideration. Indeed, my biggest challenge in the transition from child to adult is to put into balance the importance of how others see me. Children define themselves entirely by how others see them. In early recovery, feedback from others was a useful tool for self-awareness, but in Deep Recovery, the opinion of others does not matter so much. I keep my eye steadfastly on my target of spiritual growth. Similarly, my opinions and judgments of others is a burden I carry and my problem; I don't have to make it theirs.

"I'm not entangled in shaping my work according to other people's views of how I should have done it."

Toni Morrison (1931-2019)

Kübler-Ross
1926 - 2004

a) Quote for Morning Contemplation

**"People are like stained-glass windows. They sparkle and shine when the sun is out, but when the darkness sets in, their true beauty is revealed only if there is a light from within."
(Kübler-Ross)**

Reflection for Deep Recovery (Sharabi)

It is easy to be jovial when everything is going my way. I slap people on the back, joke with them, ask them what they are up to, and am even generous with my time. But when darkness sets in—that is the time when my spiritual fitness is tested. Recovery is about preparing me for those difficulties which are sure to come. I will encounter injustice, helplessness, feelings of being overwhelmed, isolation, and dejection. Can I absorb all that and still show my true nature, illuminated by the light that is in me?

"A woman is like a tea bag; you never know how strong it is until it's in hot water."

Eleanor Roosevelt (1884 - 1962)

---

b) Quote for Evening Contemplation

"Should you shield the canyons from the windstorms, you would never see the true beauty of their carvings." (Kübler-Ross)

Reflection for Deep Recovery (Sharabi)

The windstorms of our lives have carved us into the beautiful people we are today. I see this and announce that I am grateful to be an alcoholic. But the real question—the question that distinguishes the genuine spiritual student from the ones just along for the ride—is whether I can be grateful for the difficulties I am facing today, not just the difficulties I have recovered from. These difficulties are here now, and they will help me grow. I must know this and believe this in order to accept them—even welcome them—as friends along my journey.

"We are like blocks of stone out of which the sculptor carves forms of men. The blows of His chisel, which hurt so much, are what make us perfect.

C. S. Lewis (1898 - 1963)

Kübler-Ross
1926 - 2004

a) Quote for Morning Contemplation

"I have learned there is no joy without hardship. There is no pleasure without pain. Would we know the comfort of peace without the distress of war?" (Kübler-Ross)

Reflection for Deep Recovery (Sharabi)

Would I know the joy of sobriety without knowing the distress of alcoholism? Some believe that difficulties are necessary for growth; indeed, that growth will not occur without them. If I take the attitude that I can learn from every event, I can approach the future without requiring it to turn out any particular way. I will then have truly surrendered my will and my life over to the care of a Higher Power.

"The highest reward for a person's toil is not what they get for it, but what they become by it

John Ruskin (1819 - 1900)

---

b) Quote for Evening Contemplation

"The five stages—denial, anger, bargaining, depression, and acceptance—are a part of the framework that makes up our learning to live with the one we lost. They are tools to help us frame and identify what we may be feeling. But they are not stops on some linear timeline in grief." (Kübler-Ross)

Reflection for Deep Recovery (Sharabi)

I denied that I could be an alcoholic; I said I just drank too much last night. Later, I was angry that alcohol was not amenable to my peace overtures. I bargained with it, pleaded with it, tried to limit myself, switched drinks, drinking only on weekends, etc. Nothing worked. Then, depressed, I dragged myself to a meeting, not intending to stay long. Finally, I accepted my alcoholism. My journey mirrors the stages of a dying person. The death was of my old alcoholic self and of that way of living. But this journey does not happen automatically; I must move myself along it with effort. Recovery is not an escalator ride; I must work the Steps.

"It is not God's will merely that we should be happy, but that we should make ourselves happy."

Immanuel Kant (1724 - 1804)

Kübler-Ross
1926 - 2004

a) Quote for Morning Contemplation

"We often assume that if we are good people, we will not suffer the ills of the world." (Kübler-Ross)

Reflection for Deep Recovery (Sharabi)

Alcoholism is the universal leveler because it occurs equally among good people and bad people, among brilliant people and among idiots, among honest people and among crooks. In recovery, we all strive to move towards goodness and compassion. Still, it is not enough. If only "good" people recovered, most of us would be doomed. Nor do we seek out all our "badness" and beat ourselves down in order to recover. Recovery is not a reward for being good and obedient. It is an act of mercy and grace. Yet, the conscious and deliberate attempt to lead a "good" and moral life provides the backbone for my new journey in recovery.

"Truth is everybody is going to hurt you; you just gotta find the ones worth suffering for."

Bob Marley (1845 - 1981)

b) Quote for Evening Contemplation

"In Switzerland, I was educated in line with the basic premise: work, work, work. You are only a valuable human being if you work. This is utterly wrong. Half working, half dancing—that is the right mixture. I myself have danced and played too little." (Kübler-Ross)

Reflection for Deep Recovery (Sharabi)

Dancing 90% of the time or working 90% of the time are both wrong—life out of balance. Too much self-examination degenerates into self-obsession. For half the time, I need to forget the work and just dance. All over the world and in all cultures, joyful people take to dance; it is a universal symbol of celebration, of freeing oneself from a suffocating self-focus. Sometimes our recovery is too much talk and not enough dancing. Addiction is a physical craving and needs a physical solution, not just a mental offering. Even a walk in the woods can be a dance; you can hop, skip, and jump along. Consider it an essential part of recovery.

"An addiction is never purely "psychological"; all addictions have a biological dimension."

Gabor Maté (born 1944)

Lao-Tzu
604 BC - 531 BC

a) Quote for Morning Contemplation

**"The journey of a thousand miles begins with a single step."
(Lao-Tzu)**

Reflection for Deep Recovery (Sharabi)

When I came into recovery, the changes needed appeared overwhelming, but they told me all I had to do was to take the First Step. A thousand days of sobriety begins with one day—today. A lifetime of committed action is built on a moment of commitment now—and now, now, now, and yet again, now. I have accumulated thousands of days of sobriety with this approach, but what really matters today are the steps I am going to take today. Now.

"Whatever you can do or dream you can—begin it. Boldness has genius, power, and magic in it!'"

Goethe (1749 - 1832)

"The earth was once molten rock. Now it sings operas."

Brian Swimme (born 1950)

b) Quote for Evening Contemplation

**"Simplicity, patience, compassion.
These three are your greatest treasures.
Simple in actions and thoughts,
you return to the source of being.
Patient with both friends and enemies,
you accord with the way things are.
Compassionate toward yourself,
you reconcile all beings in the world" (Lao-Tzu)**

Reflection for Deep Recovery (Sharabi)

Recovery is a slow process; I can get disheartened if I demand immediate results. The secret to sustained recovery is simplicity and patience. "Keep it Simple." "Give Time Time." And compassion is contained in the saying: "Live and Let Live." Be accepting of others and gentle towards yourself. It is futile to try for happiness directly; instead, we strive for simplicity, patience, and compassion. With these three pearls of Lao-Tzu's wisdom, life becomes less complicated, less frenzied, and less agitating.

"Science is organized knowledge. Wisdom is organized life."

Immanuel Kant (1724 - 1804)

Lao-Tzu
604 BC - 531 BC

a) Quote for Morning Contemplation

"A good traveler has no fixed plans and is not intent on arriving."
(Lao-Tzu)

Reflection for Deep Recovery (Sharabi)

I have learned to enjoy the journey, to become a good traveler on this road we all are on. I enjoy working towards goals, but I realize: whether I am successful or not is a property of the future and need not intrude into my enjoyment today of the work itself. There is no end-point to sobriety; recovery is the journey itself.

"Happiness is not the end of the rainbow. Happiness is the beginning of the rainbow. Following the rainbow is happiness, not getting to the end of it."

Werner Erhard (born 1935)

"Self-knowledge has no end - you don't come to an achievement, you don't come to a conclusion. It is an endless river."

Krishnamurti (1895 - 1986)

b) Quote for Evening Contemplation

"Life is a series of natural and spontaneous changes.
Don't resist them: that only creates sorrow.
Let reality be reality.
Let things flow naturally forward in whatever way they like."
(Lao-Tzu)

Reflection for Deep Recovery (Sharabi)

Can I can allow my life to change in natural and spontaneous ways without resisting the changes? Do I get overly attached to things turning out a particular way; do I suffer from rigidity and an exaggerated need to be in control? If I let life unfold gently and naturally (in the way it always does), it often works out better than the way I was trying to force it. I remind myself that the stream flows easily and gently around the rocks, never into them.

"We must be willing to let go of the life we have planned, so as to have the life that is waiting for us."

Joseph Campbell (1904 - 1987)

Lao-Tzu
604 BC - 531 BC

a) Quote for Morning Contemplation

**"Those who know do not speak.
Those who speak do not know." (Lao-Tzu)**

Reflection for Deep Recovery (Sharabi)

The loud and strident people at the meeting often have less to offer than the ones who are sitting quietly. Just being in their presence is an experience that contributes to my sobriety and serenity. I must thank people for coming and sitting at meetings, not just the people who make comments or give speeches.

"They also serve who only stand and wait."

John Milton (1608 - 1674)

b) Quote for Evening Contemplation

"When you are content to be simply yourself and don't compare or compete, everyone will respect you" (Lao-Tzu)

Reflection for Deep Recovery (Sharabi)

My journey is unique. There is no need to compare myself to others or to compete with anyone. No matter how long I have been sober, there are people who have been sober longer; I do not wish to overtake them. And the people who have been sober less or have trouble staying sober: I do not look down on them. I am not better than them. God willing, in the fellowship, we all will continue to increase our sobriety one day at a time. There is no competition—only collaboration.

"Be yourself. Everyone else is already taken."

Oscar Wilde (1854 - 1900)

Lao-Tzu
604 BC - 531 BC

a) Quote for Morning Contemplation

"When I let go of what I am, I become what I might be." (Lao-Tzu)

Reflection for Deep Recovery (Sharabi)

Surrender. Surrender. Surrender. I cannot hang on to who I have been; I must let go of the old ways. I also need to let go of my notions of who I am in order to become what I might be. I allow myself to become... to emerge in recovery... to "recover" a possible self that had become hidden and lost over years of misuse. What is important is not "who I am," but who I am trying to be.

"I don't feel that it is necessary to know exactly what I am. The main interest in life and work is to become someone else that you were not in the beginning."

Michel Foucault (1924 - 1986)

---

b) Quote for Evening Contemplation

**"Time is a created thing.
To say "I don't have time" is like saying, "I don't want to."
(Lao-Tzu)**

Reflection for Deep Recovery (Sharabi)

Modern life is busy and demanding. It is easy to tell oneself: "I don't have time to go to meetings." But one does not look to see if one has time for meetings: one makes the time. If I believe meetings are necessary and worthwhile, and that I have something essential to gain from meetings, then I will make time to attend meetings. Time cannot be managed; there is no such thing as Time Management. We all get twenty-four hours a day, but what we can manage are our activities during those twenty-four hours. For myself, I simply include one and a half hours for a meeting three times a week (or more,) and then I look around and see what else I have time for.

"The butterfly counts not months but moments, and has time enough."

Rabindranath Tagore (1861 - 1941)

Lao-Tzu
604 BC - 531 BC

a) Quote for Morning Contemplation

"Care about what other people think, and you will always be their prisoner." (Lao-Tzu)

Reflection for Deep Recovery (Sharabi)

I am not free as long as I concern myself with what others think of me, especially as I seek their respect, love, and admiration. Freedom to be spontaneous requires me not to worry about consistency or reputation. I discover myself as I emerge each moment, trusting that the right values are already embedded in me. I can examine people's feedback and opinions to see if there are some useful insights, but I cannot allow them to crush me or to elevate me. What people speak about me says more about them than about me.

"The character truest to itself becomes eccentric rather than immovably centered... We are more subject to invasions, less able to mobilize defenses, less sure of who we really are."
James Hillman (1926 - 2011)

b) Quote for Evening Contemplation

"Because one believes in oneself, one doesn't try to convince others. Because one is content with oneself, one doesn't need others' approval. Because one accepts oneself, the whole world accepts him or her." (Lao-Tzu)

Reflection for Deep Recovery (Sharabi)

A central purpose of recovery is to arrive at acceptance—self-acceptance. We make amends, not for approval but to set things right. Seeking approval from others only means I have not accepted myself—a decision that I can take any moment without waiting. When I catch myself beating myself up over something or "feeling bad," I tell myself: "I did what I did because that is who I am, or at least who I was back then." From this place of self-acceptance, there is never any guilt or false notions about how good I am. Change can happen without guilt or shame—without violence towards myself. I can just behave differently next time, do the next right thing. Deep Recovery engages with "from now on;" it is not obsessively mired in the past, except for information.

"It never ceases to amaze me: we all love ourselves more than other people but care more about their opinions than our own."
Marcus Aurelius (121 - 180 A.D.)

Lao-Tzu
604 BC - 531 BC

a) Quote for Morning Contemplation

"Be content with what you have; rejoice in the way things are. When you realize nothing is lacking, the whole world belongs to you." (Lao-Tzu)

Reflection for Deep Recovery (Sharabi)

I am missing nothing by giving up drinking; in fact, I have "gained" sobriety. The sober life I have contains everything necessary for a rich, happy, and complete life, no matter what the conditions of life. If my "problems" can be solved with money, it means that I don't have serious problems. Everyone has money problems, no matter how rich or how poor; money problems are the "stuff" of life. Expecting to go through life without money problems, difficult emotional periods, or challenges in general is a child's dream.

"The difficulties which I meet with in order to realize my existence are precisely what awaken and mobilize my activities, my capacities."

Jose Ortega y Gasset (1883 - 1955)

b) Quote for Evening Contemplation

"Stop thinking and end your problems." (Lao-Tzu)

Reflection for Deep Recovery (Sharabi)

Problems are all creations of the mind declaring, "It shouldn't be so!" Regret, fear, worry, resentment—these are all created by my thinking. It is possible to ruin a perfectly good present by worrying about a presently nonexistent "future" or filling it with regrets about a presently nonexistent "past." Worrying does not help the future, but it does ruin the present. This is what thinking is all about: removing me from the present. Once I turn my will and my life over to the care of God—and this is an act of heart and soul, not just an act of the thinking mind—I will have acceptance of whatever constitutes the present. No more will things show up as problems or as "good" things and "bad" things—at best only as things that need attending to. I will become present to life as it is.

"There is really no such thing as bad weather, only different kinds of good weather. Sunshine is delicious, rain is refreshing, wind braces us up, snow is exhilarating."

John Ruskin (1819 - 1900)

Lao-Tzu
604 BC - 531 BC

a) Quote for Morning Contemplation

"Do you have the patience to wait till your mud settles and the water is clear? Can you remain unmoving till the right action arises by itself?" (Lao-Tzu)

Reflection for Deep Recovery (Sharabi)

Hasty reactions and impulsive actions characterized me when I was drinking. My first thought was almost always wrong, generated by my ingrained character defects, past memories, and past coping strategies. Recovery calls for conscious, deliberate, moral, and measured effort on a consistent basis. It has taught me to think my way past the urges that arise automatically, but instead, to choose the next "right" thing. But it takes discipline over the years to correct these default settings.

"Human freedom involves our capacity to pause, to choose the one response toward which we wish to throw our weight."

Rollo May (1909 - 1994)

---

b) Quote for Evening Contemplation

**"Manifest plainness,
  Embrace simplicity,
  Reduce selfishness,
  Have few desires." (Lao-Tzu)**

Reflection for Deep Recovery (Sharabi)

Humble, simple, unselfish, and contented with what I have: that is the creature I am striving to become in recovery. These thoughts would have made no sense to me in my drinking days, and it is a sign of how much I have moved that they speak to me now. I walk along this spiritual path with God and with my fellows. However, it is also necessary to be able to walk alone. I understand that society glorifies desires and the achievement of lofty dreams, but this is not the path for me in recovery. My dreams today are not just for material achievement or fame, but for simplicity. My desires were and are—at some level—the source of unhappiness. Fulfilling my desires only provides temporary happiness. Recovery offers me a long-term foundation for living by telling me not to focus on desires. Drinking, I sought excitement; sober, I seek contentment.

Lao-Tzu
604 BC - 531 BC

a) Quote for Morning Contemplation

**"If you are depressed, you are living in the past.
If you are anxious, you are living in the future.
If you are at peace, you are living in the present." (Lao-Tzu)**

Reflection for Deep Recovery (Sharabi)

*"We will neither regret the past nor wish to shut the door on it.
"Fear of people and of economic insecurity will leave us.
"We will comprehend the word serenity, and we will know peace."*

The Promises, BIG BOOK, Ch. 6

In so many ways, recovery is a Taoist path. (Taoism is a Chinese philosophy based on the writings of Lao-Tzu.)

b) Quote for Evening Contemplation

"Act without expectation." (Lao-Tzu)

Reflection for Deep Recovery (Sharabi)

We learn in the program to act as if it is all up to us—to put in our full effort—but we treat the result as if it is all up to God. We feel no entitlement to any particular result; our focus is on the work.

"The wise man lets go of all results, whether good or bad, and is focused on the action alone."

Krishna to Arjuna in the Bhagavad Gita (circa 500 - 200 B.C.)

a) Quote for Morning Contemplation

"If you do not change direction, you may end up where you are heading." (Lao-Tzu)

Reflection for Deep Recovery (Sharabi)

Does this quote sound as if Lao-Tzu was speaking to a practicing alcoholic? In recovery we tell you: if you want to know where the train is heading, you shouldn't look at the train; you should look at the tracks. You must not just look where you have ended up; you must look at how you got here and where you seem to be going.

According to a study published in the National Academy of Sciences (USA), chemical analyses of ancient organics absorbed into pottery jars from the village of Jiahu in Henan province in China have revealed that a mixed fermented beverage of rice, honey, and fruit was being produced as early as 7000 B.C.

b) Quote for Evening Contemplation

"Stop trying to control. Let go of fixed plans and concepts, and the world will govern itself." (Lao-Tzu)

Reflection for Deep Recovery (Sharabi)

The CEO of my brain often entertains a feverish concern that unless he (or she) stays in tight control of everything, it will all fall apart. But this rigid clutching often has the opposite effect. In recovery, we have a phrase: "Let go and let God!" Let the world flow, let go of fixed ideas of how things must proceed, and I will find that things turn out alright, perhaps even better than if I had been in charge. I must let go of the illusion that I manage life—that the executive part of my brain is running me. My job is simply to make the best decisions I can, and then I must let go of things that are outside my control.

"Adulthood brings with it the pernicious illusion of control, perhaps even depends on it."

Juan Gabriel Vásquez (born 1973)

Lao-Tzu
604 BC - 531 BC

a) Quote for Morning Contemplation

"Thus, the Master is content to serve as an example and not to impose his will. He is pointed but doesn't pierce; straightforward, but gentle; radiant, but easy on the eyes."
(Lao-Tzu)

Reflection for Deep Recovery (Sharabi)

As a sponsor in recovery, I serve as an example but do not impose my will. I can ask questions and make comments to raise the consciousness of the person I am sponsoring, but I must not get angry when disobeyed or ignored. Humility is a necessity for the Master, Teacher, or sponsor. The willingness to shine bright in recovery comes not from pride at our own refulgence but to illuminate others along the path.

"Don't walk behind me; I may not lead. Don't walk in front of me; I may not follow. Just walk beside me and be my friend."
Albert Camus (1913 - 1960)

---

b) Quote for Evening Contemplation

"Men are born soft and supple; dead, they are stiff and hard. Plants are born tender and pliant; dead, they are brittle and dry. Thus whoever is stiff and inflexible is a disciple of death. Whoever is soft and yielding is a disciple of life. The hard and stiff will be broken. The soft and supple will prevail." (Lao-Tzu)

Reflection for Deep Recovery (Sharabi)

The need to be controlling and rigid comes from fear and from being frozen with fear. Change requires me to be open, accepting, and flexible. I am soft and supple, evolving constantly and easily.

"The green reed which bends in the wind is stronger than the mighty oak which breaks in a storm."
Confucius (559 - 459 B.C.)

"Blessed are the hearts that can bend; they shall never be broken."
Albert Camus (1913 - 1960)

Lao-Tzu
604 BC - 531 BC

a) Quote for Morning Contemplation

"What the caterpillar calls the end, the rest of the world calls a butterfly." (Lao-Tzu)

Reflection for Deep Recovery (Sharabi)

When I had to quit drinking, I thought my life was over. Now I have been reborn into a new life. What were the things I was holding on to, from fear that I—as I knew myself—would cease to exist if I let go? Even today, I need to see these identities and perspectives I am clutching. For me, they appear as reality, as me, not as false notions or superstition. Only when I become willing to die to the identity I think of as "me"—will a new life open up for me.

"Life begins on the other side of despair."

Jean-Paul Sartre (1905 - 1980)

"The bird fights its way out of the egg. The egg is the world. Whoever will be born must destroy a world."

Hermann Hesse (1877 - 1962)

b) Quote for Evening Contemplation

**"Your own positive future begins in this moment.
All you have is right now. Every goal is possible from here." (Lao-Tzu)**

Reflection for Deep Recovery (Sharabi)

Recovery happens one day at a time. This is the first day of the rest of my sober life. In this moment, my future begins, and in this moment are contained the kernels of all possible futures. If sobriety is to be summed up in one word, that word would be "possibility." Everything is possible now. Recovery is not about obsessing over the past. It is about not worrying over things that are out of my control and cannot be changed. It truly does not matter who I have been; what matters is who I am willing to be.

"To bring forth possibility is to bring forth a domain in which new options become possible. It is not simply finding new options within the same range of options; it actually produces whole new ranges of options."
Werner Erhard (born 1935)

"The greatest personal limitation is to be found not in the things you want to do and can't, but in the things you've never considered doing."
Richard Bandler (born 1950)

Lao-Tzu
604 BC - 531 BC

a) Quote for Morning Contemplation

**"The wise man is one who knows what he does not know."
(Lao-Tzu)**

Reflection for Deep Recovery (Sharabi)

I realize that no matter how wise I am, there are things I do not know. I might have accumulated a lot of information, but not true "knowledge." This awareness makes me open to learning. Taking it one step further, I realize there may be things I don't even know that I don't know. This awareness makes me open to transformation. And ultimately, there is the broader question: is knowing even possible, or only the illusion of knowledge and understanding? I must be careful about claiming certainty about anything. Such certainty is not necessary for a full, engaged, and satisfying life.

"The only true wisdom is in knowing that you know nothing."

Socrates (470 - 399 B.C.)

b) Quote for Evening Contemplation

**"Stop leaving, and you will arrive.
Stop searching, and you will see.
Stop running away, and you will be found." (Lao-Tzu)**

Reflection for Deep Recovery (Sharabi)

Stop fighting and you will win. Stop searching and things will be revealed. Admit powerlessness over alcohol and sobriety can be yours. Stop battling your feelings and you will find yourself. Stop wrestling with the porcupine and it will go away. If you want to be rid of your character defects and shortcomings, stop struggling with them. Stop even naming them; just do the next right thing.

The supreme art of war is to subdue the enemy without fighting.

Sun Tzu (544 - 496 B.C)

Lao-Tzu
604 BC - 531 BC

a) Quote for Morning Contemplation

**"He who controls others may be powerful
but he who has mastered himself is mightier still." (Lao-Tzu)**

Reflection for Deep Recovery (Sharabi)

In recovery, I am learning to let others be. They have the freedom
to make their decisions—to own their life; my job is to adjust
myself to who they are and how they are. Sure, I can try and
influence them as they choose, but I have to accept what they
choose. In recovery, I accept others and manage myself. This
involves carefully avoiding "shoulds" and "shouldn't" for them.
Even my own shoulds and shouldn't about myself come, not from
the inner me, but are values I have swallowed from others. They
are protests by the self-appointed CEO of my brain. I consider that
voice but choose my own path. I do not need to justify my path.

*"Self reverence, self-knowledge, self-control; these three alone lead life to
sovereign power."*

Alfred Lord Tennyson (1809 - 1892)

b) Quote for Evening Contemplation

**"If you correct your mind, the rest of your life will fall into place."
(Lao-Tzu)**

Reflection for Deep Recovery (Sharabi)

My default settings were wrong, and my journey in recovery has
been to identify these errors and gradually correct them. But
until they are corrected, I must consciously choose what thoughts
to dwell on and what thoughts to distract myself from, not just
engage with the thought that popped up uninvited. Then my life
will fall into place. I cannot choose to just "not think" a certain
thought. (Try not thinking of elephants!) However, I can replace it
with a different thought. I cannot simply "not think" of drinking,
but I can replace it with thoughts of how to be grateful, how to be
helpful, and how to improve my conscious contact with the Deep
Spirit. And I cannot directly "stop beating myself up." When the
self-loathing thought begins, I must immediately distract myself
and focus on something else—something pleasant, something
present, something useful, something constructive and uplifting.

*"The mind is its own place and in itself, can make a Heaven of Hell, a Hell
of Heaven."*

John Milton (1608 - 1674)

Lao-Tzu
604 BC - 531 BC

a) Quote for Morning Contemplation

"As soon as you have made a thought, laugh at it." (Lao-Tzu)

Reflection for Deep Recovery (Sharabi)

I must stop believing that my thoughts are significant. They are just thoughts... my thoughts... random thoughts... appearing from nowhere... then gone. Who knows, they may not even be "my" thoughts; they simply appeared in my head. I don't agree that I "made" these thoughts, but I have some choice on how long I dwell on them. As soon as a thought of drinking appears, I laugh at it... ha ha ha... It will go away. It is trying to find someone who will actually engage with it. I don't wish to engage with it.

"Give thy thoughts no tongue..."
Shakespeare (1564 - 1616) (Polonius, in 'Hamlet.')

---

b) Quote for Evening Contemplation

"One who is too insistent on his own views finds few to agree with him." (Lao-Tzu)

Reflection for Deep Recovery (Sharabi)

But he (or she) will probably quote something from the Big Book to support his point! I do not need to engage with such people who get angry when people disagree with them. Wanting to convince others is a sign of uncertainty and fear. Recovery is not a religious group where everyone takes on the same beliefs. Even things I consider "fundamental principles of recovery" may not be perceived as such by everyone. Recovery is a vast and diverse community where each person is trying to find his or her own path. We show others the path we have walked, but it is up to them from then on. I cannot insist that others walk my path, and I avoid people who demand that I walk their path.

"We must love them both, those whose opinions we share and those whose opinions we reject, for both have labored in the search for truth, and both have helped us in finding it."
Thomas Aquinas (1224 - 1274)

Lao-Tzu
604 BC - 531 BC

a) Quote for Morning Contemplation

"Perfection is the willingness to be imperfect." (Lao-Tzu)

Reflection for Deep Recovery (Sharabi)

Perfection in recovery is: making progress. Perfection is the journey itself, not the destination. Not having a drink today is perfection, for it cannot get any better than that. Perfection is not about shoulds and shouldn't. Perfection simply is what is. Perfection is acceptance of my imperfection, even as I am trying to do the next right thing. Nothing more can be asked of me. To be perfect is to be okay in my own skin, to be in total acceptance, completely immersed in the moment.

"God loves you unconditionally as you are, and not as you should be because nobody is as they should be."

Brennan Manning (1934 - 2013)

---

b) Quote for Evening Contemplation

"Hope and fear are both phantoms that arise from thinking of the self. When we don't see the self as self, what do we have to fear?" (Lao-Tzu)

Reflection for Deep Recovery (Sharabi)

Not seeing the self as self means rising above the ego, being relieved of the bondage of self, no longer a miserable ball of trivial, self-centered concerns arising from fear. Success and failure are equally dangerous; praise and criticism are both feeding the ego. I can stop getting "offended" by people and things and demanding respect. Nor do I demand that people see me the way I see myself. Hopes for outcomes recede into the background, and the present begins to occupy me. Both fear and hope focus on virtual realities—bad images and good images involving me. Ultimately, all that exists is the Tao of the now, without a "me."

"What is needed, rather than running away or controlling or suppressing or any other resistance, is understanding fear; that means, watch it, learn about it, come directly into contact with it. We are to learn about fear, not how to escape from it."

Krishnamurti (1895 - 1986)

Lao-Tzu
604 BC - 531 BC

a) Quote for Morning Contemplation

"Knowing others is intelligence. Knowing yourself is true wisdom. Mastering others is strength. Mastering yourself is true power."
(Lao-Tzu)

Reflection for Deep Recovery (Sharabi)

As a drunk sitting at the bar, I may have been brilliant in psychoanalyzing all the others sitting around me. But as a sober person in recovery, I now know my own tendencies: my tendency to rationalize and justify, my tendency to present myself more favorably than I am, my desire to be a "big shot," my desire to be never wrong and my tendency to get angry at someone who is pointing out an uncomfortable truth. In other words, I am beginning to know myself.

"Never mistake knowledge for wisdom. One helps you make a living; the other helps you make a life."

Eleanor Roosevelt (1884 - 1962)

---

b) Quote for Evening Contemplation

"Respond intelligently even to unintelligent treatment." (Lao-Tzu)

Reflection for Deep Recovery (Sharabi)

Intelligence is the ability to respond thoughtfully rather than to react impulsively—as I used to in those drinking days. Let my treatment of others reflect who I choose to be, not who they are; let it be governed by the principles of recovery—not by their behavior, and not by my own personality traits. I stop and think, "What is underneath my reaction here? What am I trying to achieve here? Am I feeling shame because I am exposed? Do I think I am in danger here? Am I hiding my fear by showing my power? " I can consciously declare that, at a deep level, I am safe, no matter what my autonomic nervous system thinks.

"Between stimulus and response, there is a space.
In that space is our power to choose our response.
In our response lies our growth and our freedom."

Viktor Frankl (1905 - 1997)

"Teach me to behave like the orange which, though crushed and bitten, fails not to impart its sweetness."

Parmahansa Yogananda (1893 - 1952)

Lao-Tzu
604 BC - 531 BC

a) Quote for Morning Contemplation

"The sage does not hoard. The more he helps others, the more he benefits himself, The more he gives to others, the more he gets himself." (Lao-Tzu)

Reflection for Deep Recovery (Sharabi)

Wisdom, love, and sobriety—we keep it by giving it away. The more willing I am to love, the more love I will experience. The more I help others, the more I benefit myself; the more I give to others, the more I have for myself. This is a well-known principle of recovery today—but enunciated by Lao-Tzu over twenty-five hundred years ago.

"The meaning of life is to find your gift. The purpose of life is to give it away."

Pablo Picasso (1881 - 1973)

b) Quote for Evening Contemplation

"Perseverance is the foundation of all action." (Lao-Tzu)

Reflection for Deep Recovery (Sharabi)

Sobriety is not an event. "Not drinking" is not an event. Nothing major "happened" on that first day that I did not drink. There had been many such days when I "quit" drinking, and they did not last. But where sobriety happens is: in each day following. Sobriety is founded on perseverance. It is accomplished by practicing abstinence over and over and over again... and over again, one day at a time. I am never done. All I have to do is: not drink now! Perseverance is only called for in the moment. The rest takes care of itself.

"When you're at the end of your rope, tie a knot and hold on."

Theodore Roosevelt (1858 - 1919)

"Quiet minds cannot be perplexed or frightened but go on in fortune or misfortune at their own private pace, like a clock during a thunderstorm."

Robert Louis Stevenson (1850 - 1894)

Lao-Tzu
604 BC - 531 BC

a) Quote for Morning Contemplation

**"If you would take, you must first give,
this is the beginning of intelligence." (Lao-Tzu)**

Reflection for Deep Recovery (Sharabi)

If I seek love I must give love. If I am seeking wealth, I must be
generous with my money. If I want to keep sobriety, I must try
to help another alcoholic get sober. I must share what I have and
what I have learned. This is the essence of recovery, the beginning
of intelligence. Rather than trying to achieve wealth so we can
practice generosity, let us be generous first, so we can experience
what wealth feels like.

"Let us try to teach generosity and altruism because we are born selfish."
Richard Dawkins (born 1941)

*"Better to illuminate than merely to shine; to deliver to others
contemplated truths than merely to contemplate."*
Thomas Aquinas (1224 - 1274)

b) Quote for Evening Contemplation

**"We shape clay into a pot, but it is the emptiness inside that holds
what we want." (Lao-Tzu)**

Reflection for Deep Recovery (Sharabi)

Nothing new can flow into an already filled vessel. We need to
create an emptiness inside of us so that recovery can enter. This
cleansing out of the garbage that we have filled ourselves with is
initiated by the act of surrender. Our excuses, rationalizations,
justifications, arguments, and distortions are the things that must
be thrown out so we can present ourselves empty and stripped
of defenses, ready to learn. We must let go, absolutely, all our old
ideas. The correct ones will come back in, sprouting fresh buds.

"We turn not older with years but newer every day."
Emily Dickinson (1830 - 1886)

Lao-Tzu
604 BC - 531 BC

a) Quote for Morning Contemplation

"The Tao is (like) the emptiness of a vessel; in our employment of it we must be on our guard against all fullness." (Lao-Tzu)

Reflection for Deep Recovery (Sharabi)

I must not get attached to my opinions and points of view. Instead, I stay loose and empty, remembering, "Easy Does It." The less I claim to "know," the more open I will be to learning. Some practical advice can be useful, but claims of "knowing" abstract things are, of necessity, dishonest. Only uncertainty and admission of not knowing can be honest. Beliefs are not in the realm of honesty or dishonesty; there is no distinction between "honest" beliefs and "dishonest" beliefs; they are just "beliefs"—poof! I stay on guard against people who are pressing their beliefs, opinions, and self-proclaimed "knowledge." They are tiresome. I hope I do not become like them.

"The greatest deception men suffer is from their own opinions."

Leonardo da Vinci (1452 - 1519)

b) Quote for Evening Contemplation

"If anyone should wish to get the kingdom for himself... he will not succeed. The kingdom is a spirit-like thing and cannot be got by active doing. He who would so win it destroys it; he who would hold it in his grasp loses it." (Lao-Tzu)

Reflection for Deep Recovery (Sharabi)

The kingdom of sobriety cannot be possessed. It cannot be gotten by active doing; I cannot "earn" it. It cannot be won as a prize for completing the Steps or by driving an alcoholic to a meeting—even driving hundreds of alcoholics to hundreds of meetings. Sobriety is more than mere abstinence; it is an ephemeral spirit-like thing that visits me daily, and I accept its visitations as Grace. And I cannot grasp sobriety and attempt to keep it for myself; we only have sobriety together, and we have it only in this moment.

"We're all just walking each other home."

Baba Ram Dass (1931 - 2019)

Nietzsche
1844 - 1900

a) Quote for Morning Contemplation

"God is Dead." (Nietzsche)

Reflection for Deep Recovery (Sharabi)

Arguments abound about the intended meaning of this most famous saying of Nietzsche's. For us in recovery, "God is dead," could mean that we have killed God by becoming literal and dogmatic—preaching blind belief and mindless obedience. The sacred beauty—the sublime mystery of God as an alive Presence inside each of us—has been rendered lifeless by the literalists and the fundamentalists. They have created ideas, dogma, stories, and concepts about God; they have killed the spirit of wonder and ecstasy associated with personal discovery. In the process, one could say, religion has killed man.

"In the nineteenth century the problem was that God is dead. In the twentieth century the problem is that man is dead."

Erich Fromm (1900 - 1980)

---

b) Quote for Evening Contemplation

"What does not destroy me makes me stronger." (Nietzsche)

Reflection for Deep Recovery (Sharabi)

Alcoholism destroys most people, but we in recovery are the ones who did not get destroyed by it. Instead, it has made us wiser, deeper, more honest, and more robust. It has made us stronger. Our strength today derives from the fact that we can admit powerlessness over alcohol and commit ourselves to live a life requiring conscious, courageous, moral effort on a daily basis. Our strength comes from our willingness to deal with difficulties one day at a time; our courage from a willingness to take on difficulties in the future as they arise.

"It doesn't matter if the water is cold or warm if you're going to have to wade through it anyway."

Pierre Teilhard de Chardin (1881 - 1955)

Nietzsche
1844 - 1900

a) Quote for Morning Contemplation

"You have your way. I have my way. As for the right way, the correct way, and the only way, it does not exist." (Nietzsche)

Reflection for Deep Recovery (Sharabi)

There is no "correct" interpretation of the Steps. Yet, we will encounter people who thunder and proclaim that their path in recovery is the only correct path, that their interpretation is the only true interpretation, and that their direction is the one we must follow. We can listen to them, but we realize that the meaning of the Steps must sprout and blossom within each of us. Until and unless we make personal meaning of the Steps—absorb them and make them a part of who we are—they are not useful. And therefore, we must remain humble while trying to "guide" others.

"Anyone who conducts an argument by appealing to authority is not using his intelligence; he is just using his memory."

Leonardo da Vinci (1452 - 1519)

b) Quote for Evening Contemplation

"The individual has always had to struggle to keep from being overwhelmed by the tribe. If you try it, you will be lonely often, and sometimes frightened. But no price is too high to pay for the privilege of owning yourself." (Nietzsche)

Reflection for Deep Recovery (Sharabi)

In the beginning, I found my seat at the meeting, sat in silence and listened. I was doing what everyone was doing and saying what everyone was saying. But at some point, I had to get up and start wandering—intellectually, philosophically, and spiritually. It had been okay for a while to walk in step with the others, but there came a time when I had to leave the crowd and walk my own path. I needed to find my own way through recovery and through life while staying true to the principles. As I do this, I am lonely sometimes and frightened sometimes, but I am engaging in being true to myself; I will have the privilege of owning myself.

"If a man does not keep pace with his companions, perhaps it is because he hears a different drummer. Let him step to the music which he hears, however measured or far away."

Thoreau (1817 - 1862)

Nietzsche
1844 - 1900

a) Quote for Morning Contemplation

"To live is to suffer, to survive is to find some meaning in the suffering." (Nietzsche)

Reflection for Deep Recovery (Sharabi)

People exclaim in meetings: "I am so glad that I am an alcoholic." The newcomer is puzzled. But we in recovery are the ones who have found meaning in our suffering. We have acquired depth and sturdiness, added texture to our personality, and we have a rich and engaging existence today. We have found—no, we have created—meaning and purpose to life.

"Not until we are lost do we begin to understand ourselves."

Thoreau (1817 - 1862)

"Here is the test to find whether your mission on Earth is finished: if you're alive, it isn't."

Richard Bach (born 1936)

---

b) Quote for Evening Contemplation

"A casual stroll through the lunatic asylum shows that faith does not prove anything." (Nietzsche)

Reflection for Deep Recovery (Sharabi)

Anxiety about things we cannot control leads us to seek shelter in faith. But refusing to face our fears, continuing to run away from reality, seeking shelter in superstition and magical thinking: this surely is not a path to sanity. On the other hand, if we can truly turn our will and our life over and decide to accept whatever unfolds for us in life, then there is no more need for blind faith or belief. There is no investment in the future turning out any particular way, no seeking of reassurance and safety. We accept and deal with the future any way it turns out—whatever way that is—and we try to do our best with it. This is sanity.

"Perhaps everything that frightens us is, in its deepest essence, something helpless that wants our love."

Rainer Maria Rilke (1875 - 1926)

"Faith in a holy cause is to a considerable extent a substitute for the lost faith in ourselves."

Eric Hoffer (1898 - 1983)

Nietzsche
1844 - 1900

a) Quote for Morning Contemplation

"Hope in reality is the worst of all evils because it prolongs the torments of man." (Nietzsche)

Reflection for Deep Recovery (Sharabi)

I kept drinking and looking over my shoulder, "hoping" for a beautiful and wealthy woman (maybe a man in your case) to see my specialness and rescue me from my barstool. Hope prolonged my torment and misery; now, I engage with reality. Accepting "what is" means I accept life. Hope imprisons, acceptance frees. Religion offers hope; spirituality offers acceptance.

"Expecting something for nothing is the most popular form of hope."
Arnold Glasow (1905 - 1998)

"We hold on to hope, and hope robs us of the present moment. Hopelessness is the basic ground. Otherwise, we're going to make the (spiritual) journey with the hope of getting security."
Pema Chödrön (born 1936)

---

b) Quote for Evening Contemplation

"The surest way to corrupt a youth is to instruct him to hold in higher esteem those who think alike than those who think differently." (Nietzsche)

Reflection for Deep Recovery (Sharabi)

If I surround myself in recovery with people who think in just one particular way, it may work to keep me sober for a little while. But there will be no need or opportunity for me to grow. Recovery is measured by how many different perspectives I can see, by how many types of people I can accept and get along with, and by how comfortable I can be in the midst of ideas contrary to my own. I must seek out people who think differently from myself if I am to avoid complacency and stagnation in recovery. This may seem unnatural at first, and it may take effort, but the rewards and satisfaction from the growth that results are great.

"Most enjoyable activities are not natural; they demand an effort that initially one is reluctant to make. But once the interaction starts to provide feedback to the person's skills, it usually begins to be intrinsically rewarding."

Mihaly Csikszentmihalyi (born 1934)

Nietzsche
1844 - 1900

a) Quote for Morning Contemplation

"The man of knowledge must be able not only to love his enemies but also to hate his friends." (Nietzsche)

Reflection for Deep Recovery (Sharabi)

The man of knowledge is not repulsed by people who criticize him and does not react with elation for the praises heaped on him by admirers. People will appreciate us and praise us for the behaviors that are useful to them, not necessarily the qualities that are good for us. Friends can shield us from growing. We must also accept the "enemies" who create difficulties for us because in learning to handle ourselves among them, we will grow.

"Men will not accept truth at the hands of their enemies, and truth is seldom offered to them by their friends."
Alexis de Tocqueville (1805 - 1859)

"We swallow greedily any lie that flatters us, but we sip only little by little at a truth we find bitter."
Denis Diderot (1713 - 1786)

b) Quote for Evening Contemplation

"A pair of powerful spectacles has sometimes sufficed to cure a person in love." (Nietzsche)

Reflection for Deep Recovery (Sharabi)

Recovery provides those powerful spectacles so we can examine our love of alcohol and be cured of it. We see clearly the nature of the disease that had us enamored and entranced. We also see the false idols that we have been worshipping, the fantasies we have been in love with, the dreams that had us mesmerized. Today we can say we have fallen in love with the Program, the Steps, the Big Book, the Traditions. But Nietzsche will claim that we need to be cured of these too, for we must come to knowledge from the inside. We cannot merely borrow the meaning that someone else is offering us; we must create our own. We cannot just fall in love with a book that someone else has written; we need to put together our own book. Nor can we idolize the old-timers in recovery—or even the founders. They are only imperfect humans, not impeccable statues to be placed on pedestals in a frozen state and worshipped from afar, for that would make them unapproachable and untouchable.

Nietzsche
1844 - 1900

a) Quote for Morning Contemplation

"Faith: not wanting to know what is true." (Nietzsche)

Reflection for Deep Recovery (Sharabi)

The injunction to be honest and truthful in recovery is more powerful and more important than the invitation to believe—to believe in God, in "commandments" to people, and in the "program." Sobriety is not a reward for belief but for action. Many choose to hide from uncertainty, reality, and truth under the masquerade of faith, seeking the comfort of delusions and magical thinking rather than the discomfort of truth. As we progress in recovery, we will find courage and acceptance; then, we will not need faith because we will not seek guarantees that life will turn out any particular way according to our desires.

"Faith is belief without evidence and reason; coincidentally, that's also the definition of delusion."

Richard Dawkins (born 1941)

---

b) Quote for Evening Contemplation

"And we should consider every day lost on which we have not danced at least once. And we should call every truth false which was not accompanied by at least one laugh." (Nietzsche)

Reflection for Deep Recovery (Sharabi)

Once we accept a sober way of life, our goal is to affirm life and to dance with it: to play and create as children do. Alcoholism is no joke, but we in recovery have learned to laugh at ourselves and also at people who take themselves too seriously. We are not a glum lot. Initially, the truth was somber and terrifying. Then, as we stopped resisting the truth, we lost our fear of it. Truth became light, airy, and freeing; we began to experience the lightness of being. We began to laugh and dance, light on our feet, free from fear, easy on beliefs. Truth was no longer a heavy burden.

"Do not take life too seriously. You will never get out of it alive."

Elbert Hubbard (1856 - 1915)

"Man is most nearly himself when he achieves the seriousness of a child at play."

Heraclitus (circa 500 B.C.)

Nietzsche
1844 - 1900

a) Quote for Morning Contemplation

"He who would learn to fly one day must first learn to stand and walk and run and climb and dance; one cannot fly into flying." (Nietzsche)

Reflection for Deep Recovery (Sharabi)

That is why we need to work, to trudge, to climb one step at a time, before attempting to soar into serenity. There is nothing magical about recovery; We cannot fly into peace and equanimity the day after we stop drinking. Recovery calls for steady work. In fact, recovery is not just about stopping drinking; recovery is what we do after we stop drinking. Today, even after many years of sobriety, we are still working, still changing, still playful, still enjoying the fellowship. Recovery is Life.

"Drudgery is as necessary to call out the treasures of the mind as harrowing and planting is necessary to call out those of the earth."
Margaret Fuller (1810 - 1850)

---

b) Quote for Evening Contemplation

"After coming into contact with a religious man, I always feel I must wash my hands." (Nietzsche)

Reflection for Deep Recovery (Sharabi)

Excessive religiousness is a disease of people avoiding contact with themselves "as is" because they feel unclean. They try to cover their inner smell with their extreme sanctimoniousness and self-righteousness. Humility is the willingness to be in full contact with ourselves and to be present to the world just as we are, unabashed and unashamed. Then, we would have no need to postulate and believe in the existence of a being who is all clean, all pure, and all light, or to denigrate ourselves for not being that way, ourselves.

"Belief in god is bound up with submission to autocracy. The two rise and fall together, and men will never be free until the last king is strangled with the entrails of the last priest."
Denis Diderot (1713 - 1786)

Nietzsche
1844 - 1900

a) Quote for Morning Contemplation

"It is impossible to suffer without making someone pay for it; every complaint already contains revenge." (Nietzsche)

Reflection for Deep Recovery (Sharabi)

Every complaint, every resentment, is a claim that we have been wronged. It is a limp attempt to exact revenge. There may be some weird comfort available in the notion that we have been wrongfully treated, but our complaints form the walls of the prison that limit our access to joy. In recovery, we learn that one does not "work on resentment;" one simply walks away from it. We learn that it is possible to go through life without complaining, without thinking that any "wrong" has been done to us, without resentments. This is the ultimate freedom.

"So now I have sworn to bury - All this dead body of hate,
I feel so free and so clear - By the loss of that dead weight."

Alfred Lord Tennyson (1809 - 1892)

---

b) Quote for Evening Contemplation

"There are horrible people who, instead of solving a problem, tangle it up and make it harder to solve for anyone who wants to deal with it." (Nietzsche)

Reflection for Deep Recovery (Sharabi)

This does describe how many of us dealt with problems in our drinking life. When we got into a jam, we drank. Then we lied, avoided facts, drank some more, and blamed everyone around us. When confronted, we lied some more and got angry. We were invincible, but everything just kept getting worse. Now, in sobriety, we learn that the first step in solving a problem is to acknowledge that it exists and then to get honest about our role in creating it.

"Facts do not cease to exist because they are ignored."

Aldous Huxley (1894 - 1963)

"If by accident, you step into the mud, it is not therefore necessary to keep
on walking in the muddy path."

Hazrat Inayat Khan (1882 - 1927)

Nietzsche
1844 - 1900

a) Quote for Morning Contemplation

"In heaven, all the interesting people are missing." (Nietzsche)

Reflection for Deep Recovery (Sharabi)

In recovery, I am not interested in heaven because I am fully involved in life here on earth. Perhaps those who never drank and lived every moment virtuously and piously have gathered in heaven. Who wants to be lectured by them? No, not me. The interesting people—the real people, the ones who were the biggest partiers and loudmouths—have come to live here in these rooms, sober. I need the authenticity and the earthy honesty of such people, not the vacuous virtuousness and sappy self-righteousness of the white-clad, smiling inhabitants of heaven.

"Virtuous people often revenge themselves for the constraints to which they submit by the boredom which they inspire."

Confucius (559 - 459 B.C.)

---

b) Quote for Evening Contemplation

"And if you gaze for long into an abyss, the abyss gazes also into you." (Nietzsche)

Reflection for Deep Recovery (Sharabi)

I kept drinking, looking over the edge into the abyss of insanity. It looked back at me; it began to enter me. Here, in recovery, I stare at God, and God stares back at me. I look for God, and God comes looking for me. I reach for God, and God enters me.

(God here is a metaphor for something deep and moving, some archetypal presence—not the God of the religious books. No, Nietzsche wouldn't go for that!)

Nietzsche
1844 - 1900

a) Quote for Morning Contemplation

"There are no facts, only interpretations." (Nietzsche)

Reflection for Deep Recovery (Sharabi)

There are no facts, only opinions. But there will be people who will come to you claiming to know exactly what the Steps mean, what every line in the Big Book means, and exactly what you need to do to stay sober. Be wary of such people who claim to know God's will. They have immediate advice for anyone who is going through a hard time in recovery as if they themselves have mastered life. Perhaps, deep down, they are terrified of their own uncertainty. But recovery is a fellowship where people who don't "know" are willing to share their experience, strength, hope, and time with each other and somehow help each other stay sober. It is love and caring—not dogmatic advice—that can make the difference, and sometimes, even that is not enough.

"I'm humbled by my feebleness in helping this person."

Gabor Maté (born 1944)

b) Quote for Evening Contemplation

"We have art in order not to die of the truth." (Nietzsche)

Reflection for Deep Recovery (Sharabi)

I need something beyond stony truth, wooden goodness, suffocating advice, and somber spirituality. I must cultivate an art. I must let art have a presence in my life, for without art, we are no more than mechanical puppets. I can develop an appreciation of—and find a way of expressing myself in—art, music, poetry, and fantasy. This is an important part of returning to wholeness. The drudgery of constantly improving myself needs to be broken; imagination is necessary in order not to get crushed by rationality. The less useful and practical the art is, the more beautiful its practice is. Art is for art's sake—for waking the soul and for no other purpose—and through it, I am uplifted.

"You use a glass mirror to see your face. You use art to see your soul."
George Bernard Shaw (1856 - 1950)

"Art washes away from the soul the dust of everyday life."
Pablo Picasso (1881 - 1973)

Nietzsche
1844 - 1900

a) Quote for Morning Contemplation

"The most common lie is that which one lies to himself; lying to others is relatively an exception." (Nietzsche)

Reflection for Deep Recovery (Sharabi)

The most important virtue I need in recovery is the capacity to be honest with myself. This merely means dismissing the rational justification that has popped up in my mind. It is relatively easy to know when I am lying to others but quite difficult to see through my own lies. The most dangerous enemy in recovery is self-justification. It perpetuates the illusion of being right. If I am justifying something to myself, I am already lying; the truth needs no justification.

"The prisoner is not the one who has committed a crime, but the one who clings to his crime and lives it over and over."

Henry Miller (1891 - 1980)

---

b) Quote for Evening Contemplation

"The demand to be loved is the greatest of all arrogant presumptions." (Nietzsche)

Reflection for Deep Recovery (Sharabi)

No one "deserves" love—because nobody is undeserving of love. Love is an act of generosity, not of judgment. But demanding to be loved—or being bitter that someone did not love in a certain way—is a petty and foolish tantrum that generates a sense of victimhood. "If you really loved me, you would... " is an attempt to manipulate. The love-giver—not the love-taker—determines the form of love. With love, all notions of entitlement are foolish and arrogant. We cannot hold anyone guilty of not loving us, not even our parents. Instead, we should demand of ourselves that we give love, and we should feel entitled to nothing in return except the satisfaction and joy of expressing ourselves as love. And if we claim we love someone "because... —" (whatever,) then it is not love. Love is not because of reasons. The giver generates love, creates love out of nothing.

Nietzsche
1844 - 1900

a) Quote for Morning Contemplation

**"I cannot believe in a God who wants to be praised all the time."
(Nietzsche)**

Reflection for Deep Recovery (Sharabi)

Do not think that exaggerated piety, orchestrated humility, and excessive obsequiousness towards a Higher Power will please Him or Her. We praise God not to earn brownie points with God, not because God needs praise, but because it forces us to be in awe of—and grateful for—the sobriety we have. God does not need our fear or our praise, but we need an avenue to express our gratitude. By all means, praise God, but do not think that it absolves you of the responsibility to engage with life, to grow—to become a person.

"It is impossible to imagine the universe run by a wise, just, and omnipotent God, but it is quite easy to imagine it run by a board of gods."
H. L. Mencken (1880 - 1956)

---

b) Quote for Evening Contemplation

"I assess the power of a will by how much resistance, pain, torture it endures and knows how to turn to its advantage." (Nietzsche)

Reflection for Deep Recovery (Sharabi)

In recovery, I need not be afraid of difficulties because I can learn from each obstacle that life throws my way. I can welcome difficulties because I always grow from them. Freedom means not being afraid of difficulties or struggle. My difficulty with alcohol brought me here; where is my next difficulty going to take me? Difficulty brings me closer to wisdom and serenity. And serenity is not merely the seeking of calm surroundings; it is the ability to stay calm while enduring difficulties and pain, turning them to advantage. The wish for "no suffering" automatically generates fear of suffering—which is often worse than the suffering itself.

"Out of suffering have emerged the strongest souls; the most massive characters are seared with scars."
Kahlil Gibran (1883 - 1931)

"Obstacles are not really our enemies, but rather our friends.. What we call obstacles are really the way the world and our entire experience teach us where we're stuck.
Pema Chödrön (born 1936)

Nietzsche
1844 - 1900

a) Quote for Morning Contemplation

"We often refuse to accept an idea merely because the tone of voice in which it has been expressed is unsympathetic to us." **(Nietzsche)**

Reflection for Deep Recovery (Sharabi)

Sometimes—especially if the message contains a painful truth—we blame the manner in which it was offered and reject it. The tone could be generated by the ego of the messenger, but it is the ego of the receiver that has taken offense. We listen to the message, not the messenger, nor the tone. There may be a valuable diamond here if we choose not to be turned off by the crust of dirt.

"To take offense is to give offense."

Course in Miracles (1976)

"There are three classes of people: those who see, those who see when they are shown, those who do not see."
Leonardo da Vinci (1452 - 1519)

b) Quote for Evening Contemplation

"Those who cannot understand how to put their thoughts on ice should not enter into the heat of debate." **(Nietzsche)**

Reflection for Deep Recovery (Sharabi)

When I am triggered into a heated debate, I must be suspicious of the passion that has been awakened in me. I cannot merely ascribe it to "beliefs" or "convictions." My anger is never really about what I think I am angry at. Anger is a cover-up for fear, sadness, pain, or helplessness. Society glorifies anger; in recovery, we see it as a failure of self-awareness. Every time I get riled up is an opportunity to learn about myself and my fears, an opportunity to lay bare the deep structure inside me that lies hidden from me. Anger always originates within me, but my mind focuses on external things as "causing" my anger. Anger creates an illusion of power and control when I am helpless. Today, I am thankful for my anger as a channel to awareness about myself; I have a duty to shield others from it.

"Conflict cannot survive without your participation."
Wayne Dyer (1940 - 2015)

Nietzsche
1844 - 1900

a) Quote for Morning Contemplation

**"Whenever I climb, I am followed by a dog called 'Ego.' "
(Nietzsche)**

Reflection for Deep Recovery (Sharabi)

As I climb the spiritual heights, I have to deal constantly with my
ego, which follows me everywhere, barking, tugging, and urging
me to do things to make me feel powerful and righteous. I must
beware of my need to be "right," my tendency to judge people and
to punish them, my urge to feel like a victim and feel sorry for
myself; it is just my dog barking.

*"Inside of me there are two dogs. One is mean and evil, and the other is
good, and they fight each other all the time. When asked which one wins,
I answer: the one I feed the most."*

Sitting Bull (1831 - 1890)

---

b) Quote for Evening Contemplation

"Fear is the mother of morality." (Nietzsche)

Reflection for Deep Recovery (Sharabi)

Beware of highly moral (and moralistic) people in these halls
of recovery; they are merely filled with fear. Fearful people will
invent a morality and try to impose it on others. This morality will
often include repercussions—from silent condemnation to public
shaming and even lynching and burning—for the ones who fail
to follow it. Some claim that my suffering from drinking was a
natural consequence of immoral actions, thoughts, and behavior. I
reject the notion that my drinking was caused by immorality, but
I understand that in sobriety, I have to evolve my own moral and
ethical code based on love and self-awareness rather than fear. In
fact, most beliefs, philosophies, and morals are "fear management
systems." Yes, they can be useful, but they can also condemn
us to a trance. In Deep Recovery, our duty is to think, to awaken
ourselves, not to impose our morals or ethics on others.

*"... it requires less mental effort to condemn than to think... Before we can
forgive one another, we have to understand one another."*

Emma Goldman (1869 - 1940)

Nietzsche
1844 - 1900

a) Quote for Morning Contemplation

**"Is man one of God's blunders? Or is God one of man's blunders?"
(Nietzsche)**

Reflection for Deep Recovery (Sharabi)

Sincere doubt is sacred, honest, and spiritual, at least as spiritual as deep faith—possibly even more so. The doubter is expressing a brave desire for truth, while beliefs are often an attempt to escape from fear. Doubting requires intelligence and courage; believing requires neither. It is possible to be deeply spiritual without believing in God, creation, angels, heaven, hell, and so on. The idea of God has created more violence, wars, and deaths than any other invention of the human mind; it has also provided immense comfort to humble souls in recovery. Spirituality uses the idea of God as a resource, while religion uses God as a weapon.

"Skepticism is... the first step towards truth."

Denis Diderot (1713 - 1786)

---

b) Quote for Evening Contemplation

"Shared joys make a friend, not shared sufferings." (Nietzsche)

Reflection for Deep Recovery (Sharabi)

In these rooms of recovery, it may appear that we are sharing our suffering from the past; but really, we are sharing the joy of the present. The newcomer listening to stories of drunkenness might get the wrong impression of recovery. We are here uniting in the joy of freedom, and we are merely reminding each other of liberation... but liberation from what? It is easy to forget. Our ultimate freedom comes from a deep acceptance of our powerlessness, of the fragility of sobriety and life, and the gratitude for today.

"Joy is the serious business of Heaven."

C. S. Lewis (1898 - 1963)

Nietzsche
1844 - 1900

a) Quote for Morning Contemplation

"Arrogance on the part of the meritorious is even more offensive to us than the arrogance of those without merit, for merit itself is offensive." (Nietzsche)

Reflection for Deep Recovery (Sharabi)

I must not become vain about my virtues, for claiming virtuousness is itself arrogant and offensive. I cannot allow myself to feel morally superior to the poor souls still struggling with alcohol or the ones struggling with life or with feelings. I must not be arrogant about the idea that I am not bothered by things that bother others. I am not staying sober through my virtuousness or my merit. I am the recipient of good fortune; my desire to surrender to recovery came from beyond me.

"I am fond of pigs. Dogs look up to us. Cats look down on us. Pigs treat us as equals."

Winston Churchill (1874 - 1965)

---

b) Quote for Evening Contemplation

"To forget one's purpose is the commonest form of stupidity." (Nietzsche)

Reflection for Deep Recovery (Sharabi)

My purpose in recovery is to grow spiritually. My sobriety is just a base to build spirituality from. Sobriety is the platform, not the purpose of recovery.

"Nothing contributes so much to tranquilize the mind as a steady purpose - a point on which the soul may fix its intellectual eye."

Mary Shelley (1797 - 1851)

"This is the true joy in life, the being used for a purpose recognized by yourself as a mighty one, the being thoroughly worn out before you are thrown on the scrap heap; the being a force of Nature instead of a feverish, selfish little clod of ailments and grievances, complaining that the world will not devote itself to making you happy."

George Bernard Shaw (1856 - 1950)

Nietzsche
1844 - 1900

a) Quote for Morning Contemplation

**"Convictions are more dangerous foes of truth than lies."
(Nietzsche)**

Reflection for Deep Recovery (Sharabi)

If I can directly see the truth, there is no need for beliefs or convictions. Convictions are necessary only to shore myself up in the face of uncertainty, to draw more people to my side. Convictions are often indefensible lies cloaked as truth. A person with convictions makes everyone else wrong. The liar at least knows the lie and therefore glimpses the truth. But the person with convictions has stopped looking for truth, or any truth larger than the idea he(she) has gotten hold of. In many ways, he or she is even more cowardly than the liar.

"The trouble with the world is that the stupid are cocksure and the intelligent are full of doubt."

Bertrand Russell (1872 - 1970)

---

b) Quote for Evening Contemplation

"There is more wisdom in your body than in your deepest philosophy." (Nietzsche)

Reflection for Deep Recovery (Sharabi)

Who I am is an embodied presence. I exist fully even when my thoughts are silent—perhaps even more so because thoughts distract me from presence, from Being, which is, at its essence, a physical experience. The body has wisdom; it has me pass out to prevent alcohol poisoning. If it weren't for this built-in safeguard—our drunkenness preventing us from drinking more—most of us would be dead from an overdose. "Chugging" subverts this life-saving mechanism that the body has prepared. Chugging enormous quantities of alcohol faster than the body can monitor and protest can lead to death... and often does. Also, the mind can be fooled by my own lies, but the body senses it when I lie. This is the basis of the lie detector, the Breathalyzer, and the straight-line-walking test for sobriety. The body acknowledges the lie even as the mind is protesting, "I am not drunk!".

"The body is to be compared, not to a physical object, but rather to a work of art."

Maurice Merleau-Ponty (1908 - 1961)

Nietzsche
1844 - 1900

a) Quote for Morning Contemplation

"Talking much about oneself can also be a means to conceal oneself." (Nietzsche)

Reflection for Deep Recovery (Sharabi)

Then, it means we might all be in hiding because we do tend to talk a lot about ourselves in meetings—don't we? We discover ourselves in silence, but we pretend to disclose ourselves through talk. Talk can conceal me from myself, from the emptiness I feel inside. How many times did I say: "I am going to quit drinking," even with great conviction? However, there is a way of knowing myself that is an essential part of recovery; it is always one step ahead of what I fool myself, of what I want to believe myself to be. It is called "me as my gut knows me."

"What is necessary to change a person is to change his awareness of himself."

Abraham Maslow (1908 - 1970)

---

b) Quote for Evening Contemplation

"Two great European narcotics, alcohol and Christianity... " (Nietzsche)

Reflection for Deep Recovery (Sharabi)

Religion can be a drug, much like any other mood-altering chemical. It induces altered states, creates a trance, and takes someone far from reality. Religion is absorbed propaganda people take on to comfort themselves in times of pain and fear. In many cases, people's religion represents a return to the magical thinking of childhood where the parent played the role of protector and the giver of gifts, acceded to requests and entreaties, and demanded obedience with the threat of anger. Much violence in the world has been perpetrated by people in the trance of religion, also, by people drunk on alcohol. In fact, drinking —as well as beliefs and philosophies—are all "fear management systems."

"If we can acknowledge our fear, we can realize that right now, we are okay. Right now, today, we are still alive... Our eyes can still see the beautiful sky. Our ears can still hear the voices of our loved ones."

Thich Nhat Hanh (born 1926)

Nietzsche
1844 - 1900

a) Quote for Morning Contemplation

"Whoever despises himself nonetheless respects himself as one who despises." (Nietzsche)

Reflection for Deep Recovery (Sharabi)

By admitting wrong, I have suddenly become right again. By putting myself down, I immediately distinguish myself as a person of high moral character, honest and virtuous. Beware of this game the mind plays. People fill themselves up with sanctimoniousness while mouthing, "I am a liar, a cheat, and a thief." Also, dealing with the outside world, the thought enters, "I am able to acknowledge my faults—but they are not! I despise myself as a wretch and, therefore, I am spiritual while they are not!" Self-esteem and self-abasement are both contrary to humility. Humility involves no self-image at all and no should's for others.

"Self-respect: the secure feeling that no one, as yet, is suspicious."
H. L. Mencken (1880 - 1956)

---

b) Quote for Evening Contemplation

"Whatever is done for love always occurs beyond good and evil." (Nietzsche)

Reflection for Deep Recovery (Sharabi)

I spend time with newcomers, not because I wish to be "good," not for rewards, but for love. Let my actions be spurred by love and kindness rather than by "goodness" or rightness. Let me help others because they need help, not because I need to feel better. Many "good" people have perpetrated violence on others whom they consider "evil." But we don't hear of "kind" people getting mad at someone for being "unkind" or "loving" people punishing someone for being "unloving." I never wish to get into debates as to who is "right" and who is "wrong," or about "good" and "evil," because all it does is generate violence—of thought and action.

"We ought to do good to others as simply as a horse runs, or a bee makes honey, or a vine bears grapes season after season without thinking of the grapes it has borne."
Marcus Aurelius (121 - 180 A.D.)

"Kindness can become its own motive. We are made kind by being kind."
Eric Hoffer (1898 - 1983)

Nietzsche
1844 - 1900

a) Quote for Morning Contemplation

"Words are but symbols for the relations of things to one another and to us; nowhere do they touch upon absolute truth." (Nietzsche)

Reflection for Deep Recovery (Sharabi)

The Big Book is a signpost pointing to recovery. I cannot get too involved with the post; I must try to see where the sign is pointing. Studying and memorizing the sentences in the Big Book can keep me occupied and give me the illusion of progress, but real growth occurs when I lift my eyes from the pages and gaze at the horizon, for that is what the Big Book is talking about.

"The best things can't be told because they transcend thought. The second best are misunderstood because those are the thoughts that are supposed to refer to that which can't be thought about, and one gets stuck in the thoughts. The third best are what we talk about."
Heinrich Zimmer, (1890 - 1943) quoted by Joseph Campbell

---

b) Quote for Evening Contemplation

"Extreme positions are not succeeded by moderate ones, but by contrary extreme positions." (Nietzsche)

Reflection for Deep Recovery (Sharabi)

In recovery, we begin to see many issues not as black and white but as gray and diffuse. Rigidity and extreme convictions are not signs of spiritual advancement but of uncertainty, anxiety, and paralyzing fear. In these gatherings and in the group conscience meetings that occur, deciding by majority vote will lead to ignoring the needs of the minority. I try to counter extreme positions and opinions with moderate ones; I am motivated by a desire to build consensus and to arrive at solutions that everyone can live with. I do not try to vote my opinion at group conscience meetings; I try to vote for the most acceptable solution that takes everyone's needs into account. This is my responsibility in recovery.

"Democracy is two wolves and a lamb voting on what is for dinner."
Benjamin Franklin (1706 - 1790)

Nietzsche
1844 - 1900

a) Quote for Morning Contemplation

"What can everyone do? Praise and blame. This is human virtue; this is human madness." (Nietzsche)

Reflection for Deep Recovery (Sharabi)

People think their judgments of others, their opinions on issues, and their beliefs—are important. Recovery, as a movement, has no opinion on outside issues. I can model myself on that. It is human madness to have "opinions" about others. Too many opinions, too much "for" and "against;" this is the human craziness we have to live with in the world today. We have lost the ability to have a civil discourse with someone who disagrees with us; every debate becomes a fight. We have each ended up prisoners of our opinions and judgments and lost our freedom: the freedom to approach people and issues and life in the freshness of the moment.

"... one of the obvious origins of human disagreement lies in the use of noises for words."

Alfred Korzybski (1879 - 1950)

---

b) Quote for Evening Contemplation

"What is as most humane? To spare someone shame." (Nietzsche)

Reflection for Deep Recovery (Sharabi)

I must overcome the temptation to celebrate victory by humiliating the "enemy." What would it take to give up the temptation to say, "See, I told I so!" and to gloat: "I was right, and you were wrong!" Forgiveness is not about, "You were wrong, but I forgive!" Forgiveness is about giving up our condemnation of the other, about seeing that no wrong was done in the first place. This is the generosity I must use to interpret other people's actions—with kind eyes. No one is ever wrong. They are right in their world, and they don't live in mine. I must keep this in mind when I am tempted to criticize someone or to scold them in public. There is nothing so shaming for a child as to be scolded in public by his or her parents. Shame sends the child into hiding. We need to recover from our own shame, and we do this by becoming aware of how much shaming is occurring all around us, even by us.

"When I was young, I admired clever people. Now that I am old, I admire kind people."

Heschel (1907 - 1972)

Nietzsche
1844 - 1900

a) Quote for Morning Contemplation

"To use the same words is not a sufficient guarantee of understanding; one must use the same words for the same genus of inward experience; ultimately, one must have one's experiences in common." (Nietzsche)

Reflection for Deep Recovery (Sharabi)

We can identify with the words of fellow recovering alcoholics; we can use the same words in describing ourselves, but ultimately, we must resonate with their feelings and their experiences. This is only possible when one alcoholic is speaking/listening to another alcoholic, for they have experiences in common. When I listen to comments and stories, I battle my need to differentiate and disagree; they lead to feelings of isolation. Instead, I try to identify; I need that commonality to feel connected with the fellowship.

"We are like islands in the sea, separate on the surface but connected in the deep."

William James (1842 - 1910)

b) Quote for Evening Contemplation

"Sometimes people don't want to hear the truth because they don't want their illusions destroyed." (Nietzsche)

Reflection for Deep Recovery (Sharabi)

This was true in my drunkenness, but the darn thing is that it is also true in my recovery. That is why constant vigilance is needed. In recovery, I must welcome disillusionment. I must allow illusions to be shattered, especially the illusions of self, a notion created by the ego, which often causes me to get "offended" and sulk in self-righteousness. I must bravely face the stark truth about myself. Unwelcome as it may seem initially, the truth is always a friend. The truth is never wrong, and it can never be wrong to face the truth squarely. As someone has said, if the truth will kill it, maybe it deserves to die. This is the ruthless honesty with myself that is called for in recovery.

*"We would rather be ruined than changed
We would rather die in our dread
Than climb the cross of the moment
And let our illusions die."*

W. H. Auden (1907 - 1973)

Nietzsche
1844 - 1900

a) Quote for Morning Contemplation

"What is difficult? asks the spirit that would bear much, and kneels down like a camel wanting to be well loaded. What is most difficult, O heroes, asks the spirit that would bear much, that I may take it upon myself and exult in my strength?" (Nietzsche)

Reflection for Deep Recovery (Sharabi)

In recovery, we do not run from life but take it head-on, like the camel, kneeling down, willing to be loaded. We do not shirk from the idea of effort. We accept difficulties, for they make us strong; We are unafraid of disillusionment because they lift us past illusions. We remain unattached to self-image, for we seek humility. We highlight our wrongs to mock our posture of wisdom. On this path, we do not demand that recovery—or life—be easy. We are willing to do what it takes; the prize we seek is precious, exalted, well worth the difficulties along the way. Perhaps the willingness we have acquired to kneel down and take on difficulties is—itself—the prize?

---

b) Quote for Evening Contemplation

"What is great in man is that he is a bridge and not an end." (Nietzsche)

Reflection for Deep Recovery (Sharabi)

Man is not static, but he is, in essence, a crossing, forever extending in a wonderful arc. Sobriety is a bridge too, the middle rather than the ends. It is not the other end that is the prize; it is the act of reaching. What is great in each of us exists only as we are stretching... extending... growing... emerging. Recovery is not an end for us but a process: dynamic, new each moment—exciting.

"Look up at the stars and not down at your feet. Try to make sense of what you see and wonder about what makes the universe exist. Be curious."

Stephen Hawking (1942 - 2018)

Nietzsche
1844 - 1900

a) Quote for Morning Contemplation

**"You must have chaos within you to give birth to a dancing star."
(Nietzsche)**

Reflection for Deep Recovery (Sharabi)

Great stars are born in the chaos of interstellar nebulae. When order is reached, growth and change have stopped. If complacency has arrived, I have died. So I try and stay unsettled and fluid in a creative way; I try never to congeal into conclusions and firm "beliefs." Instead, I am constantly seeking new openings and new perspectives that will disrupt my stance. My beliefs, judgments, and conclusions can freeze me if I don't keep awake and participate in the dynamic dance that is existence. In Deep Recovery, I get excited when I discover I have been wrong in a view I have been holding. Then, new dancing stars come twinkling into my field of view.

"What is asserted without evidence can be dismissed without evidence."
Christopher Hitchens (1949 - 2011)

---

b) Quote for Evening Contemplation

"Whoever fights monsters should see to it that in the process he does not become a monster." (Nietzsche)

Reflection for Deep Recovery (Sharabi)

When doing a Fourth Step inventory, or a Tenth Step, I examine where my justifications pop up: "I did this because he/she did that... !" I must not fight evil with evil. The urge to retaliate may be common, but an enlightened recovering person avoids instinctively slapping back. I cannot wrong in response to wrong. All justification is suspect. We must not absorb the tactics of the "monster" we are fighting, even though it may appear effective. We maintain our principles, no matter what the personality of the opposition. We must also maintain adherence to the principles of recovery, no matter what our own personality suggests; we must not let our personality take over in our arguments, disagreements, and fights.

"The more incompetent one feels, the more eager he is to fight."
Dostoevsky (1821 - 1881)

Nisargadatta
1897 - 1981

a) Quote for Morning Contemplation

"Anticipation makes you insecure; memory, unhappy. Stop misusing your mind, and all will be well with you. You need not set it right; it will set itself right as soon as you give up all concern with the past and the future and live entirely in the now." (Nisargadatta)

Reflection for Deep Recovery (Sharabi)

Worry and regret accomplish little; yet, they fill my mind. I am misusing my mind, brooding about stuff that is in the past or future, or just abstract stuff. My regrets about the past and my worries about the future can make the stupor of alcohol appear attractive. Recovery teaches me, instead, to live one day at a time, to live in the present. The present is always welcoming, if I focus on it, this moment will open up; this day becomes luminous.

"What day is it?" asked Pooh. "It's today," squeaked Piglet. "My favorite day," said Pooh."

A. A. Milne (1882 - 1956)

---

b) Quote for Evening Contemplation

"Nothing troubles me. I offer no resistance to trouble; therefore, it does not stay with me. On your side, there is so much trouble. On mine, there is no trouble at all. Come to my side." (Nisargadatta)

Reflection for Deep Recovery (Sharabi)

When I have uncompromising ideas of the outcomes I want and hope for—when I am deeply attached to my expectations—all interference shows up as trouble. This is the space where most people operate. But, in recovery, I have learned the possibility of acceptance. I can stop trying to impose my will at every turn. I offer no resistance to "what is" in the moment. Then nothing appears as trouble. Yes, things show up requiring my attention or as indications that I may not get what I set out to get—but never as "trouble." All hopes and expectations are premeditated resentments; acceptance is freedom. It is distressingly simple.

"Whatever you are pushing against—you are stuck to."

Werner Erhard (born 1935)

"Reject your sense of injury, and the injury itself disappears."

Marcus Aurelius (121 - 180 A.D.)

Nisargadatta
1897 - 1981

a) Quote for Morning Contemplation

"The desire for truth is the highest of all desires, yet, it is still a desire. All desires must be given up for the real to be... when all search ceases, it is the Supreme State." (Nisargadatta)

Reflection for Deep Recovery (Sharabi)

Desire is the source of unhappiness. Recovery invites me to give up desire, to focus solely on improving my conscious contact with God and on doing God's will. Nisargadatta asks that we give up even the desire to please God. Leave the dualistic world of my will versus God's will, of happiness versus unhappiness, of expectations. Stop seeking, and you will reach the Supreme State—no concepts, ideas, words, opinions, desires—pure Consciousness, one with God.

"Desires are the knots that strangle the heart. When they are renounced, the mortal becomes immortal. Brahman is realized."

Upanishads (recorded 6th century B.C. or earlier)

---

b) Quote for Evening Contemplation

"All that happens is the cause of all that happens. Causes are numberless; the idea of a sole cause is an illusion." (Nisargadatta)

Reflection for Deep Recovery (Sharabi)

I spent myself trying to find "the reason" I drank so much. Then I was told: just focus on what you need to do to stop drinking. Insights and understanding about why I drink will not get me sober. Others have endured worse than me but didn't drink as I did. This reflection, in fact, also refers to all the reasons I am providing for my current unhappiness. I can stop labeling myself as "unhappy," and I can dismantle my explanations for my unhappiness. Happiness is a state of no words—just a big smile—but unhappiness is full of words and explanations. If you want to be happy, stop thinking those thoughts that lead to unhappiness. Stop having "shoulds" and "shouldn't." Happiness is simply the total absence of unhappiness, not the other way around.

"Happiness serves hardly any other purpose than to make unhappiness possible."

Marcel Proust (1871 - 1922)

Nisargadatta
1897 - 1981

a) Quote for Morning Contemplation

"In reality, there are no others, and by helping yourself, you help everybody else." (Nisargadatta)

Reflection for Deep Recovery (Sharabi)

I have been told in recovery that by helping others get sober, I am also helping my own sobriety. But the reverse is also true: by staying sober and attending meetings regularly, I am helping everybody else. My regular presence at my home group is itself a display of my faith and also a form of Twelfth Step work. Think about it: staying sober is itself Twelfth Step work. In the early days, I must focus on my own recovery. I must be very cautious in attempting to interfere in the affairs of others. "Helping" can be a form of interference; I need some wisdom, maturity, and compassion before I know to interfere fruitfully. Until then, I must limit myself to helping in simple, mechanical ways like giving rides, making coffee, setting up chairs, listening and nodding, etc.

---

b) Quote for Evening Contemplation

"It is always the false that makes you suffer, the false desires and fears, the false values and ideas, the false relationships between people. Abandon the false, and you are free of pain; truth makes you happy, truth liberates." (Nisargadatta)

Reflection for Deep Recovery (Sharabi)

Perhaps the Truth will set me free, but illusions are attractive. The illusion that I would one day control my drinking kept me going for years. The false idea that I must never admit defeat by alcohol kept me in the battle—and in the bottle. When I abandon false ideas and accept the truth about me and alcohol, I will be set free. And, in recovery, when I abandon the false ideas, explanations, desires, and values I am still hanging on to, I will come to the supreme awakening where I will see clearly. I will see that everything is all right, irrespective of the situation and the circumstances. I will stop wishing for anything to be other than how it is.

"This life is a hospital in which every patient is possessed with a desire to change his bed."

Charles Baudelaire (1821 - 1867)

Nisargadatta
1897 - 1981

a) Quote for Morning Contemplation

"When you demand nothing of the world, nor of God, when you want nothing, seek nothing, expect nothing, then the supreme state will come to you uninvited and unexpected." (Nisargadatta)

Reflection for Deep Recovery (Sharabi)

Modern culture glorifies dreams and desires. But the happiest moments involve sunning on a park bench on a spring morning: seeking nothing, expecting nothing, wanting nothing. In Step Eleven, I pray only for knowledge of God's will for me and the power to carry that out. I stop asking for anything; I want nothing. Then—Step Twelve says—a spiritual awakening will happen. That, Nisargadatta says, is the supreme state coming to me uninvited and unexpected.

"True spirituality is not fixed on faith or belief, it is the ennobling of the soul by rising above the barriers of material life."

Hazrat Inayat Khan (1882 - 1927)

---

b) Quote for Evening Contemplation

"You cannot transcend what you do not know. To go beyond yourself, you must know yourself." (Nisargadatta)

Reflection for Deep Recovery (Sharabi)

I kept drinking, but I did not know alcohol. The truth about alcohol was not available in the bars. I had to come into these meeting rooms to hear the truth. When I recognized the truth I was able to transcend my drinking. Now, to get to serenity, I must go beyond myself; I must transcend my ego-mind. I must understand its ceaseless chattering, its vanity and tendency to take offense, its obsession with self, its righteousness and need to have the last word, its need to dominate and control. If I simply keep watching the ego-mind at work, I will begin to know it, and maybe I will be able to go beyond it.

In Sufi terms, the crushing of the ego is called Nafs Kushi. And how do we crush it? When the self says, 'He ought to have done this, she ought to have said that,' we say, 'What does it matter, either this way or that way? Every person is what he is; you cannot change him, but you can change yourself.' That is the crushing. ... It is only in this way that we can crush our ego."

Hazrat Inayat Khan (1882 - 1927)

Nisargadatta
1897 - 1981

a) Quote for Morning Contemplation

"Past and future are in the mind only; I am now." (Nisargadatta)

Reflection for Deep Recovery (Sharabi)

When regrets, worries, and desire occupy my mind, I am in the past and future; I have left the present. We spent much of our conscious existence living in our commentary about life, not in life itself. Life is happening now; reality is right now. I only exist in the now. If I focus on something that is present—a flower, a bird, a touch, a melody, a smell, a face, my breathing—and direct my awareness towards it without running a commentary about it, without thinking about how it is wrong and how it needs to be fixed, my anxiety and regrets dissipate. I will be living in the now just in that moment. That is all that is possible.

"The present is the only thing that has no end."

Erwin Schrödinger (1887 - 1961)

---

b) Quote for Evening Contemplation

"If you could only keep quiet, clear of memories and expectations, you would be able to discern the beautiful pattern of events. It is your restlessness that causes chaos." (Nisargadatta)

Reflection for Deep Recovery (Sharabi)

My restlessness led me to drink; my inability to sit still caused my life to descend into chaos. I kept thinking about past memories and future expectations and failing to discern the beautiful pattern of the present. And now, in recovery, I am doing the same. Much of the work in the Steps focuses on the past, and it may be necessary for a while to do that. But the whole purpose of cleaning up the past is to dissolve my restlessness and chaos so that I am able—at will—to re-occupy the beautiful and silent present with the unblemished consciousness of a simple mind.

"The quieter you become, the more you can hear."

Baba Ram Dass (1931 - 2019)

"Give yourself a gift: the present moment."

Marcus Aurelius (121 - 180 A.D.)

Nisargadatta
1897 - 1981

a) Quote for Morning Contemplation

"Once you realize that the road is the goal and that you are always on the road, not to reach a goal, but to enjoy its beauty and its wisdom, life ceases to be a task and becomes natural and simple, in itself an ecstasy." (Nisargadatta)

Reflection for Deep Recovery (Sharabi)

Sobriety is not a goal: it is the journey. The end-point of sobriety is the end of life; therefore, sobriety is life. The intimate engagement with daily living, as suggested by the phrase, "practice these principles in all our affairs," will come naturally and effortlessly once the principles of recovery have been understood, absorbed, and become habit. Our job in recovery is to enjoy the beauty of life and its wisdom. Life becomes natural and simple, in itself an ecstasy.

"Knowledge comes, but wisdom lingers."

Alfred Lord Tennyson (1809 - 1892)

---

b) Quote for Evening Contemplation

"Desire by itself is not wrong... It is choices you make that are wrong." (Nisargadatta)

Reflection for Deep Recovery (Sharabi)

The desire to drink is a transient phenomenon, natural because I am an alcoholic. If I don't act on it, the desire will tire and go away. And if I do that repeatedly, it will even stop visiting me. The most important thing I have learned here is that I can make the right choice irrespective of my desires or impulses. Feelings or urges are not wrong; only actions can be wrong. I may feel like drinking; my mind may provide reasons for taking a drink, but I can choose not to drink, giving no reason at all for my decision. This is mindless abstinence—powerful, practical, and simple. I do not have to "think the drink through;" I can just refuse to engage with that thought when it appears. I choose sobriety just like that, not for any reason. And so too with other urges, like wanting to make them feel bad, punish, show them they can't ignore me, etc.

"I am who I am today because of the choices I made yesterday."

Eleanor Roosevelt (1884 - 1962)

Nisargadatta
1897 - 1981

a) Quote for Morning Contemplation

"To imagine that some little thing—food, sex, power, fame—will make you happy is to deceive yourself. Only something as vast and deep as the real Self can make you truly and lastingly happy." (Nisargadatta)

Reflection for Deep Recovery (Sharabi)

The "Self"—with a capital "S"—in Advaita philosophy is the same as God, Brahman, the Universal Oneness, the Tao, etc. Pursuing things like food, sex, power, fame, money, and thrills cannot give me true and lasting happiness. Nor can drugs and alcohol; these are all addictions. The way out of addictions and the frenzied pursuit of happiness and satisfaction—the cycle of desire and guilt—is to acquire consciousness of the deep Self— God-consciousness. Only this leads to true serenity, true contentment.

"Happiness is the absence of striving for happiness."

Chuang Tzu (370 - 287 B.C.)

---

b) Quote for Evening Contemplation

"Don't try to understand! It's enough if you do not misunderstand." (Nisargadatta)

Reflection for Deep Recovery (Sharabi)

"Understanding" means fitting something into pre-classified pigeonholes. I am interpreting something new with limited concepts that I already have. When I am still drinking cannot "understand" sobriety because it is outside the realm of experience. The few times I have given up drinking, I have not stuck with it long enough to glimpse what is available there. Sober living is different from anything I can conceive of or imagine, a concept so new and strange to me that it is important not to misunderstand it and reject it. For example, thinking of sobriety as "giving something up" would be a misunderstanding. Sobriety means gaining riches and freedom beyond my wildest imagination. It is not what you think of sobriety but how you think of sobriety that will determine your future.

"The essence of the independent mind lies not in what it thinks, but in how it thinks."

Christopher Hitchens (1949 - 2011)

Nisargadatta
1897 - 1981

a) Quote for Morning Contemplation

"Nothing ever goes wrong." (Nisargadatta)

Reflection for Deep Recovery (Sharabi)

I label something as "wrong" when it does not fit with my desires and expectations. But, as far as the Universe is concerned, nothing ever goes wrong in the larger scheme of things. Everything is simply what it is. I might get sad about something, but I don't have to go to, "It's sad that I'm sad," or, "It's unfair and wrong." If I let it be, let go of my interpretation that something has gone wrong, let go of labels—I am free. Deep acceptance means: nothing is wrong. It does not mean anything is right either or that it was meant to be. Acceptance means just no interpretation.

"To be blind is not miserable; not to be able to bear blindness, that is miserable."

John Milton (1608 - 1674)

---

b) Quote for Evening Contemplation

"All else will happen rightly once your mind is quiet. As the sun on rising makes the world active, so does self-awareness affect changes in the mind. In the light of calm and steady self-awareness, inner energies wake up and work miracles without any effort on your part." (Nisargadatta)

Reflection for Deep Recovery (Sharabi)

As I quieten the mind through sobriety and meditation, I begin to acquire self-awareness, and the miracle of serenity happens effortlessly. Everything occurs naturally. Just as the birds and animals and flowers naturally wake up with the rising sun, if I just keep attending meetings paying little attention to my wild thoughts and ideas, inner energies will wake up. My mind will quieten naturally; I will feel centered and grounded, and I will automatically know what to do next without having to figure it out. I will acquire self-awareness which, paradoxically, means the removal of focus on self.

"Silence is not the absence of sound, but the absence of self."

Anthony de Mello (1931 - 1997)

Nisargadatta
1897 - 1981

a) Quote for Morning Contemplation

**"To deal with things, knowledge of things is needed."
(Nisargadatta)**

Reflection for Deep Recovery (Sharabi)

To deal with alcoholism, knowledge of alcohol is needed. Alcohol is cunning, baffling, and powerful, and it takes time to get to know, deep in my bones, that I am incapable of controlling my drinking. This is the turning point: powerlessness. I cannot deal with alcohol, but I can deal with alcoholism. I do this by acquiring knowledge of alcohol, which leads me to understand that I cannot take that first drink.

"First you take a drink, then the drink takes a drink, then the drink takes you. "

F. Scott Fitzgerald (1896 - 1940)

b) Quote for Evening Contemplation

**"Your expectation of something unique and dramatic, of some wonderful explosion, is merely hindering and delaying your Self Realization. You are not to expect an explosion, for the explosion has already happened—at the moment when you were born—when you realized yourself as Being-Knowing-Feeling."
(Nisargadatta)**

Reflection for Deep Recovery (Sharabi)

Self-Realization, God-Realization, spiritual awakening: three names for the same thing. Nisargadatta (or "Maharaj") tells us that we need not await an explosion of white light. Our spiritual awakening has already occurred the moment we stopped being in a trance with our experience of this "world" but became conscious of experience—conscious of consciousness. When we stand in awareness of Being-Knowing-Feeling, it is truly stunning. It is not a state to "get to" but simply to notice; we are already there.

"The very desire to seek spiritual enlightenment is, in fact, nothing but the grasping tendency of the ego itself, and thus, the very search for enlightenment prevents it."

Ken Wilber (born 1949)

Nisargadatta
1897 - 1981

a) Quote for Morning Contemplation

"Absolute perfection is here and now, not in some future, near or far... Disregard whatever you think yourself to be and act as if you were absolutely perfect—whatever your idea of perfection may be." (Nisargadatta)

Reflection for Deep Recovery (Sharabi)

I cannot await perfection in some abstract and mythical future. It is what it is—perfect as what it is. I can disregard my story about my defects and act as if I already am what I wish to be. I can give up my story about myself and just engage with life in the moment. I focus on my character and furthering it, not on character defects.

"Do not think of your faults, still less of other's faults; look for what is good and strong, and try to imitate it. Your faults will drop off, like dead leaves, when their time comes."

John Ruskin (1819 - 1900)

---

b) Quote for Evening Contemplation

"When the center of selfishness is no longer, all desires for pleasure and fear of pain cease. One is no longer interested in being happy; beyond happiness, there is pure intensity, inexhaustible energy, the ecstasy of giving from a perennial source." (Nisargadatta)

Reflection for Deep Recovery (Sharabi)

When I cease to be involved with my petty concerns about myself and my temporary condition; when I completely let go of my frenzied insistence that things turn out a certain way or of my fear that they will turn out a different way; when I stop pursuing that elusive and brief high called happiness; when I can gaze with clarity and awareness but without thought or feeling, into that intensity of pure existence—then I am freed. When I can indulge in an activity intensely and fully without thoughts of ego and without ulterior selfish motives, then I can reach a state of "flow" which is the ultimate ecstasy.

"It is by being fully involved with every detail of our lives, whether good or bad, that we find happiness, not by trying to look for it directly."

Mihaly Csikszentmihalyi (born 1934)

Nisargadatta
1897 - 1981

a) Quote for Morning Contemplation

"Truth is not a reward for good behavior, nor a prize for passing some tests. It cannot be brought about. It is the primary, the unborn, the ancient source of all that is. You are eligible because you are. You need not merit truth. It is your own... stand still, be quiet." (Nisargadatta)

Reflection for Deep Recovery (Sharabi)

Sobriety is my own truth, my deepest clarity. I do not "merit" sobriety, but I can stand still, be quiet, and receive it. Sobriety is not a reward for good behavior; it is not something I "deserve," nor can it be brought about purely by my efforts. It is an act of grace. It is impossible that some people deserve sobriety and others do not. We are all eligible for sobriety simply because we exist. "I am." "We are." Sobriety is available to anyone and everyone.

"Abundance is not something we acquire. It is something we tune into."
Wayne Dyer (1940 - 2015)

---

b) Quote for Evening Contemplation

"All you need is already within you; only, you must approach your self with reverence and love. Self-condemnation and self-distrust are grievous errors." (Nisargadatta)

Reflection for Deep Recovery (Sharabi)

All I need to stay sober is within me—not as some thought or idea or concept or formula, but as something profound: my core Self. I must approach this Self with reverence and love, not beat myself up. It may be true that I reach incorrect conclusions sometimes, do "wrong" things sometimes, or say unkind words. At these times, the ego might seek to justify itself, and I must watch out against that. I distrust all the reasons and justifications that well up in me, but I do not distrust that deep awareness that I possess: my deep self-acceptance and self-reverence. I may "do" wrong, but I never "am" wrong, for who I "am"—my core Being—is sacred, divine.

SELF-LOVE PRAYER: "Lord, please interrupt me when I am beating myself up; remind me that I am a precious child of yours, worthy of acceptance and love as I am; that knowing this is what will give me the freedom to change."

from DEEP RECOVERY

Nisargadatta
1897 - 1981

a) Quote for Morning Contemplation

"When I look within and see that I am nothing, that is Wisdom. When I look outside and see that I am everything, that is Love. Between the two my life flows." (Nisargadatta)

Reflection for Deep Recovery (Sharabi)

When I look within: "Who am I?" I encounter that deep and sacred emptiness at my core. And when I look outside in rapture at everything, from the lowliest creature and insect to the highest mountain and cloud, I know: I am Love. Many make life about "finding love." But Wisdom is about realizing that who I am is love itself; who I am is everything. Existence is happening and life is flowing in the world of time, between these two eternal banks of everything and nothing, of Wisdom and Love.

"Man is equally incapable of seeing the nothingness from which he emerges and the infinity in which he is engulfed."

Blaise Pascal (1623 - 1662)

---

b) Quote for Evening Contemplation

"Steady faith is stronger than destiny. Destiny is the result of causes, mostly accidental, and is therefore loosely woven." (Nisargadatta)

Reflection for Deep Recovery (Sharabi)

Faith is stronger than a mere belief that some result will happen or even a willingness to accept whatever happens. What happens is the result of causes and decisions and, therefore, loosely woven. I do not accept what happens as pre-destined; I do not mistake my shallow rational explanations for what happens as faith. Steady faith soars in a different space. It is a deep reverence for what is, but it is unaffected by what happens or does not happen. It is not propped up by events or explanations, by hope or desire; it is not proven by miracles. It is not a property of the mind or observation. Faith is transcendent.

"To one who has faith, no explanation is necessary. To one without faith, no explanation is possible."

Thomas Aquinas (1224 - 1274)

"To ask for an explanation is to explain the obscure by the more obscure."

Maurice Merleau-Ponty (1908 - 1961)

Nisargadatta
1897 - 1981

a) Quote for Morning Contemplation

**"The mind creates the abyss;
the spirit crosses it." (Nisargadatta)**

Reflection for Deep Recovery (Sharabi)

There are logical barriers to this path to sobriety: statistical declamations, skeptical denials, unanswerable arguments. Any reasonable person examining the program of recovery will conclude that it is unlikely to succeed. There is a big gap in logic. But the spirit can power a leap of faith into a world where the impossible happens. My problems and my drunkenness were unsolvable at the level of mind and emotion. The mind sees the abyss—indeed created the abyss. But sanity lies on the other side of this abyss. What can be done? The spirit sees possibility and calls: I leap!

"All growth is a leap in the dark, a spontaneous unpremeditated act without benefit of experience."

Henry Miller (1891 - 1980)

b) Quote for Evening Contemplation

"A quiet mind is all you need." (Nisargadatta)

Reflection for Deep Recovery (Sharabi)

All problems: regret, anxiety, resentment, worry, expectation, uncertainty, fear, hope, self-loathing, pessimism, optimism, pride, and depression are creations of the mind. Rather than creating the problem in the mind and then trying to solve it at the level of mind, stop! Stop before creating the problem; silence the mind. Silence can be one of three kinds: a focus on thoughts, a focus on feelings, and a focus on nothing at all. Only the last is true silence. A quiet mind is one that is not thinking about anything. Imagination subsides, and all problems disappear. If I am conscious that I am meditating, then I am not really meditating. So don't try to meditate, and don't ever check if you are meditating. Just meditate.

"All of humanity's problems stem from man's inability to sit quietly in a room alone."

Blaise Pascal (1623 - 1662)

Nisargadatta
1897 - 1981

a) Quote for Morning Contemplation

"You have put so much energy into building a prison for yourself. Now spend as much on demolishing it. In fact, demolition is easy, for the false dissolves when it is discovered." (Nisargadatta)

Reflection for Deep Recovery (Sharabi)

I have spent so much energy and time rationalizing and justifying myself, justifying drinking. Now I can spend as much on going to meetings and contemplating recovery, demolishing the false arguments for drinking. Even today, I build a prison around myself. The walls are made up of my opinions, my judgments, my justifications—all the words and concepts I barricade myself with. Many of the things I think I know are not really so. How can I see my blindness? Only by acknowledging that I have latched onto many false things that I am not aware of... yet.

"Experience teaches only the teachable."

Aldous Huxley (1894 - 1963)

---

b) Quote for Evening Contemplation

"Between the banks of pain and pleasure, the river of life flows. It is only when the mind refuses to flow with life and gets stuck at the banks that it becomes a problem." (Nisargadatta)

Reflection for Deep Recovery (Sharabi)

I notice that the river never flows into the rocks or into the banks—only around the rocks and past the banks. When I go with the flow of life, it all becomes easier. On the other hand, when I try to impose my will at every turn, I will end up getting bashed into rocks or getting stuck at the banks. Therefore, if I learn to accept pain and pleasure graciously as part of life without getting stuck in either, I will flow along with the river of life.

"While the river of life glides along smoothly, it remains the same river; only the landscape on either bank seems to change."

Max Muller (1823 - 1900)

Nisargadatta
1897 - 1981

a) Quote for Morning Contemplation

"It is your fixed idea that you must be something or other, that blinds you. Give up all ideas about yourself and simply be." (Nisargadatta)

Reflection for Deep Recovery (Sharabi)

My ideas about how I must be and what I must achieve are based on my notion of who I am and what others expect from me. But I can give up ideas of myself; how I want to be seen or acknowledged, that I should be admired, respected, or valued, and my concern about being disrespected, criticized, or ridiculed. These blind me to the beauty and freedom of my experience here and now. The entire notion of "who I am" is an illusion. The mind makes things complicated and convoluted. Instead, I can just Be. It is simple. Being is available without figuring out how to be.

"What you think you are is a belief to be undone."

Course in Miracles (1976)

---

b) Quote for Evening Contemplation

"Real happiness is not vulnerable because it does not depend on circumstances." (Nisargadatta)

Reflection for Deep Recovery (Sharabi)

"Most folks are as happy as they make up their minds to be."

Abraham Lincoln (1809 - 1865)

The "real happiness" that Nisargadatta is speaking of does not lie in the realm of the mind or feeling. It does not depend on the circumstances; it is not situational and does not depend on desires being fulfilled. It is an untouchable bliss that lies at the very base of existence and consciousness—a Divine Ecstasy. I must reach for that place rather than trying to arrange the people, things, and circumstances in my life. I must stop trying to evaluate how each day is going, how my life is going. I can clean my car joyfully without complaining about the snow.

"Happiness, in fact, is a condition that must be prepared for, cultivated, and defended privately by each person. People who learn to control inner experience will be able to determine the quality of their lives, which is as close as any of us can come to being happy."

Mihaly Csikszentmihalyi (born 1934)

Nisargadatta
1897 - 1981

a) Quote for Morning Contemplation

"Once you know with absolute certainty that nothing can trouble you but your own imagination, you come to disregard your desires and fears, concepts and ideas, and live by truth alone." (Nisargadatta)

Reflection for Deep Recovery (Sharabi)

Anxiety, worries, desires, and regrets are products of the human imagination—creations of the mind. Once I understand this, I can disregard my desires and my fears. I can rise above mind and live in "presence," beyond ideas and concepts, beyond words, beyond this physical world, beyond time. This is Truth, not as a concept but as an absolute. I can access Truth any moment I choose to and linger there as long as I like. I can take care of my worldly responsibilities while operating from this state as a "base camp."

"The objective level is not words and cannot be reached by words alone. We must point our finger and be silent, or we will never reach this level."
Alfred Korzybski (1879 - 1950)

b) Quote for Evening Contemplation

"In my world, love is the only law. I do not ask for love, I give it." (Nisargadatta)

Reflection for Deep Recovery (Sharabi)

Love as a state of being, is an overflowing of the heart and soul; such love knows no object but illuminates all objects. To give love is to receive love. To give an embrace is to receive an embrace. When I embrace existence—all of existence and everything and everyone—existence embraces me. I am giving love and receiving love. In that moment, I am love.

"For true love is inexhaustible; the more you give, the more you have. And if you go to draw at the true fountainhead, the more water you draw, the more abundant is its flow."
Antoine de Saint-Exupéry (1900 - 1944)

Nisargadatta
1897 - 1981

a) Quote for Morning Contemplation

"Words and questions come from the mind and hold you there. To go beyond the mind, you must be silent and quiet. Peace and silence; silence and peace: this is the way beyond. Stop asking questions." (Nisargadatta)

Reflection for Deep Recovery (Sharabi)

The mind says, "Why? Why stop asking questions?" Meditation is the cessation of words, of thoughts, of questions. When I quieten the mind and approach in silence; when I enter that calm, still place that is at the core of every being, then I transcend thoughts and compulsions. Words disappear; all questions, reasons, explanations and objections drop away. There is peace and silence.

THE DISTURBANCE PRAYER: "Lord, when I am agitated, anxious, disturbed, or craving, remind me to seek comfort in the immense stillness within me, so I do not get lost in my chattering thoughts and mind."

from DEEP RECOVERY

---

b) Quote for Evening Contemplation

"There is nothing to practice. To know yourself, be yourself. To be yourself, stop imagining yourself to be this or that. Just be. Let your true nature emerge. Don't disturb your mind with seeking." (Nisargadatta)

Reflection for Deep Recovery (Sharabi)

Initially, I have to remember consciously: "practice these principles in all my affairs." But once I have integrated the principles, they become my natural self. I stop seeking, and "being" becomes effortless.

"The Void needs no reliance; Mahamudra rests on naught. Without making an effort but remaining natural, one can break the yoke, thus gaining liberation... Cease all activity; abandon all desire; let thoughts rise and fall as they will like the ocean waves."

Tilopa's song (11th century)

[NOTE: "Mahamudra" (Sanskrit) = "the Grand Gesture." It is a seal or symbol in Tibetan Buddhism representing the Great Emptiness.]

Nisargadatta
1897 - 1981

a) Quote for Morning Contemplation

"Just as every drop of the ocean carries the taste of the ocean, so does every moment carry the taste of eternity." (Nisargadatta)

Reflection for Deep Recovery (Sharabi)

"To see the world in a grain of sand,
And heaven in a wild flower,
Hold infinity in the palm of your hand
And eternity in an hour."

William Blake (1757 - 1827)

Every day contains all of life in it. Live this day fully. Each day of sobriety— indeed every moment—carries within it the taste of eternity. This moment is as good and as exquisite as any moment that has ever existed, or will ever exist anywhere in the world, at any point in time. In fact, it is all one moment: now.

---

b) Quote for Evening Contemplation

"What you seek is so near you,
that there is no place for 'a way.'" (Nisargadatta)

Reflection for Deep Recovery (Sharabi)

There are a thousand ways to drink, a thousand reasons for drinking and a thousand drinks to choose from. Drinking is a "thing," an act, a doing. But sobriety itself is nothing; it is a non-thing. There is no such thing as a sober life; there is life, and there is life with drinking. There is no "way" to sobriety because it is not a place to get to or to work towards. Sobriety is simply life—right here, right now. It is so near, always present, that there is no place for "a way." There is no way to get to where I already am standing, but there are a thousand ways to leave. I already possess the gift of sobriety each day until I lose it by drinking.

Nisargadatta
1897 - 1981

a) Quote for Morning Contemplation

"When you travel in a car, are you the car?" (Nisargadatta)

Reflection for Deep Recovery (Sharabi)

Just because my consciousness inhabits my body, do I think I am the body? Just because I go to the railway station every day and drink tea with travelers, do I think I am a traveler? Can I sit in a garage for five years and become a car? Can I go and sit in the chair with sober people at meetings and claim I am in recovery? What does it take to be in recovery? I must think about this.

"You can't cross the sea by merely standing and staring at the water."
Rabindranath Tagore (1861 - 1941)

"From a hundred rabbits, you cannot make a horse."
Dostoevsky (1821 - 1881)

b) Quote for Evening Contemplation

"In the mirror of your mind, all kinds of pictures appear and disappear. Knowing that they are entirely your own creations, watch them silently come and go. Be alert, but not perturbed." (Nisargadatta)

Reflection for Deep Recovery (Sharabi)

I must not get disturbed by things just because I can imagine them or think of them. I can watch images and thoughts appear and disappear; they are creations of my mind-factory. So, I will have drinking thoughts and drinking dreams; what do I expect? I am an alcoholic. I can also have fantasies of wealth and power, fame and adulation. I can have critical thoughts, mean thoughts, even self-deprecating thoughts. Yes, I am alert but not perturbed or excited, for these pictures just appear and disappear. There is no "truth" necessarily associated with any of them. Recovery is rooted in the now while thoughts and images belong to the future or past, or an imagined world— never in the "now."

"Live quietly in the moment and see the beauty of all before you. The future will take care of itself."
Parmahansa Yogananda (1893 - 1952)

154

Nisargadatta
1897 - 1981

a) Quote for Morning Contemplation

"Until we can look at fear and accept it as the shadow of personal existence, as persons, we are bound to be afraid." (Nisargadatta)

Reflection for Deep Recovery (Sharabi)

As long as my ego keeps proposing the notion that an "I" exists in "time" as a consciousness, not just as a body—I will have fear, for it is about "existence" ceasing. Hinduism considers the notion of "self"—indeed the whole idea of "personal existence" and separateness—as an illusion created by the mind. Nisargadatta is talking about an enlightened consciousness where the concept of "self," the idea of "personal existence," and the notion of time have been transcended. But this perspective makes sense, perhaps, only to people who have arrived there.

"If time is not real, then the dividing line between this world and eternity, between suffering and bliss, between good and evil, is also an illusion."
Hermann Hesse (1877 - 1962)

---

b) Quote for Evening Contemplation

"There is nothing to do. Just be. Do nothing. Be. No climbing mountains and sitting in caves. I do not even say: 'be yourself,' since you do not know yourself. Just be. Having seen that you are neither the 'outer' world of perceivables, nor the 'inner' world of thinkables, that you are neither body nor mind, just be." (Nisargadatta)

Reflection for Deep Recovery (Sharabi)

"You do not need to leave your room. Remain sitting at your table and listen. Do not even listen, simply wait. Do not even wait, be quiet, still, and solitary. The world will freely offer itself to you to be unmasked: it has no choice; it will roll in ecstasy at your feet."
Franz Kafka (1883 - 1924)

"Every culture teaches egoic consciousness in different ways. At that level, it is all about me, my preferences, my choices, my needs, my desires and me and my group as the central reference point."
Richard Rohr (born 1943)

Nisargadatta
1897 - 1981

a) Quote for Morning Contemplation

"Once you arrive at the source, you come to know that actually there is no water, the water is purely the taste." (Nisargadatta)

Reflection for Deep Recovery (Sharabi)

"Sugar" is just a concept. I can never directly experience sugar—only sweetness. Similarly, I never directly experience sobriety—only bliss. I never directly experience recovery—only serenity. I never experience myself, only life. And I never directly experience spirituality or God; only completeness, only oneness, only infinity.

"My Lord, when I don't know who I am, I serve you. When I know who I am, I am you."

from Ramayana (circa 300 B.C.)

---

b) Quote for Evening Contemplation

"You are too much concerned with past and future. It is all due to your longing to continue, to protect yourself against extinction. And as you want to continue, you want others to keep you company, hence your concern with their survival. But what you call survival is but the survival of a dream." (Nisargadatta)

Reflection for Deep Recovery (Sharabi)

I am much too concerned about past and future because I have not realized that this moment is timeless and contains all of eternity. Rather than enjoying this "now"—which is where I will ever live—I fill myself with anxiety about survival: mine and others whose company I want. Nisargadatta (from Hinduism) considers this physical world and the notion of time to be a sort of dream, an illusion (Maya) from which awakening is possible. Then my anxiety vanishes; all is Perfect. I am a perfect consciousness awakened in a perfect moment, dreaming of this world: of problems, of desire, craving, misery, impermanence, change, and death.

"Your life is just about craving and making something else tremendously more important than you."

Sadhguru (born 1957)

Epictetus
55 AD - 135 AD

a) Quote for Morning Contemplation

"There is only one way to happiness, and that is to cease worrying about things which are beyond the power of our will." (Epictetus)

Reflection for Deep Recovery (Sharabi)

God grant me the serenity to accept the things I cannot change and the wisdom not to agonize about them. That wisdom comes from the Third Step. When we turn our will and my life over to a Higher Power, we are, in essence, agreeing to abide by the will of the universe; We will deal with it as best as we can. We are not going to sit here fretting about all the possibilities that may or may not ever happen. And when something does happen, we will accept it in that present moment as part of "what is." Our responsibility only is to make the best decisions we can. Sanity is accepting that we manage our decisions and choices, not how it turns out.

"If your happiness depends on what somebody else does, I guess you do have a problem."

Richard Bach (born 1930)

b) Quote for Evening Contemplation

"Don't explain your philosophy. Embody it." (Epictetus)

Reflection for Deep Recovery (Sharabi)

There is no point in just reciting the Steps and expounding on their meaning. There is no point just understanding them; the Steps exist only in the practice of the Steps in all my affairs—to absorb them and embody them in my life, to live the Steps, even outside these rooms. The Steps provide a complete blueprint for daily living and daily "being;" they are not just philosophy or metaphysics. They can be incorporated into who I am—mentally, emotionally, psychologically, and spiritually. You have to "be" the Steps, don't just "do" the Steps.

"Metaphysics is a restaurant where they give you a thirty thousand page menu and no food."

Robert M. Pirsig (1928 - 2017)

"Philosophy is not the reflection of a pre-existing truth, but, like art, the act of bringing truth into being."

Maurice Merleau-Ponty (1908 - 1961)

Epictetus
55 AD - 135 AD

a) Quote for Morning Contemplation

"Wealth consists not in having great possessions, but in having few wants." (Epictetus)

Reflection for Deep Recovery (Sharabi)

I want... I want... I want... It is my "wanting" that makes me poor; desires are the source of unhappiness. The more wants I have, the poorer I am; the fewer wants I have, the richer. I can notice my desires, but I don't have to glorify them or put them on a pedestal and go over them every morning. There is never any contentment possible if the underlying desire is for "more"—more drink, more money, more happiness. In my sobriety, I have everything I need—right here and right now—to have a full and rich life.

"I have no money, no resources, no hopes. I am the happiest man alive."
Henry Miller (1891 - 1980)

"The only truly affluent are those who do not want more than they have."
Erich Fromm (1900 - 1980)

---

b) Quote for Evening Contemplation

"If anyone tells you that a certain person speaks ill of you, do not make excuses about what is said of you but answer, "He was ignorant of my other faults, else he would not have mentioned these alone." (Epictetus)

Reflection for Deep Recovery (Sharabi)

Do I think I have to be faultless to survive? Why else am I constantly arguing that I am right—that I am not wrong? Why am I so invested in my self-image? Why is criticism intolerable; why can I not allow someone to think poorly of me? Perhaps I can learn to examine what was said with humor and with honesty: "That is how he or she sees me. There is probably some truth to it." It is a sign of humility not to have to maintain an image of myself in the world—not to have an image in my own "image"-ination.

"The cleverest of all, in my opinion, is the man who calls himself a fool at least once a month."
Dostoevsky (1821 - 1881)

"All faults may be forgiven of him who has perfect candor."
Walt Whitman (1819 - 1892)

Epictetus
55 AD - 135 AD

a) Quote for Morning Contemplation

**"First, say to yourself what you would be,
and then do what you have to do." (Epictetus)**

Reflection for Deep Recovery (Sharabi)

First, say to yourself: "I wish to be sober," and then do what you
have to do to be sober: go to meetings, work the Steps, whatever.
Or maybe you are in a more primitive place and are only able to
say, "I want to be free of trouble in my life." You will then see
that what you have to do is stop drinking. Maybe there are other
complex and convoluted solutions to your problems in life, but the
simplest solution which is right in front of you is sobriety. Then,
there are changes in attitude and changes in the way you behave
in the world that go with being in recovery. These, too, you can
embrace.

"Any man can ride a train. Only a wise man knows when to get off."
Eric Hoffer (1898 - 1983)

---

b) Quote for Evening Contemplation

**"Don't just say you have read books. Show that through them, you
have learned to think better, to be a more discriminating and
reflective person. Books are the training weights of the mind.
They are very helpful, but it would be a bad mistake to suppose
that one has made progress simply by having memorized their
contents." (Epictetus)**

Reflection for Deep Recovery (Sharabi)

It would be a bad mistake to suppose that I have made progress
simply by having read or memorized the contents of the Big Book.
People have relapsed and ended up in the detox ward, people who
could quote every line in the Big Book. What is worse, still—and
common   is believing that possessing a copy and having
intentions of reading it is sufficient.

*"... the purchase of books is mistaken for the appropriation of their
contents."*

Arthur Schopenhauer (1788 - 1860)

Epictetus
55 AD - 135 AD

a) Quote for Morning Contemplation

"Man is not worried by real problems so much as by his imagined anxieties about real problems." (Epictetus)

Reflection for Deep Recovery (Sharabi)

Our ability to imagine catastrophes far exceeds the ability (or the inclination) of the universe to produce them. Sure, problems can crop up unexpectedly, but most of the things we worry about never happen. Worry is simply the sign of a rich and dour imagination that wastes time projecting horrible outcomes into the future. Nothing useful comes from worrying, but the anxiety must somehow be comforting, or we wouldn't indulge in it so much.

"Present fears are less than horrible imaginings."
Shakespeare (1564 - 1616) (Macbeth)

"Treat all disasters as if they were trivialities but never treat a triviality as if it were a disaster."
Quentin Crisp (1908 - 1999)

---

b) Quote for Evening Contemplation

"If you want to improve, be content to be thought foolish and stupid." (Epictetus)

Reflection for Deep Recovery (Sharabi)

The first step to becoming a better person is just to stop behaving badly. "Do no harm" is the beginning of change; just stop making things worse. Later, you begin actively trying to do good. But here, concern about looking bad can prevent you from owning up to errors, from acknowledging defects, from ever admitting that you were wrong. Heck, it even prevented you from coming to recovery for a long time, for you thought it foolish and stupid to call yourself an alcoholic. Growth in the program requires you to pursue certain paths madly and foolishly without worrying about how you might appear to others. Don't avoid praying just because you are embarrassed about kneeling. Whenever you are learning something new, you are likely to appear clumsy and stupid. But bigger things are at stake here than just looking good.

"A man should never be ashamed to own that he has been in the wrong, which is but saying... that he is wiser today than yesterday."
Jonathan Swift (1667 - 1745)

Epictetus
55 AD - 135 AD

a) Quote for Morning Contemplation

"The key is to keep company only with people who uplift you, whose presence calls forth your best." (Epictetus)

Reflection for Deep Recovery (Sharabi)

I avoid people who try to make me feel bad about myself under the guise of feedback to help me grow. I prefer to stick around people who encourage me, who believe in me, and whose company I leave feeling better than when I came in. And, as a corollary, I try and make people feel better about themselves after talking with me. I try to inspire them to do their best, not with criticism or advice or preaching, but by seeing the best in them, seeing them as sacred, and ignoring the traits that are triggering my annoyance. If they want criticism, there are plenty in recovery who are willing to provide them that.

"Preach always. Use words only when necessary."

Thomas Aquinas (1224 - 1274)

---

b) Quote for Evening Contemplation

"It's not what happens to you, but how you react to it that matters." (Epictetus)

Reflection for Deep Recovery (Sharabi)

I accept whatever comes my way. I focus on how to play the cards life has dealt me, not on whether the cards were fair or unfair, easy or difficult. Luck may have played a role in what happened, but character is how I deal with things that happen. Difficulties and challenges are necessary to make me grow; I am willing to take them on. I am not going to sit here in fear of what I imagine might befall me. If there is preparation to be made for the future, I work on it without obsessing about it. Whatever happens, I have the support of people in the fellowship and the wisdom of recovery.

"Happiness is beneficial for the body, but it is grief that develops the powers of the mind."

Marcel Proust (1871 - 1922)

"I have always believed, and I still believe, that whatever good or bad fortune may come our way, we can always give it meaning and transform it into something of value."

Hermann Hesse (1877 - 1962)

Epictetus
55 AD - 135 AD

a) Quote for Morning Contemplation

"Any person capable of angering you becomes your master; he can anger you only when you permit yourself to be disturbed by him." (Epictetus)

Reflection for Deep Recovery (Sharabi)

No one can "make you angry." When you are angry, irritated, annoyed, petulant, or filled with rage, you must ask yourself: "How am I causing myself to get annoyed? What is my role in this, and what am I getting by getting myself riled up? Why am I invested in feeling righteous or in feeling like a victim? Do I really wish this person to have so much power over my insides, to determine my mood?" You don't want to be a slave of your default reactions over which you have no say and over which you have no control.

"If you are distressed by anything external, the pain is not due to the thing itself, but to your estimate of it, and this you have the power to revoke at any moment."

Marcus Aurelius (121 - 180 A.D.)

b) Quote for Evening Contemplation

"If you are careless and lazy now and keep putting things off and always deferring the day after which you will attend to yourself, you will not notice that you are making no progress, but you will live and die as someone quite ordinary." (Epictetus)

Reflection for Deep Recovery (Sharabi)

I used to tell myself: "I will quit someday, but not right now. Maybe tomorrow, but not today." Recovering alcoholics tell themselves, "I will work on my Fourth Step when I am ready. Maybe I'll start tomorrow... or next week. Actually, let me do it after the summer..." It is possible to postpone sobriety and keep drinking. But even after getting sober, it is possible to postpone recovery—one day at a time—postpone meaningful change day by day, until one day, you die—sober, perhaps, but not recovered.

"If you won't be better tomorrow than you were today, then what do you need tomorrow for?"

Nachman (1772 - 1810)

"Only put off until tomorrow what you are willing to die having left undone."

Pablo Picasso (1881 - 1973)

Epictetus
55 AD - 135 AD

a) Quote for Morning Contemplation

**"He who laughs at himself never runs out of things to laugh at."
(Epictetus)**

Reflection for Deep Recovery (Sharabi)

We alcoholics understand this; we are more adept at laughing at ourselves than any other group of people in the world. That is why our meetings are filled with merriment. We are laughing not at each other but with each other, laughing at ourselves. We see the absurdity of the world and the way it works, and we laugh at the silly solutions we came up with to the problems life posed us.

"My pain may be the reason for somebody's laugh, but my laugh must never be the reason for somebody's pain."

Charlie Chaplin (1889 - 1977)

b) Quote for Evening Contemplation

"Nature hath given men one tongue but two ears, that we may hear from others twice as much as we speak." (Epictetus)

Reflection for Deep Recovery (Sharabi)

If I come to a meeting, give my opinion, and then leave without having changed my opinion or my perspective: nothing has changed; no growth has occurred. But if I come to a meeting, listen, take in things that are contrary to what I thought before, and thereby change my opinion on something—or change my way of looking at something—then something has changed, something has been accomplished. No one grows by rigidity, by holding on to a particular point of view, and trying to consolidate it and spread it. No growth occurs when everyone agrees to the same thing. Gaining followers is not the purpose of recovery; they are not here to find leaders. And listening to everything that is said simply with the idea of agreeing or disagreeing means I am impervious to change; I have already consolidated all my opinions. This attitude will also prevent you from learning anything from this book too.

Epictetus
55 AD - 135 AD

a) Quote for Morning Contemplation

"All religions must be tolerated... for every man must get to heaven in his own way." (Epictetus)

Reflection for Deep Recovery (Sharabi)

My God and my heaven—or my lack of God and heaven—are not to be judged by your God or even by you. And your God is not to be judged by me. In recovery, we furiously defend the right of every individual to have a God entirely of his or her understanding... or even lack of understanding. Every alcoholic must get to the heaven of sobriety in his or her own way. Recovery includes religious fanatics and atheists mingling together, nudging each other, accepting each other, growing together.

"We are all atheists about most of the gods that societies have ever believed in. Some of us just go one god further."

Richard Dawkins (born 1941)

---

b) Quote for Evening Contemplation

"Circumstances don't make the man; they only reveal him to himself." (Epictetus)

Reflection for Deep Recovery (Sharabi)

The things that happen to me in life and the situations I land in: they help me discover who I am. Let me approach life with this spirit of excitement and self-discovery and not get entangled in posturing myself as a victim of circumstances. We are the ones who were dealt the card of alcoholism; we are being revealed to ourselves in recovery.

"A single event can awaken within us a stranger totally unknown to us."

Antoine de Saint-Exupery (1900 - 1944)

"Life is not a matter of holding good cards but of playing a poor hand well."

Robert Louis Stevenson (1850 - 1894)

Epictetus
55 AD - 135 AD

a) Quote for Morning Contemplation

"First, learn the meaning of what you say, and then speak."
(Epictetus)

Reflection for Deep Recovery (Sharabi)

Then, when you have spoken, stop, and sit down. Don't go on and on.

---

b) Quote for Evening Contemplation

"Attach yourself to what is spiritually superior, regardless of what other people think, or do. Hold to your true aspirations, no matter what is going on around you." (Epictetus)

Reflection for Deep Recovery (Sharabi)

You should attach yourself to the principles of recovery as guidelines on how to carry yourself through life. Hold on to these principles in all your affairs, no matter what is going on around you, no matter how others are behaving, and no matter how tempted you are to be reactive. Let your behavior be guided by these spiritually superior principles, not by your personality, your complexes, or your character defects. Your first reaction is your personality; your character is what you do with that reaction. Recovery means laying the first thought aside—which is the default setting—and examining your options. Your "personality" is just your default setting; you are not stuck with it; you can reset it.

SECOND THOUGHT PRAYER: "God, please help me pause and not rush to action after my first reaction or first thought, over which I have no control. Help me take my first thought into a second thought, and a third thought..."

from DEEP RECOVERY

Epictetus
55 AD - 135 AD

a) Quote for Morning Contemplation

"He is a wise man who does not grieve for the things which he has not, but rejoices for those which he has." (Epictetus)

Reflection for Deep Recovery (Sharabi)

When I make a list of what I want, it will invariably be a list of things I don't have. Therefore, it is bound to make me dissatisfied, to give me a sense of what is missing. Instead, if I make a list of what I have and express gratitude for these things, I will rejoice in what I have. In recovery, we refer to this as a "gratitude list," but we could equally well call it a "joy list." What are the things in life that I feel joy about? It is impossible to be grateful (joyful) and miserable at the same time.

"A person, however learned... in whom gratitude is absent, is devoid of that beauty of character which makes personality fragrant."

Hazrat han (1882 - 1927)

---

b) Quote for Evening Contemplation

"If evil be said of thee, and if it be true, correct thyself; if it be a lie, laugh at it." (Epictetus)

Reflection for Deep Recovery (Sharabi)

In Deep Recovery, I try to treat people's comments and judgments about me as feedback and be thankful to them for pointing it out. If they are off the mark, I try to laugh about it rather than get riled up about it. And, of course, if I am riled up, I must suspect that there may be some unpleasant truth behind it that is hard for me to acknowledge. Now, I am getting to a place where I am not overly affected by what people say or think of me. I have realized that these comments often say more about them than about me. I do consider what they are saying, but I don't let the arrows pierce my heart; I have a choice here. The challenge is to remember all this in the heat of the moment.

"To avoid criticism, say nothing, do nothing, and be nothing."

Elbert Hubbard (1856 - 1915)

"Talk about your failures without apologizing."

Brené Brown (born 1965)

166

Epictetus
55 AD - 135 AD

a) Quote for Morning Contemplation

"Don't seek to have events happen as you wish, but wish them to happen as they do happen, and all will be well with you." (Epictetus)

Reflection for Deep Recovery (Sharabi)

When I turn my will and my life over to the care of God (in the Third Step), I commit to accepting whatever happens. Acceptance is different from resignation. Resignation involves helplessness plus a silent complaint. Acceptance means I have no cries of "it shouldn't have happened this way," and no complaint. It is insufficient merely to keep my mouth shut; I must not complain, even internally; I embrace what is. Recovery's goal is to engage with life as it is without whining. When I stop complaining, the air becomes clear and unclouded; "what next?" becomes easy to see.

"To have courage for whatever comes in life—everything lies in that."
Teresa of Avila (1515 - 1582)

---

b) Quote for Evening Contemplation

"Events do not just happen but arrive by appointment." (Epictetus)

Reflection for Deep Recovery (Sharabi)

Epictetus believed in destiny. In these recovery rooms, we sometimes hear: "Everything that happens, happens for a reason; nothing happens by accident." Whether I am willing to believe in such a planned and orchestrated universe or not, this perspective will allow me to accept whatever has happened and whatever may happen. One possibility is to consider that I can actively learn something valuable from everything that happens. Instead of sitting there just passively bemoaning fate, I ponder: "How can I make use of this experience? What can I learn from this? How can I grow?"

"There is no end to education. It is not that you read a book, pass an examination, and finish with education. The whole of life—from the moment you are born to the moment you die—is a process of learning."
Krishnamurti (1895 - 1986)

Epictetus
55 AD - 135 AD

a) Quote for Morning Contemplation

"Do not try to seem wise to others." (Epictetus)

Reflection for Deep Recovery (Sharabi)

Do not emptily mouth lines from the Big Book when you haven't spent time absorbing them. That would be just your attempt to appear wise. Nor should you try and avoid seeming wise, for that would be fake too. In fact, you must not try to be humble either, for it is even worse—more hypocritical—to try to seem humble. Think about this: trying to "seem" anything to others is inauthentic, orchestrated—a lie. What would drive this? Is it to get an advantage of some kind that you do not deserve, or perhaps to hide your shame about who you really are underneath? If you know you are dishonest, you might try to "appear" sincere; if grandiose: humble, and if ignorant: wise.

"Nothing is more deceitful than the appearance of humility. It is... an indirect boast."

Jane Austen (1775 - 1817)

b) Quote for Evening Contemplation

"Difficulty shows what men are. Therefore when a difficulty falls upon you, remember that God, like a trainer of wrestlers, has matched you with a rough young man. Why? So that you may become an Olympic conqueror, but it is not accomplished without sweat." (Epictetus)

Reflection for Deep Recovery (Sharabi)

The greatest difficulty you have wrestled with has been alcoholism, and it has helped you become who you are today. But success will not be accomplished without sweat. Expect the seas to be stormy and, therefore, do not complain to everyone about the waves. "Getting sober is so hard!" someone muttered. "Oh, you'll only do it if it's easy?" was the retort. "Life is difficult," someone complained. "Difficult compared to what? God made life the way it is, so you will keep coming to meetings!" was the retort. One of the promises ought to be: we will lose our fear of future difficulties.

"Please subdue the anguish of your soul. Nobody is destined only to happiness or to pain. The wheel of life takes one up and down by turn."

Kalidasa (5th century)

Epictetus
55 AD - 135 AD

a) Quote for Morning Contemplation

"Make the best use of what is in your power, and take the rest as it happens." (Epictetus)

Reflection for Deep Recovery (Sharabi)

"... change what I can and accept what I cannot change." Your responsibility as a human being is not to make sure that everything will work out. Your calling is to act just as a normal and responsible human being would; you do what you can to affect the outcome, make the best decisions you can, and turn the rest over to God. You are responsible for the effort; God is responsible for the result. It is an enduring and inarguable belief is that everything will work out exactly the way it is going to work out. Then you will not be afraid of change, of the inevitability of things changing, of putting in the effort.

"Plans are only good intentions unless they immediately degenerate into hard work."

Peter Drucker (1909 - 2005)

b) Quote for Evening Contemplation

"If you suppose that only to be your own which is your own, and what belongs to others such as it really is, then no one will ever compel you or restrain you. Further, you will find fault with no one or accuse no one. You will do nothing against your will. No one will hurt you, you will have no enemies, and you will not be harmed." (Epictetus)

Reflection for Deep Recovery (Sharabi)

Manage yourself, not others! Others have the right to their own decisions, to live life as they choose. My internal voice screams at everyone: "Why aren't you more like me?" Do you have such a voice too? It is the source of all resentment: the idea that others should behave (or should have behaved) the way you think they should. Dropping "shoulds" and "shouldn't" for others—and for the world—will lead to harmonious relations. Your job in Deep Recovery is not to change others but to adjust yourself.

"You have power over your mind - not outside events. Realize this, and you will find strength."

Marcus Aurelius (121 - 180 A.D.)

169

Epictetus
55 AD - 135 AD

a) Quote for Morning Contemplation

"The condition and characteristic of a vulgar person is that he never expects either benefit or hurt from himself, but from externals. The condition and characteristic of a philosopher is that he expects all hurt and benefit from himself." (Epictetus)

Reflection for Deep Recovery (Sharabi)

Broadly speaking, there are two kinds of people: those who tend to blame others—Epictetus calls these vulgar people—and those who tend to blame themselves—Epictetus calls these philosophers. The "vulgars" have a hard time taking responsibility; it is always somebody else's fault. The Fourth Step inventory is an attempt to get them to acknowledge their role in the matter. The inventory comes easier for the self-blamers or "philosophers," but these have to then make sure that the Fourth Step does not become an exercise in self-bashing and self-deprecation. A philosopher must start with self-acceptance; that is what allows him to take responsibility for himself as the source.

---

b) Quote for Evening Contemplation

"The marks of a proficient are, that he censures no one, praises no one, blames no one, accuses no one, says nothing concerning himself as being anybody, or knowing anything: when he is, in any instance, hindered or restrained, he accuses himself; and, if he is praised, he secretly laughs at the person who praises him; and, if he is censured, he makes no defense." (Epictetus)

Reflection for Deep Recovery (Sharabi)

In contrast to the "vulgar person" and the "philosopher" described in the previous quote, Epictetus defines a "proficient" in terms that mirror our goal in Deep Recovery. We strive to be humble, criticize no one, worship no one, and avoid presenting ourselves as important or wise. We do not let praise inflate our ego and, when criticized, offer no defense. We stop rationalizing and justifying our actions to others (and to ourselves.) Anonymity is the spiritual foundation of recovery, ridding ourselves of "personality." As "garden-variety" alcoholics, no one shines brighter or grovels lower; we are all equal, though different, and we accept ourselves.

"Self-actualized people are independent of the good opinion of others."
Wayne Dyer (1940 - 2015)

Montaigne
1533 - 1592

a) Quote for Morning Contemplation

"The most certain sign of wisdom is cheerfulness." (Montaigne)

Reflection for Deep Recovery (Sharabi)

I used to think that I drank because I had a profound and poignant understanding of the futility of life. I thought torment was a sign of intellect and depth. Then, I came to a meeting and found everyone in good cheer. "These people either are shallow or have gotten religion and become delusional," I told myself. But today, I am part of that cheerful crowd the newcomer encounters. Some of us are religious, and some are not. Sure, we have some dark moments—life is like that—but we learn not to stay down. The path of Deep Recovery contains a sense of gay abandon and the realization that everything does not have to be solved for me to be completely happy. Therefore, cheerfulness and joy are available even in the presence of uncertainty.

---

b) Quote for Evening Contemplation

"He who fears he shall suffer, already suffers what he fears." (Montaigne)

Reflection for Deep Recovery (Sharabi)

Fear of suffering—arising from the anticipation of suffering—is itself the greatest suffering of all. Surrendering to recovery and turning my life and my will over to the care of God (and the Universe) has allowed me to let go of anxiety about the future. I have stopped agonizing over things that might happen that I have no control over. I live in today with the understanding that each day, I will have the resources to deal with what that day may hold. I may make some preparations for tomorrow, but I will deal with tomorrow, tomorrow. If I am fearful of future pain, I tell myself that I will deal with pain as best as I can when it arrives, not now. The fear of cloudy days ahead must not stop me from enjoying the sunshine today.

"I am touched by your beautiful anxiety about life... "
Rainer Maria Rilke (1875 - 1926)

171

Montaigne
1533 - 1592

a) Quote for Morning Contemplation

"I do not care so much what I am to others as I care what I am to myself." (Montaigne)

Reflection for Deep Recovery (Sharabi)

What we call "self-esteem" essentially comes from believing that others esteem us and approve of us. It is precarious because these others are capricious and inconsistent. Self-esteem can quickly crumble if we fail, if we make a fool of ourselves, or if we become the object of ridicule from others. Self-acceptance, on the other hand, comes from being rather unconcerned with what others think. I can decide to accept myself at any moment, to never beat up on myself or "feel bad" about myself. Self-improvement is fine, but it is not the path to self-acceptance, for you can simply accept yourself as you are. In fact, with self-acceptance, self-improvement comes easily and naturally, without a struggle.

"No one can make you feel inferior without your consent."
Eleanor Roosevelt (1884 - 1962)

---

b) Quote for Evening Contemplation

"If I speak of myself in different ways, that is because I look at myself in different ways." (Montaigne)

Reflection for Deep Recovery (Sharabi)

Shaking off the shackles of a forced appearance of consistency, I can discover and create myself each moment, anew, based on what life presents me. I have the potential to be anything as long as I am not a dead and crusted being, frozen into a solid and unchanging "this is who I am!" In recovery I have the ability to twinkle, to shimmer, to leap as the context requires. I am constantly discovering, changing, emerging—creating myself fresh in the moment about to be.

"Do I contradict myself? Very well, then I contradict myself, I am large, I contain multitudes."

Walt Whitman (1819 - 1892)

Montaigne
1533 - 1592

a) Quote for Morning Contemplation

"When I am attacked by gloomy thoughts, nothing helps me so much as running to my books. They quickly absorb me and banish the clouds from my mind." (Montaigne)

Reflection for Deep Recovery (Sharabi)

Montaigne was a lover of books and literature, and a fan of creating a reading habit which, surely, will generate a rich inner life in anyone who perseveres with it. If we are to become deep, we must reach into the wisdom and thoughts of others. The more widely read a man or woman is, the more evolved he or she becomes. The evolution of the human soul is the central point of Deep Recovery. We have, therefore, a responsibility to reach out to books not only when we are feeling gloomy, but also to provide a steady spiritual and contemplative diet for sustaining in us, "joie de vivre:" an exultation of spirit and the buoyant enjoyment of the richness of life.

---

b) Quote for Evening Contemplation

"Learned we may be with another man's learning: we can only be wise with wisdom of our own." (Montaigne)

Reflection for Deep Recovery (Sharabi)

I can become learned (as far as recovery is concerned) by gathering information, reading books, memorizing passages in recovery literature, studying the history of the movement, and listening to stories of drunken foolishness and redemption. But to become wise, I must identify and relate to my own encounters with alcohol and the perceptual distortions it created in my view of myself and the world. I must become willing to face the consequences of my behavior. It is my intimate knowledge of the ravages of drinking, and my understanding of the path out of it that makes me wise. That wisdom is my own. Learning can be impersonal; wisdom is personal. Wisdom is learning applied to myself.

"Sooner or later, everyone sits down to a banquet of consequences."
Robert Louis Stevenson (1850 - 1894)

"Wisdom can be learned, but it cannot be taught."
Anthony de Mello (1931 - 1997)

Montaigne
1533 - 1592

a) Quote for Morning Contemplation

"Obsession is the wellspring of genius and madness." (Montaigne)

Reflection for Deep Recovery (Sharabi)

We gather and talk incessantly about our obsession with drinking—our madness. We stare at where we came from, but there is no point in "feeling bad" about what we have done unless it is to understand how to be different in the future. Obsessing about our character defects is self-absorption—another madness. Instead, we must focus on where we are going. This is a good obsession—the genius of recovery. Indeed, our mad commitment to recovery and to this fellowship is an obsession that is genius.

"Madness need not be all breakdown. It may also be a break-through. It is potential liberation and renewal as well as enslavement and existential death."

R. D. Laing (1927 - 1989)

---

b) Quote for Evening Contemplation

"Nothing fixes a thing so intensely in the memory as the wish to forget it." (Montaigne)

Reflection for Deep Recovery (Sharabi)

I decide to stop beating myself up, and when I fail at that, I end up beating myself for beating myself up. I find myself in this vortex. What is the way out? I need to be alert and distract myself the moment that self-demeaning voice starts; it is not a friend. I must immediately direct my focus on something or someone that is real, tangible, and physically present. This can help me get out of my thoughts; beating myself up is just a thought. It is necessary to walk away from thoughts because trying to wrestle a thought down is like wrestling with a porcupine. Recovery calls on me to examine myself in places as called for, but I must not indulge in a constant and brooding self-rage. My very attempt to forget the past attaches me to it.

"Our errors perish before we do. Let's not mummify them and keep them around."

Emile Chartier (1868 - 1951)

Montaigne
1533 - 1592

a) Quote for Morning Contemplation

"I prefer the company of peasants because they have not been educated sufficiently to reason incorrectly." (Montaigne)

Reflection for Deep Recovery (Sharabi)

The "peasants" can often get the program more easily than the "professors." There is a saying: "No one is too dumb to get sober, but you can be too smart to get sober." There is also this profound and simple truth: "If you don't take that first drink, you will never be drunk." To get it, you need to approach recovery with the simplicity of a "peasant"—with the empty mind of the Zen beginner.

"When my guru wanted to compliment me, he called me simple; when he wanted to criticize me, he called me clever."

Baba Ram Dass, (1931 - 2019) referring to Neem Karoli Baba

---

b) Quote for Evening Contemplation

"Confidence in others' honesty is no light testimony of one's own integrity." (Montaigne)

Reflection for Deep Recovery (Sharabi)

I used to lie so much myself that I never believed anyone. Now I have slowly become capable of trusting, capable of believing that people can behave with honesty and integrity because I have seen that possibility in myself. Recovery is making me aware of muscles I never knew existed, making me capable of movements I had not imagined.

"It is better to suffer wrong than to do it, and happier to be sometimes cheated than not to trust."

Samuel Johnson (1709 - 1784)

Montaigne
1533 - 1592

a) Quote for Morning Contemplation

"The great and glorious masterpiece of man is to live with purpose." (Montaigne)

Reflection for Deep Recovery (Sharabi)

To live with purpose, I have to work towards the desired goal. Simple longing requires no effort. Purpose brings meaning and satisfaction to life; longing brings fantasy, disappointment, and bitterness. Those purposeless drinking days were filled with wistful longing. Now, I focus on the purpose of my life and the daily striving required to move towards it. I am blessed to be in the company of others traveling the same path.

"Continuous effort—not strength or intelligence—is the key to unlocking our potential."
Winston Churchill (1874 - 1965)

"He who has a why to live can bear almost any how."
Nietzsche (1844 - 1900)

---

b) Quote for Evening Contemplation

"Let us give Nature a chance; she knows her business better than we do." (Montaigne)

Reflection for Deep Recovery (Sharabi)

In contrast to those frantic attempts to control an unmanageable lifestyle, I am now willing to let life unfold in its natural course. Yes, life can be stormy sometimes, and I want to intervene and direct its course, but I don't really know what is best for me. When I have let go, I have found things often to turn out better than I expect. The program has taught me the wisdom of letting go, of accepting the natural way that life unfolds. I find that my consternation, worry, and panic were unfounded. God—and Nature—can do quite well without my frantic banging on the door, complaining, whining, and demanding at every turn. I now pray for the ability to deal with whatever happens with calmness and with an appreciation for the wisdom of nature. We cannot "conquer" nature; we are part of it.

"Some of us think holding on makes us strong, but sometimes it is letting go."

Hermann Hesse (1877 - 1962)

Montaigne
1533 - 1592

a) Quote for Morning Contemplation

"To practice death is to practice freedom. A man who has learned how to die has unlearned how to be a slave." (Montaigne)

Reflection for Deep Recovery (Sharabi)

Surrender was a death to the old life; also, a new beginning. In Deep Recovery I am practicing dying in different ways so I can be reborn continually. I let die: my need to explain myself all the time, be right always, and justify myself in every situation. I am willing to accept criticism even if it feels like dying. I have learned not to be a slave to my feelings, moods, wishes, desires, impulses, and reactions. I am willing to let die the "me" that identifies with these. I am no longer dominated; I am free.

"The call of death is a call of love. Death can be sweet if we answer it in the affirmative; if we accept it as one of the great eternal forms of life and transformation."

Hermann Hesse (1877 - 1962)

---

b) Quote for Evening Contemplation

"Every man has within himself the entire human condition." (Montaigne)

Reflection for Deep Recovery (Sharabi)

Every alcoholic who walks in, no matter how far down the scale he or she has gone... represents me. I am that man or woman. Within me exists the entire human condition; within me rests the alcoholism and degradation that any of my fellows has suffered. "We" are alcoholic—all of us, together. And, within me, also rests the deepest recovery that is possible, the most peaceful serenity that anyone has attained, and the most complete contentment that can come from this path. It is there already; I merely need to step into it.

"If a person loves only one other person, and is indifferent to his fellow men, his love is not love but a symbiotic attachment, or an enlarged egotism."

Erich Fromm (1900 - 1980)

Montaigne
1533 - 1592

a) Quote for Morning Contemplation

"No-one is exempt from speaking nonsense — the only misfortune is to do it solemnly." (Montaigne)

Reflection for Deep Recovery (Sharabi)

I would speak at meetings often. I was not saying much, but I would say it solemnly, hoping that people would be impressed. I would throw in words like "God," and "gratitude," "principles," and "surrender." Then, I would glare at others in the room, particularly the newcomers. Finally, I would take every opportunity to lecture my sponsees. Looking back, I see that it was a pathetic attempt to feel good about myself by orchestrating a personality to present to others.

"It is no use walking anywhere to preach unless our walking is our preaching."

Saint Francis of Assissi (1181 - 1226)

---

b) Quote for Evening Contemplation

"There is no knowledge so hard to acquire as the knowledge of how to live this life well and naturally." (Montaigne)

Reflection for Deep Recovery (Sharabi)

I went to bars, and I consulted many people for this knowledge of how to live life. I did not know where else to look. Guess what? Going to the bars worked for me because it led me to recovery. And here, I am finally being taught how to live life naturally and well. Yes, this knowledge is hard to acquire, but I have plenty of time now; there is no "last call" here in recovery.

"Knowledge doesn't really form part of human nature... Knowledge is not instinctive; it is counter-instinctive, just as it is not natural but counter-natural."

Michel Foucault (1924 - 1986)

"Everything has been figured out, except how to live."

Jean-Paul Sartre (1905 - 1980)

Montaigne
1533 - 1592

a) Quote for Morning Contemplation

"No wind favors he who has no destined port." (Montaigne)

Reflection for Deep Recovery (Sharabi)

People would look at my drinking and exclaim: "Poor fellow! He is a lost soul." They were wrong. I was not lost because there was no place or destination I was trying to get to. I was not a failure because I had no goals to measure success or failure by. I was bringing a different meaning to the phrase: "living one day at a time." In fact, I was just trying to have a good time for a few hours.

"You've got to be very careful if you don't know where you are going because you might not get there."

Yogi Berra (1925 - 2015)

b) Quote for Evening Contemplation

"There were many terrible things in my life, and most of them never happened." (Montaigne)

Reflection for Deep Recovery (Sharabi)

My anxiety is just my habit of imagining terrible things and then picturing a future where these things have occurred. Worry needs a vivid imagination. Someone said to me, "Worry is good; I have tried it. When I worry about something, it usually doesn't happen! You too ought to worry about things that you don't want to happen." Instead, if I only pay attention to what is in front of me—living one day at a time—I could avoid worry and anxiety. If there is something to be done, I do it today, but if there is nothing I can do to affect it, I try not to worry about it. The best way to deal with anxiety about the future is to focus on the work for today... one day at a time.

"The reason why worry kills more people than work is that more people worry than work."

Robert Frost (1874 - 1963)

"The act of birth is the first experience of anxiety, and thus the source and prototype of the affect of anxiety."

Sigmund Freud (1856 - 1939)

Montaigne
1533 - 1592

a) Quote for Morning Contemplation

"He who establishes his argument by noise and command shows that his reason is weak." (Montaigne)

Reflection for Deep Recovery (Sharabi)

He who starts shouting has already lost the argument. When I find myself riled up about something and feel a desire to raise my voice, recovery teaches me to shut my mouth. But it does not stop there. I have a duty to examine why my helplessness to make the other see and acknowledge my point of view was so scary? What is it reminding me of? Is my life really in danger here? If not, why am I behaving as if it is?

"Education is the ability to listen to almost anything without losing your temper or your self-confidence."

Robert Frost (1874 - 1963)

"Where there is shouting, there is no true knowledge."
Leonardo da Vinci (1452 - 1519)

---

b) Quote for Evening Contemplation

"Not being able to govern events, I govern myself." (Montaigne)

Reflection for Deep Recovery (Sharabi)

God, grant me the serenity to accept the things I cannot change (events); the courage to change the things I can (myself); and the wisdom to remember this when I need it. Yes, it is frustrating to realize that I cannot run the world and people exactly as I desire to. When something happens differently from how I want it—when I don't get my way—my initial reaction is rage, irritation, annoyance—even despair. But gradually, I have realized that events unfold in their own way and in their own time. Interruptions, distractions, and annoyances are part of life; all I can influence is the way I react to them. Sometimes, even my reactions are not of my choosing; I cannot be held responsible for my feelings—but certainly my actions. Some of us who have numbed ourselves will need to get more in touch with feelings, but some may need to tone down our sensitiveness. We use sensitivity like a knob on the radio: to turn up the volume and sometimes to turn down the volume of our feelings.

"Intelligence is the ability to adapt to change."
Stephen Hawking (1942 - 2018)

Montaigne
1533 - 1592

a) Quote for Morning Contemplation

"Don't discuss yourself, for you are bound to lose; if you belittle yourself, you are believed; if you praise yourself, you are disbelieved." (Montaigne)

Reflection for Deep Recovery (Sharabi)

And yet, it seems fashionable for some people to stand up and publicly belittle themselves in meetings. They are just asking to be loved in spite of their defects. The great thing is that whether they are belittling themselves or subtly praising themselves (look, I am so honorable, I can acknowledge my defects!), we can see both as a cry for acceptance. We accept them and love them, not because of who they are, but because of who they are trying to be. In time—their own time, not mine or yours—they will stop performing their act.

b) Quote for Evening Contemplation

"The finest souls are those that have the most variety and suppleness." (Montaigne)

Reflection for Deep Recovery (Sharabi)

When the strong wind blows, it is the rigid trees that break, not the supple ones. The finest souls are the ones who are flexible and open; the most impoverished souls are the ones who are rigid and frozen. Religious fanatics can be dogmatic and shrill; they have established rules, ceremonies, and punishment. Spiritually evolved souls have a gentleness and ease about them. The one thing that we are inflexible about here in recovery is the impossibility of that first drink. All else is negotiable.

"The fools of the world have been those who have established religions, ceremonies, laws, faith, rules of life."

Giordano Bruno (1548 - 1600)

Montaigne
1533 - 1592

a) Quote for Morning Contemplation

"Kings and philosophers defecate, and so do ladies." (Montaigne)

Reflection for Deep Recovery (Sharabi)

I do not put my sponsor on a pedestal, nor do I require others to think that I always smell wonderful. I do not worship the old-timers as deities, but I pay attention to their message. I think for myself but allow myself to be moved by the insights and wisdom of others. After all, we are just human beings who used to be drunks—each of us. There are no Saints or Angels in recovery, and all people have to get rid of their smelly parts regularly on the toilet, just like doing a daily inventory. In recovery, my job is to recover my human-ness and to accept it, not claim to be a saint or become Godly.

"One does not become fully human painlessly."

Rollo May (1909 - 1994)

---

b) Quote for Evening Contemplation

"Once conform, once do what others do because they do it, and a kind of lethargy steals over all the finer senses of the soul." (Montaigne)

Reflection for Deep Recovery (Sharabi)

It is easy to slip into lethargy in recovery, repeating the same old cliches, recycling comments—meeting after meeting. Conformity, obedience, and compliance are useful in the early days, but complacency in later years indicates stagnation and leads to dullness. Now that my head has cleared, I have a responsibility to keep pushing, discover and explore new ideas and insights, delight in new ways of expressing previously unspoken truths, and find joy and excitement in spiritual discovery. Sobriety is but a base camp from which I can set out to climb the spiritual peaks that will determine my vision of life.

"The majority cannot reason; it has no judgment. It has always placed its destiny in the hands of others; it has followed its leaders even into destruction. The mass has always opposed, condemned, and hounded the innovator, the pioneer of a new truth."

Emma Goldman (1869 - 1940)

182

Montaigne
1533 - 1592

a) Quote for Morning Contemplation

"Every other knowledge is harmful to him who does not have knowledge of goodness." (Montaigne)

Reflection for Deep Recovery (Sharabi)

If love, compassion, kindness, humility, and—above all—human goodness are not present, all attempts to help the newcomer are suspect and can be harmful. Many people go from the First Step directly to the Twelfth Step without doing the internal work necessary to prepare them to serve as soldiers for recovery. They admit powerlessness over alcohol, and then they rush to help the newcomers battle the disease. They shower advice and party-line cliches, even criticism, trying to convince the newcomer to surrender to their "program." Self-awareness is often missing.

"Part of being awake is slowing down enough to notice what we say or do. The more we witness our emotional chain reactions and understand how they work, the easier it is to refrain (from harm).

Pema Chödrön (born 1936)

---

b) Quote for Evening Contemplation

"The value of life lies not in the length of days, but in the use we make of them." (Montaigne)

Reflection for Deep Recovery (Sharabi)

It is not the length of sobriety that is important, but how much we have changed and grown in our sobriety, how we have used the days we have been sober, and who we have become. What matters is what we are doing today with all that learning.

"Not how long, but how well you have lived, is the main thing."

Seneca (4 B.C. to 65A.D.)

"Be a Columbus to whole new continents and worlds within you, opening up channels, not of trade, but of thought... live deep and suck out all the marrow out of life."

Thoreau (1817 - 1862)

Montaigne
1533 - 1592

a) Quote for Morning Contemplation

"My business is only to keep myself in motion, whilst motion pleases me; I only walk for the walk's sake." (Montaigne)

Reflection for Deep Recovery (Sharabi)

My business is to enjoy the journey; there is no destination in sobriety. I get pleasure from the movement. Sobriety is the art of applying focused attention and effort to create something new on a daily basis: an individual who has never existed before. The art—for me—lies in the effort: the gestures and flourishes we put on our daily walk, the style we bring to our daily climbing.

"To live only for some future goal is shallow. It's the sides of the mountain that sustain life, not the top."

Robert M. Pirsig (1928 - 2017)

"People often say that motivation doesn't last. Well, neither does bathing; that's why we recommend it daily."

Zig Ziglar (1926 - 2012)

b) Quote for Evening Contemplation

"It is putting a very high price on one's conjectures to have someone roasted alive on their account." (Montaigne)

Reflection for Deep Recovery (Sharabi)

Let me not wish evil to befall those who disagree with my ideas and my conjectures on what recovery is and what life is about, or those who are following a different path. Even if someone is not following the "program" at all, let me sincerely hope and pray—for their sake—that they succeed in their life. My desire to see others fail when they are not practicing my brand of "recovery," and my insistence that they are not happy: these are signs that I myself am not convinced. I am seeking proof of the correctness of my path in the failure of others. In particular, I must never wish anyone to fail at sobriety or at life, no matter how different his or her approach is to mine; this would be a form of meanness—and of madness. How I accommodate and honor others whom I disagree with—now, that is a measure of my spiritual growth.

"Difference in opinions has cost many millions of lives: for instance, whether flesh be bread, or bread be flesh; whether the juice of a certain berry be blood or wine ."

Jonathan Swift (1667 - 1745)

Montaigne
1533 - 1592

a) Quote for Morning Contemplation

"There is no conversation more boring than the one where everybody agrees." (Montaigne)

Reflection for Deep Recovery (Sharabi)

Even though we have much in common and we agree on basics, the paths we follow are varied, textured, and colorful. No two people in recovery are the same. It is surprising that we do not gouge out each other's eyes, given our deep discussions and the committed viewpoints we express. Let us not become a fellowship where everyone agrees on everything and mouths the same old clichés at every meeting. Unity in recovery means that I accept, include, and honor my fellows who think differently from me, and I hope that they will extend the same generosity to me.

"I am alone in the midst of these... reasonable voices... explaining, realizing happily that they agree with each other. In Heaven's name, why is it so important to think the same things, all together?"
Jean-Paul Sartre (1905 - 1980)

b) Quote for Evening Contemplation

"Age imprints more wrinkles in the mind than it does on the face." (Montaigne)

Reflection for Deep Recovery (Sharabi)

Age and maturity permit us to see that "truth" is not one frozen, lifeless statement or fact but has many wrinkles and twists. In my youth, I was simplistic, opinionated, and rigid; older, I have begun to appreciate the legitimacy of diverse positions on the same subject. It is a form of intellectual poverty—and fear—to see and support only one side of an argument; to perceive only in black and white; to express highly polarized views. Generosity and wisdom require honoring the opposing viewpoint. "God will constantly disclose more to you and to us." the Big Book says. I must leave every meeting a different person than the one who arrived, for that is the proof that I am still learning, still open, still capable of being moved, and still willing to change. As I leave the meeting, or at the end of each day, I should contemplate: "What have I learned? How have I changed?" It is a daily inventory.

"Live as if you were to die tomorrow. Learn as if you were to live forever."
Mahatma Gandhi (1869 - 1948)

Maya Angelou
1928 - 2014

a) Quote for Morning Contemplation

"You may not control all the events that happen to you, but you can decide not to be reduced by them." (Maya Angelou)

Reflection for Deep Recovery (Sharabi)

Unbelievable as it seemed at first, I now understand that no one and no happening can force me to feel or act in any particular way. How I respond to events and people is determined by me, not by the events or by people or by their attitude towards me. How much I allow an event or a situation to outrage me, to reduce me, is a matter of decision, not just a matter of feeling. Yes, I fall sometimes, but I can pick myself up and start walking again.

"There is perhaps no phenomenon which contains so much destructive feeling as moral indignation, which permits envy or hate to be acted out under the guise of virtue."

Erich Fromm (1900 - 1980)

---

b) Quote for Evening Contemplation

"We delight in the beauty of the butterfly but rarely admit the changes it has gone through to achieve that beauty." (Maya Angelou)

Reflection for Deep Recovery (Sharabi)

In recovery, each of us has come through a journey that has made us beautiful. The people in recovery are beautiful in who they have become. Today, I merely present myself to the world how I am, true to who I am, and in that authenticity, there is beauty. I had to go through a lot of changes to get here. I must also be generous in acknowledging the beauty of the person sitting next to me at the meeting, for they too have been through a lot while getting to their truth; of that, I can be sure. My job is to get them to see the beauty of where they are, not criticize them for what they are not. This is what it means to love them while they learn to love themselves.

" 'Beauty is truth, truth beauty,' - that is all ye know on earth, and all ye need to know."

John Keats (1795 - 1821)

186

Maya Angelou
1928 - 2014

a) Quote for Morning Contemplation

"The need for change bulldozed a road down the center of my mind." (Maya Angelou)

Reflection for Deep Recovery (Sharabi)

In the beginning, I thought I needed to behave better when drinking; then. I felt I had to cut down my drinking; finally, I realized that I had to quit drinking entirely. In addition to all that, I now see that I have to make large changes in attitude and perspective. Life kept knocking me down and running me over until I finally understood the need to break down all my structures. I am now busy constructing a new road to travel along in recovery.

"There is nothing noble in being superior to your fellow man; true nobility is being superior to your former self."

Ernest Hemingway (1899 - 1961)

---

b) Quote for Evening Contemplation

"While I know myself as a creation of God, I am also obligated to realize and remember that everyone else and everything else are also God's creation." (Maya Angelou)

Reflection for Deep Recovery (Sharabi)

Everyone I have developed a resentment towards is also a creation of God. Recovery teaches me to pray for the person I resent. I distinguish the person from the behavior and acknowledge that God loves that person. I also understand that the behavior appears justifiable to that person, just like my behavior seems right to me. I try not to justify or honor my negative feelings towards a creation of God, but to manage my feelings within myself. My feelings are not real; they are just feelings. Recovery has taught me an invaluable possibility: that of not having to behave the way my feelings are urging me to. It has also taught me that people are not who I think they are.

"We see people not as they are, but as we are."

Anthony de Mello (1931 - 1997)

Maya Angelou
1928 - 2014

a) Quote for Morning Contemplation

**"Words mean more than what is set down on paper. It takes the human voice to infuse them with shades of deeper meaning."
(Maya Angelou)**

Reflection for Deep Recovery (Sharabi)

This is why we do the Fifth Step after the Fourth Step. When we read our written inventory to another person, when we speak it and acknowledge it to God, we infuse it with shades of deeper meaning. Truth becomes real when it is declared rather than when it resides mutely in some corner of the brain. So we need to declare our love, not just feel it. And our declarations about who we are going to be and what we are going to do will define us in recovery—where we develop the habit of keeping our word.

"Kind words do not cost much. Yet, they accomplish much."
Blaise Pascal (1623 - 1662)

---

b) Quote for Evening Contemplation

"One isn't necessarily born with courage, but one is born with potential. Without courage, we cannot practice any other virtue with consistency. We can't be kind, true, merciful, generous, or honest." (Maya Angelou)

Reflection for Deep Recovery (Sharabi)

In our drinking days, people looked at us and shook their heads at all the potential being wasted. Potential is simply ability that is not realized. But we changed. We are the ones who developed the courage to change and to begin to fulfill our potential. I can use that same courage to be kind, true, merciful, generous, and honest even when my feelings are screaming to do otherwise. The central requirement for discipline is to act consistently, irrespective of how we feel and to detach action from feelings. Doing the next right thing—consistently—requires courage and discipline. Not acting on my feelings can come from cowardice or courage. Here we are talking about the courage and discipline needed to stay consistent with the moral principles of recovery.

"Doing the right thing is more important than doing the things right."
Peter Drucker (1909 - 2005)

Maya Angelou
1928 - 2014

a) Quote for Morning Contemplation

"If our children are to approve of themselves, they must see that we approve of ourselves." (Maya Angelou)

Reflection for Deep Recovery (Sharabi)

Some folks have egos so frail that they cannot look at themselves honestly. Such people often present themselves as faultless. Some of us were children born to such "perfect parents." We grew up facing their constant criticism, never feeling good enough or acceptable. Continuing to seek the approval of such parents is a dour, suffocating, and demeaning journey that we undertake in adult life. We have to break free from our need for parental approval—all "approval"—if we are going to be ourselves.

"There are only two lasting bequests we can hope to give our children. One of these is roots, the other, wings."

Goethe ((1749 - 1832)

---

b) Quote for Evening Contemplation

"My great hope is to laugh as much as I cry; to get my work done and try to love somebody and have the courage to accept the love in return." (Maya Angelou)

Reflection for Deep Recovery (Sharabi)

Recovery is achieved only when passion has returned to life. During my drinking years, the only times of passion involved rage and self-sorrow, and I numbed these with alcohol. Then, in early recovery, I was slinking through these rooms, apprehensive of all strong feelings; I had muted my reactions. But, in Deep Recovery, I have learned not to be afraid of feelings; that serenity is not just the numbing of feeling but requires embracing the ups and downs of life—the willingness to be moved by life, by events, and by people. The goal of recovery is to become human and vulnerable once more—to live from the heart rather than in the abstract world of ideas. Our challenge is to stay as feeling individuals in a world that is often unfeeling—even scared of feelings.

"We think too much and feel too little... What do you want a meaning for? Life is a desire, not a meaning."

Charlie Chaplin (1889 - 1977)

Maya Angelou
1928 - 2014

a) Quote for Morning Contemplation

"Nature has no mercy at all. Nature says, 'I'm going to snow. If you have on a bikini and no snowshoes, that's tough. I am going to snow anyway.' " (Maya Angelou)

Reflection for Deep Recovery (Sharabi)

And nature says: if you are an alcoholic and you choose to continue drinking, I will show no mercy, I will do my thing, and I will destroy you.

"I am become Death, the destroyer of worlds... "
Quote from the Bhagavad Gita (circa 500 - 200 B.C.)
paraphrased by J. Robert Oppenheimer.

b) Quote for Evening Contemplation

"Love is that condition in the human spirit so profound that it allows me to survive, and better than that, to thrive with passion, compassion, and style." (Maya Angelou)

Reflection for Deep Recovery (Sharabi)

As long as I know how to love, I will survive. Whether I love a pet, a plant, a poem, a song, a symphony, a child, a mate, a stream, the forest, the mountains, sunshine, the warmth of spring, hot chocolate, ice cream, a warm bath—any love contains the essential fire to kindle my soul. I have grown not to be afraid of sadness, for even sadness is a form of love. But the one love that must be quenched, destroyed, and thrown out is the love of alcohol. For that was not love at all; it was a perversion.

"You have within you more love than you could ever understand."
Rumi (1207 - 1273)

Believe that life is worth living, and your belief will help create the fact.
William James (1842 - 1910)

Maya Angelou
1928 - 2014

a) Quote for Morning Contemplation

"Not everything you do is going to be a masterpiece, but you get out there and you try, and sometimes it really happens. The other times you're just stretching your soul." (Maya Angelou)

Reflection for Deep Recovery (Sharabi)

I need not try to make the Fourth Step inventory a masterpiece; the work is there just to stretch my soul. Unfortunately, many of us suffer from a malady called "perfectionism." We avoid trying rather than offering something that may be criticized. To understand this, we reflect: "Can I survive if I am less than perfect? In childhood, what consequences occurred if I made an error or a mistake?" Today, criticism will not kill me; before rushing to protest, I must pause: "You might be right!"

"The final proof of greatness lies in being able to endure criticism without resentment."

Elbert Hubbard (1856 - 1915)

---

b) Quote for Evening Contemplation

"Self-pity in its early stage is as snug as a feather mattress. Only when it hardens does it become uncomfortable." (Maya Angelou)

Reflection for Deep Recovery (Sharabi)

Grieving can be an authentic expression of pain: a part of healing. But I turned to alcohol and drugs to avoid genuine grieving. I went to self-pity, which contains notions of unfairness and victimhood. When entertained too long, it turned into self-centered bitterness and despair, becoming a straight-jacket that prevented me from touching and feeling life and people—even feeling myself. Such despair boils down to a lack of humility, an unwillingness to accept what is, a romantic adherence to a dark pessimism, and an unwillingness to turn my will and my life over to the care of God.

"But the man who is truly humble cannot despair because in the humble man, there is no longer any such thing as self-pity."

Thomas Merton (1915 - 1968)

"While injustice is the worst of sins, despair is the most dangerous; because when you are in despair, you care neither about yourself nor about others."

Thomas Aquinas (1224 - 1274)

Maya Angelou
1928 - 2014

a) Quote for Morning Contemplation

"There's a world of difference between truth and facts. Facts can obscure truth." (Maya Angelou)

Reflection for Deep Recovery (Sharabi)

Facts exist in the material world, but truth is the essence of things. Facts are scientifically proven; truth is what is effective, what works, beyond proof. I must not mistake my evaluations, judgments, and opinions for the truth. It is possible to love everyone, but some facts I remember can obscure this truth. Truth resides at a spiritual level, not at the level of scientific facts or words, not even at the level of ideas and thoughts. Our Higher Power is a truth that is beyond ideas and thoughts, beyond our puny "understanding." Spirituality soars in expanses outside our limited minds, beyond concepts, conflicts, and contradictions.

"Everything we hear is an opinion, not a fact;
Everything we see is a perspective, not the truth."

Marcus Aurelius (121 - 180 A.D.)

---

b) Quote for Evening Contemplation

"Tragedy, no matter how sad, becomes boring to those not caught in its addictive caress." (Maya Angelou)

Reflection for Deep Recovery (Sharabi)

"Tragedy" exists not in the event itself but in the commentary I create about the event. I must not impose my personal "tragedy" upon everyone who will stop to listen. Nor must I brood in private, thinking myself a romantic figure. I do not need to label every disappointment, anxiety, concern, and vexation as sobriety-threatening. There is no such thing as a sobriety-threatening event or situation unless I decide to call it that. Life itself is sobriety-threatening, and one can decide to use any disappointment as an excuse to drink. The Steps give me the tools to deal with anything that life throws at me. How "hard" or tragic life appears is determined not just by the events, circumstances, and facts of my life but also my expectations and how I react to life.

"One may not reach the dawn save by the path of the night."
Kahlil Gibran (1883 - 1931)

"Disdappointment requires adeuate planning."
Richard Bandler (born 1950)

Maya Angelou
1928 - 2014

a) Quote for Morning Contemplation

"There is a very fine line between loving life and being greedy for it." (Maya Angelou)

Reflection for Deep Recovery (Sharabi)

Loving life means enjoying the simple things, being able to linger in its moments, taking the time to smell the flowers and smile at strangers. Being greedy for life means not wanting to miss anything, not wanting to embrace anyone fully for fear of missing someone else who may show up. It also means not choosing any one path for fear of missing things that lie on the other paths. This kept me drinking, greedy, fearful I might miss something. But now I realize: if I stay sober I might miss some things, but if I drink, I will be missing out on life itself.

"Fools stand on their island of opportunities and look toward another land. There is no other land; there is no other life but this."

Thoreau (1817 - 1862)

b) Quote for Evening Contemplation

"I am convinced that most people do not grow up. We find parking spaces and honor our credit cards. We marry and dare to have children and call that growing up. I think what we do is mostly grow old. We carry accumulation of years in our bodies and on our faces, but generally our real selves, the children inside, are still innocent and shy as magnolias." (Maya Angelou)

Reflection for Deep Recovery (Sharabi)

In recovery, we become willing to show our inner selves to the world. We no longer attempt to prop up a false image. Instead, we take off our masks, and become honest and authentic; we freely admit uncertainties and fears; we do not pretend to be "grown-up" any more than we are. Nowhere else in the world do I see people openly exposing themselves in front of a roomful of others, honestly admitting their defects and their vulnerabilities, knowing that they will be accepted as they are. In recovery, I have the possibility of becoming simple and innocent as a child once again.

"It takes a very long time to become young."

Pablo Picasso (1881 - 1973)

Maya Angelou
1928 - 2014

a) Quote for Morning Contemplation

"If you don't like something—change it. If you can't change it, change your attitude. Don't complain." (Maya Angelou)

Reflection for Deep Recovery (Sharabi)

In recovery, our job is to accept people the way they are, whether we "understand" them or not. We adjust ourselves and our attitude towards them; we stop complaining. We tell ourselves: "The world is imperfect, and I am imperfect. I need to figure out how to live in an imperfect world without complaining." But later, in Deep Recovery, we stop seeing anything as imperfect; we begin to see the world as simply what it is and people just as they are. Our complaints fade away. All we focus on is: what to do next.

"There would be no society if living together depended upon understanding each other."

Eric Hoffer (1898 - 1983)

---

b) Quote for Evening Contemplation

"If God loved me, then I could do wonderful things, I could try great things, learn anything, achieve anything. For what could stand against me with God, since one person, any person with God, constitutes the majority? That knowledge humbles me, melts my bones, closes my ears, and makes my teeth rock loosely in their gums. And it also liberates me. I am a big bird winging over high mountains, down into serene valleys. I am ripples of waves on silver seas. I'm a spring leaf trembling in anticipation." (Maya Angelou)

Reflection for Deep Recovery (Sharabi)

I'm a spring leaf, trembling in anticipation of meeting my real self, of discovering what recovery holds for me. For God and I, together, can tackle anything life hurls at me. This attitude is not arrogant; on the other hand, it is the essence of humility. Being authentic requires the courage to let go of control, of plans and outcomes.

"Staying vulnerable is a risk we have to take if we want to experience connection."

Brené Brown (born 1965)

Virginia Satir
1916 - 1988

a) Quote for Morning Contemplation

"We must not allow other people's limited perceptions to define us." (Virginia Satir)

Reflection for Deep Recovery (Sharabi)

No matter what I do or what I say, someone will say I should have done it differently. I will go crazy if I try to please everyone. I need to strike a balance, though, between completely shutting out feedback and being overly concerned about the opinion of others. I do not let every arrow fired at me pierce my heart. I accept their opinion gracefully, but I assert my autonomy. I will not be crushed, nor will I be angry with them for having their perceptions and opinions.

"We have to dare to be ourselves, however frightening or strange that self may prove to be."

May Sarton (1912 - 1995)

b) Quote for Evening Contemplation

"Life is not what it's supposed to be. It's what it is. The way you cope with it is what makes the difference. Your responses to the events of life are more important than the events themselves." (Virginia Satir)

Reflection for Deep Recovery (Sharabi)

I find it necessary for sanity to accept that things are exactly the way they are. Then, I can decide how to deal with life—given that things are the way they are. When I am having a strong reaction—indignation, panic, annoyance or rage—it is usually because I am in a trance or a frenzy, in the grip of some past memory triggered. I try to calm myself by repeating the phrase: "It is what it is. It is what it is." Am I really entitled to things going smoothly? Are not interruptions and obstructions part of life? I choose how to respond thoughtfully to the events rather than furiously going with my first reaction. Recovery has taught me to slow down, examine my options, and choose an action based on principles rather than my personality.

"I define nothing... I take each thing as it is, without prior rules about what it should be."

Bob Dylan (born 1941)

Virginia Satir
1916 - 1988

a) Quote for Morning Contemplation

"I want to love you without clutching, appreciate you without judging, join you without invading, invite you without demanding, leave you without guilt, criticize you without blaming, and help you without insulting. If I can have the same from you, then we can truly meet and enrich each other." (Virginia Satir)

Reflection for Deep Recovery (Sharabi)

The distinctions made here by Virginia Satir are delicate: loving from strength, not neediness; appreciating without approving; criticizing without disapproving; requesting without demanding; getting close without crowding. And with the newcomer, I must try to support and help without advising or judging. These are the highest standards, and they come from healthy, mature boundaries.

"Whatever is received is received according to the nature of the recipient."
· *Thomas Aquinas (1224 - 1274)*

---

b) Quote for Evening Contemplation

"However I look and sound, whatever I say and do, and whatever I think and feel at a given moment in time is authentically me. If later some parts of how I looked, sounded, thought, and felt, turn out to be unfitting, I can discard that which is unfitting, keep the rest, and invent something new for that which I discarded." (Virginia Satir)

Reflection for Deep Recovery (Sharabi)

It is not sufficient merely to admit my "wrongs" and move on. I must examine my behavior to decide what would have been right. Not only must I discard the old behavior, I must discard the views that led me to behave that way. My behavior is an authentic representation of my deep structure at that time—information about my insides. I need to invent a new set of principles, perspectives, and ethics to replace the old ones, so the next time I face with the same situation, I will behave differently. Recovery calls for change beyond a mere apology or an admission of wrong: a rearrangement of my deep internal structure.

"Do not let your sins turn into bad habits."
Teresa of Avila (1515 - 1582)

Virginia Satir
1916 - 1988

a) Quote for Morning Contemplation

"The problem is never the problem! It is only a symptom of something much deeper." (Virginia Satir)

Reflection for Deep Recovery (Sharabi)

When I was feeling lousy in the early days, I would bring myself to a meeting, and I would feel much better. Today I look and think, "Oh, what a lost opportunity." Because my "lousy feelings" are precisely where my unfinished business is. My eagerness to run away from unpleasant feelings led me to bars and alcohol; today, I run to a meeting to avoid feelings. Is it different? In Deep Recovery, I must cultivate an ability to sit with my discomfort and work to change my deep structures by shining a light on them.

"Generally speaking, we regard discomfort in any form as bad news... but feelings like disappointment, embarrassment, irritation, resentment, anger, jealousy, and fear... are like messengers that show us, with terrifying clarity, exactly where we're stuck."

Pema Chödrön (born 1936)

b) Quote for Evening Contemplation

"Over the years, I have developed a picture of what a human being living humanely is like. She is a person who understands, values and develops her body, finding it beautiful and useful; a person who is real and is willing to take risks, to be creative, to manifest competence, to change when the situation calls for it, and to find ways to accommodate to what is new and different, keeping that part of the old that is still useful and discarding what is not." (Virginia Satir)

Reflection for Deep Recovery (Sharabi)

Recovery literature seems to call for a total demolition of the old self. Satir here is more respectful of everything that the human being is, enjoining the recovering person to examine and discard only those parts that are not working while keeping parts that are still useful. In recovery, the focus is often placed on thoughts and feelings while the body is ignored. Noteworthy is Satir's invitation to accept, understand, and value the body for what it is. Loving myself is impossible if I hate my body or any part of it. So I treat my body gently, with honor and love. If I think I am beautiful, I will behave well, do beautiful things and see beauty in others. If I judge myself as ugly, I will be miserable and make others miserable.

Virginia Satir
1916 - 1988

a) Quote for Morning Contemplation

**"I want you to get excited about who you are, what you are, what you have, and what can still be for you. I want to inspire you to see that you can go far beyond where you are right now."
(Virginia Satir)**

Reflection for Deep Recovery (Sharabi)

Sobriety brings with it the excitement of waking up with a clear head, of discovering that I am conscious and free to be who I wish to be. Sobriety gives me the freedom to make choices, take risks, go far beyond where I am right now and where I thought I could go. I can be authentic, strong, persevering, bold, generous and loving; things I couldn't even dream of, burdened under the weight of my disease and my compulsions. So in recovery, I am now free to become.

"One is not born, but rather, becomes a woman."

Simone de Beauvoir (1908 - 1986)

---

b) Quote for Evening Contemplation

**"To see and hear what is here, instead of what should be, was, or will be. To say what I feel and think instead of what I should. To feel what I feel instead of what I ought. To ask for what I want instead of always waiting for permission. To take risks on my behalf, instead of choosing to be safe and not rock the boat."
(Virginia Satir)**

Reflection for Deep Recovery (Sharabi)

The "shoulds" in recovery may be useful initially, but they cannot be a basis for life. We are responsible for finding and defining ourselves, not allowing others to define us. We cannot be resigned to obeying our sponsors mindlessly, to satisfying everyone in the community, or to be drowned by the cliches that surround us. In Deep Recovery, I have stopped asking for advice and also stopped giving it. It can irk those who want me to submit myself to their "suggestions." But this is the only way to find myself, to become myself. It is a bold and risky path,

"Immaturity is the incapacity to use one's intelligence without the guidance of another."

Immanuel Kant (1724 - 1804)

Virginia Satir
1916 - 1988

a) Quote for Morning Contemplation

"Taste everything, but swallow only what fits." (Virginia Satir)

Reflection for Deep Recovery (Sharabi)

In recovery, I have heard the phrase: "Take what you want and leave the rest." They don't say destroy the rest, for someone else may find a use for it. The problem is that what I don't want is sometimes the right thing for me. I will hear things I don't want to hear, but at a gut level, I know that it fits me. So, I am careful not to spit something out just because of the way it tastes. Some bitter medicine is good; it fits my ailment. So, before I reject the offered medicine, I check around with others, and I check deep within myself. I am not too hasty rejecting things, for my initial reaction is often wrong.

"What progress we are making. In the Middle Ages they would have burned me. Now they are content with burning my books."

Sigmund Freud (1856 - 1939)

---

b) Quote for Evening Contemplation

"The symbol in Chinese for crisis is made up of two ideographs: one means danger, the other means opportunity. This symbol is a reminder that we can choose to turn a crisis into an opportunity or into a negative experience." (Virginia Satir)

Reflection for Deep Recovery (Sharabi)

A crisis can provide an opportunity to grow, become strong, and develop resilience. I accept gracefully the difficulties that life presents, for where there is danger, there is opportunity. A breakdown must happen before a breakthrough. Any and all past experiences I have labeled as "negative" need to be revisited. I may have seen myself as a victim and blamed others; perhaps I need to take responsibility and see my role in the matter. Every experience has contributed to making me who I am today. I can change the meaning I have made of that experience to learn something different from it and even get to a place of gratitude for it.

"Gratitude bestows reverence, allowing us to encounter everyday epiphanies, those transcendent moments of awe that change forever how we experience life and the world."

John Milton (1608 - 1674)

Virginia Satir
1916 - 1988

a) Quote for Morning Contemplation

"People prefer the certainty of misery to the misery of uncertainty." (Virginia Satir)

Reflection for Deep Recovery (Sharabi)

A miserable, familiar, and manageable situation is often preferred to the anxiety of the unknown, even though the unknown may contain powerful possibilities. I stayed in the pit of drunkenness for years, afraid of the uncertainty contained in a sober life. Today, I must balance my aversion to risk with the urge to explore, to keep growing and developing. After all, anything new can be expected to create discomfort. In recovery and life, I have become willing to go into zones of discomfort; I do not merely restrict myself to things I am "comfortable" with.

"The psychic task we must set for ourselves is not to feel secure, but to be able to tolerate insecurity."

Erich Fromm (1900 - 1980)

---

b) Quote for Evening Contemplation

"Our biggest problem as human beings is not knowing that we don't know." (Virginia Satir)

Reflection for Deep Recovery (Sharabi)

It is not just the things I don't know that hurt me; it is the things I don't know that I don't know, and the things I think I know that ain't so. For years I drank, not knowing about alcohol and not knowing that I didn't know. Eventually, some of the truth about alcohol penetrated into my sodden brain, and I decided to quit. Then I found that just deciding was not enough; I had to admit I was powerless. And then I discovered that powerlessness was just the entry point into recovery. It takes much more than stopping drinking to stop drinking. That is the education I have received in recovery.

"Beware of false knowledge. It is more dangerous than ignorance."

George Bernard Shaw (1856 - 1950)

"In a time of drastic change, it is the learners who inherit the future. The learned usually find themselves equipped to live in a world that no longer exists."

Eric Hoffer (1898 - 1983)

Virginia Satir
1916 - 1988

a) Quote for Morning Contemplation

"We get together on the basis of our similarities; we grow on the basis of our differences." (Virginia Satir)

Reflection for Deep Recovery (Sharabi)

If I only hang out with people like myself, I will become limited. If I go only to meetings where I feel comfortable, I will become lazy. I must go to meetings outside my zip code and talk to people who look different from me, who think differently from me, to connect with the larger recovery community and with the larger world. My recovery can be measured by the wide variety of people I connect with, find interesting, and enjoy interacting with. It is wonderful that this fellowship brings such a broad cross-section of humanity to me.

"One of the signs of passing youth is the birth of a sense of fellowship with other human beings as we take our place among them."

Virginia Woolf (1882 - 1941)

---

b) Quote for Evening Contemplation

"All meaning is self-created." (Virginia Satir)

Reflection for Deep Recovery (Sharabi)

The human mind is a meaning-making machine. No matter what happens, it immediately begins to interpret, comes up with some explanation, jumps to some conclusion. I have done this with all my past events. So the question becomes: does the meaning I have created about this serve me well, or is it reducing my world? In particular, I must be careful about interpreting the actions of others in a way that I take offense or build resentment. Often, they just did something thoughtlessly, and I think they intentionally meant me harm. "It's not all about you!" I hear in these rooms. And I catch myself wondering: was that statement crafted specifically for me?

"What matters in life is not what happens to you but what you remember and how you remember it."

Gabriel García Márquez(1927 - 2014)

"The Universe is under no obligation to make sense to you."

Neil deGrasse Tyson (born 1958)

Virginia Satir
1916 - 1988

a) Quote for Morning Contemplation

"Hugging is good medicine. It transfers energy and gives the person hugged an emotional boost. We need four hugs a day for survival. We need eight hugs a day for maintenance. We need twelve hugs a day for growth. " (Virginia Satir)

Reflection for Deep Recovery (Sharabi)

Intimacy and connection ultimately derive from physicality; a child learns acceptance from being held by the mother. A clean hug is a deep and intimate way of connecting with someone, being present to them, and declaring that we care about each other. It is a great balancer for all the talk and words produced at meetings. All judgments are wiped clean in a hug.

"Go then if you must, but remember, no matter how foolish your deeds, those who love you will love you still."

Sophocles (496B.C.- 406 B.C.)

---

b) Quote for Evening Contemplation

"Feelings of worth can flourish only in an atmosphere where individual differences are appreciated, mistakes are tolerated, communication is open, and rules are flexible—the kind of atmosphere that is found in a nurturing family." (Virginia Satir)

Reflection for Deep Recovery (Sharabi)

The fellowship of recovery is a nurturing family, where individual differences are appreciated, mistakes are tolerated, communication is open, and rules are flexible. We have no leaders or authorities, only colleagues and equals. And we care about each other and will go out of our way to be there for each other. And the fundamental characteristic of such a healthy family, and indeed any healthy organization, is the absence of arguments about who is right and who is wrong. We do not try to prove anyone wrong; only they can decide what is right and what is wrong for them. We encourage self-examination, and we allow them to come to their own realization. Learning is voluntary

"We are one, after all, you and I, together we suffer, together exist, and forever will recreate each other."

Pierre Teilhard de Chardin (1881 - 1955)

Virginia Satir
1916 - 1988

a) Quote for Morning Contemplation

"I believe the greatest gift I can conceive of having from anyone is to be seen, heard, understood, and touched by them. The greatest gift I can give is to see, hear, understand and touch another person." (Virginia Satir)

Reflection for Deep Recovery (Sharabi)

The greatest gift we can give newcomers is to make them feel seen, heard, understood, and touched. It is essential to speak to the listening of the new person, not just cater to our own need to spew wisdom like an erupting volcano. We must not thrust help on people who are suspicious of us. We must first accept them as they are and we honor their autonomy, always. After that, they can choose to follow us—or not—on this sacred journey of redemption, reclamation, and recovery.

"Love is the... willingness to allow those that you care for to be what they choose for themselves without any insistence that they satisfy you."
Wayne Dyer (1940 - 2015)

b) Quote for Evening Contemplation

"I have talked about choosing rather than acting from compulsion. When you feel that you have to live according to someone else's direction or live so that you never disappoint or hurt anybody, then your life is a continual assessment of whether or not you please other people." (Virginia Satir)

Reflection for Deep Recovery (Sharabi)

For some of us, our drinking and drugging started as a rebellious attempt to break out of the oppression of other people's rules and direction. We just wanted to do the opposite of what they wanted us to do. Now, in recovery, I have the ability to choose carefully and consciously, my path in life. Neither have I to surrender to other people's values and wishes for me nor am I compelled to do the opposite. Instead, I can craft my life on Higher Principles. This is true choosing; I am free.

"Forget not that the earth delights to feel your bare feet and the winds long to play with your hair."

Kahlil Gibran (1883 - 1931)

Virginia Satir
1916 - 1988

a) Quote for Morning Contemplation

"Adolescents are not monsters. They are just people trying to learn how to make it among the adults in the world, who are probably not so sure themselves." (Virginia Satir)

Reflection for Deep Recovery (Sharabi)

Adults are not sure, themselves, but they have no hesitation telling adolescents how to be. And adolescents often drink to show that they are now adults. Sponsors, too, may succumb to the pressure to appear knowledgeable about life. Ultimately, we are all kids pretending to be adults, pretending to know things, trying to make it among the so-called adults in the world. And then, suddenly we find ourselves "seniors," and we say, "Thank God! Now I don't have to pretend to be mature any more; I can be eccentric."

"The distance between the adolescent and the true adult is about five thousand miles, but the distance between the adult and the elder is almost as large."

Robert Bly (1926 - 2021)

b) Quote for Evening Contemplation

"Problems are not the problem; coping is the problem." (Virginia Satir)

Reflection for Deep Recovery (Sharabi)

Life is always full of problems and challenges: things to be taken care of. Alcohol does not take care of anything, yet I turned to it as a way of "coping" with this life. And this "coping" became my biggest problem. As they say in recovery, "We are not so concerned about your problems, but we are worried about your solutions." It was my "solutions" that got me into trouble. In Deep Recovery I see that there are no problems—only things to be taken care of. And I am not just trying to "cope" with life; I am trying to exult in life and I celebrate living.

"Do not worry about your difficulties in mathematics. I can assure you mine are still greater."

Albert Einstein (1879 - 1955)

Emerson
1803 -1882

a) Quote for Morning Contemplation

"Adopt the pace of nature; her secret is patience." (Emerson)

Reflection for Deep Recovery (Sharabi)

Why am I in such a hurry to get to wisdom and serenity? As long as I walk briskly in the right direction, it is sufficient; there is no need to run. I must be patient about recovery. Everything takes time; I am exactly where I need to be today. I will work steadily and let life unfold at her own pace.

"Patience is the companion of wisdom."
                                        Saint Augustine (354 - 430 A.D.)

"The key to everything is patience. You get the chicken by hatching the egg, not by smashing it."
                                        *Arnold Glasow (1905 - 1998_*

---

b) Quote for Evening Contemplation

"Our greatest glory is not in never falling, but in rising up every time we fall." (Emerson)

(also attributed to Confucius, Oliver Goldsmith, and others)

Reflection for Deep Recovery (Sharabi)

We are all bathed in glory because we are the ones who have finally made it to these rooms after failing and falling countless times. And, even in recovery, I will have setbacks—guaranteed. It is okay. I struggle to my feet each time and start trudging again. It is struggle that contains the texture of existence, that fashions my character, that brings sturdiness to my existence. If I am not afraid to engage in struggles, life will be enthralling and invigorating.

"If you can't fly, then run; if you can't run, then walk; if you can't walk, then crawl; but whatever you do, you have to keep moving forward."
                                        Martin Luther King Jr. (1929 - 1968)

"Our business in life is not to succeed but to continue to fail in good spirits... The saints are the sinners who keep on trying."
                                        Robert Louis Stevenson (1850 - 1894)

Emerson
1803 -1882

a) Quote for Morning Contemplation

"I cannot remember the books I've read any more than the meals I have eaten; even so, they have made me." (Emerson)

Reflection for Deep Recovery (Sharabi)

Every comment I have heard, every speaker I have listened to, every passage in the Big Book I have examined—they all have gone in somewhere and altered the neural connections in my brain... little by little. Over the years, I have been transformed because I have come to know many things that I may not even be able to acknowledge. These are the things that have made me who I am today, and this is the reason I keep coming to meetings—to be changed in ways I do not realize and may not remember.

"A real book is not one that we read, but one that reads us."
W. H. Auden (1907 - 1973)

---

b) Quote for Evening Contemplation

"The glory of friendship is not the outstretched hand, nor the kindly smile, nor the joy of companionship; it is the spiritual inspiration that comes to one when you discover that someone else believes in you and is willing to trust you with a friendship." (Emerson)

Reflection for Deep Recovery (Sharabi)

The recovery community readily gives me the outstretched hand and the friendly smile. But the real jewel is the fellowship that comes from people who believe in me and in my effort to get sober. So I too must reach out to others with encouragement, trust, and friendship; support the newcomer to think and listen to his/her internal voice and acquire confidence in the correctness of his path. Just as you cannot pull on a sapling to make it grow, I cannot pull on the newcomer to make him grow. I water the newcomer and provide fertilizer and sunshine, and I marvel at how well he or she is growing. Friendship is rooted in acceptance—not needs, not expectations.

"Let there be no purpose in friendship, save the deepening of the spirit."
Kahlil Gibran (1883 - 1931)

Emerson
1803 -1882

a) Quote for Morning Contemplation

"People do not seem to realize that their opinion of the world is also a confession of their character." (Emerson)

Reflection for Deep Recovery (Sharabi)

What I see out there is a reflection of what exists in me. My judgments and comments about the world and people in it say something about me, not necessarily about the world. I must not get stuck in my opinions and judgments; I must not insist that reality is defined by the way I see it. Many aspects of reality are fluid, not rigid, and can be changed by my stance towards them, just as changing the way I look at the world changes the world itself. When I sobered up and changed my attitude, gave up my complaints about people, the people in the world were all suddenly nicer.

"The real voyage of discovery consists not in seeking new landscapes, but in having new eyes."

Marcel Proust (1871 - 1922)

b) Quote for Evening Contemplation

"What lies behind us and what lies before us are tiny matters compared to what lies within us." (Emerson)

Reflection for Deep Recovery (Sharabi)

When we become still and tune in, we can sense the depth of what lies within. Our regrets about the past and our anxiety about the future both become puny concerns compared to this vast infinity that lies within us in the present moment. Some call it God, and some choose to leave it nameless. A constant awareness of, and a connection with this sense of the deep, is the essential pillar of life in recovery. And must become present to this sense of what lies within us without defining it, explaining it, or pushing it on others. We merely point out its presence; they must connect with their own.

"The little space within the heart is as great as the vast universe. The heavens and the earth are there, and the sun and the moon and the stars. Fire and lightning and winds are there, and all that now is and all that is not."

Upanishads (recorded 6th century B.C. or earlier)

Emerson
1803 -1882

a) Quote for Morning Contemplation

"To be yourself in a world that is constantly trying to make you something else is the greatest accomplishment." (Emerson)

Reflection for Deep Recovery (Sharabi)

I used to think that recovery was trying to make me into something else, someone else, trying to change me from "who I am." But it was my drinking that had been making me into somebody else. I had become false, desperately trying to figure out who to be to be accepted. I used alcohol to numb the pain, and said I didn't care. Now, recovery wishes me to be true to myself, to recover and return to my "original self."

"The liberty of the individual is no gift of civilization. It was greatest before there was any civilization."

Sigmund Freud (1856 - 1939)

"What did your face look like before your parents were born?"

Zen Koan

b) Quote for Evening Contemplation

"Do not go where the path may lead, go instead where there is no path and leave a trail." (Emerson)

Reflection for Deep Recovery (Sharabi)

The great spirits of the past were not merely compliant or obedient. They did not meekly follow someone's direction or walk in someone else's path. They created their own path, and they kept their fire. Each "I" of us is a Great Spirit. Once I have achieved some years of sobriety, my responsibility in Deep Recovery is to strike out on my own and find my spiritual path. I let the fire inside guide me. But I leave a trail to show others the path until they too are ready to strike out on their own. Yes, they say it takes courage to be a firefighter, but it takes even more courage to be fire itself.

"Be careful how quickly you give away your fire."

Robert Bly (1926 - 2021)

"The opinion of 10,000 men is of no value if none of them knows anything about the subject."

Marcus Aurelius (121 - 180 A.D.)

Emerson
1803 -1882

a) Quote for Morning Contemplation

"The mind, once stretched by a new idea, never returns to its original dimensions." (Emerson)

Reflection for Deep Recovery (Sharabi)

Recovery will stretch my mind and yours by planting the idea of sobriety, by showing the possibility that recovery contains. After hearing these stories, your relationship with that drink will never be the same again. You can never again not know what has been revealed to you even once. Even if we do not get you sober, we will dent your drinking.

"Everyone should have their mind blown once a day. "

Neil deGrasse Tyson (born 1958)

---

b) Quote for Evening Contemplation

"Make your own Bible. Select and collect all the words and sentences that in all your readings have been to you like the blast of a trumpet." (Emerson)

Reflection for Deep Recovery (Sharabi)

I can underline and select those phrases and passages in recovery literature that really speak to me. But in my spiritual quest, I also go far and wide, looking always for that special pearl that lifts my mood, that sonorous blast of a trumpet that suddenly awakens me, that inspired phrase that shocks me and makes me gasp in recognition of a truth that feels familiar, something I have known all along.

"Just like the honey bee gathers nectar from many flowers to make its unique honey, so too must the seeker collect wisdom from many Gurus to create his own knowledge."

Gaudapada (6th century)

"Beware of the person of one book."

Thomas Aquinas (1224 - 1274)

Emerson
1803 -1882

a) Quote for Morning Contemplation

**"What you do speaks so loudly that I cannot hear what you say."
(Emerson)**

Reflection for Deep Recovery (Sharabi)

I am being judged now by my actions. Integrity in recovery simply
means doing what I say; there is consistency between my words,
behavior, and who I am inside. But as they say, what counts is not
talking the talk; it is walking the walk. It is one thing to present
myself as earnest, generous, humble, compassionate, kind,
and committed in meetings, but do I really act this way in my
interaction with my family and with the "outside" world?

"Kindness is in our power even when fondness is not."
Samuel Johnson (1709 - 1784)

b) Quote for Evening Contemplation

**"Whatever you do, you need courage. Whatever course you decide
upon, there is always someone to tell you that you are wrong.
There are always difficulties arising that tempt you to believe
your critics are right." (Emerson)**

Reflection for Deep Recovery (Sharabi)

I will always find people who criticize me, belittle me, and tell
me that I am wrong. Sometimes these critics are among the ones
closest to me—like my parents or my own family. Even people
in recovery want me to toe the line—their line, not mine. Never
mind. I just remind myself that I am courageous and, in sobriety,
I will need a private courage to keep to this path of honesty,
purity, humility, and love. It also takes courage to let people have
whatever opinions they have of me; getting riled up is an act of
cowardice.

*"Great spirits have always encountered violent opposition from mediocre
minds. The mediocre mind is incapable of understanding the man who
refuses to bow blindly to conventional prejudices."*
Albert Einstein (1879 - 1955)

Emerson
1803 -1882

a) Quote for Morning Contemplation

"Life is a succession of lessons which must be lived to be understood." (Emerson)

Reflection for Deep Recovery (Sharabi)

I do not need to avoid anything that God (or life) puts in my way; I can simply accept it and deal with it. If I consider that there is a message and lesson in everything, I will no longer live in fear of what might await me around the corner. I can look forward to everything, and I will neither seek out—nor seek to avoid—anything. What looks fearsome from afar may provide rich lessons and rewards when approached and engaged with.

"I never lose. Either I win, or I learn."

Nelson Mandela (1918 - 2013)

"Learning is the only thing the mind never exhausts, never fears, and never regrets."

Leonardo da Vinci (1452 - 1519)

---

b) Quote for Evening Contemplation

"The purpose of life is not to be happy. It is to be useful, to be honorable, to be compassionate, to have it make some difference that you have lived and lived well." (Emerson)

Reflection for Deep Recovery (Sharabi)

I wanted to get sober, thinking that sobriety would make me happy. But I learned that happiness is not sustainable, a booby prize, an empty goal, a selfish and self-centered obsession fueled by fear of unhappiness. Nothing can be done with happiness once I have achieved it because the next moment awaits where life begins once again. "Lasting happiness" is a fantasy, just like "they lived happily ever after." But if I focus on service, a deep joy will settle on me without my directly striving to be happy.

"The best way to find yourself is to lose yourself in the service of others."

Mahatma Gandhi (1869 - 1948)

Emerson
1803 -1882

a) Quote for Morning Contemplation

"It is not the length of life, but the depth." (Emerson)

Reflection for Deep Recovery (Sharabi)

It is not the length of sobriety but the depth. Deep Recovery goes beyond being good, moral, and obedient. We commit to awakening, to exploring beyond language and beyond intellect. We seek the numinous, and we make spiritual awakening—becoming conscious—the central purpose of our lives.

(We) must find ways and means of penetrating into the sphere of the spiritual, a domain which cannot be perceived with outer physical senses nor apprehended with the intellect which is bound to the brain.

Rudolf Steiner (1861 - 1925)

b) Quote for Evening Contemplation

"Cultivate the habit of being grateful for every good thing that comes to you, and to give thanks continuously. And because all things have contributed to your advancement, you should include all things in your gratitude." (Emerson)

Reflection for Deep Recovery (Sharabi)

I celebrate my existence today by being grateful for everything in my life, even for the very things I complained about. These things I am complaining about today will give me character and contribute to making me the person I will be tomorrow. One moment of supreme happiness and contentment—and that could even occur on my deathbed—would justify everything that happened in my life up to that point. Therefore, the idea of labeling things today as "good" and "bad" seems presumptuous and ignorant on my part.

"Health and sickness, enjoyment and suffering, riches and poverty, knowledge and ignorance, power and subjection, liberty and bondage, civilization and barbarity: have all their offices and duties. All serve for the formation of character."

William Paley (1743 - 1805)

Emerson
1803 -1882

a) Quote for Morning Contemplation

"You cannot do a kindness too soon, for you never know how soon it will be too late." (Emerson)

Reflection for Deep Recovery (Sharabi)

I am told in recovery to admit my wrongs promptly. But there is another side to this; it is not just "wrongs" that have to be dealt with promptly; it is also right things. When I think of doing something good and kind, I must do it right away; I must not wait. It is not just about apologizing promptly; I also need to compliment promptly, express my appreciation and love promptly, acknowledge their goodness and their magnificence—promptly—and if I have been thinking of doing something for them, I must do it today.

"Be kind to others so that you may learn the secret art of being kind to yourself."

Paramahansa Yogananda (1893 - 1952)

---

b) Quote for Evening Contemplation

"Our chief want is someone who will inspire us to be what we know we could be." (Emerson)

Reflection for Deep Recovery (Sharabi)

I would sit in the bar, drinking, waiting for a woman (maybe, a man in your case) to come in and inspire me to be what I knew I could be. Then I got sober and looked around for a sponsor who would inspire me to be what I knew I could be. Now I just look for a newcomer to get involved with, so that in helping him or her, I can be what I know I can be. The other things I used to want: fame, success, respect, adulation, love, loyalty, etc. was just my ego talking, expressing its most prominent qualities: the ego is insecure, grandiose, and lazy.

"You begin saving the world by saving one man at a time; all else is grandiose romanticism or politics."

Charles Buchowski (1920 - 1994)

Emerson
1803 -1882

a) Quote for Morning Contemplation

"Unless you try to do something beyond what you have already mastered, you will never grow." (Emerson)

Reflection for Deep Recovery (Sharabi)

I must make sure I do not stick to only things I am comfortable with. I seek to stretch; I seek discomfort, and I learn that I can survive—even grow—by enduring. There is no growth in complacency, comfort or smugness. I must venture out to meetings beyond my area, mingle at gatherings outside of recovery, and I must learn to get along and connect with people who have never heard of the Twelve Steps. If I only seek to hang out with people in recovery—and even there, limit myself to people who think like me—I will remain forever smug: I will never grow to my full possibility.

"You have to make something different out of yourself, rather than just find a new supply of energy."

Peter Drucker (1909 - 2005)

b) Quote for Evening Contemplation

"There is creative reading as well as creative writing." (Emerson)

Reflection for Deep Recovery (Sharabi)

There are a thousand ways to read a book. One way to read is to forget everything I have known, to encounter ideas as if for the first time, discover new meaning and nuances in every paragraph. Another way to read is to keep only what I agree with and throw away everything I disagree with. I must beware of this latter way of engaging: only with things I agree with, for I will never grow. If I am creative in reading, even in reading something I had read before, I will find things I might swear were not there the last time. And if I get into the habit of keeping a journal of recovery, I can learn and change and grow through writing, not just through reading and thinking. Any serious student of recovery must carry a notebook to meetings. Writing is more powerful, a stronger agent of change than mere speaking.

"May I write words more naked than flesh, stronger than bone, more resilient than sinew, sensitive than nerve."

Sappho (620 B.C. - 550 B.C.)

Emerson
1803 -1882

a) Quote for Morning Contemplation

"That which we persist in doing becomes easier to do, not that the nature of the thing has changed but that our power to do has increased." (Emerson)

Reflection for Deep Recovery (Sharabi)

The longer I persist in not drinking, the easier it becomes to stay sober. I do not have to resist the temptation to drink, constantly. It is just a matter of doing the next right thing—routinely, repeatedly, and effortlessly. This is the formation of habit. In recovery, there is a saying: "The road gets narrower." What this means is that there will be fewer crossroads; my decisions are always clear. We will intuitively know how to deal with situations that used to baffle us.

"I never resist temptation because I have found that things that are bad for me do not tempt me."

George Bernard Shaw (1856 - 1950)

---

b) Quote for Evening Contemplation

"For everything you have missed, you have gained something else, and for everything you gain, you lose something else." (Emerson)

Reflection for Deep Recovery (Sharabi)

With this realization, I am able to let go of my rigid ideas about how life ought to turn out. And I am able to turn my will and my life over to the care of God—with no qualms—as asked for in the Third Step. I think of how much I have gained by losing alcohol from my life, and at that moment, it seemed like such a big loss! I was so concerned about missing out on life. So today, I do not fear losing anything or missing out on anything. Sure, I might miss out on some grand vistas because I did not sign up for that expedition to climb Mount Everest. But then, by staying home, I might have a numinous encounter with a deer in the woods near here this evening, or even a tree.

"...we must address trees as we must address all things, confronting them in the awareness that we are in the presence of numinous mystery."

Brianne Swimme (born 1930)

Emerson
1803 -1882

a) Quote for Morning Contemplation

"A foolish consistency is the hobgoblin of little minds." (Emerson)

Reflection for Deep Recovery (Sharabi)

"Consistency is contrary to nature, contrary to life. The only completely consistent people are dead."

Aldous Huxley (1894 - 1963)

But the one consistency that keeps us from being dead is that mindless consistency of refusing the drink that may be available. Other than that, I am free—indeed invited—to generate myself spontaneously in the moment, unhampered by the weights I gathered in the past, unfettered by the notions people have of who I used to be.

---

b) Quote for Evening Contemplation

"All my best thoughts were stolen by the ancients." (Emerson)

Reflection for Deep Recovery (Sharabi)

A thought or idea may have been around for thousands of years; I may have come across it, myself, recently. But it is always a special moment—a sacred moment—when that idea penetrates me. It enters, and suddenly, I am not the same anymore. It is like an unexpected bird that has been flying around and suddenly decides to alight on my shoulder—an unexpected gift or random insight. I do not worry about who invented the idea, but I let it in and allow myself to be transformed. The idea of sobriety existed long before the recovery movement. I have allowed the idea of sobriety to penetrate me.

"The great and rare mystics of the past... were, in fact, ahead of their time, and are still ahead of ours. In other words, they most definitely are not figures of the past. They are figures of the future."

Ken Wilber (born 1949)

Emerson
1803 -1882

a) Quote for Morning Contemplation

"If the stars should appear but one night every thousand years how man would marvel and adore." (Emerson)

Reflection for Deep Recovery (Sharabi)

After the spiritual awakening, the individual "dull" moments of life begin to sparkle with the luminosity of existence itself. I look with fresh eyes; I don't take things for granted, and I marvel at the ordinary. I am moved every time I see a friend. The person greeting me at the door when I return home is not the same one I left in the morning. I look at the stars like they have never been here before. I marvel at this moment, for it has never been here before.

"As I get older, I sit on the park bench more often, and even the clumsy walk of the pigeons becomes fascinating."

James Hillman (1926 - 2011)

b) Quote for Evening Contemplation

"You will always find those who think they know what is your duty better than you know it. It is easy in the world to live after the world's opinion; it is easy in solitude to live after our own; but the great man is he who, in the midst of the crowd, keeps with perfect sweetness the independence of solitude." (Emerson)

Reflection for Deep Recovery (Sharabi)

I sit amidst people, listening to them. Some of them are telling me how to be—what my duty is in recovery—and I can live my life trying to please them. Or, I can withdraw into the mountains and live only to please myself—heck with the people in recovery. Both these are easier than the middle way: balance. I sit in the middle of the crowd, present to others but thinking at the same time, "Ah, how sweet my independence and the privacy of my solitude!"

"You cannot find peace by avoiding life."

Virginia Woolf (1882 - 1941)

Emerson
1803 -1882

a) Quote for Morning Contemplation

**"What I need is someone who will make me do what I can."
(Emerson)**

Reflection for Deep Recovery (Sharabi)

We alcoholics are notorious for letting ourselves off the hook.
Our sponsor's job—or our coach's job—is to elicit promises from
us and to hold us accountable for what we promise. Our sponsor
does not tell us what to promise; he/she only helps us keep the
promises we make to ourselves. Recovery makes me take action so
I am the best I can be—so I am whomever I want to be. So why do I
need to fight it?

*"The trouble with the future is that it usually arrives before we're ready
for it."*

Arnold Glasow (1905 - 1998)

---

b) Quote for Evening Contemplation

**"Don't waste life in doubts and fears; spend yourself on the work
before you, well assured that the right performance of this hour's
duties will be the best preparation for the hours or ages that
follow it." (Emerson)**

Reflection for Deep Recovery (Sharabi)

When I am doing the "next right thing," I need to focus on that
thing only, and not on all the other things I am not doing, not on
all my worries and anxieties about how the future will turn out. I
avoid getting agitated about things that have already happened. No
amount of agitation will change the past; I am training my brain
to understand this at the level of deep structure. The antidote to
worry and fear is to focus today on the Steps and do well the thing
that is in front of me, right now. Taking care of the present is the
best preparation for the future, and also the path to freedom from
the past.

*"We are here, and it is now. Further than that, all human knowledge is
moonshine."*

H. L. Mencken (1880 - 1956)

Emerson
1803 -1882

a) Quote for Morning Contemplation

"We aim above the mark to hit the mark." (Emerson)

Reflection for Deep Recovery (Sharabi)

This is true in archery as in life. We aim for perfection in order to make progress. If we start out aiming for half-measures, we will accomplish only a quarter, and a quarter can buy us a cup of coffee at the meeting but not much else. Half measures avail us nothing, anyway, as the Big Book tells us. In fact, there is a huge difference between being 99% committed to recovery and being 100% committed. Only 100% gets the job done here.

"One must think like a hero to behave like a merely decent human being."
May Sarton (1912 - 1995)

"There are no traffic jams on the extra mile."

Zig Ziglar (1926 - 2012)

---

b) Quote for Evening Contemplation

"Sorrow looks back; Worry looks around; Faith looks up." (Emerson)

Reflection for Deep Recovery (Sharabi)

If I look back with sorrow, I will encounter regret—even resentment— and I may feel like reaching for a drink to drown these unpleasant memories. Or, if I look around, worried, I may find myself filled with anxiety and despair about the state of the world and about the condition of my life. Ah, that drink looks attractive. But if I look up in Faith, I will find calmness and inspiration so that the drink is no longer in the field of consciousness.

"Faith is the bird that feels the light when the dawn is still dark."
Rabindranath Tagore (1861 - 1941)

"Faith means belief in something concerning which doubt is theoretically possible."

William James (1842 - 1910)

Emerson
1803 -1882

a) Quote for Morning Contemplation

"It is one of the beautiful compensations of life that no man can sincerely try to help another without helping himself." (Emerson)

Reflection for Deep Recovery (Sharabi)

This is the great principle of recovery that Bill and Bob discovered in Akron years ago. Perhaps they had not read Emerson, but the truth expressed in this simple statement came through to them, and with that, a path to recovery from alcoholism: we can stay sober by helping others. We are all the richer for their discovery. And in our service efforts, we must strive to be sincere and earnest. Sincerity and earnestness in everything we do is "honesty in action," as opposed to honesty in thought and contemplation, which is also called for in recovery.

"The greatness of a man is not in how much wealth he acquires, but in his integrity and his ability to affect those around him positively."
Bob Marley (1845 - 1981)

---

b) Quote for Evening Contemplation

"This is my wish for you:
comfort on difficult days,
smiles when sadness intrudes,
rainbows to follow the clouds,
laughter to kiss your lips, sunsets to warm your heart,
hugs when spirits sag, beauty for your eyes to see,
friendships to brighten your being,
faith so that you can believe,
confidence for when you doubt, courage to know yourself,
patience to accept the truth, love to complete your life."
(Emerson)

Reflection for Deep Recovery (Sharabi)

This is our collective wish for you from us in recovery. Read it over. Paste it on your bathroom mirror so that it can greet you every morning and remind you that you are not alone, that there is a fellowship out there: people wishing you well and sending you blessings every day.

Simone Weil
1909 - 1943

a) Quote for Morning Contemplation

"In struggling against anguish, one never produces serenity; the struggle against anguish only produces new forms of anguish." (Simone Weil)

Reflection for Deep Recovery (Sharabi)

Struggle against the anguish of a drunken life only provides more anguish; serenity is never the end-point of any struggle. I was resisting, struggling with my helplessness. But accepting powerlessness over alcohol—rather than struggling with it—is the most effective way of dealing with it. This acceptance immediately transforms my anguish and sets me on the path to serenity. Similarly, accepting life on life's terms—perhaps even accepting my anguish as just where I am today—relieves my frenzy.

"True strength lies in submission which permits one to dedicate his life, through devotion, to something beyond himself."
Henry Miller (1891 - 1980)

---

b) Quote for Evening Contemplation

"A hurtful act is the transference to others of the degradation which we bear in ourselves." (Simone Weil)

Reflection for Deep Recovery (Sharabi)

Punishing others, wanting to "get even," or seeking revenge—these can provide temporary glee at best, but the soul can suffer long and deep from this momentary illusion of victory. When I feel like punishing or hurting others—emotionally or physically—it is an outward expression of pain, resentment, and self-hate that I may be carrying deep inside me from long ago. This resentment degrades me. In recovery, I do not dwell on resentment, but take it as an opportunity to discover and heal ancient hurts. I do not hate myself for being hateful, but I ask God to remove this shortcoming. As I heal, the desire to see others suffer goes away. Deep Recovery calls me to be healthier, wiser, more generous, and more compassionate than regular people. I have compassion even for the hateful people, for they are lost, unable to see the beauty of the world.

"An eye for an eye will make the whole world blind."
Mahatma Gandhi (1869 - 1948)

Simone Weil
1909 - 1943

a) Quote for Morning Contemplation

"Humility is attentive patience." (Simone Weil)

Reflection for Deep Recovery (Sharabi)

Humility has to happen naturally; it takes time, like snowflakes gently settling on trees. It is futile to try directly to become humble, futile to try to acquire it quickly. The statement above provides us with a practical way to cultivate humility. We cannot pull humility out of ourselves, much like we cannot speed up the growth of a sprout by pulling on it. Humility is cultivated through painstaking care afforded to every task in life and patience and attention to every caring service we perform.

"Care is a state in which something does matter; it is the source of human tenderness."

Rollo May (1909 - 1994)

---

b) Quote for Evening Contemplation

"An atheist may be simply one whose faith and love are concentrated on the impersonal aspects of God." (Simone Weil)

Reflection for Deep Recovery (Sharabi)

An atheist might reject the notion of a personal God: a God as a separate entity or intelligence with personality and aspects of a "person." But the atheist could be focused on honesty, generosity, compassion, love, and service. His ethics could be thought of as the impersonal aspects of God. The agnostics or atheists may "pray" in their own way. There may be no mention of God in their prayerful life and no appeal to God to deliver certain results; yet, they may have a deeply spiritual existence. Such a path, too, is consistent with the principles of recovery.

"Prayer is not asking. It is a longing of the soul. It is daily admission of one's weakness. It is better in prayer to have a heart without words than words without a heart."

Mahatma Gandhi (1869 - 1948)

"The first gulp from the glass of natural sciences will turn you into an atheist, but at the bottom of the glass, God is waiting for you."

Werner Heisenberg (1901-1976)

Simone Weil
1909 - 1943

a) Quote for Morning Contemplation

**"Whenever one tries to suppress doubt, there is tyranny."
(Simone Weil)**

Reflection for Deep Recovery (Sharabi)

Enforcing compliance by outlawing doubt and questioning has
been used by oppressive regimes, oppressive authorities, and by
some religions. In recovery, we welcome your examination, and
we provide our experience as evidence of the effectiveness of
this path. Doubts are natural for the discriminating; skepticism
is healthy. But beware: the "disease"—which wants to keep you
drinking—could be generating doubts to obscure the truth. Your
doubt about one thing should not lead you to discredit everything
else.

*"The philosopher has never killed any priests, whereas the priest has
killed a great many philosophers."*

Denis Diderot (1713 - 1786)

---

b) Quote for Evening Contemplation

"The highest ecstasy is the attention at its fullest." (Simone Weil)

Reflection for Deep Recovery (Sharabi)

The most we can expect from life is to be fully occupied with
something that engrosses us and dominates our full attention in
the moment. Nothing lies deeper than this; it is complete, and we
are complete. In this moment is the highest ecstasy. Since God is
always with us, attention to God is the highest ecstasy. Since the
present moment is always with us, full attention to the "is-ness" of
the moment, the "am-ness" of "I am," is the highest ecstasy.

*"And what delights can equal those
That stir the spirit's inner deeps..."*

Alfred Lord Tennyson (1809 - 1892)

Simone Weil
1909 - 1943

a) Quote for Morning Contemplation

"It is an eternal obligation toward the human being not to let him suffer from hunger when one has a chance of coming to his assistance." (Simone Weil)

Reflection for Deep Recovery (Sharabi)

"I am Responsible. When anyone, anywhere, reaches out for help, I want the hand of A.A. always to be there, and for that, I am responsible!"
A.A. Responsibility Pledge

It is not sufficient to be willing to help; I must actually come to the assistance of the hungry—whether the hunger is for food, for love, for a sober life, or for a connection with God. And this desire to assist is rooted in relatedness, which is the basic truth of the human race.

"Most people do not really want freedom because freedom involves responsibility, and most people are frightened of responsibility."
Sigmund Freud (1856 - 1939)

b) Quote for Evening Contemplation

"All sins are attempts to fly from emptiness." (Simone Weil)

Reflection for Deep Recovery (Sharabi)

Alcoholism and addiction are my attempt to run from emptiness, to fill a void in my soul—a feeble and disastrous effort to make myself whole. I had a dark, empty hole where I carried my shame, anxiety, self-hate and feelings of worthlessness. I tried to fill that hole with pride, haughtiness, and a high self-image, but inside, I knew I was bankrupt. So I drank. In recovery, this emptiness has been filled with spirit, with fellowship, with community, with love, with goodness, and with knowledge of—and gratitude for—God's Grace. This is what has allowed humility to envelop me; now, there is no need for self-image or self-esteem.

"All sins tend to be addictive, and the terminal point of addiction is damnation."
W. H. Auden (1907 - 1973)

Simone Weil
1909 - 1943

a) Quote for Morning Contemplation

"The intelligent man who is proud of his intelligence is like the condemned man who is proud of his large cell." (Simone Weil)

Reflection for Deep Recovery (Sharabi)

Intelligence can imprison us by denying access to certain perspectives and some movement. Intelligence is useful, but it is not clear that it can chart a path to ultimate Truth and Wisdom. Let us not be proud of our intelligence but seek instead, to become wise. Wisdom is not mere knowledge; wisdom contains awe, respect, reverence, and compassion. Intelligence may try to understand and explain recovery, but wisdom is simply present to its awesomeness.

"Three-quarters of the sicknesses of intelligent people come from their intelligence. They need at least a doctor who can understand this sickness.."

Marcel Proust (1871 - 1922)

---

b) Quote for Evening Contemplation

"Attachment is the great fabricator of illusions; reality can be attained only by someone who is detached." (Simone Weil)

Reflection for Deep Recovery (Sharabi)

For many people, achieving worldly goals and financial success are the things that matter. Even finding love becomes a self-centered endeavor to find attachment. On this path, temporary satisfaction is possible but no lasting contentment. In recovery, what matters to me is the inner journey and the engagement with spiritual matters. Turning my will and my life over to the care of God is the commencement of detachment. I am detached not just from lust for material things but from entitlement to outcomes. Hope is good, but what if what I hoped for does not materialize? That is also good. Once I realize this, I am detached from hope itself because nothing in the future concerns me that much; all I will ever have is the present. Serenity and contentment come from the absence of desire and attachment, the willingness to accept and to engage with "what is" without any demand that it be different.

"Even in heavenly pleasures, he finds no satisfaction, the disciple who is fully awakened delights only in the destruction of all desires."

Max Muller (1823 - 1900)

Simone Weil
1909 - 1943

a) Quote for Morning Contemplation

"The love of our neighbor in all its fullness simply means being able to say, 'What are you going through?' " (Simone Weil)

Reflection for Deep Recovery (Sharabi)

The love of my fellow alcoholic is best expressed by an interest in, and concern for, what he or she may be going through. My ability to ask and to listen is the highest expression of my love. I must not listen passively, just making a show of listening. I listen actively and with interest, as a witness, not merely waiting to inject my opinions and advice. If I find myself getting impatient, I regard it as a lack of generosity. Nor must not be overcome by sorrow for his or her plight; that would merely be a form of self- indulgence on my part, for the focus, then, is my feelings and my reaction: me and not the person in front of me. .

"The first duty of love is to listen."

Paul Tillich (1886 - 1965)

---

b) Quote for Evening Contemplation

"Those who are unhappy have no need for anything in this world but people capable of giving them their attention." (Simone Weil)

Reflection for Deep Recovery (Sharabi)

Many problems arise from getting insufficient attention in childhood: the adults who failed to be present to us, who got lost in their ideas of what we "should" be, who failed to see us for who we were. They showed no patience and interest in us or in our brand new world. We learned to cope by giving attention to ourselves; by becoming self-absorbed. This is at the root of selfishness, self-centeredness, and narcissism. Now, in recovery, the most valuable thing I can offer the newcomer is my attention—not my advice. I do this by honoring him (or her) with my quiet and accepting presence, my curiosity, and my full attention to his or her being, by being excited about the fact that he (or she) has arrived here—just like any family is excited about the arrival of a new baby.

"Wherever I look, I see signs of the commandment to honor one's parents and nowhere of a commandment that calls for the respect of a child."

Alice Miller (1923- 2010)

Simone Weil
1909 - 1943

a) Quote for Morning Contemplation

"Culture is an instrument wielded by teachers to manufacture teachers, who, in their turn, will manufacture still more teachers." (Simone Weil)

Reflection for Deep Recovery (Sharabi)

The cult of sponsorship manufactures more sponsors, who, in turn, manufacture still more sponsors, some of whom mindlessly spout off phrases from the Big Book as a lazy way of passing on recovery culture. The job of a good teacher is not merely to pass on information or beliefs but to make the student think for himself or herself. Swallowing the Big Book without chewing on it will result in indigestion. A teacher does not just teach; he encourages learning. The job of a good sponsor is to make himself or herself redundant.

"I am not a teacher but an awakener."

Robert Frost (1874 - 1963)

---

b) Quote for Evening Contemplation

"It is only the impossible that is possible for God. He has given over the possible to the mechanics of matter and the autonomy of his creatures." (Simone Weil)

Reflection for Deep Recovery (Sharabi)

Doctors, scientists, and psychologists can make happen only things that are possible and reasonable. But God can make the impossible happen. If I stop insisting on dry scientific explanations of happenings, stop insisting that only "explainable" things are possible, then I will be opening myself to the possibility of miracles. Awe and wonderment, inspiration and hope—these emotions move humanity in ways that logic and reason do not. God moves Man in ways that reason cannot. These are often termed miracles. Every alcoholic who is sober now is a walking miracle: no amount of intelligence, reason, and sense could have got him or her to this place.

"Miracles are a retelling in small letters of the very same story which is written across the whole world in letters too large for some of us to see."

C. S. Lewis (1898 - 1963)

227

Simone Weil
1909 - 1943

a) Quote for Morning Contemplation

**"The future is made of the same stuff as the present."
(Simone Weil)**

Reflection for Deep Recovery (Sharabi)

Am I wondering about the future? I used to wonder about the future. Well, they tell me, here it is: here is how the future has turned out for you. I am in it today; all I can do is seize the day.

"Today is the tomorrow you worried about yesterday."
Dale Carnegie (1888 - 1955)

b) Quote for Evening Contemplation

"A mind enclosed in language is in prison." (Simone Weil)

Reflection for Deep Recovery (Sharabi)

We can get fascinated with words and concepts, syntax and semantics. We can become occupied with ideas and arguments and completely miss the experience itself. Many of us live, not in the present, but in our commentary about the present. We become slaves to language—to the words and sentences in the Big Book—and lose sight of the wonderful liberation it is pointing to. If I relate to God as a concept, I will miss the presence of God. If I get occupied with the finger pointing at the moon, I might fail to see the moon.

"Words are not the things we speak about... there is no such thing as an object in total isolation. The map is not the territory; the menu is not the meal."

Alfred Korzybski (1879 - 1950)

Simone Weil
1909 - 1943

a) Quote for Morning Contemplation

"A test of what is real is that it is hard and rough. Joys are found in it, not pleasure. What is pleasant belongs to dreams."
(Simone Weil)

Reflection for Deep Recovery (Sharabi)

If I give up the pursuit of pleasure, my real life begins. I can derive immense joy from the texture of life—all of it, including the hard and rough parts—and not lust after some imaginary and easy pleasure. Pleasure is something experienced momentarily, but joy is a state of being. Something may be worth doing, but it may not be "pleasant." Pleasure is only skin-deep; joy is felt in the bones. If I limit myself only to things that please me, I will not find joy or happiness.

"If you say, 'It is hard to get up in the morning,' or, 'It is hard to cease smoking,' then you are using hypnotic suggestion on yourself."
Richard Bandler (born 1950)

---

b) Quote for Evening Contemplation

"The mysteries of faith are degraded if they are made into an object of affirmation and negation, when in reality they should be an object of contemplation." (Simone Weil)

Reflection for Deep Recovery (Sharabi)

God is a mystery, not to be described, believed in, or rejected but available as an object of contemplation. Similarly, the quotations in this book are degraded if I examine them solely from the perspective of choosing ones to agree with and ones to reject. I can judge based only on the structure already installed in my mind, and I will become impervious to new structures and new ideas. When encountering something new, I must sit with it, expose myself to it, and make it an object of contemplation without interference from my ego, my past knowledge, or my "logic."

"It is the mark of an educated mind to be able to entertain a thought without accepting it."
Aristotle (384 -322 B.C.)

"The ability to observe without evaluating is the highest form of intelligence."
Krishnamurti (1895 - 1986)

Simone Weil
1909 - 1943

a) Quote for Morning Contemplation

"In the Church, considered as a social organism, the mysteries inevitably degenerate into beliefs." (Simone Weil)

Reflection for Deep Recovery (Sharabi)

A belief is the action of freezing the Great Mystery and rendering it lifeless. Spreading beliefs while discouraging contemplation, meditation, and inquiry is contrary to the spirit of recovery. Recovery is not a Church where I am merely taught to believe. Instead, I must engage with, question, and ponder every line in the Big Book. This will cause me to affirm it in a deep way, so the knowledge becomes my own as opposed to mere hearsay. And I may find that the mystery itself is the answer to the question.

"Contemplation is an alternative consciousness that refuses to identify with or feed what are only passing shows. It is the absolute opposite of addiction, consumerism, or any egoic consciousness."

Richard Rohr (born 1943)

---

b) Quote for Evening Contemplation

"Life does not need to mutilate itself in order to be pure." (Simone Weil)

Reflection for Deep Recovery (Sharabi)

I stay away from people who think that degrading themselves and mutilating their character in public is some sign of sincerity, humility, and earnestness. Indeed, it is a form of perversion practiced by some recovering alcoholics in the name of self-honesty. I do not speak of myself unkindly in these rooms—indeed, do not allow it even in my private thoughts; I am aware that God loves me, and I am made of sacred stuff. I attribute the same sacredness to everyone who walks into these rooms. Some have suffered verbal and emotional—or even more severe forms of—abuse, and they may be drawn to people who treat them poorly. Nobody gets better through being put down by others or through self-flagellation; no, that is not the path here.

"But if a mirror ever makes you sad, you should know that it does not know you."

Kabir (1440 - 1518)

Simone Weil
1909 - 1943

a) Quote for Morning Contemplation

**"One cannot imagine St. Francis of Assisi talking about rights."
(Simone Weil)**

Reflection for Deep Recovery (Sharabi)

The notion of individual rights was a great step for progress
and has become the basis for a just society. The talk of rights
stems directly from legal entitlement but is sometimes presented
as a moral entitlement also. However, there is a price to pay:
when someone is protesting about their "right," they are usually
operating from a feeling of being wronged and posturing
themselves as a victim. It furthers a feeling of helplessness and
complaint of the unfairness of this world. In recovery, we are
urged to consider everything as a privilege, not as a right. This will
lead to eternal gratitude and tranquility.

*"When you arise in the morning, think of what a precious privilege it is to
be alive: to breathe, to think, to enjoy, to love."*

Marcus Aurelius (121 - 180 A.D.)

b) Quote for Evening Contemplation

**"Unless one has placed oneself on the side of the oppressed, to
feel with them, one cannot understand." (Simone Weil)**

Reflection for Deep Recovery (Sharabi)

We each have experienced the severe oppression that alcohol
creates. Now that I am sober and free, I must still remember and
understand; I must feel with the still struggling alcoholic. I must
not hold myself as higher than them; I must not judge or condemn
them for struggling; I must not make myself the judge of how
sincere their efforts are. I must always be an understanding and
encouraging presence. My failure to remember this shows up when
disappointment turns to anger and caring turns to scorn at the
newcomer. Disappointment comes from expectations; it could
be a sign of caring, but such disappointment must be managed
internally. My expectations and my disappointment should never
be the other person's burden to carry.

"There can be no deep disappointment where there is not deep love."

Martin Luther King Jr. (1929 - 1968)

Simone Weil
1909 - 1943

a) Quote for Morning Contemplation

"We can only know one thing about God—that he is what we are not." (Simone Weil)

Reflection for Deep Recovery (Sharabi)

All I need to know about God is that I am not God. All I need to understand about a Higher Power is that this Power is larger than and beyond the forces that can be generated by my ego and my conscious will. Contrary to popular misconception, recovery is not a "self-help" program.

"We will not find the inner strength to evolve to a higher level if we do not inwardly develop this profound feeling that there is something higher than ourselves."
Rudolf Steiner (1861 - 1925)

"Obeying the ego leads to bondage; obeying the soul brings liberation."
Parmahansa Yogananda (1893 - 1952)

---

b) Quote for Evening Contemplation

"If we are suffering illness, poverty, or misfortune, we think we shall be satisfied on the day it ceases. But there too, we know it is false; so soon as one has got used to not suffering, one wants something else." (Simone Weil)

Reflection for Deep Recovery (Sharabi)

When we are parched and thirsty in the desert, a glass of water seems like heaven. But once we have found that water, we will seek something else. It is the nature of the human mind to seek the next missing thing: this is the source of endless dissatisfaction. Remember the days when we longed for sobriety? Now we are taking it for granted, desiring something else, fretting over relatively inconsequential trivialities. I need to realize that with sobriety, my life is whole, pure, simple, and complete; the rest is all adornment. We seek not satisfaction, which is always fragile and temporary, but contentment which is lasting and does not depend on circumstance.

"Acceptance of what has happened is the first step to overcoming the consequences of any misfortune."
William James (1842 - 1910)

Simone Weil
1909 - 1943

a) Quote for Morning Contemplation

**"Attention is the rarest and purest form of generosity."
(Simone Weil)**

Reflection for Deep Recovery (Sharabi)

If I wish to be generous with the people around me, let me offer
them my attention. Let me listen rather than talk; let me inquire
and wait rather than advice and demand; let me accompany them
where they want to go rather than push or pull them to my path.
My attention offered as silent listening is the purest form of
generosity; miracles can occur in the space created.

*"When you are listening to somebody, completely, attentively, then you
are listening not only to the words, but also to the feeling of what is being
conveyed, to the whole of it, not part of it."*

Krishnamurti (1895 - 1986)

b) Quote for Evening Contemplation

**"If we go down into ourselves, we find that we possess exactly
what we desire." (Simone Weil)**

Reflection for Deep Recovery (Sharabi)

If we did not already possess a particular quality, we would not
be familiar enough with it even to imagine it or to desire it. It
is merely a question of letting it rise to the surface. If we desire
sobriety, it means that deep down, we imagine and possess
the possibility. It is merely a matter of unveiling it. And if we
genuinely desire sobriety for another, then the two of us, together,
possess this possibility and can make it happen. This principle is
the cornerstone of recovery.

Another way of interpreting this quote is to realize there is
nothing to seek; we already have it. We do not need to seek
sobriety; we already have sobriety. We merely need to avoid giving
it away by taking a drink.

*"The fabled musk deer searches the world over for the source of the scent
which comes from itself."*

Sri Ramakrishna (1836 - 1886)

Simone Weil
1909 - 1943

a) Quote for Morning Contemplation

"To be rooted is perhaps the most important and least recognized need of the human soul." (Simone Weil)

Reflection for Deep Recovery (Sharabi)

I went to the bar daily, seeking a home, seeking roots among the regulars who frequented the place. I drank in an attempt to belong. But now, I have grown roots within the fellowship of recovery—permanent and lasting roots in the community. An important need of my soul that I myself may not have recognized fully has been satisfied in a deep and abiding way.

"Because true belonging only happens when we present our authentic, imperfect selves to the world, our sense of belonging can never be greater than our level of self-acceptance."

Brené Brown (born 1965)

b) Quote for Evening Contemplation

"Even if our efforts of attention seem for years to be producing no result, one day a light that is in exact proportion to them will flood the soul." (Simone Weil)

Reflection for Deep Recovery (Sharabi)

Some people, in early sobriety, are not drinking, but their mood is dark. I tell them not to be discouraged; they should not judge the effectiveness of their work by the mood they are in. I tell them to wait. One day they may be flooded with the payment for all their work, and their attention to the detailed requirements of the Steps will have borne fruit. So they should be patient and keep focusing on the work, enjoying the engagement with the process of recovery. I tell them they should not sit impatiently awaiting the promises; they should just do the work and be surprised, delighted, and amazed when the promises materialize.

"It is at the edge of a petal that love waits."

William Carlos Williams (1883 - 1963)

Simone Weil
1909 - 1943

a) Quote for Morning Contemplation

"God's love for us is not the reason for which we should love him. God's love for us is the reason for us to love ourselves." (Simone Weil)

Reflection for Deep Recovery (Sharabi)

"We love you until you learn to love yourself, and then we continue loving you," the new person is told. But the newcomer who thinks of himself or herself as unlovable has a difficult time accepting love from others. Loving myself in recovery is very different from the self-centered and narcissistic self-focus that occupied me as a drinking man. The courage to love ourselves can only come from the knowing that God loves us.

"Selfish persons are incapable of loving others, but they are not capable of loving themselves either."

Erich Fromm (1900   1980)

---

b) Quote for Evening Contemplation

"Compassion directed toward oneself is true humility." (Simone Weil)

Reflection for Deep Recovery (Sharabi)

Humble people do not degrade themselves or speak poorly of themselves. They simply see themselves the way they are; they are compassionate and understanding of themselves the same way they would be towards a child. Seeing myself as a child in recovery is the ultimate sign of compassion, of humility. Beating up on myself is a form of grandiosity and violence; it comes from saying, "I should be better than that!" while not accepting that—perhaps—I am not better than that. It is the opposite of humility. It comes from self-will, from believing that I have the power to remove my character defects by myself rather than needing God's help in removing my shortcomings.

"Nothing is a greater impediment to being on good terms with others than being ill at ease with yourself."

Honore de Balzac (1799 - 1850)

Simone Weil
1909 - 1943

a) Quote for Morning Contemplation

"Grace fills empty spaces, but it can only enter where there is a void to receive it, and it is grace itself, which makes this void." (Simone Weil)

Reflection for Deep Recovery (Sharabi)

In my drinking days, there was a dark and empty hole in my soul that I was constantly attempting to fill with alcohol. Only when I surrendered did I make space for Grace to come in and fill this void. But it had never struck me that it was Grace itself that allowed this emptiness to occur in the first place. I was just filling it with the wrong spirit(s).

---

b) Quote for Evening Contemplation

"We have to endure the discordance between imagination and fact. It is better to say, 'I am suffering,' than to say, 'This landscape is ugly.' " (Simone Weil)

Reflection for Deep Recovery (Sharabi)

It is better to say, "I am in pain," rather than, "The world has hurt me." Even saying, "I don't like it," is better than saying, "It is bad and wrong and unfair!" I do not ever want to blame others—people, places, and things—for the pain I might be feeling inside myself. Imagining that someone or something must change in order for me to be happy is a certain path to misery. I now know how to accept and transcend the pain I may be feeling without ever requiring anything or anybody out there to change or be different. Most of all, I cannot attribute my suffering to someone else; it is solely my responsibility to heal.

"One can't carry one's father's corpse about everywhere."

Apollinaire (1880 - 1918)

Simone Weil
1909 - 1943

a) Quote for Morning Contemplation

"We cannot take a step toward the heavens. God crosses the universe and comes to us." (Simone Weil)

Reflection for Deep Recovery (Sharabi)

It is not just we who are seeking God; when we become ready to receive, God comes to us. God is seeking us! God had been seeking me even when I had no thought of Him and was drowning myself in the bottle.

"The breeze of God's grace is always blowing.
Set your sails to catch the breeze."

Sri Ramakrishna (1836 - 1886)

b) Quote for Evening Contemplation

"Love of God is pure when joy and suffering inspire an equal degree of gratitude." (Simone Weil)

Reflection for Deep Recovery (Sharabi)

Once we have completed and realized the Third Step and turned our will and our life over to the care of God, we are no longer this feeble ball of anxiety, wishing that certain things will happen and hoping that other things do not. Today I have no investment in my future turning out any way other than how God wishes for me. I no longer need to label events as "good" and "bad;" I no longer have to ask God to explain. In striving for total acceptance, I have become aware of a place where I can welcome equally both joy and suffering in life; each has value, and all comes from God.

"Sometimes allowing yourself to cry is the scariest thing you will ever do... and the bravest... But it is the only way to cleanse your wounds and prepare them for healing. God will take care of the rest."

Barbara Johnson (1927 - 2007)

Simone Weil
1909 - 1943

a) Quote for Morning Contemplation

"The only way into truth is through one's own annihilation; through dwelling a long time in a state of extreme and total humiliation." (Simone Weil)

Reflection for Deep Recovery (Sharabi)

The way into truth has been opened for the alcoholic through the extreme and total humiliation that drinking has exposed him or her to for a long time. All efforts to conquer this monster fail until the ego and will are annihilated. Only then are powerlessness and total surrender—initially perceived as humiliation—exposed to us as the path to truth and the doorway to freedom and liberation, to love.

"Of all forms of caution, caution in love is perhaps the most fatal to true happiness."

Bertrand Russell (1872 - 1970)

b) Quote for Evening Contemplation

"We must not wish for the disappearance of our troubles but for the grace to transform them." (Simone Weil)

Reflection for Deep Recovery (Sharabi)

With a spiritual awakening, troubles appear in my consciousness illuminated by a different light. Then they no longer look like useless troubles. In grappling with these, I can be moved and transformed. I can embrace my troubles as the path to my transformation. This is the wonderful gift that the program offers but alas! Too many are content just to not drink, and they go to meetings hoping for troubles to disappear. They are counting the days of sobriety that they have accumulated—much like the miser counts his coins—but they are not getting any closer to the real liberation that is possible. If a situation is causing us anguish and suffering, we could just conclude that we have yet to attain that spiritual sturdiness that will give us the ability to deal graciously with life—however life is.

"Most men lead lives of quiet desperation and go to the grave with the song still in them."

Thoreau (1817 - 1862)

Carl Jung
1875 - 1961

a) Quote for Morning Contemplation

"The word 'belief' is a difficult thing for me. I don't believe. I must have a reason for a certain hypothesis. If I know a thing—and then I know it—I don't need to believe it. I don't allow myself to believe a thing just for the sake of believing it." (Carl Jung)

Reflection for Deep Recovery (Sharabi)

There is a huge difference between believing and knowing. Belief is based on personal needs and on what people or books have told me, not on personal knowledge. If it is part of my experience, then it is no longer a mere "belief." I am powerless over alcohol; it is not just a belief—I know it. And it is not sufficient to merely "believe" in God. One must know God, and connect with God—relate to God as a deeply personal experience. Knowing God is completely different from knowing about God or reading about God. This is the foundation of long term recovery.

"Nothing that is worth knowing can be taught."

Oscar Wilde (1854 - 1900)

---

b) Quote for Evening Contemplation

"God is not a statistical truth; hence it is just as stupid to prove the existence of God as to deny Him... Belief and disbelief in God are mere surrogates. The naive primitive doesn't believe, he knows, because the inner experience means as much to him as the outer.. He has no theology and hasn't yet let himself be befuddled by booby trap concepts." (Carl Jung)

Reflection for Deep Recovery (Sharabi)

The experience of a "Higher Power," whether we call it God, Love, the Universe, Brahman, the Tao, the Nameless—whatever—this inner experience has been available to, and held as sacred, by primitive people for thousands of years. Reaching deep and connecting with this archetypal presence is the core of the Twelve Step programs. Here, God is not a concept but an experience. I do not concern myself with intellectual arguments about the existence of God—leave that to the theologians—but instead, I just make use of this sublime, transcendent energy for my own recovery.

"Theology is the effort to explain the unknowable in terms of the not worth knowing."

H. L. Mencken (1880 - 1956)

Carl Jung
1875 - 1961

a) Quote for Morning Contemplation

"The first half of life is devoted to forming a healthy ego; the second half is going inward and letting go of it." (Carl Jung)

Reflection for Deep Recovery (Sharabi)

We talk a lot, here in recovery, of the ego with all its negative connotations—pride, vanity, grandiosity, self-absorption, self-justification, indignation, and self-righteousness. Our character defects—things the ego tries to hang on to for survival—keep us from our urge to achieve "union with God." But psychologists say that a healthy ego—a sense of self—is the thing that prevents us from getting crushed by criticism and gives us the strength to persevere under adversity. Both these definitions have some usefulness. Jung is talking about getting to a stage where the ego of the individual surrenders itself to a higher Self—a Higher Power. The individual is no longer dominated by the petty concerns of the ego but is answering the call of something larger.

---

b) Quote for Evening Contemplation

"It all depends on how we look at things, and not how they are in themselves." (Carl Jung)

Reflection for Deep Recovery (Sharabi)

The ability to change my attitude and my perspective on anything has given me immense freedom. The language and concepts that I use end up defining my "reality," and the notion of a fixed reality imprisons me in an inflexible world that exists out there, one that I can only helplessly react to. Rather than complaining about "reality," if I become willing to change my attitude and to change how I look at things, the "reality" out there changes. Reality is not "what is" but the meaning we have made of it. We choose this meaning; we choose our attitude. Some say that A.A. stands for Attitude Adjustment. Ultimately, what counts is not how I claim life "is," but how I deal with life. The fellowship of recovery has given me tools—many tools. My universe is benevolent and friendly today, not unfair and dangerous as I held it to be.

"Everything can be taken from a man but one thing: the last of the human freedoms—to choose one's attitude in any given set of circumstances, to choose one's own way."

Viktor Frankl (1905 - 1997)

Carl Jung
1875 - 1961

a) Quote for Morning Contemplation

"God is the name by which I designate all things which cross my willful path violently and recklessly, all things which alter my subjective views, plans, and intentions, and change the course of my life, for better or for worse." **(Carl Jung)**

Reflection for Deep Recovery (Sharabi)

God is merely the gap between possibility and probability. Of all the things that could possibly happen, the force in the universe that selects the thing that happens—is God. Instead of saying that God is the plan behind the universe, I can consider God as a manifestation of the randomness and unpredictability of the universe. How freeing it is to see God not just in order but in chaos! It all is God. Since alcohol sabotaged all my plans, it, too, is a God. All the sabotage I have experienced of my plans are divine.

"You are free, and that is why you are lost."

Franz Kafka (1883 - 1924)

---

b) Quote for Evening Contemplation

"Meaninglessness inhibits fullness of life and is therefore equivalent to illness. Meaning makes a great many things endurable—perhaps everything." **(Carl Jung)**

Reflection for Deep Recovery (Sharabi)

Initially, I wanted sobriety just to avoid the problems drinking had brought me. But later, I had to find meaning in recovery to overcome the empty meaninglessness that permeated my life in those drinking days. So I had to honor my yearning for something higher; I had to find meaningful activities and pursuits that got me out of myself and answered a spiritual calling. This included helping other alcoholics, reaching for sobriety and growth, expressing myself in art, and trying to improve my conscious contact with God—in whatever way and however I understood God. Pursuing spiritual awakening brings meaning to my life in recovery.

"As the hart panteth after the water brooks, so panteth my soul after thee, O God."

Bible, Psalm 42 King James Version.

Carl Jung
1875 - 1961

a) Quote for Morning Contemplation

"If I accept the fact that a God is absolute and beyond all human experiences, he leaves me cold. I do not affect Him, nor does he affect me. But if I know that a God is a powerful impulse in my soul, at once I must concern myself with Him, for then He can become important... like everything belonging to the sphere of reality." (Carl Jung)

Reflection for Deep Recovery (Sharabi)

My alcoholism was a powerful impulse in my body and mind, and also in my soul, where it was beyond the reach of my intellectual thoughts and will. Only another powerful impulse in my soul could help me: God. As long as I stay connected with my God-impulse, He is as real as anything else in the sphere of material reality, like apples, cheese, hunger, pain, and alcoholism.

"The demon that you can swallow gives you its power, and the greater life's pain, the greater life's reply."
Joseph Campbell (1904 - 1987)

b) Quote for Evening Contemplation

"No science will ever replace myth, and a myth cannot be made out of any science. For it is not that 'God' is a myth, but that myth is the revelation of a divine life in man. It is not we who invent myth, rather it speaks to us as a Word of God." (Carl Jung)

Reflection for Deep Recovery (Sharabi)

Jung considered myth and mythology as the sacred emerging of preexisting archetypes in the Collective Unconscious—symbolic images that mankind was born with. So, when Jung says "God is a myth," he implies that "God" is an intrinsic and fundamental presence in the unconscious of man. Therefore, this God of my understanding is not just an invention of mine nor a fact to be ascertained from texts or from science. A sense of God is a deep part of me that has been there all along from prehistoric times. I had covered up God with my drinking and my cynicism; now, this divine presence has pushed out and uncovered itself. It is available to me as a resource for me to lean on in recovery.

"Mythology is not a lie; mythology is poetry, it is metaphorical...mythology is the penultimate truth--penultimate because the ultimate cannot be put into words... what can be known but not told.
Joseph Campbell (1904 - 1987)

Carl Jung
1875 - 1961

a) Quote for Morning Contemplation

"Every form of addiction is bad, no matter whether the narcotic be alcohol or morphine or idealism." (Carl Jung)

Reflection for Deep Recovery (Sharabi)

Every addiction to one thing is an attempt to avoid something else. Every addiction is an immersion in unconsciousness. Every problem started out as the solution to some other problem. The recovery movement has bred some "fanatics" who thunder and expound from the pulpits. In the beginning, witnessing such passionate demonstrations may serve to distract the listener from using, but it can also turn off many newcomers who feel pressured to join in the fanaticism. We each have a responsibility to wake up and open our eyes at some point, to not hide behind fanaticism or idealism or "recovery-ism," but to move to a higher plane.

"A problem cannot be solved from the same level of consciousness that created it.

Albert Einstein (1879 - 1955)

---

b) Quote for Evening Contemplation

"The attainment of wholeness requires one to stake one's whole being. Nothing less will do." (Carl Jung)

Reflection for Deep Recovery (Sharabi)

Recovery calls for total surrender: 100% commitment. Half measures avail us nothing. Success is for those who "let go absolutely" and who "thoroughly follow" the path with "complete abandon." (Big Book: How it Works.) Many spiritual paths around the world also call for total surrender to the path. However, the modern human mind trained to be scientific and skeptical will carefully protest: "Let me think about it." Thinking is all about objections and reservations. The mind cannot leap across the chasm; only the heart can, crazy-mad after sobriety, abandoning all reservations and objections.

"People wish to learn to swim and at the same time to keep one foot on the ground."

Marcel Proust (1871 - 1922)

"All of us are in desperate need of the restoration of our wholeness through union with our inmost self."

Stephan Hoeller (born 1931)

Carl Jung
1875 - 1961

a) Quote for Morning Contemplation

**"Who looks outside, dreams;
who looks inside, awakes." (Carl Jung)**

Reflection for Deep Recovery (Sharabi)

A spiritual awakening is the fruit of a journey inward. When our
focus is exclusively on external and material success, or even
on the God outside, we are dreaming. When we focus on the
God inside, we are awakened. But it takes courage to awaken:
are we prepared to see whatever it is that shows up when we
open our eyes? Or do we prefer to hide behind a veil of stories,
delusions, and beliefs given to us by others just because they
are "comforting?" Deep Recovery calls for ruthless awakening, a
willingness to encounter the truth "as is."

"Is awareness bearable?"

Sonia Nevis (1927 - 2017)

---

b) Quote for Evening Contemplation

**"God, an inner experience, not discussable as such but impressive.
Psychic experience has two sources, the outer world and the
unconscious. All immediate experience is psychic. There is
physically transmitted (outer world) experience and inner
(spiritual) experience. The one is just as valid as the other."
(Carl Jung)**

Reflection for Deep Recovery (Sharabi)

I would be wasting everyone's time if I were to stand up and
proclaim either my belief in God or my arguments against God,
for God is not discussable. God is a deep and personal inner
experience that has either made a profound individual impact on
me or not (or maybe, not yet.) Recovery is not a religion where
we promulgate certain beliefs. Recovery is a space for people to
have their individual experience of this Higher Self. And this inner
spiritual experience is just as real as scientific facts about the
outer world. We can seek agreement about facts, but not about the
Truth of God.

"We do not talk about God. We talk to God."

Viktor Frankl (1905 - 1997)

244

Carl Jung
1875 - 1961

a) Quote for Morning Contemplation

"We cannot change anything until we accept it. Condemnation does not liberate, it oppresses... What you resist not only persists but will grow in size." (Carl Jung)

Reflection for Deep Recovery (Sharabi)

The condemnation of the alcoholic by well-meaning "others" does not push him or her to recovery. My own condemnation of my alcoholism only oppressed me; it did not liberate me. I kept drinking, but I added "feeling bad about it" to the mix. It is only when I accepted my alcoholism that I was able to impact it. I was then able to move to the larger sphere of accepting life as it is. Then I ceased to be a little ball of objections, complaints, regrets, petulance, and anxiety. The clouds disappeared, and the skies opened up.

"The cave you fear to enter holds the treasures you seek."
Joseph Campbell (1904 - 1987)

---

b) Quote for Evening Contemplation

"Everything that irritates us about others can lead us to an understanding of ourselves... Knowing your own darkness is the best method for dealing with the darknesses of other people." (Carl Jung)

Reflection for Deep Recovery (Sharabi)

When I point one finger at others, three are pointing back at me. When I get aroused by the darkness of others, I now know that I am hiding my own darkness and projecting it on the outer world. I would never be able to notice something in others if it was not already present in me. Therefore, I can use my irritation as a tool to disclose things about myself that I have pushed deep down. I must pay attention, not only when I am triggered to anger or annoyance, but to things that humiliate me or evoke shame in me. What is it I am trying to protect, I must ask myself, and what is intolerable if the world were to see in me? This is the steady and continuing work needed in the pursuit of self-awareness.

"Good character is not formed in a week or a month. It is created little by little, day by day. Protracted and patient effort is needed.
Heraclitus (circa 500 B.C.)

Carl Jung
1875 - 1961

a) Quote for Morning Contemplation

"Man needs difficulties; they are necessary for health. There's no coming to consciousness without pain." (Carl Jung)

Reflection for Deep Recovery (Sharabi)

The process of working through my difficulties will lift me to new heights; I will see new lands. Deep Recovery tells me to accept difficulties—to face them instead of just protesting. Difficulty with alcohol brought me to consciousness. This is also true of difficulty watching loved ones suffer. Sometimes all we can do is keep them company, be present to their suffering and pray for them. We must ensure our "pain" is not merely a form of self-focus.

"Do you not see how necessary a world of pains and troubles is to school an intelligence and make it a soul?"

John Keats (1795 - 1821)

"One may not reach the dawn save by the path of the night."

Kahlil Gibran (1883 - 1931)

---

b) Quote for Evening Contemplation

"Why not go into the forest for a time, literally? Sometimes a tree tells you more than can be read in books." (Carl Jung)

Reflection for Deep Recovery (Sharabi)

The deep changes that occur in recovery are not merely intellectual or even understandable. We focus on words, sit around, talk incessantly, and talk about ourselves. But the significant changes in recovery are really occurring at the level of Being, and there is no better way to connect with Being than when we are out in nature. As a civilization, we are all nature-starved—suffering from "nature-deficit disorder." A walk through the woods or even a park, a chance encounter with a tree, or with a deer in the forest, can itself become a numinous episode, full of meaning and significance beyond words. Today, I seek out nature and treasure these special gifts that sobriety has to offer, even when I am unable to explain them to anyone. But the mountain brook understands. Being in nature allows me to experience my own perfection.

"You will always find an answer in the sound of water."

Chuang Tzu (370 - 287 B.C.)

246

Carl Jung
1875 - 1961

a) Quote for Morning Contemplation

"The shoe that fits one person pinches another; there is no recipe for living that suits all cases." (Carl Jung)

Reflection for Deep Recovery (Sharabi)

Beware of a sponsor who has the same advice for everybody: "prayer," or "acceptance," or "more meetings," and, "This too shall pass." Some cliches may fit certain situations and pinch painfully in others. The key to recovery is to know when to refuse to accept; instead, to object, and to protest, to resist —and when to just accept and move on. Sometimes it is useful to just sit with feelings without trying to change anything. There is no universal answer.

"To a man who only has a hammer, everything he encounters begins to look like a nail."

Abraham Maslow (1908 - 1970)

b) Quote for Evening Contemplation

"I cannot love anyone if I hate myself. That is the reason why we feel so extremely uncomfortable in the presence of people who are noted for their special virtuousness, for they radiate an atmosphere of the torture they inflict on themselves. That is not a virtue but a vice." (Carl Jung)

Reflection for Deep Recovery (Sharabi)

My need to present myself as virtuous, as "all good," is a vice in itself: a perverted distortion arising from desperation, a self-torture stemming from my inability to accept all parts of myself. Even when I stand up and publicly declare my imperfections, I am trying to become "all good" once again, feel superior once more. But really, I must not be concerned with the defects that I see in myself, but with those that I am unaware of. As long as I know defects exist in me, I am saying that I am human, and accepting my human-ness is the first step to recovering my wholeness. Even "trying" to be virtuous is fake. Just be natural, and the change will happen naturally. And it will not even feel like "change" because you are always present as you are, simply doing the next right thing—naturally, as best as you can.

Carl Jung
1875 - 1961

a) Quote for Morning Contemplation

"Enlightenment is not imagining figures of light but making the darkness conscious." (Carl Jung)

Reflection for Deep Recovery (Sharabi)

Enlightenment is not merely about standing, bathed in light, and being happy ever after. Recovery calls on me to accept both the light and the darkness in me so that I am fully conscious to all aspects of life and of myself. In Deep Recovery we are called to take on a larger, more complex perspective than simplistic two-dimensional notions of good and bad, right and wrong. Certain behavior that readily elicits approval from others may be the "wrong" thing for the growth of my soul and for my process of individuation.

"People get the idea that enlightened beings never have bad days. If you've got that idea, you've got a false standard against which to measure the quality of your life."

Werner Erhard (born 1935)

b) Quote for Evening Contemplation

"Through pride, we are ever deceiving ourselves. But deep down below the surface of the average conscience, a still, small voice says to us, something is out of tune." (Carl Jung)

Reflection for Deep Recovery (Sharabi)

When I feel proud that I have gotten myself sober, a still, small voice whispers to me: "Something is out of tune." That is the sacred and gentle voice of humility, of sanity, of God-consciousness. Recovery sometimes leads me to pride and one-upmanship as in: "I can look at myself, but he/she cannot." "I can acknowledge my defects, but he/she always has to be right." "I have a spiritual program, but he/she does not." But pride in myself—pride itself—is suspect, a compensation for low-self esteem: "Don't they know who I think I am?" High self-esteem is always built on a foundation of shame. Hence the phrase heard often in recovery: "egomaniac with an inferiority complex."

"Pride is pleasure arising from a man's thinking too highly of himself."

Spinoza (1632 - 1677)

"Every man has a sane spot somewhere."

Robert Louis Stevenson (1850 - 1894)

Carl Jung
1875 - 1961

a) Quote for Morning Contemplation

"An inflated consciousness is always egocentric and conscious of nothing but its own existence. It is incapable of learning from the past, incapable of understanding contemporary events, and incapable of drawing right conclusions about the future. It is hypnotized by itself and therefore cannot be argued with." (Carl Jung)

Reflection for Deep Recovery (Sharabi)

The alcoholic's consciousness—indeed, the consciousness of the average human being—is full of ego and grandiosity. Grandiosity cannot be argued with; it is the barrier to knowledge and awareness. Be careful of grandiosity aroused by successful abstinence: this is not sobriety. I am wary of the inflated voice in meetings of someone who has been sober a few years and now considers himself or herself an authority. However, I am also aware that when someone's ego is bothering me, it is my own ego that has been aroused to ire.

b) Quote for Evening Contemplation

"The acceptance of oneself is the essence of the whole moral problem and the epitome of a whole outlook on life. The most terrifying thing is to accept oneself completely... I myself am the enemy who must be loved." (Carl Jung)

Reflection for Deep Recovery (Sharabi)

The ultimate goal of recovery is unconditional self-acceptance. Self-love, when it manifests itself as self-acceptance is not a selfish indulgence, but just the refusal to put oneself down, the refusal to beat oneself up, is the beginning of compassion towards the whole universe. In recovery, I must learn to love myself with my character defects as they are, not wait to attain sainthood before I love myself. Only after acknowledging and accepting myself the way I am does change begin. It is not easy to change myself, but my self-acceptance provides favorable conditions for change to happen.

"The courage to Be is the courage to accept oneself in spite of being unacceptable."

Paul Tillich (1886 - 1965)

Carl Jung
1875 - 1961

a) Quote for Morning Contemplation

"The greatest and most important problems of life are all fundamentally insoluble. They can never be solved but only outgrown." (Carl Jung)

Reflection for Deep Recovery (Sharabi)

In recovery, we do not solve the problem of how we react to alcohol. Instead, we outgrow this problem by focusing instead, on the Steps and the principles of correct living. Similarly, I may never completely heal from the traumas of my childhood, but I can outgrow them. Further, I can stop viewing life as a problem to be solved—as a problem that can be solved. My vast and unquenchable need for safety, security, reassurance, and control can never be fulfilled, but it can be transcended—a process Jung refers to as "individuation."

"Trauma is not what happens to you. Trauma is what happens inside you as a result of what happens to you."

Gabor Maté (born 1944)

b) Quote for Evening Contemplation

"Nothing has a stronger influence psychologically on their environment and especially on their children than the unlived life of the parent." (Carl Jung)

Reflection for Deep Recovery (Sharabi)

Many parents want their children to do better than them; this is not unusual. But it puts pressure on the kids to excel, to be extraordinary, and they experience being judged, often found lacking. In recovery, I need to understand that I am staying sober for myself, not to make my parents proud, not to make my teachers and my preachers happy, nor to satisfy my family. If I am getting sober from guilt, at some point, I might be tempted to drink—just to get back them. For guilt usually conceals anger. I also need to examine what pressures I am placing on my own children: whether I am willing just to be present to them and to give them my attention. Then, they can feel loved without conditions and experience the world as safe.

"A Sunday school is a prison in which children do penance for the evil conscience of their parents."

H. L. Mencken (1880 - 1956)

Carl Jung
1875 - 1961

a) Quote for Morning Contemplation

"However, it will not kill your body because it is imaginary. But it will eventually kill your soul."(About a patient who imagines he has cancer) (Carl Jung)

Reflection for Deep Recovery (Sharabi)

Some people say, "I have stopped drinking, but I am sick to the core. I am a liar, a thief, and a cheat. I look in the mirror every day and say, 'There is my problem!' " Such vicious self-hate may not kill my body, but it will eventually kill my soul. I do not accumulate any brownie points in recovery for standing up and publicly proclaiming that I am a terrible person. Indeed, these public declarations of my wretchedness serve as announcements of how honest, repentant, and wonderful I have become—a star in recovery. I do not get brownie points for telling you how horrible I am or how wonderful I am. These are both sicknesses cancers of the soul—and will eventually kill my soul if I persist.

---

b) Quote for Evening Contemplation

"Loneliness does not come from having no people about one, but from being unable to communicate the things that seem important to oneself, or from holding certain views which others find inadmissible." (Carl Jung)

Reflection for Deep Recovery (Sharabi)

Even though we share views on alcoholism, recovery, and life, there will always be things about which my personal perspective will differ from others. I can give myself permission to be different without frantically trying to get them to see my views. I tell myself I am safe and okay alone; I can manage myself socially. If I identify with the great ocean of common goodness this fellowship represents, I will not be so concerned with my views being accepted. I will feel part of a worldwide family even if I am different; the "we" coexisting with the separate "I"s. My communications will be driven by my desire to contribute rather than my need to be seen, appreciated, accepted, or admired.

"People who lead a lonely existence always have something on their minds that they are eager to talk about."
Anton Chekhov (1860 - 1904)

Carl Jung
1875 - 1961

a) Quote for Morning Contemplation

"There can be no transforming of darkness into light and of apathy into movement without emotions." (Carl Jung)

Reflection for Deep Recovery (Sharabi)

Every feeling and emotion—whether light or dark—is a signpost on the path to recovery. It is the numbness we were seeking through drinking that spells death. I must be grateful for and rejoice in every feeling I have, in every emotion I experience, because it declares that I am human, that I have rejoined the human race. All feelings are here merely to provide me with information about my insides; I accept them and treat them as my friends.

"Neuroscience research shows that the only way we can change the way we feel is by becoming aware of our inner experience and learning to befriend what is going on inside ourselves."

Bessel van der Kolk (born 1943)

---

b) Quote for Evening Contemplation

"You are what you do, not what you say you'll do... I am not what happened to me; I am what I choose to become. ... the privilege of a lifetime is to become who you truly are." (Carl Jung)

Reflection for Deep Recovery (Sharabi)

I am not what happened to me in my drinking, nor what happened to me in childhood. I am what I choose to become in sobriety and recovery. I have learned how to respond thoughtfully based on principles I have come across in the program. Earlier I would react mindlessly based on whatever feelings got aroused in me. The greatest thing recovery has taught me about living is that I do not have to go with the first thought or the first impulse that is triggered in me. Recovery has given me the privilege of a lifetime: to be present to my feelings and emotions but, at the same time, not be governed by them; to choose in a deliberate manner how I show up in the world. Here, in recovery, I am judged not by what I did but by who I am trying to be.

"The deeds you do may be the only sermon some persons will hear today."

Saint Francis of Assisi (1181 - 1226)

252

Carl Jung
1875 - 1961

a) Quote for Morning Contemplation

"Nobody, as long as he moves among the chaotic currents of life, is without trouble." (Carl Jung)

Reflection for Deep Recovery (Sharabi)

We have ended up purchasing life "as is;" there are no warranties. It is not true that if I get sober, all my troubles will go away. Yes, I entertained hopes that this would happen, but life is still life. There will be testing times—guaranteed—unless I can arrange to die young. But I now have the resources to deal with these troubles when they appear. And as I work the Steps, my troubles begin to show up merely as things to be handled in the process of living.

"I love the man that can smile in trouble, that can gather strength from distress, and grow brave by reflection."
Thomas Paine (1737 - 1809)

b) Quote for Evening Contemplation

"Where love rules, there is no will to power, and where power predominates, love is lacking. The one is the shadow of the other." (Carl Jung)

Reflection for Deep Recovery (Sharabi)

Power and domination are the polar opposites of love. Those seeking to love will not seek power. To them, God is a Higher Love rather than a Higher Power. Choosing love is how an individual manifests his or her humanity. If I am to love, I must support and protect every person's right to choose for themselves. Getting mad at them for making their choices—any choice—is not love, but power and domination. Sometimes their choices may not be "wise" as I see it, and may be hard to watch, but I cannot treat adults as children. In recovery, I do not try to change others but make space for them to change themselves—if they wish. This is the part that requires constant vigilance: walking away from the urge to advise, control, and dominate others and the world.

"Power intoxicates men. When a man is intoxicated by alcohol, he can recover, but when intoxicated by power, he seldom recovers."
Sappho (620 B.C. - 550 B.C.)

Carl Jung
1875 - 1961

a) Quote for Morning Contemplation

"If there is anything that we wish to change in the child, we should first examine it and see whether it is not something that could better be changed in ourselves." (Carl Jung)

Reflection for Deep Recovery (Sharabi)

The things we are eager to advise the newcomer about are perhaps things we are trying to tell ourselves. The things we want to criticize others for: these are defects we are still struggling with, ourselves. When we feel the urge to change someone, we should resist. We must sit on the urge and not act on it. It will mutate and transform; it will turn into an insight into ourselves.

"Wise men don't need advice. Fools won't take it."
Benjamin Franklin (1706 - 1790)

"Sometimes people say, 'One day you are going to look back at this and laugh.' My question is: why wait?
Richard Bandler (born 1950)

---

b) Quote for Evening Contemplation

"There are as many nights as days, and the one is just as long as the other in the year's course. Even a happy life cannot be without a measure of darkness, and the word 'happy' would lose its meaning if it were not balanced by sadness." (Carl Jung)

Reflection for Deep Recovery (Sharabi)

Serenity does not imply a muted existence. I must not wish to live the rest of my life in a frozen state of existential numbness, even if it appears attractive compared to the wild emotional swings and nights of despair I used to have. Joyful serenity has a place for poignant sadness, which is necessarily part of any full experience in life. I try to experience loss and grieve things, and I can do this with an aliveness that brings texture and taste to life. I must neither worship joy nor be terrified of sadness. Like the poet, I should welcome both and linger in their presence as humanity blossoms in me. I take things as they come along, with patience, humility, and equanimity.

"We should feel sorrow but not sink under its oppression."
Confucius (559 - 459 B.C.)

Carl Jung
1875 - 1961

a) Quote for Morning Contemplation

"Wholeness is not achieved by cutting off a portion of one's being, but by integration of the contraries." (Carl Jung)

Reflection for Deep Recovery (Sharabi)

In recovery, I must focus not just on the goodness and light but must also accept my darkness. I drank in order to forget the parts I was unable to accept; I lied, rationalized, and I justified and defended myself in order to avoid facing all that I really was. But now, all of me is here—the good, the bad, and the ugly; my virtues and my shortcomings—and by accepting and integrating all, I can become whole in recovery. The times I am feeling "bad" provide important clues to the work that remains to be done in recovery. I must not rush out—to the bar or to the meeting—just to get out of there, but I must become curious about what is going on that I am feeling this.

b) Quote for Evening Contemplation

"I have frequently seen people become neurotic when they content themselves with inadequate or wrong answers to the questions of life. They seek position, marriage, reputation, outward success or money, and remain unhappy and neurotic even when they have attained what they were seeking. Such people are usually confined within too narrow a spiritual horizon. Their life has not sufficient content, sufficient meaning." (Carl Jung)

Reflection for Deep Recovery (Sharabi)

In recovery, the ones who define sobriety merely as not drinking remain unhappy and neurotic even when they have attained what they might have sought: position, marriage, reputation, outward signs of success, money, material things, and abstinence. Deep Recovery is truly about seeking a higher spiritual purpose to life; concern about not drinking ceases to be the focus of our existence.

"Life is without meaning. You bring the meaning to it. The meaning of life is whatever you ascribe it to be. Being alive is the meaning."

Joseph Campbell (1904 - 1987)

Carl Jung
1875 - 1961

a) Quote for Morning Contemplation

"As far as we can discern, the sole purpose of human existence is to kindle a light in the darkness of mere being." (Carl Jung)

Reflection for Deep Recovery (Sharabi)

Many of us live in darkenss, just enduring the existence that has been thrust upon us. We claim that drinking is helping us cope. But recovery has shown me the possibility of a higher consciousness, an awakening where life appears not as something to be endured but celebrated.

"Man alone is born crying, lives complaining, and dies disappointed."
Samuel Johnson (1709 - 1784)

"So black was the way ahead that my progress consisted of long periods of inert despondency punctuated by spasmodic lurches forward towards any small chink of light that I thought I saw...As the years went by, it did not get lighter but I became accustomed to the dark"
Quentin Crisp (1908 - 1999)

---

b) Quote for Evening Contemplation

"Don't hold on to someone who's leaving; otherwise you won't meet the one who's coming." (Carl Jung)

Reflection for Deep Recovery (Sharabi)

It is natural to hold on to the familiar, to resist change, to stay with what is comfortable. But recovery calls for the willingness to change, and the change is something I may not fully understand yet, or know exactly where it will lead. "Willing to change" requires a willingness to go wherever it takes me, to let go of things I am clutching. Fortunately, people in the fellowship who have promised to accompany me on this journey give me the courage to change.

"Any time you're going to grow, you're going to lose something. You're losing what you're hanging on to... to keep safe. You're losing habits that you're comfortable with; you're losing familiarity."
James Hillman (1926 - 2011)

"If you want something new, you have to stop doing something old."
Peter Drucker (1909 - 2005)

Gurdjieff
1886 - 1949

a) Quote for Morning Contemplation

"Conscious faith is freedom. Emotional faith is slavery. Mechanical faith is foolishness." (Gurdjieff)

Reflection for Deep Recovery (Sharabi)

Gurdjieff is distinguishing between three types of faith: an awakened faith that comes from enlightened consciousness, a faith motivated by emotions like fear and anxiety, and an archaic faith that originates in mechanical stupidity. Recovery encourages thoughtful self-examination—seeing, not closing my eyes. Blind faith can provide temporary comfort, just like alcohol, but is untenable as a basis for long-term recovery. Even as a newcomer, awakened faith is what will liberate me from the grip of this disease.

"We are all born ignorant, but one must work hard to remain stupid."
Benjamin Franklin (1706 - 1790)

---

b) Quote for Evening Contemplation

"It is very difficult also to sacrifice one's suffering. A man will renounce any pleasures you like, but he will not give up his suffering." (Gurdjieff)

Reflection for Deep Recovery (Sharabi)

Alcoholics have become used to misery and suffering. The suffering in my life served some curious purpose; sometimes, it provided a familiar structure and generated a sense of martyrdom and victimhood. I was invested in believing that I had been wronged, that I had "problems." I was not willing suddenly to drop the suffering and the complaining and say: "I am happy!" Happiness can feel empty and precarious to someone used to misery. Perhaps we can reassure them that there will be challenges and suffering in recovery—indeed, in life.

"Why do we focus so intensely on our problems? What draws us to them? Why are they so attractive? What would a life be without them? Completely tranquilized and loveless... There is a secret love hiding in each problem."
James Hillman (1926 - 2011)

Gurdjieff
1886 - 1949

a) Quote for Morning Contemplation

"Awakening is possible only for those who seek it and want it, for those who are ready to struggle with themselves and work on themselves for a very long time and very persistently in order to attain it." (Gurdjieff)

Reflection for Deep Recovery (Sharabi)

Recovery is a long, engrossing journey, an awakening into consciousness. Everything else recedes into the background in the presence of this huge and sanctifying mission. In fact, recovery and spiritual awakening become the purpose of living, become life itself. I could content myself just with not drinking, going to meetings, and helping other alcoholics. These are fine, but this is just a doorway on the journey of awakening—which I seek and for which I am willing to struggle with myself and work on myself for a very long time, with persistence (as Gurdjieff states.) And once I attain the awakened state, I will begin to see things as they are, not through my desires and distortions.

---

b) Quote for Evening Contemplation

"Man has no individual i. But there are, instead, hundreds and thousands of separate small "i"s, very often entirely unknown to one another, never coming into contact, or, on the contrary, hostile to each other, mutually exclusive and incompatible. Each minute, each moment, man is saying or thinking, "i." And each time his i is different: just now it was a thought, now it is a desire, now a sensation, now another thought, and so on, endlessly. Man is a plurality." (Gurdjieff)

Reflection for Deep Recovery (Sharabi)

"Who I am" is an entity that is constantly emerging each moment, only to disappear immediately. Each day is a new day different from past days; each instant is new and has to be lived afresh. The resentments and anxieties of yesterday do not need to reappear today. Everything is in passage. When the static "i" disappears, there is freedom and vitality.

"Life isn't about finding yourself. Life is about creating yourself."

George Bernard Shaw (1856 - 1950)

Gurdjieff
1886 - 1949

a) Quote for Morning Contemplation

"Two things in life are infinite; the stupidity of man and the mercy of God." (Gurdjieff)

Reflection for Deep Recovery (Sharabi)

I am assured that the stupidity I displayed is not uncommon among man and that forgiveness and exoneration are possible, given God's infinite mercy and generosity. It is only we humans who are unforgiving—of ourselves and of others. We nurture our resentments, and we keep alive the embers of self-hate. Recovery gently turns us around: let go, let go, let go... and let God. We are completely forgiven on this path to a new wholeness.

"If you never condemned, you would never need to forgive."
Anthony DeMello (1931 - 1997)

"Perhaps we've never been visited by aliens because they have looked upon Earth and decided there's no sign of intelligent life."
Neil deGrasse Tyson (born 1958)

b) Quote for Evening Contemplation

"I will tell you one thing that will make you rich for life. There are two struggles: an Inner-world struggle and an Outer-world struggle... you must make an intentional contact between these two worlds; then you can crystallize data for the Third World, the World of the Soul." (Gurdjieff)

Reflection for Deep Recovery (Sharabi)

The inner struggle with my feelings and emotions, and the pursuit of serenity, and the outer struggle around my finances, job, situation in life, and other worldly issues: these are often in conflict. Our struggle is to reconcile the tension between these, and to manage them and bring them together, to generate growth that makes us soulful and deep. Therefore, we welcome the struggle(s) that life poses. This struggle provides data for the journey of the Soul, which is what recovery is. In recovery, we live simultaneously on these three different planes. The first ten Steps address our outer world struggles and our inner world struggles, but the Eleventh Step is the entry to the World of the Soul. Once we get here, the path feels like no struggle.

Gurdjieff
1886 - 1949

a) Quote for Morning Contemplation

"Common aim is stronger than blood." (Gurdjieff)

Reflection for Deep Recovery (Sharabi)

That is why my recovery family is, in many ways, stronger than my blood family. My recovery family understands me better, accepts me more readily, criticizes me less, offers me insights for growth, and creates fewer problems. The fellowship of recovery gives me love, and through that, the strength to love and support my blood family.

b) Quote for Evening Contemplation

"I ask you to believe nothing that you cannot verify for yourself." (Gurdjieff)

Reflection for Deep Recovery (Sharabi)

Once you look back at your own life, you will see that your experience with alcohol verifies what people in recovery are saying: yes, you are indeed powerless over alcohol after that first drink, and yes, unless you commit to a spiritual approach to living, you will go back to drinking. But the disease itself wants you to ignore your experience and go back to drinking. If you do, it will serve to verify the truth, but you must understand that you can destroy yourself in the process of verification: it is dangerous territory. So maybe our stories will convince you so you can spare yourself further experimentation? Think with an open mind of the things we are telling you, but watch out that it is your own thinking as opposed to the disease using your thinking for its own ends.

"Take the risk of thinking for yourself; much more happiness, truth, beauty, and wisdom will come to you that way."

Christopher Hitchens (1949 - 2011)

Gurdjieff
1886 - 1949

a) Quote for Morning Contemplation

"Remember you come here having already understood the necessity of struggling with yourself — only with yourself. Therefore, thank everyone who gives you the opportunity." (Gurdjieff)

Reflection for Deep Recovery (Sharabi)

My struggle is not with people; my struggle is with my reactions. Recovery is, ultimately, a struggle with myself. And we are all sanctified by this struggle. Rather than complaining about the struggle, I see that it purifies me, makes me grow, takes me beyond. I should thank the people who have given me a hard time in life, made me struggle with myself, and provided this opportunity to grow.

" ...the redeeming things (in life) are not happiness and pleasure but the deeper satisfactions that come out of struggle."

F. Scott Fitzgerald (1896 - 1940)

---

b) Quote for Evening Contemplation

"Knowledge can be acquired by a suitable and complete study, no matter what the starting point is. Only one must know how to 'learn.' What is nearest to us is man, and you are the nearest of all men to yourself. Begin with the study of yourself; remember the saying 'Know thyself.' " (Gurdjieff)

Reflection for Deep Recovery (Sharabi)

In recovery, I will meet and study a very interesting individual, fascinating to know and understand—myself. I will begin to know myself but not as the drunken fool that emerged from the bar, nor the enraged coward nor the petty and self-centered knot of problems, the pitiful creature that alcohol had reduced me to. Yes, in recovery, the real me emerges. I will "Know myself" beyond my selfish dreams, beyond my miserly fears and hopes, beyond my scared attempts to gather things and people and clutch them to myself. My instrument in this study is humility; without it, the world will always be distorted.

"Remember always that you have not only the right to be an individual, but an obligation to be one... It's your life—but only if you make it so."

Eleanor Roosevelt (1884 - 1962)

261

Gurdjieff
1886 - 1949

a) Quote for Morning Contemplation

"Religion is doing; a man does not merely think his religion or feel it. He lives his religion as much as he is able. Otherwise, it is not religion but fantasy or philosophy. Whether he likes it or not, he shows his attitude towards religion by his actions, and he can show his attitude only by his actions." (Gurdjieff)

Reflection for Deep Recovery (Sharabi)

Recovery stresses choices over feelings; action over concerns, desires, fears, and resentments. The Steps are relevant only so far as I incorporate the principles into daily living. I have been taught that gratitude is not something to be felt but something to be shown. Our religion is gratitude, humility, and goodness, manifesting in action—not just in philosophy or in theology.

"One's philosophy is not best expressed in words; it is expressed in the choices one makes."

Eleanor Roosevelt (1884 - 1962)

---

b) Quote for Evening Contemplation

"Let us take some event in the life of humanity—for instance, war. There is a war going on at the present moment. What does it signify? It signifies that several millions of sleeping people are trying to destroy several millions of other sleeping people. They would not do this, of course, if they were to wake up. Everything that takes place is owing to this sleep." (Gurdjieff)

Reflection for Deep Recovery (Sharabi)

In my drinking life, I was in a trance. It seems that most people go through life in a trance; recovery is a commitment to waking up. Recovery represents the largest community of people in the world who are pursuing "awakening." We can no longer indulge in the kinds of behavior that "sleeping" people do, many of which might be considered "normal" by outside society. We are living to a higher standard, marching to a heavenly music, and we have a responsibility to live conscious and thoughtful lives. And awakening is not an "event." Awakening is an ongoing process, pursued with persistence each day, for it is possible for me to fall asleep on any given day, at any time.

Gurdjieff
1886 - 1949

a) Quote for Morning Contemplation

"It is impossible to recognize a wrong way without knowing the right way." (Gurdjieff)

Reflection for Deep Recovery (Sharabi)

Sometimes it is not clear to me what is right. In those moments, I can ask myself: what could not possibly be "wrong?" If I am sitting in the parking lot of the church on a Friday night wondering whether to go join my friends at the bar for a good time or walk into the recovery meeting that is about to start, I can just ask myself: "Could this be wrong? What could not be wrong?" In this exploration, my instrument is humility—not power, not grandiosity, not self-will.

"Half of the harm that is done in this world is due to people who want to feel important."

T. S. Eliot (1888 - 1965)

---

b) Quote for Evening Contemplation

"Man lies to himself a lot." (Gurdjieff)

Reflection for Deep Recovery (Sharabi)

How often did the chattering monkey inside my head say: "I'm going to quit drinking... tomorrow!" But Gurdjieff is referring not just to alcoholics but to humans in general. The CEO of our brain is constantly offering press releases that are lies. It is not always easy to see them as such, but the decision to be honest with ourselves elevates us from common humanity. We are held to higher standards in recovery. We commit to such honesty that we can no longer continue fooling ourselves the way we did to keep drinking, and the way a lot of humanity does—and gets away with. My job here is to be honest with myself, not to confront others about their dishonesty. Only they get to decide when they will become honest with themselves. When I stop pushing my standards on others, the relationships in my life will improve dramatically.

"The truth will not necessarily set you free, but truthfulness will."

Ken Wilber (born 1949)

Gurdjieff
1886 - 1949

a) Quote for Morning Contemplation

"A man can keep silence in such a way that no one will even notice it. The whole point is that we say a good deal too much. If we limited ourselves to what is actually necessary, this alone would be keeping the silence." (Gurdjieff)

Reflection for Deep Recovery (Sharabi)

Silence makes people anxious. So they talk a lot, or they drink, or they drink and talk (to others or to themselves.) Alcohol is a way of avoiding contact with myself; true internal silence is necessary for contact with myself—and with God. I can gain by just being silent in a meeting; indeed, I do not even have to listen to the words. I can simply breathe the recovery air—lots of pure molecules from sober lungs—and I will have a new experience of the sacredness of meetings, a new sense of Godliness.

"Don't talk unless you can improve the silence."

Jorge Luis Borges (1899 - 1986)

---

b) Quote for Evening Contemplation

"In properly organized groups, no faith is required; what is required is simply a little trust and even that only for a little while, for the sooner a man begins to verify all he hears, the better it is for him." (Gurdjieff)

Reflection for Deep Recovery (Sharabi)

In recovery, I do not necessarily have to have faith in God, but I have to trust the process of recovery as outlined in the Steps and practiced in the fellowship. This is the simplest requirement: trust the process! And as I experience things improving, I will be able to verify all I am hearing. I am being asked to believe only in the beginning; after that, my data will verify the effectiveness of this program. For some of us, all that is required is to believe that these people mean well, that they are not out to fool me or take something from me, or get me to commit to their cult for their benefit.

"We can't have full knowledge all at once. We must start by believing; then afterwards, we may be led on to master the evidence for ourselves."

Thomas Aquinas (1224 - 1274)

264

Gurdjieff
1886 - 1949

a) Quote for Morning Contemplation

"A man may be born, but in order to be born, he must first die, and in order to die, he must first awake." (Gurdjieff)

Reflection for Deep Recovery (Sharabi)

Recovery is about dying to the old life of addiction and being reborn into sobriety. Gurdjieff distinguishes between having life and actually being alive—between existing and actually living. We must awaken to our powerlessness and to how unmanageable our life—and our lifestyle—has become. Then we surrender to this program of recovery; we die willingly. Our egotistical self is sacrificed. And then—and only then—are we born into our new form: sober alcoholics pursuing sanity and an awakened life.

"I exist, that is all, and I find it nauseating... It is up to you (me/us) to give [life] a meaning... Freedom is what we do with what is done to us... We are our choices"

Composite quote from Jean-Paul Sartre (1905 - 1980)

---

b) Quote for Evening Contemplation

"Death must come before rebirth. But what must die? False confidence in one's own knowledge, self-love, and egoism." (Gurdjieff)

Reflection for Deep Recovery (Sharabi)

Recovery tells me I must let go completely rather than hang on to my old ideas. And my self-love—manifesting as self-centeredness, false pride, grandiosity, and an air of "knowing it all"— must be replaced by humility. Finally, egotistic thoughts and perspectives must be banished; the "I" must be replaced by a "We." Recovery is the process of dying and being reborn: dying to isolation and being reborn to fellowship and community.

"Wine gives a man nothing... it only puts in motion what had been locked up in frost. It makes a man mistake words for thoughts. Wine makes a man more pleased with himself; I do not say it makes him more pleasing to others. I have no objection to a man's drinking wine if he can do it in moderation. I found myself apt to go to excess in it, and therefore... I thought it better not to return to it. Every man is to judge for himself, according to the effects which he experiences.
(written or said around 1760!)

Samuel Johnson (1709 - 1784)

Gurdjieff
1886 - 1949

a) Quote for Morning Contemplation

"Man such as we know him is a machine." (Gurdjieff)

Reflection for Deep Recovery (Sharabi)

As an alcoholic, I was a machine. The moment I felt the itch, I scratched. Anytime the slightest discomfort or unpleasant sensation appeared, I reached for a drink. When criticized, I flew into a rage or was completely crushed (or both.) When someone questioned anything, I would automatically explain, justify, and defend myself. If I felt uncomfortable around somebody, I decided I disliked them. These automatic patterns constituted my character defects. In fact, acting by my feelings and desires—even my thoughts—amounts to behaving like a machine. For I don't really "choose" my feelings, thoughts, or wants; they just show up, uninvited, and I am whipped around by them. Recovery is the attempt to change myself from such a mindless machine into an awakened person who engages in self-examination and chooses actions intentionally—not just on feelings, desires, impulses, or first thoughts, all of which arise on their own.

b) Quote for Evening Contemplation

"Without self-knowledge, without understanding the working and functions of his machine, man cannot be free, he cannot govern himself, and he will always remain a slave." (Gurdjieff)

Reflection for Deep Recovery (Sharabi)

All my life, I have been a slave to reactions rising in me. That was a machine-like response, requiring no thought, no choice, and no processing. I did not have self-knowledge—that these reactions were based on my past wounds and the defenses I had invented to deal with challenges I faced. Today, I realize that people "show up" in my life based on my attitude and posture towards them. The stories and commentary I have created about them and the world constitute my "reality." Can I change it? Can I approach each person with a welcome, supporting, and appreciative posture? Can I have sympathy and compassion for his or her struggle? "Liking" someone—anyone—and appreciating their complexity is a choice that I can make at any moment. It does not merely have to be the passive reporting of a reaction that arose spontaneously in me.

"When you meet anyone, remember it is a holy encounter."

Course in Miracles (1976)

Gurdjieff
1886 - 1949

a) Quote for Morning Contemplation

"It is very difficult to explain what takes place in me when I see or hear anything majestic, which allows no doubt that it proceeds from the actualization of Our Maker Creator. Each time, my tears flow of themselves. I weep, that is to say, it weeps in me, not from grief, no, but as if from tenderness." (Gurdjieff)

Reflection for Deep Recovery (Sharabi)

A sense of awe that I feel when I see anything majestic like a huge mountain, or the vast sea, or the myriad stars of the sky, or when I witness a new life being born—that sense of awe that moves me and can bring me to tears—that is the opening through which I experience God as the source of magnificence in the universe.

"It was morning; through the high window I saw the pure, bright blue of the sky as it hovered cheerfully over the long roofs of the neighboring houses. It too seemed full of joy, as if it had special plans and had put on its finest clothes for the occasion."

Hermann Hesse (1877 - 1962)

---

b) Quote for Evening Contemplation

"He can be called a remarkable man who stands out from those around him by the resourcefulness of his mind, and who knows how to be restrained in the manifestations which proceed from his nature, at the same time conducting himself justly and tolerantly towards the weaknesses of others." (Gurdjieff)

Reflection for Deep Recovery (Sharabi)

I must be restrained in expressing my natural tendency to judge, criticize, and condemn—others and myself. My first thought is a default reaction, often based on a misreading of the situation; it is usually (always?) wrong, and I should not honor that first thought. When someone does not think as I do, does not conform to the way they "should" be, my limbic brain panics. In recovery, I must discredit the criticisms and judgments that spontaneously pop up in my head and recommit to acceptance: to treat others justly and with tolerance and myself with compassion.

"Compassion for others is not a simple virtue because it avoids snap judgments of right or wrong, good or bad, hero or villain: It seeks truth in all its complexity."

Brennan Manning (1934 -2013)

Gurdjieff
1886 - 1949

a) Quote for Morning Contemplation

**"If you want to lose your faith, make friends with a priest."
(Gurdjieff)**

Reflection for Deep Recovery (Sharabi)

Recovery proposes direct contact with a "God of my understanding," not contact through an intermediary. The God of my parents or the God of my priest cannot get me sober. What is required is a spiritual experience that brings me in direct contact with the sublime, the mysterious, and the transcendent. Gurdjieff is advocating against people who claim to be "men of God." He was a strong believer in a personal awakening, as opposed to mindless subservience to people in authority and to books, to succumbing to dogma and doctrine.

"The priest is an immense being because he makes the crowd believe astonishing things."

Charles Baudelaire (1821 - 1867)

---

b) Quote for Evening Contemplation

"Sincerity is the key which will open the door... You must go on trying to be sincere. Each day you put on a mask, and you must take it off little by little." (Gurdjieff)

Reflection for Deep Recovery (Sharabi)

Each day, I have become used to putting on suitable masks as I prepare to meet the outside world. The masks come from concern that I am inadequate for the task at hand, that my authentic self is unacceptable and defective, and that I have to hide who I truly am. I am portraying myself as better than I am. Fear is at the root and arises from the notion that the world is unsafe. But as I progress in recovery, I feel safer, and the mask wears away; more of the real me begins showing. Sincerity is the key to making this happen over time—a combination of authenticity, simplicity, and integrity. When I accept myself, there is nothing I need to hide from others or myself. I will honor myself as I am, and I will also see qualities in others that are worthy of honor as they are.

"If you spend your life sparing people's feelings and feeding their vanity, you get so you can't distinguish what should be respected in them."

F. Scott Fitzgerald (1896 - 1940)

Gurdjieff
1886 - 1949

a) Quote for Morning Contemplation

"Only help him who is not an idler." (Gurdjieff)

Reflection for Deep Recovery (Sharabi)

People in recovery are willing to help those who have a sincere desire to stop drinking. In fact, we will go out of our way. But those who come here unwilling and disgruntled, forced by some family or legal pressure—those who come expecting us to cure them or solve their problems—we welcome them to sit and listen, but we cannot help them until they are willing to get up and begin the effort. There is no "treatment" for the disease; in other words, no cure that can be delivered to a passive "I." What was offered to me was training to keep me sober, and I was welcome to join them and train with them. Thirty years later, I am still training with them.

"In short, the important thing is to get started, no matter how; then there will be time to ask yourself where you are going."

Emile Charlier (1868 - 1951)

b) Quote for Evening Contemplation

"Here there are neither Russians nor English, Jews nor Christians, but only those who pursue one aim — to be able to be." (Gurdjieff)

Reflection for Deep Recovery (Sharabi)

" ... able to be," or "Being," as defined by Gurdjieff here, is not merely passive existence; it is an awakened consciousness attained through an effort of mind, body, and soul. It equates to the spiritual awakening that can occur as the result of the Steps. "Being" is available to every human consciousness that is willing to work for it. So whatever background I come from—however I choose to identify myself—I understand that we are all here to pursue one aim: an awakening. Sobriety is a by-product of working the Steps and focusing on spiritual growth, on awakening, but this awakening extends far beyond sobriety.

"Times are difficult globally; awakening is no longer a luxury or an ideal. It's becoming critical. We don't need to add more depression, more discouragement, or more anger to what's already here... The earth seems to be beseeching us to connect with joy and discover our innermost essence."

Pema Chödrön (born 1936)

Gurdjieff
1886 - 1949

a) Quote for Morning Contemplation

"By teaching others, you will learn yourself. (Gurdjieff)

Reflection for Deep Recovery (Sharabi)

I will learn much about my own sobriety through working with the new person; this is a crucial ingredient of the program. It is not sufficient just to be willing to help others; I must actually seek people out. And I must seek them out, but not to lecture them about the program or their character defects, or what to do and how to be. Instead, I must listen and help them discover who they really are. Life has beaten them, distorted their view of themselves, taught them to beat themselves up. For some, drinking became a way of punishing themselves. Here, by teaching them to accept themselves, I will learn to accept myself.

"We teach best what we need to learn."

Richard Bach (born 1936)

---

b) Quote for Evening Contemplation

"A man is never the same for long. He is continually changing. He seldom remains the same even for half an hour." (Gurdjieff)

Reflection for Deep Recovery (Sharabi)

By this count, within a recovery meeting lasting an hour, a man—or woman—must have changed at least twice in some way. This is a program of change. Stopping drinking is a big "change," but we are not talking about that here. Instead, we are talking about the constant and persistent change required to develop into full and awakened human beings. There is no point going to a meeting and listening with those same old ears that have heard it all before, expressing stale ideas, and recycling comments, and leaving unchanged. In every meeting, I must notice the humanity and vulnerability of people, hear something new, realize something fresh, and allow myself to be moved. I go to each meeting looking to be altered in some way by what I encounter there. Cultivating the ability to be touched and moved—intellectually and emotionally—is a fundamental requirement for recovery.

Martin Buber
1878 - 1965

a) Quote for Morning Contemplation

"Journeys have secret destinations of which the traveler is unaware." (Martin Buber)

Reflection for Deep Recovery (Sharabi)

I came here to stop drinking and to get out of my difficulties. But I am staying here now for different reasons—larger reasons. My spiritual journey has taken on a life of its own and is leading me to destinations I had never imagined.

"The real treasure, that which we all seek, is never very far... , for it lies buried within our own hearts. And yet, there is this strange and persistent fact that it is only after a journey in a distant region, in a new land, that the way to that treasure becomes clear."

Heinrich Zimmer (1890 - 1943)

"One's destination is never a place but rather a new way of looking at things."

Henry Miller (1891 - 1980)

b) Quote for Evening Contemplation

"When two people relate to each other authentically and humanly, God is the electricity that surges between them." (Martin Buber)

Reflection for Deep Recovery (Sharabi)

There is no experience more affirming than that of one alcoholic being present authentically and fully with another—indeed, one human with another. What happens in that moment of contact and connection between two people is sacred. Buber refers to that electric thrill of the breakdown of the ego-boundary as a taste of God. God manifests as relatedness. While we cannot set out directly to "conquer" ego, we can attempt to relate authentically with our fellows. Recovery stresses community and commonality: the "we" of the fellowship over the individualism rampant in modern society, which says you can get sober by pulling yourself up by your bootstraps. Hence the importance of anonymity as the spiritual foundation of recovery, the idea that "we" get sober collectively, and the value of working one-on-one with another alcoholic.

Martin Buber
1878 - 1965

a) Quote for Morning Contemplation

**"The atheist staring from his attic window is often nearer to God than the believer caught up in his own false image of God."
(Martin Buber)**

Reflection for Deep Recovery (Sharabi)

The atheist who is living a principled and observant life and staring quietly from his attic window in an attitude of contemplative silence is closer to God than the loud and strident believer screaming his ideas about God from the rooftops.

"I think being an atheist is something you are, not something you do."
Christopher Hitchens (1949 - 2011)

"Atheism represents a concept of life without any metaphysical Beyond or Divine Regulator... an actual, real world with its liberating, expanding and beautifying possibilities, against an unreal world with its spirits, oracles, and mean contentment which has kept humanity in helpless degradation.
Emma Goldman (1869 - 1940)

---

b) Quote for Evening Contemplation

**"Everyone must come out of his Exile in his own way."
(Martin Buber)**

Reflection for Deep Recovery (Sharabi)

My drinking life was a self-imposed sentence of exile from normal humanity. Others could not get me sober; I had to acquire that desire in my own way, and I had to find my own path out of that hole, even though there were many willing to give me a hand. Deciding to become sober is a deep and lonely decision of the heart, and even that decision is often not sufficient. I need the Steps and the fellowship to craft a path for me out of the hole.

"Every person's life is worth a novel."
Erving Polster (born 1922)
(... or at least a chapter at the end of the Big Book!)

Martin Buber
1878 - 1965

a) Quote for Morning Contemplation

"... what is required is a deed that a man does with his whole being." (Martin Buber)

Reflection for Deep Recovery (Sharabi)

Total surrender and commitment are required for recovery: I need to jump in with my whole being, not hold anything back. I must give completely to this simple program. Half-measures will avail me nothing. And, how fully I have given myself is not measured just by how many meetings I attend. It is measured by how completely I embrace this path and incorporate these spiritual principles into my daily behavior. Recovery must enter into my bones.

"As soon as you learn to never give up, you have to learn the power and wisdom of unconditional surrender, and that one doesn't cancel out the other; they just exist as contradictions. The wisdom of it comes as you get older."

Kris Kristofferson (born 1936)

b) Quote for Evening Contemplation

"All real living is meeting." (Martin Buber)

Reflection for Deep Recovery (Sharabi)

Living occurs in the meetings and in the conversations I have with people; all else is internal fantasy and preparation. What are the conversations I am currently having? Not the ones in my head—I mean the real conversations with live people? That is what defines me. Conversation with others includes the words I say as well as the actions I do that impact others. I am defined by my interactions, the places where I meet others, not my intentions.

"The meeting of two personalities is like the contact of two chemical substances: if there is any reaction, both are transformed."

Carl Jung (1875 - 1961)

Martin Buber
1878 - 1965

a) Quote for Morning Contemplation

"The world is not comprehensible, but it is embraceable: through the embracing of one of its beings." (Martin Buber)

Reflection for Deep Recovery (Sharabi)

Life is not something to be understood; it is something to be embraced. The fellowship exists because alcoholics embrace each other and, through this community, embrace life. Let me learn to embrace my fellow alcoholic instead of trying to comprehend how recovery works.

"Lord... grant that I may not so much seek
to be consoled as to console,
to be understood as to understand,
to be loved, as to love."

Saint Francis of Assisi (1181 - 1226)

---

b) Quote for Evening Contemplation

"Solitude is the place of purification." (Martin Buber)

Reflection for Deep Recovery (Sharabi)

You hear recovery talk of how it is dangerous to isolate oneself. The individual in solitary confinement without the benefit of interaction and feedback from others can end up with very distorted views and in a very perverted reality. The community is especially important to the new person. However, in Deep Recovery, the spiritual value of spending time with myself—maybe taking a walk in the woods or spending time in meditation— becomes very real. Meditation is the practice of isolating myself from my chattering mind, taking a much-needed respite from the constant judging, opining, criticizing, and raging that this voice in my head is doing all the time, taking time just to be.

"Your solitude will be a support and a home for you, even in the midst of very unfamiliar circumstances, and from it, you will find all your paths."

Rainer Maria Rilke (1875 - 1926)

Martin Buber
1878 - 1965

a) Quote for Morning Contemplation

"You can rake the muck this way, rake the muck that way—it will always be muck. Have I sinned, or have I not sinned? In the time I am brooding over it, I could be stringing pearls for the delight of Heaven." (Martin Buber)

Reflection for Deep Recovery (Sharabi)

People told me that I had been spending all my time thinking about myself. Now I spend my time thinking about how self-absorbed I am. It doesn't feel like much of an improvement. Self-examination can easily become an extension of self-centeredness. Talking about my self-centeredness is a further form of self-absorption. Thinking about what others need—now, that is an answer to self-absorption.

"A man wrapped up in himself makes a very small bundle."
Benjamin Franklin (1706 - 1790)

---

b) Quote for Evening Contemplation

"I do not accept any absolute formulas for living. No preconceived code can see ahead to everything that can happen in a man's life. As we live, we grow, and our beliefs change. They must change. So I think we should live with this constant discovery. We should be open to this adventure in heightened awareness of living." (Martin Buber)

Reflection for Deep Recovery (Sharabi)

"Willing to change" means I must be flexible and allow who I am to emerge fresh based on the needs of the moment. I must give up the notion of "who I am" based on historical stories. I am a living, breathing, responsive aliveness, not a cold and frozen rigidity. I am not the same person I was a year ago or even yesterday. The program also breathes and changes constantly, depending on where I am, where each of us is. I cannot use the same frozen lines of a book to tell me how to behave in all situations. Life is being created constantly.

"The task is not to see what has never been seen before, but to think what has never been thought before about what you see every day."
Erwin Schrödinger (1887 - 1961)

Martin Buber
1878 - 1965

a) Quote for Morning Contemplation

"When people come to you for help, do not turn them off with pious words, saying, 'Have faith and take your troubles to God.' Act instead as though there were no God, as though there were only one person in the world who could help, only yourself."
(Martin Buber)

Reflection for Deep Recovery (Sharabi)

When someone comes to me for help, I must not just tell him or her to go away and pray, nor must I offer editorial comments about their situation. There is value in just listening without providing any solutions. I must stay involved as if I am the last person on this planet, the last one they can go to for help, the only one who has a shot at helping them.

"On the outskirts of every agony sits some observant fellow who points."
Virginia Woolf (1882 - 1941)

---

b) Quote for Evening Contemplation

"When we see a great man desiring power instead of his real goal, we soon recognize that he is sick, or more precisely that his attitude to his work is sick." (Martin Buber)

Reflection for Deep Recovery (Sharabi)

There are many who are attempting to give and to help others in recovery. Some of these attempts arise from humility and generosity, but in some, it may be a hidden desire for public esteem and power originating in the ego. How do I tell the difference? Simple. The ego gets annoyed and angry if its ideas are not accepted, but the humble servant will feel no anger if his/ her ideas are rejected—maybe disappointment, maybe sorrow, but not anger. Power, fame, and respect are sought by people as compensation for lack of inner grounding. I must examine how I react when my "advice" is not taken, when my attempts to play "director," are rebuffed.

"The ego is not master in its own house."
Sigmund Freud (1856 - 1939)

Martin Buber
1878 - 1965

a) Quote for Morning Contemplation

"A person cannot approach the divine by reaching beyond the human. To become human is what this individual person has been created for." (Martin Buber)

Reflection for Deep Recovery (Sharabi)

I must not seek to be among the Gods but must have compassion for my own imperfections, my own fallibility, my own humanness. At the end-point of recovery lies not a sober saint but a simple and sincere human with many flaws who is being contemplative and seeking progress, not perfection. My recovery is about returning to the human race. And if I develop this compassionate attitude towards myself, I will uncover my compassion towards others.

"There is no need to be perfect, but are you a constant striving to be better. That is all that matters."

Sadhguru (born 1957)

b) Quote for Evening Contemplation

"The origin of all conflict between me and my fellow-men is that I do not say what I mean and I don't do what I say." (Martin Buber)

Reflection for Deep Recovery (Sharabi)

Authenticity, Integrity, Kindness, and Generosity are the Four Essentials of sobriety. Recovery requires us to be consistent and disciplined in practicing these virtues. Authenticity is saying what I mean, and Integrity is doing what I say. Kindness is looking at myself and others with soft eyes, and Generosity is the willingness to give time and attention to others. The Essentials represent the Truth about me, point to the essence of me. Integrity is about living a life consistent with who I am. How I treat others is entirely up to me, based on my values. I do not have to treat others the way they have treated me, nor do I expect others to treat me the way I would treat them. They are entirely free and autonomous creatures. They do not have to live by my values. This way, I will be free of resentment. It is not my place to teach them these essentials; those values are only for me; they are between my God and me.

Martin Buber
1878 - 1965

a) Quote for Morning Contemplation

"God is the *mysterium tremendum* that appears and overthrows, but he is also the mystery of the self-evident, nearer to me than my I." (Martin Buber)

Reflection for Deep Recovery (Sharabi)

Mysterium tremendum is a Latin phrase referring to a mystery that inspires awe and trembling. God can be revealed in such a spiritual awakening that terrifies us and overthrows our perspective. But God is also revealed in the simplicity and beauty of existence as pure Presence. He is even closer to me than the awareness of myself. Awareness of God comes first; it is there as the backdrop to my awareness of self. Consciousness itself comes first, prior to the consciousness of the self, or consciousness of anything. God is the ultimate riddle, and I keep coming to meetings to solve this riddle; in the process, I stay sober.

---

b) Quote for Evening Contemplation

"When a human being turns to another as another, as a particular and specific person to be addressed, and tries to communicate with him through language or silence, something takes place between them which is not found elsewhere in nature." (Martin Buber)

Reflection for Deep Recovery (Sharabi)

The central aspect of the recovery program is not the Steps; it is one alcoholic working with another. We cannot be concerned about alcoholics in general: only particular alcoholics. It is in our one-on-one work with other alcoholics—talking with them or just being with them—that we encounter something deep and special that is not found anywhere else in nature. And this special connectedness, this profound relatedness, is what recovery is based upon. If you do not see this and know this, you might merely be watching recovery, not participating in it. Your growth in recovery is measured by how related you feel to each person in recovery, to each person in this world.

"It is easier to love humanity as a whole than to love one's neighbor."
Eric Hoffer (1898 - 1983)

278

Martin Buber
1878 - 1965

a) Quote for Morning Contemplation

"Everything depends on the teacher as a man, as a person. He educates from himself, from his virtues and his faults, through personal example and according to circumstances and conditions. His task is to realize the truth in his personality and to convey this realization to the pupil." (Martin Buber)

Reflection for Deep Recovery (Sharabi)

The sponsor must present himself to his sponsees as a human—as a humble, imperfect and thoughtful alcoholic trying to live an examined life—not as a demi-God or as a wise and perfect master. This way, the truth about recovery is transmitted by personal connection, through sharing and revealing how he is without pride or apology, modeling self-acceptance. The sponsor does not try to change the pupil; rather, he helps the pupil apply his or her own unique personality, talents, and strength to the task at hand: the monumental task of changing his own outlook and attitude on life, just as the sponsor has himself done.

b) Quote for Evening Contemplation

"The teacher must... not know him as a mere sum of qualities, strivings, and inhibitions; he must be aware of him as a whole being and affirm him in this wholeness." (Martin Buber)

Reflection for Deep Recovery (Sharabi)

The sponsor must be aware of the sponsee as a whole being, not merely as a collection of qualities, desires, and frustrated dreams. He must affirm this wholeness in the person he sees before him. Total respect for the sponsee is the first requirement for being a sponsor for it is through this that the newcomer meets himself or herself, recovers himself or herself. If I cannot be this for the new person, I should be careful about accepting the responsibility of sponsorship. There may be work I need to do on myself, first.

"Correction does much, but encouragement does more."

Goethe (1749 - 1832)

"If you go looking for a friend, you're going to find they're very scarce. If you go out to be a friend, you'll find them everywhere."

Zig Ziglar (1926 - 2012)

Martin Buber
1878 - 1965

a) Quote for Morning Contemplation

"What has to be given up is not the I but that false drive for self-affirmation, which impels man to flee from the... world of relations into the having of things." (Martin Buber)

Reflection for Deep Recovery (Sharabi)

When we talk about conquering ego, we do not mean giving up the sense of "I," but of giving up the drive for fame, recognition, and admiration—for I-affirmation. This drive takes me to concern about how others see me, to valuing reputation, and to the accumulation of things as symbols of success in order to cover up an essential hollowness. I relate to the person in front of me on three different planes simultaneously: (1) ego to ego (I - It) seeking affirmation; (2) person to person (I - Thou) seeking to accept; and (3) divine Beings connected (We) transcending separateness.

"Quantum physics thus reveals a basic oneness of the universe."
Erwin Schrödinger (1887 - 1961)

---

b) Quote for Evening Contemplation

"Some would deny any legitimate use of the word God because it has been misused so much. Certainly, it is the most burdened of all human words. Precisely for that reason, it is the most imperishable and unavoidable." (Martin Buber)

Reflection for Deep Recovery (Sharabi)

Everyone who mentions "God" in a recovery meeting probably means it in a different way. It is necessary to avoid detailed explanations of our personal God and to avoid oppressing others with our beliefs so that we all make space for them to discover their own Higher Power. Even though it has been much misused, mention of the word God is unavoidable in recovery. When I use that word, I need to make sure that everyone understands they can interpret the word in their own way, not necessarily the way I might have intended. And even those who reject the notion of God are only rejecting one particular representation that they have issues with, that they find oppressive in some way.

"Second-order effects, such as belief in belief, makes fanaticism."
Alfred Korzybski (1879 - 1950)

Martin Buber
1878 - 1965

a) Quote for Morning Contemplation

"To be old can be glorious if one has not unlearned how to begin."
(Martin Buber)

Reflection for Deep Recovery (Sharabi)

Even when I am old, even if I have lived through many, sober days
and years, I must begin each day fresh, and I must learn how
to live that day. This day is new, it has never been here before,
and each day is a beginning and an opportunity to begin. I am
always working on something about myself, no matter how old
I am because there is always some learning possible, some new
awareness, some changing, an awakening: some new path that has
shown itself. I am always beginning. The sun rises anew every day.

"The beginning is always today."

Mary Shelley (1797 - 1851)

*"A man, though wise, should never be ashamed of learning more, and
must unbend his mind."*   *Sophocles (496 B.C.- 406 B.C.)*

---

b) Quote for Evening Contemplation

"Every person born in this world represents something new,
something that never existed before, something original
and unique, and every man or woman's foremost task is the
actualization of his or her unique, unprecedented, and never
recurring possibilities." (Martin Buber)

Reflection for Deep Recovery (Sharabi)

I am one in a billion—just like each and everyone else. Not only
am I different from anyone who has ever existed, but I am also
different from everyone who will exist in the future. Yes, we are
each ordinary too, but in our own special way. We can be ordinary
without being mediocre. Each of us is filled with possibility and to
discover and fulfill that unique possibility through getting sober
and working in recovery—that is the most exciting thing. Being
myself calls for bravery because it requires giving up the desire for
approval.

*"Human beings are not born once and for all on the day their mothers
give birth to them, but... life obliges them over and over again to give
birth to themselves."*

Gabriel García Márquez (1927 - 2014)

Martin Buber
1878 - 1965

a) Quote for Morning Contemplation

"I do, indeed, close my door at times and surrender myself to a book, but only because I can open the door again and see a human face looking at me." (Martin Buber)

Reflection for Deep Recovery (Sharabi)

In recovery, it is necessary to study and contemplate. However, I must not get lost exclusively in the reading of books and in the consideration of ideas. It is unbalanced to indulge in obsessive self-examination, or in a private pursuit of God or of a sacred life. I must periodically open the door to meet my fellow alcoholic face-to-face, to see a human face looking at me. Above all other things, recovery is the fellowship—a meeting with and a connecting with—human beings just like me.

"I define connection as the energy that exists between people when they feel seen, heard, and valued... when they derive sustenance and strength from the relationship."

Brené Brown (born 1965)

b) Quote for Evening Contemplation

"The real struggle is not between east and west, or capitalism and communism, but between education and propaganda." (Martin Buber)

Reflection for Deep Recovery (Sharabi)

There is no struggle between the believers and the non-believers; between people telling me to include myself in the amends list and those that tell me not to; between people saying I should list my virtues in the Fourth Step inventory and those who say only list my drawbacks and defects. The real struggle is between people offering this program to me as education, teaching me to think for myself, and those merely pushing it on me as propaganda, telling me to shut up, not to think, and to listen to them. This is a program of attraction and education, not publicity and propaganda. It cannot be packaged as a set of frozen platitudes. It is alive, dynamic, and dangerous—dangerous to complacency, rigidity, and certainty. Waking up can be dangerous to sleep.

Plato
474 B.C. - 348 B.C.

a) Quote for Morning Contemplation

"Good actions give strength to ourselves and inspire good actions in others." (Plato)

Reflection for Deep Recovery (Sharabi)

This is a program of doing, of action, not just of dreaming, philosophizing, or preaching. We choose right action rather than yield to the temptation to be mean, petty, dishonest, or selfish. Consistent good action strengthens our character. It is called discipline. On the other hand, each time we let ourselves off the hook, we weaken. Each relapse weakens us. In recovery, we teach by example, through action; we model for others how to be. And as we walk the path, we make it easier for others to walk the path.

"Knowing is not enough; we must apply;
Willing is not enough; we must do."

Goethe (1749 - 1832)

"The truth is lived, not taught."

Hermann Hesse (1877 - 1962)

---

b) Quote for Evening Contemplation

"Be kind, for everyone you meet is fighting a hard battle." (Plato)

(Also attributed to Ian McLaren)

Reflection for Deep Recovery (Sharabi)

I can be quick to condemn people because I do not see the battle they have been—and are—fighting; how far they have come from their difficult beginnings. I do not see the demons they are fighting even right now. If I could follow everyone from their baby-hood and I got to watch the impact of each event in their lives, I would understand how they have turned out the way they are. I must remember to be respectful and kind to everyone who is struggling with this disease—with life itself. And I must believe that the decisions they are taking are the best they are capable of, given where they are standing. My job is just to help them not lose their spirit, to keep encouraging them no matter what.

"In the depth of winter, I finally learned that within me, there lay an invincible summer."

Albert Camus (1913 - 1960)

Plato
474 B.C. - 348 B.C.

"Come then, and let us pass a leisure hour in storytelling, and our story shall be the education of our heroes." (Plato)

Reflection for Deep Recovery (Sharabi)

Ancient cultures used myth and storytelling to educate and to create future heroes. In recovery, we transmit wisdom through stories, not through advice. A meeting is a leisure hour devoted to storytelling. Stories work surreptitiously because our intellect cannot put up barriers; there is nothing to disagree with. Deep wisdom is absorbed mindlessly. My mind thinks these stories belong to the teller—comparing—but my soul is hearing it as a story about me—identifying. There is much value in attending speaker meetings, not just discussion meetings. I am also healing the storyteller by listening.

"There is no greater agony than bearing an untold story inside you."
Maya Angelou (1928 - 2014)

---

b) Quote for Evening Contemplation

"The beginning is the most important part of the work." (Plato)

Reflection for Deep Recovery (Sharabi)

I must watch my beginnings in recovery well, for that is where I am building my foundation. Recovery is a magnificent palace, but we begin by working on the basement. It is the most important part of the work. Until now, all my instincts were focused merely on avoiding pain; I had no understanding of the benefit of enduring pain for future rewards. The first step to dealing with procrastination is to begin the work I have been avoiding. I must also not lament about the phase that is ending, but I must become excited about the change that is coming. Committing to recovery with all my being, I must climb into the middle of the bed where I will be less likely to fall off instead of living on the fringes of recovery, peering out over the edge.

"New beginnings are often disguised as painful endings."
Lao-Tzu (6th century B.C.)

Plato
474 B.C. - 348 B.C.

a) Quote for Morning Contemplation

"We can easily forgive a child who is afraid of the dark; the real tragedy of life is when men are afraid of the light." (Plato)

Reflection for Deep Recovery (Sharabi)

Sometimes I am scared of discovering who I really can be. For years I holed up in dark spaces and slunk through life, avoiding the responsibility that existence brings. I hid in my drunken isolation, afraid of the light, afraid to see myself for the sacred soul I was, and we all are, afraid to see my world itself in the glory that it can be. This is the tragedy and delusion of the chronic drunk, slinking around dark barrooms, neither alive nor dead.

"Our deepest fear is not that we are inadequate. Our deepest fear is that we are powerful beyond measure. It is our light, not our darkness, that most frightens us."

Marianne Williamson (born 1952)

---

b) Quote for Evening Contemplation

"Never discourage anyone... who continually makes progress, no matter how slow." (Plato)

Reflection for Deep Recovery (Sharabi)

I teach the newcomer not to get discouraged by the slowness of recovery. As long as they are making progress—no matter how slow—they are doing well. And every time they stumble and fall, (it will happen,) I encourage them to get up and start walking again. It does not matter how fast they are going as long as they are walking in the right direction. It does not matter if they appear to be going backward at times; this is part of progress. If I have a thought that they won't make it, I consider it a statement at that moment about me than about them. I remind myself to see them not where they are right now but as the possibility they contain.

"Curious that we spend more time congratulating people who have succeeded than encouraging people who have not."

Neil deGrasse Tyson (born 1958)

Plato
474 B.C. - 348 B.C.

a) Quote for Morning Contemplation

"A sensible man will remember that the eyes may be confused in two ways—by a change from light to darkness or from darkness to light; and he will recognize that the same thing happens to the soul." (Plato)

Reflection for Deep Recovery (Sharabi)

After years spent huddled in the corner of a dark bar, the newcomer will be disoriented and intimidated by the transition to daylight and open air. The confusion when he or she first enters the program may just be light trying to penetrate the darkness of existence. They might be tempted to shut their eyes and go back to the life they came from. It is just like how longtime prisoners are confused and disoriented by the world when their cell doors are suddenly thrown open. But I tell them: don't make premature judgments. Stay in these rooms of recovery! You will soon adjust to this new life and this new freedom.

---

b) Quote for Evening Contemplation

"We do not learn, and that which we call learning is only a process of recollection." (Plato)

Reflection for Deep Recovery (Sharabi)

Thoughts can be a recollection, or thoughts can be imagination. But "thinking" is what we do with the thoughts that show up. Thinking is what allows us to separate the bad thoughts from the good and useful thoughts. We do not act on the first thought that appears. Thinking is conscious and purposeful activity; having thoughts is mere recollection. Memorizing and recollecting phrases from the Big Book will not keep me sober in the long run. Unless I have accepted and integrated the wisdom into my bones, it is not useful. Only that would be true learning.

"Education is what remains after one has forgotten what one has learned in school."

Albert Einstein (1879 - 1955)

"Knowledge can be communicated, but not wisdom. One can find it, live it, be fortified by it, do wonders through it, but one cannot communicate and teach it."

Hermann Hesse (1877 - 1962)

Plato
474 B.C. - 348 B.C.

a) Quote for Morning Contemplation

"I am the wisest man alive, for I know one thing, and that is that I know nothing." (Plato)

Plato, ascribed to Socrates.

Reflection for Deep Recovery (Sharabi)

People know many little things, but I, in recovery, know one big thing: if I don't pick up that first drink, I will never be drunk! But beyond that, I know darn little, except the stuff I have made up. We must all beware of people who mistake opinions for knowledge, of people frantic to believe that they "know" things. There are no authorities on recovery, no authorities on the future. We stay sober one day at a time, with humility and with gratitude.

"Words are but wind, and learning is nothing but words; therefore, learning is nothing but wind."

Jonathan Swift (1667 - 1745)

---

b) Quote for Evening Contemplation

"Wisdom is knowing what not to fear." (Plato)

Reflection for Deep Recovery (Sharabi)

My past life was beset with fears, often unfounded and implausible. But when I turned my will and my life over to the care of God as I understand God, my fear of the future left me. Fear of economic insecurity left me. Fear of not knowing what to do in situations left me. Fear that I was somehow defective and useless left me. Fear that I had to manage everything in life all by myself left me. Ultimately, even the fear that I would be afraid left me. With fear of the future put in its place, I was able to concentrate on living in the present.

"I have been through some terrible things in my life, some of which actually happened."

Mark Twain (1835 - 1910)

"Fear is simply because you are not living life - you are living in your mind."

Sadhguru (born 1957)

Plato
474 B.C. - 348 B.C.

a) Quote for Morning Contemplation

"Every heart sings a song, incomplete until another heart whispers back. Those who wish to sing always find a song. At the touch of a lover, everyone becomes a poet." (Plato)

Reflection for Deep Recovery (Sharabi)

Everyone who wishes to sing the song of sobriety can find a willing partner in recovery. The entire fellowship becomes our lover in recovery, whispering the song of sobriety, serenity, peace, goodness, acceptance, and service into our heart. Touched by the love of recovery, we all become poets; our sober life itself becomes a poem.

"The lover of life makes the whole world into his family."

Charles Baudelaire (1821 - 1867)

b) Quote for Evening Contemplation

"Character is simply habit long continued." (Plato)

Reflection for Deep Recovery (Sharabi)

"We are what we repeatedly do. Excellence, then, is not an act, but a habit."

Will Durant, paraphrasing Aristotle (384 -322 B.C.)

"The acquisition of a new habit, or the leaving off of an old one, we must take care to launch ourselves with as strong and decided an initiative as possible... Never suffer an exception to occur till the new habit is securely rooted in your life... every day during which a breakdown is postponed adds to the chances of it not occurring at all."

William James (1842 - 1910)

William James' injunction to "never suffer an exception to occur..." is the most sacred principle of recovery from alcoholism. It makes sobriety easy because it allows no compromise on complete abstinence.

Plato
474 B.C. - 348 B.C.

a) Quote for Morning Contemplation

"Good people do not need laws to tell them to act responsibly, while bad people will find a way around the laws." (Plato)

Reflection for Deep Recovery (Sharabi)

In recovery, people act responsibly not because there are laws, but because recovery has helped us heal and connect with our inherent goodness. Recovery has made us into good people who have developed good habits and good ethics. I will no longer try to find ways to justify and rationalize my bad behavior. Once I assimilate the principles of recovery, I will intuitively know how to behave in situations without needing to consult a manual or call my sponsor.

"Society needs a return to spiritual values—not to offset the material but to make it fully productive."

Peter Drucker (1909 - 2005)

b) Quote for Evening Contemplation

"Education is teaching our children to desire the right things." (Plato)

Reflection for Deep Recovery (Sharabi)

In the program of recovery, I have been educated to desire the right thing: to be of maximum service to God and to fellow human beings. The desires that fall off are the ones that were generated by a perceived deficit or void—desires for fame, respect, admiration, financial "success," etc. The good life follows as a by-product of the right desire. And such right desire only comes to happy people because unhappy people desire things only to relieve their unhappiness in the moment.

"The best way to make children good is to make them happy. Don't be discouraged if your children reject your advice. Years later, they will offer it to their own offspring. Children begin by loving their parents; after a time they judge them; rarely, if ever, do they forgive them."

Oscar Wilde (1854 - 1900)

Plato
474 B.C. - 348 B.C.

a) Quote for Morning Contemplation

"There are two things a person should never be angry at, what they can help, and what they cannot." (Plato)

Reflection for Deep Recovery (Sharabi)

When we truly contemplate it, we will understand the arrogance of anger. Instead of dealing with what "is," we are ranting about what it should be—according to us—and ranting about our helplessness. Anger is just an instinctive reaction to a perceived threat. Righteous anger might be the "dubious luxury" of regular folks, but we in recovery have no "right" to be angry anywhere, about anything. We are taught here to deal with what is, not whine about it, but take action if possible. We manage ourselves in that moment, not other people and the things "out there." God, grant me the serenity to accept the things I cannot change—without getting angry or whining—the courage to change the things I can—without getting angry or whining—and the wisdom to know the difference.

b) Quote for Evening Contemplation

"People are like dirt. They can either nourish you and help you grow as a person, or they can stunt your growth and make you wilt and die." (Plato)

Reflection for Deep Recovery (Sharabi)

I select carefully the people I surround myself with. I avoid those who feel threatened by the changes I am making but instead hang out with people who support me in my efforts to keep growing. I have had to avoid some old friends who found my attempt at sobriety threatening to their drinking life. When you are ready, you must disentangle from sponsors who require you to consult them on everything; they will stunt your growth and make you wilt and die. Individuation requires—at some point—that you leave the herd and venture out. Turning over your decisions and attitudes to the group or a sponsor or even to a book of instructions, will prevent you from taking responsibility for your growth. You will be dead even if you are walking around, shaking hands.

"We may become strangers to those who thought they knew us, but at least we are no longer strangers to ourselves."

James Hollis (born 1940)

Plato
474 B.C. - 348 B.C.

a) Quote for Morning Contemplation

"You should not honor men more than truth." (Plato)

Reflection for Deep Recovery (Sharabi)

We cannot place old-timers on a pedestal; we should not respect
or honor them more than the truth. The truth is that they are
just human beings, just like you and me. Not drinking for a long
time does not automatically bring wisdom, spiritual awakening,
or direct access to truth. Each of us in recovery must honor the
truth we are after more than any personality. We cannot lie about
ourselves in order to maintain our image of honor. Truth is
entirely shameless.

"I would prefer even to fail with honor than win by cheating."
Sophocles (496 - 406 B.C.)

b) Quote for Evening Contemplation

**"Wise men speak because they have something to say; Fools
because they have to say something." (Plato)**

Reflection for Deep Recovery (Sharabi)

When I have something to say, I say it. When I have said it, I
stop and sit down. And if I have nothing to say, I don't take five
minutes of everyone's time to prove it.

Plato
474 B.C. - 348 B.C.

a) Quote for Morning Contemplation

"An empty vessel makes the loudest sound, so they that have the least wit are the greatest babblers." (Plato)

Reflection for Deep Recovery (Sharabi)

We have all been subjected to comments that have gone on and on, degenerating into mini-leads. Some people stand up proclaiming an arduous and tortured humility, piousness, in a public show of self-degradation. They repeating themselves, recycling the same comments they have trumpeted before. We may have been guilty of this at times ourselves when we were experiencing an inner emptiness. It is easy while speaking to get entranced with one's own "truth." Self-awareness in the fellowship really stands for "other-awareness" and thoughtfulness about other people.

"Let a man get up and say, Behold, this is the truth, and instantly I perceive a sandy cat filching a piece of fish in the background. Look, you have forgotten the cat, I say."

Virginia Woolf (1882 - 1941)

b) Quote for Evening Contemplation

"Do not train a child to learn by force or harshness; but direct them to it by what amuses their minds, so that you may be better able to discover with accuracy the peculiar bent of the genius of each." (Plato)

Reflection for Deep Recovery (Sharabi)

Sometimes we treat newcomers as children who know nothing. This is ignorant, arrogant, and stupid on our part. The newcomer is, in actuality, a whole person, quite sophisticated, with his or her own thoughts, perspectives, and genius—a full human being. We must always be respectful towards the newcomers, and we should not treat them with harshness and condescension or try to manipulate them with force or cunning. We should especially avoid trying to change people by making them feel bad about who they are. Instead, we teach with "I" statements, not with "you" statements. Each newcomer should be encouraged to develop and uncover his or her own genius through the search for sober living.

"Learning is finding out what you already know; doing is demonstrating that you know it; teaching is reminding others that they know it as well as you do. We are all learners, doers, and teachers."

Richard Bach (born 1936)

Plato
474 B.C. - 348 B.C.

a) Quote for Morning Contemplation

"The soul takes flight to the world that is invisible but there arriving she is sure of bliss and forever dwells in paradise." (Plato)

Reflection for Deep Recovery (Sharabi)

I realize that the pursuit of a spiritual life and the arrival of a spiritual awakening can bring bliss. I can be dwelling in paradise even though the material world has its own problems that are being addressed on a different plane. In Deep Recovery, we live in this world, but we are not of it. We exist as spiritual beings, taking care of material obligations without complaining.

"You are not a human being in search of a spiritual experience. You are a spiritual being immersed in a human experience."

Pierre Teilhard de Chardin (1881 - 1955)

b) Quote for Evening Contemplation

"The greatest wealth is to live content with little." (Plato)

Reflection for Deep Recovery (Sharabi)

The mindless pursuit of "more," which characterizes our society has to be replaced. I must cultivate in recovery the ability to appreciate the little things in life: simple things that I encounter through the day. The more I desire things I don't have, the poorer I am. Rather than moan over what I don't have, I try and delight in what I have. I become rich by forgetting my desires. I have learned that every life, no matter how barren, contains all the ingredients for supreme happiness. If I want to be happy, I just have to focus on something different—to listen for that melody playing in the background rather than the chatter in the foreground.

"Many men go fishing all of their lives without knowing that it is not fish they are after."

Thoreau (1817 - 1862)

"Happiness is a how; not a what. A talent, not an object."

Hermann Hesse (1877 - 1962)

Plato
474 B.C. - 348 B.C.

a) Quote for Morning Contemplation

"Bodily exercise, when compulsory, does no harm to the body; but knowledge which is acquired under compulsion obtains no hold on the mind." (Plato)

Reflection for Deep Recovery (Sharabi)

We cannot force our knowledge and our beliefs down the newcomer's throat. There are many things they have to discover by themselves for these are the things that will have a hold on their mind. However, in recovery, bodily exercise and physical actions—like setting up the chairs at a meeting, making coffee, and going for a walk in the woods—will benefit even the "unwilling."

"Truth can be tolerated only if you discover it yourself because then, the pride of discovery makes the truth palatable."

Fritz Perls (1883 - 1970)

---

b) Quote for Evening Contemplation

"Poets utter great and wise things which they do not themselves understand." (Plato)

Reflection for Deep Recovery (Sharabi)

The depth of the ideas contained in the Big Book may not have been realized even by the writers themselves. Today we are constantly discovering more in those same sentences. The ultimate meaning of something that is said or written lies not in the person who said it but in the person who receives it—how he receives it, what meaning he makes of it, and how he uses it. The knowledge contained in the Big Book is not static but changing; its meaning evolves as recovery itself evolves. Knowledge is too large to be contained in sentences.

"Knowledge has to be improved, challenged, and increased constantly, or it vanishes."

Peter Drucker (1909 - 2005)

"Men honor what lies within the sphere of their knowledge but do not realize how dependent they are on what lies beyond it."

Chuang Tzu (370 - 287 B.C.)

Plato
474 B.C. - 348 B.C.

a) Quote for Morning Contemplation

"The first and best victory is to conquer self." (Plato)

Reflection for Deep Recovery (Sharabi)

The ego is the biggest barrier to self-knowledge; it is the strongest impediment to acquiring humility. He who has conquered the ego has achieved a great victory. Paradoxical as it may sound, humility is the greatest achievement possible in recovery. Unfortunately, once it is achieved, the humble person does not even know that he or she is humble. All she finds is that she does not take personal offense at things. The ultimate in recovery is to arrive at this transparency so that the self is only minimally conscious of "self." There is no attachment to any particular "self-image" or attempts to protect "self-esteem." Such monumental anonymity is the spiritual goal of deep recovery.

"When the ego is gone, Realisation results by itself. There are neither good nor bad qualities in the Self. The Self is free from all qualities."

Ramana Maharshi (1879 - 1950)

---

b) Quote for Evening Contemplation

"Man is a being in search of meaning." (Plato)

Reflection for Deep Recovery (Sharabi)

I spent years at the bar wondering: who am I? What am I supposed to do? What is my purpose? What happens when I die? Each evening I found answers, but they would be gone by morning. Today I can glimpse the meaning of these questions, the meaning of life itself. Who I am is an alcoholic committed to sobriety. What I am supposed to do is to live life by the principles. And my purpose in life is to develop my spiritual side, help other alcoholics and constantly move closer to God in whatever way I picture God and godliness. And I don't waste energy on what will happen to me when I die. I live simply, one day at a time.

"Time is a river which sweeps me along, but I am the river; it is a tiger which destroys me, but I am the tiger; it is a fire which consumes me, but I am the fire."

Jorge Luis Borges (1899 - 1986)

"Success isn't a result of spontaneous combustion. You must set yourself on fire."

Arnold Glasow (1905 - 1998)

Plato
474 B.C. - 348 B.C.

a) Quote for Morning Contemplation

"He was a wise man who invented God." (Plato)

Reflection for Deep Recovery (Sharabi)

They were wise who saw that a God of our understanding could provide a path out of our alcoholism. We need to access our sense of something deeper, our sense of awe, mystery and wonder, to give us the strength and courage to remain sober, and to take on life on life's terms. We call this "God," but each person will explain this sense differently.

"Let man live at a distance from God, and the universe remains neutral or hostile to him. But let man believe in God, and immediately all around him, the elements, even the irksome, (inevitably) organize themselves into a friendly whole, ordered to the ultimate success of life."

Pierre Teilhard de Chardin (1881 - 1955)

b) Quote for Evening Contemplation

"All is flux; nothing stays still." (Plato)

Reflection for Deep Recovery (Sharabi)

No matter what is happening in the moment, I can tell myself: "This Too Shall Pass." I am not to be content seeking happiness, for happiness is only momentary: things will change. Serenity cannot be based on things being any particular way because the world is always changing. Therefore, serenity is unconditional; it cannot have to do with the condition of my present world or with the feelings I am presently feeling.

"Feelings come and go like clouds in a windy sky. Conscious breathing is my anchor."

Thich Nhat Hanh (born 1926)

"Nevertheless, whether in occurrences lasting days, hours or mere minutes at a time, I have experienced happiness often, and have had brief encounters with it in my later years, even in old age."

Hermann Hesse (1877 - 1962)

Plato
474 B.C. - 348 B.C.

a) Quote for Morning Contemplation

"Let parents then bequeath to their children not riches but the spirit of reverence." (Plato)

Reflection for Deep Recovery (Sharabi)

Of the things that helped me, the thing that really saved my soul was my reverence for sobriety, for this fellowship of recovery, and for God. That capacity to feel awe and reverence—to be moved by things— was a posture that I had learned from my parents and by their own reverential attitude. I was fortunate to have such parents, and I thank them. But for those who did not have such kind and good parents, I tell them: a parent's job is to wound. The wounds from your parents are what have made you deeper; thank them anyway.

"Hold dear to your parents, for it is a scary and confusing world without them."

Emily Dickinson (1830 - 1886)

b) Quote for Evening Contemplation

"The unexamined life is not worth living." (Plato)

(Plato possible quoting from Socrates)

Reflection for Deep Recovery (Sharabi)

In recovery, we live examined lives; we take inventory at the end of each day, and we reflect on our motives; we examine our character defects and our tendencies. We examine the wrongs we have done, and we make amends where possible. We can also benefit from reflecting at the end of each day on what we have learned; what insights and openings the day has provided; in what ways we have been changed. This constant examination that recovery demands, provides texture, structure, and meaning to my day-to-day life. It enriches me—and us. Contemplating and wondering about the powers that are driving us is a fulfilling alternative to the mindless pursuit of pleasure, prestige, possessions, and power. We have to make things matter that are outside the "things" in our life.

"We are lived by powers we pretend to understand:
They arrange our loves; it is they who direct at the end..."

W. H. Auden (1907 - 1973)

Plato
474 B.C. - 348 B.C.

a) Quote for Morning Contemplation

"There is no such thing as a lovers' oath." (Plato)

Reflection for Deep Recovery (Sharabi)

Love of sobriety eliminates the need for willpower. Those fruitless resolutions you made to stop drinking arose from your ego, your grandiosity, and the need to think you were in control. What you do for love does not need an oath. As a lover of sobriety and of this fellowship, I no longer need to take an oath not to drink. Indeed, taking an oath not to drink acknowledges the possibility of drinking, and suggests that willpower can work. As for me, I just know that I am done with drinking.

"Integrity has no need of rules."

Albert Camus (1913 - 1960)

"Temptation usually comes in through a door that has been deliberately left open."

Arnold Glasow (1905 - 1998)

---

b) Quote for Evening Contemplation

"Those who are able to see beyond the shadows and lies of their culture will never be understood, let alone believed, by the masses." (Plato)

Reflection for Deep Recovery (Sharabi)

The ultimate job in recovery is to find my own truth. There are many shadows and lies being mouthed—mindlessly—by the larger society as well as within the rooms of the fellowship. When I clearly see truth, I will not seek others to validate it, nor will I necessarily be understood or believed by the masses. But if I am merely embracing beliefs, the lack of support will disturb me. As has been said, "To be ahead of others is to invite a flogging."

"Few people are capable of expressing with equanimity opinions which differ from the prejudices of their social environment. Most people are incapable of forming such opinions."

Albert Einstein (1879 - 1955)

"When a true genius appears, you can know him by this sign: that all the dunces are in a confederacy against him."

Jonathan Swift (1667 - 1745)

Osho
1931 - 1990

a) Quote for Morning Contemplation

"A man who really wants to be free has to accept immense responsibilities. He cannot dump his responsibilities on anybody else. Whatever he does, whatever he is, he is responsible." (Osho)

Reflection for Deep Recovery (Sharabi)

My drinking was my way to avoid responsibility; I kept procrastinating sobriety even though I knew it was inevitable. Now, in sobriety, I have accepted immense responsibility: for myself and my acts, for my conduct, for my decisions, and for my character. Accepting responsibility for sobriety is the very essence of the program of recovery. It is quite different from taking credit for my sobriety or blaming myself for drinking.

"If you could kick the person in the pants responsible for most of your trouble, you wouldn't sit for a month."

Theodore Roosevelt (1858 - 1919)

---

b) Quote for Evening Contemplation

"Each individual passing through a rebellion is not fighting with anybody else but is only fighting with his own darkness. Swords are not needed; bombs are not needed. What is needed is more alertness, more meditativeness, more love, more prayerfulness, more gratitude. Surrounded by all these qualities, you are born anew." (Osho)

Reflection for Deep Recovery (Sharabi)

Here we are not rebelling against parents or bosses, against authority, against sponsors, or against society. We are rebelling against domination by alcohol. We are rebelling against our own darkness and our self-condemnation. Our weapons are not determination and willpower, not swords, not guns, and not bombs; we do not need stubbornness or obstinacy. Our weapons are kindness, alertness, contemplation, prayer, meditation, humility, service, love, gratitude, willingness, and total surrender.

"For prayer is nothing else than being on terms of friendship with God."

Teresa of Avila (1515 - 1582)

Osho
1931 - 1990

a) Quote for Morning Contemplation

"To be in tune with yourself is the only way to be in tune with existence. Nobody needs personal guidance because all personal guidance is a beautiful name for dependence on somebody, and he is going to distort you." (Osho)

Reflection for Deep Recovery (Sharabi)

I cannot become a blind follower of any spiritual guide or sponsor; I cannot become anyone's puppet. I do not depend on someone or some book to tell me how to live. That would be substituting alcohol-dependence with person-dependence, with sponsor-dependence, with book-dependence. Let the wisdom of the ages be my spiritual guide. Let my inner knowledge and conscious contact with the Deep Spirit illuminate my path; inside is knowledge of what is needed. In Deep Recovery, I am guided to what is good and correct by my own inquiry and alertness, not by instructions from others.

---

b) Quote for Evening Contemplation

"Meditation is a totally different affair. You have to become aware of your mind stuff. Whatever goes on in your mind, you have to become a watcher, and the watcher has to be so deep-rooted that slowly, slowly, your mind disappears and only the watcher remains. Then all possibilities of tension, anxiety, anguish disappear, and you will not find even the conflict." (Osho)

Reflection for Deep Recovery (Sharabi)

Most of us are living in our commentary about life, not in life itself. The chattering monkey inside our head won't leave us alone, and we mistake that voice for "me." When I see that I am not my thoughts—that I am not the commentator but the observer—the thoughts disappear into the background. Tension, anxiety, conflicts, and anguish disappear during meditation; all that is left is the watcher experiencing the stillness of pure Being, a plane that transcends feelings, thoughts, compulsions, urges, conflicts, anxiety, worry, fear, and desires. Here is true freedom.

"Where can I find a man who has forgotten words so I can have a word with him?"

Chuang Tzu (370 - 287 B.C.)

300

Osho
1931 - 1990

a) Quote for Morning Contemplation

"A meditator, on the contrary, needs only one thing: the atmosphere of meditation. He needs other meditators; he needs to be surrounded by other meditators. Because whatever goes on happening within us is not only within us, it affects people who are close by." (Osho)

Reflection for Deep Recovery (Sharabi)

Sitting silently in the presence of a roomful of alcoholics is a profound meditation in itself. Each person's presence has an impact on every other person. Meditation requires an atmosphere of meditation, a community of meditators who will leave you alone, yet be present to you. I am also respectful in the meeting of the need for others to be in a meditative space.

"I hold this to be the highest task for a bond between two people: that each protects the solitude of the other."

Rainer Maria Rilke (1875 - 1926)

---

b) Quote for Evening Contemplation

"Find ecstasy within yourself. It is not out there. It is in your innermost flowering. The one you are looking for is you." (Osho)

Reflection for Deep Recovery (Sharabi)

Recovery is the task of looking for my lost self, of recovering original Self, of becoming once more who I always have been and was meant to be. Recovery means recovering my soul, uncovering my core. There is ecstasy in finding myself, whether happy or bittersweet—it is I.

"When pain, misery, or anger happen, it is time to look within you, not around you."

Sadhguru (born 1957)

"And the end of all our explaining will be to arrive where we started And to know the place for the first time."

T. S. Eliot (1888 - 1965)

Osho
1931 - 1990

a) Quote for Morning Contemplation

"You cannot surrender ego because it does not exist. You can bring a little awareness, a little consciousness, a little light. Forget completely about the ego; concentrate totally on bringing alertness into your being. And the moment your consciousness has become a flame, concentrated, you will not be able to find the ego." (Osho)

Reflection for Deep Recovery (Sharabi)

When people talk about conquering ego, it is worth asking: who is the entity that wishes to do the conquering? Is that not ego itself? When I concentrate on alertness and awareness, the notion of ego disappears; there is nothing to battle and conquer. All that is present is awareness itself—a flame, a pure illumination. There is no "I," for "I" is merely a concept generated by the ego to try and gain survival in time, some permanence. But in the moment, there is no time and no "I"—only consciousness; not consciousness "of" something, like "me" or "the world" but just pure consciousness.

---

b) Quote for Evening Contemplation

"It is simply sitting silently, witnessing the thoughts, passing before you. Just witnessing, not interfering, not even judging, because the moment you judge, you have lost the pure witness. The moment you say "this is good, this is bad," you have already jumped onto the thought process." (Osho)

Reflection for Deep Recovery (Sharabi)

An inventory merely means examining the present state, just noting what is without judgment—without condemning myself or patting myself on the back. And it is an inventory not just of actions but also of tendencies, of thought patterns and behavior patterns that have been running my life without my permission. I may not be able to control my thoughts, but I can watch them. The purpose of an inventory is to become a witness to myself, not to condemn myself. For if I start condemning myself, I will also automatically begin justifying myself. I will be unable to see myself clearly when I am distracted with justifying myself. And justifying myself often involves making someone else wrong.

"Once you create a self-justifying storyline, your emotional entrapment within it quadruples."

Pema Chödrön (born 1936)

Osho
1931 - 1990

a) Quote for Morning Contemplation

"Sadness gives depth. Happiness gives height. Sadness gives roots. Happiness gives branches. Happiness is like a tree going into the sky, and sadness is like the roots going down into the womb of the earth. Both are needed, and the higher a tree goes, the deeper it goes, simultaneously. The bigger the tree, the bigger will be its roots. In fact, it is always in proportion. That's its balance." (Osho)

Reflection for Deep Recovery (Sharabi)

It is our suffering and our sadness that give us a depth of character. Our capacity to be sad gives us, also, the ability to be immensely joyful. It is the roots of sadness that allow the tree of happiness to grow to great heights, well-supported by a base of wide experience. If we try to create a life that is all happy, all positive, all light, it is in danger of crashing down when the inevitable storms come. This is when we need our roots that go into the earth.

---

b) Quote for Evening Contemplation

"You feel good, you feel bad, and these feelings are bubbling from your own unconsciousness, from your own past. Nobody is responsible except you. Nobody can make you angry, and nobody can make you happy." (Osho)

Reflection for Deep Recovery (Sharabi)

When I live an examined life, I am asking not only, "How am I feeling?" but, "How am I creating this feeling? How am I getting myself all riled up over that? How have I maneuvered myself into thinking that I cannot live without this?" I must look beyond feelings, underneath feelings. Nobody can make me angry. I even stop thinking in phrases like, "He annoys me," or "She makes me happy!" "You hurt me." Nobody can make me happy or unhappy. Anger is simply a feeling contained within my skin. I am never "angry at..." or "angry about..." somebody or something; I am just angry. I can process anger by becoming aware of my body sensations, by breathing deeply, by avoiding any mental commentary about the anger. The anger then dissipates, without the fuel of justification propping it up. Pain may be real but "You hurt me," comes from a stance of victim, a blaming of other.

Osho
1931 - 1990

a) Quote for Morning Contemplation

"If you love a flower, don't pick it up." (Osho)

Reflection for Deep Recovery (Sharabi)

If I love a flower, I should let it be—let it grow and flourish where
it is planted, water it where it is. The flower is life, its own life,
and I am mine. I must not imprison or try to possess what I love. I
must approach the newcomer, too, with appreciation and joy first,
not with advice or criticism. A person's changing is up to him or
her and sometimes even willingness is not enough; God's help is
necessary. We cannot just blame people for the way they are; even
molecular biologists and congitive scientists today are debating
where there is any such thing as free will in humans.

*"He who binds to himself a joy Does the winged life destroy; But he who
kisses the joy as it flies Lives in eternity's sunrise."*

William Blake (1757 - 1827)

---

b) Quote for Evening Contemplation

**"That is the simple secret of happiness. Whatever you are doing,
don't let past move your mind; don't let future disturb you.
Because the past is no more, and the future is not yet. To live
in the memories, to live in the imagination is to live in the non-
existential. Naturally, you will be miserable because you will miss
your whole life." (Osho)**

Reflection for Deep Recovery (Sharabi)

People who are unhappy are always asking themselves, "Am I
happy?" People who are truly happy are occupied with life, not
with questions about their happiness. Would it be okay for you to
be happy without knowing that you are happy?

*"Look to this day! For it is life, the very life of life. In its brief course
lie all the verities and realities of your existence: the bliss of growth; the
glory of action; the splendor of achievement.*

*"For yesterday is but a dream, and tomorrow is only a vision. But
today, well-lived, makes every yesterday a dream of happiness, and every
tomorrow a vision of hope."*

Sanskrit poem attributed to Kalidasa (5th century)

Osho
1931 - 1990

a) Quote for Morning Contemplation

"Be realistic: Plan for a miracle." (Osho)

Reflection for Deep Recovery (Sharabi)

Rarely have we seen a person fail who has thoroughly followed our path. When a hopeless drunk, wallowing in misery, catches a glimpse of sobriety and grabs the chance, it is truly a miracle. We are—each of us—a walking miracle. So get ready and expect the miracle. You might find you have a full and satisfying life, even without that thing you thought you couldn't live without.

"To hope means to be ready at every moment for that which is not yet born, and yet not become desperate if there is no birth in our lifetime."

Emily Dickinson (1830 - 1886)

b) Quote for Evening Contemplation

"It is not so cheap to reach the ultimate realization of truth. You will have to create the path by walking yourself; the path is not ready-made, lying there and waiting for you. It is just like the sky; the birds fly, but they don't leave any footprints. You cannot follow them; there are no footprints left behind." (Osho)

Reflection for Deep Recovery (Sharabi)

People will accompany me in the beginning and point me in the right direction, even suggest a program and Steps. But, in Deep Recovery, there is no trail that I can follow, no footprints. Each has to create his or her own path, find his own meaning. I must discover the unique path that is beckoning me. And as I walk along it, I must stop looking intermittently for approval and reassurance.

"Two roads diverged in a wood, and I—
I took the one less traveled by..."

Robert Frost (1874 - 1963)

"Unless you roar like a lion against the teachings of your Guru, that knowledge will never be your own."

Gaudapada (6th century)

Osho
1931 - 1990

a) Quote for Morning Contemplation

"Truth is not something outside to be discovered; it is something inside to be realized." (Osho)

Reflection for Deep Recovery (Sharabi)

Facts may exist in the outside world, but Truth lives inside us. To discover facts we study the outside world; to realize Truth we must go on an inward journey, discover beauty and depth in ourselves, deep inside our heart. God does not need me to tell the truth; after all, He already knows the truth. What recovery calls for is ruthless honesty with myself. But we might need to modulate what we reveal to others; it is called good boundaries.

"My guru gave a single precept:
Turn your gaze from the outside
Fix it on the hidden self inside
I, Lalla, took this to heart and naked set forth to dance."
Lal Ded/Lalleshwari (1320 - 1392)

---

b) Quote for Evening Contemplation

"Whenever you are self-conscious, you are simply showing that you are not conscious of the self at all. You don't know who you are. If you had known, then there would have been no problem—then you are not seeking opinions. Then you are not worried what others say about you—it is irrelevant!" (Osho)

Reflection for Deep Recovery (Sharabi)

Self-consciousness and shyness come from an exaggerated sense of one's own importance. "How am I? I'm sure they are all looking at me!" We go through this phase in adolescence, and many of us never grow out of it. No, they are not all looking at me and commenting; they are all busy being self-conscious themselves! When I don't know myself, I look to others; their opinion is what will define me.

"Literature is strewn with the wreckage of men who have minded beyond reason the opinions of others."
Virginia Woolf (1882 - 1941)

"True guilt is guilt at the obligation one owes to oneself to be oneself.
False guilt is guilt felt at not being what other people feel one ought to be."
R. D. Laing (1927 - 1989)

Osho
1931 - 1990

a) Quote for Morning Contemplation

"Listen to your being. It is continuously giving you hints; it is a still, small voice. It does not shout at you, that is true. And if you are a little silent, you will start feeling your way." (Osho)

Reflection for Deep Recovery (Sharabi)

Now, in sobriety, I am able to sit quietly, and I can hear God whispering from deep inside me. God's voice is always small and still; I need to silence my own chatter to hear it. Whether I call it my internal wisdom or I call it God, it is the voice I must trust in guiding me to sobriety. During my drinking days, I drowned out this voice, but now that I have learned to be silent, I hear it clearly. It is helping me feel my way, telling me to start along a new path.

"What is not started today is never finished tomorrow."

Goethe (1749 - 1832)

---

b) Quote for Evening Contemplation

"Nobody has the power to take two steps together; you can take only one step at a time." (Osho)

Reflection for Deep Recovery (Sharabi)

This is true for walking as much as it is true for working the Steps. I cannot take two steps at a time. I do not get to skip the next Step because I did great on the previous Step. And there are no rewards for completing the Steps quickly and efficiently. The education system rewards learning quickly and efficiently, but life rewards learning thoroughly. In recovery, doing the Steps quickly may or may not be wise. However, there are great rewards for doing the Steps thoroughly, doing one Step at a time, and doing the maintenance Steps on an ongoing basis.

"... the most pressing task is to teach people how to learn."

Peter Drucker (1909 - 2005)

Osho
1931 - 1990

a) Quote for Morning Contemplation

"I'm simply saying that there is a way to be sane. I'm saying that you can get rid of all this insanity created by the past in you, just by being a simple witness of your thought processes." (Osho)

Reflection for Deep Recovery (Sharabi)

I can be restored to sanity if I just cooperate: become willing to examine my thought processes without attachment or condemnation. In the Fifth Step, I have to expose my insanity to myself, to another human being, and to God without explaining or defending. Why do I try to "explain" or justify my thought processes to people? And to myself? Isn't that suspicious? Is it necessary?

"Never explain—your friends do not need it, and your enemies will not believe you anyway."

Elbert Hubbard (1856 - 1915)

---

b) Quote for Evening Contemplation

"I live my life based on two principles. One, I live as if today was my last day on earth. Two, I live today as if I am going to live forever." (Osho)

Reflection for Deep Recovery (Sharabi)

One, I live my life as if everyone is watching. Two, I live my life as if no one is watching. I can also live as if today was my last day on earth. Then, I clean up unfinished business, admit my wrongs, repair my relationships, express my love and my gratitude. And I can live today as if I am going to live forever. Then, I take time off to smell the flowers, smile at people, and give them my undivided and unhurried attention. I can take extra time with my meditation; I can enjoy a long, leisurely walk and linger, communing with the tree I encounter. The idea that I could die in my sleep tonight should not lessen my ability to enjoy the fullness of my life today.

"The most beautiful moments in life are moments when you are expressing your joy, not when you are seeking it."

Sadhguru (born 1957)

Osho
1931 - 1990

a) Quote for Morning Contemplation

"The moment you become miserly, you are closed to the basic phenomenon of life: expansion, sharing. The moment you start clinging to things, you have missed the target." (Osho)

Reflection for Deep Recovery (Sharabi)

I must not be miserly with my time when it comes to recovery and service. The more time I give to recovery and to the people in it, the more leisurely my life becomes. How would I live today if I knew I was going to live forever? If I knew that time was infinite? By clinging to things, I create a sense of scarcity; by being generous, I generate abundance. I must meditate at least fifteen minutes a day—unless I am too busy, in which case I should meditate for half an hour.

"Only those who have a real and lasting sense of abundance can be truly charitable."

Course In Miracles (1976)

---

b) Quote for Evening Contemplation

"Freedom is not license and does not mean no structure. It simply means flexibility, that one can move from one structure to another easily—from no-structure to structure, from structure to no-structure. If your freedom is afraid of being in a structure, then it is not freedom at all." (Osho)

Reflection for Deep Recovery (Sharabi)

Repression can occur from outside, or it can occur from inside, from my own rigidity. As I progress along the path of recovery, I will find that it is not willpower or rigidity that keeps me from drinking; it is simply rejoicing in the freedom to not drink. Sobriety in Deep Recovery is freedom of the deepest kind—even recognizing that I have the freedom to drink if I choose to. Of course, what happens after that drink is not in my control. I can move from rules to no rules and back to rules. When I get stuck to rigid external "rules," or I get stuck on "no rules"— either way, I have lost my freedom.

Osho
1931 - 1990

a) Quote for Morning Contemplation

"I speak to help you to be silent. I use words to help you to go into wordlessness. But then people became intoxicated with my words. That was not my purpose. I continuously insisted: don't be concerned with my words. Be concerned with my silences, the gaps between the words, the gaps between the lines." (Osho)

Reflection for Deep Recovery (Sharabi)

Sobriety is wordless, but the fuss I make about being sober is full of chatter. Meditation is the gap between words; I must learn to focus on this enormous silence that exists between the words. Much of recovery happens in the silences between comments. You can agree or disagree with the words someone is using, but you cannot disagree with their silences.

"He who does not understand your silence will probably not understand your words."

Elbert Hubbard (1856 - 1915)

b) Quote for Evening Contemplation

"For thousands of years, what man has done to woman is simply monstrous. She cannot think of herself as equal to man. She has been conditioned so deeply... that she is less in everything. And the man who has reduced the women to such a state cannot love her because love can exist only in equality, in friendship." (Osho)

Reflection for Deep Recovery (Sharabi)

In the early days, they considered keeping women out of the recovery movement. The Big Book is written for men with a condescending chapter entitled: "To Wives." God is a "Him," as in all patriarchal religions. But I can make a decision to turn my will and my life over to the care of a feminine God—the Divine Mother or Kali, the fierce warrior Goddess—God, anyway I choose to understand Her.

"The best thermometer to the progress of a nation is its treatment of its women."

Swami Vivekananda (1863 - 1902)

"I do not wish women to have power over men but over themselves."

Mary Shelley (1797 - 1851)

Osho
1931 - 1990

a) Quote for Morning Contemplation

"The moment a child is born, the mother is also born. She never existed before. The woman existed, but the mother, never." (Osho)

Reflection for Deep Recovery (Sharabi)

The moment powerlessness was born, a Higher Power was also born, the possibility of recovery was born. Before I came to the program, I was just someone who had " ... a little bit too much to drink last night." But now, I am an alcoholic. The day "alcoholic" was born into my vocabulary, recovery was also born. The moment I accept I am going to die, my awakened life is born.

"My greatest blessing has been the birth of my son. My next greatest blessing has been my ability to turn people into children of mine."

Maya Angelou (1928 - 2014)

---

b) Quote for Evening Contemplation

**"They say: think twice before you jump.
I say: Jump first and then think as much as you want!" (Osho)**

Reflection for Deep Recovery (Sharabi)

I must jump into the program, and then—later, when I am sober—I can think as much as I want about whether it was the right decision or not. You need not wait—you cannot wait—for a desire to get sober. Get sober first, and the desire for sobriety will take hold of you later. You ought to stay sober for a year, and then you can think of leaving and going back to drinking—if you wish. We will not stop you, but you will stop yourself when you glimpse what sobriety has to offer. And when it comes to the Third Step, don't waste time debating whether to turn your will and your life over, whether to surrender to the path suggested by recovery. Just do it. Later, after you have some period of sobriety under your belt, you can think about it.

"If there is a fear of falling, the only safety consists in deliberately jumping."

Carl Jung (1875 - 1961)

Osho
1931 - 1990

a) Quote for Morning Contemplation

"Each person comes into this world with a specific destiny—he or she has something to fulfill, some message that has to be delivered, some work that has to be completed. You are not here accidentally—you are here meaningfully. There is a purpose behind you. The whole intends to do something through you." (Osho)

Reflection for Deep Recovery (Sharabi)

I am not in recovery accidentally; I am here for a reason. Indeed, I could say there was a reason I became an alcoholic. God—or the Universe—intends to do something with me, through me. I search for my purpose; I stay alert and embrace my purpose when it is revealed to me. Otherwise, I am living life like in a bumper car at an amusement park. My petty complaints about life will disappear when I find purpose. Right now, it is to engage in spiritual growth and to help fellow alcoholics.

---

b) Quote for Evening Contemplation

"These are the two paths from the valley leading to the peak. One path is of awareness, meditation, and the other is the path of love, the path of the devotees. These two paths are separate when you start the journey... by the time you have reached the ultimate, they are one." (Osho)

Reflection for Deep Recovery (Sharabi)

I can practice the pursuit of truth and awareness, or I can pursue the path of love and devotion. These are different paths leading to the same end: a spiritual awakening. The lovers of God do not need to attack the "truth-seeking" rationalists, and these, in turn, do not need to demean the God-lovers: the seekers of love and beauty. Their destinations are the same; they will all arrive at the same place. Whichever group I identify with, I need to be conscious that the fellowship includes all: not just the ones I agree with and think I understand.

"Beauty is truth's smile when she beholds her own face in a perfect mirror."

Rabindranath Tagore (1861 - 1941)

Osho
1931 - 1990

a) Quote for Morning Contemplation

"You exist in time, but you belong to eternity. You are a penetration of eternity into the world of time." (Osho)

Reflection for Deep Recovery (Sharabi)

There was an urgency associated with stopping drinking, but now that I have stopped drinking, I cannot hurry to achieve "time" in sobriety. I can only be sober now—sober today. How long I have been sober is a calculation, an abstract concept, ultimately not rooted in tangible reality—which is today and now. Sobriety appears to exist in time, but it really is a penetration of eternity, a shadow cast on a screen of time that is hung by the mind. Only today's sobriety is real and eternal; today's life contains all of life.

"I existed from all eternity and, behold, I am here; and I shall exist till the end of time, for my being has no end."

Kahlil Gibran (1883 - 1931)

---

b) Quote for Evening Contemplation

"When you understand life in its totality, only then can you celebrate; otherwise not. Celebration means: whatsoever happens is irrelevant—I celebrate. Celebration is not conditional on certain things: 'When I am happy, then I will celebrate,' or, 'When I am unhappy, I will not celebrate.' No. Celebration is unconditional; I celebrate life." (Osho)

Reflection for Deep Recovery (Sharabi)

The Third Step is the beginning of celebration. Once I turn my will and my life over to the care of the Universe, I am able to celebrate existence without laying down conditions. In the old days, when I was feeling down, I drank to cheer myself; when I was feeling up, I drank to celebrate. Today I celebrate sobriety itself, irrespective of the things in my life. I turn my paints over to God and say: paint my world in any colors you wish—while I dance to celebrate! Celebration is the antidote to misery.

"The misery of a child is interesting to a mother, the misery of a young man is interesting to a young woman, the misery of an old man is interesting to nobody."

Eric Hoffer (1898 - 1983)

Osho
1931 - 1990

a) Quote for Morning Contemplation

"You will find meaning in life only if you create it." (Osho)

Reflection for Deep Recovery (Sharabi)

All my life, I tried to find meaning and failing to find meaning, I drank. I did not want to work; I wanted to drink. But in recovery, I have discovered that meaning is not there to be found; it is sculpted, moment to moment. I have made sobriety and spiritual growth the most important thing in my life, and I spend time contemplating what that means for me. All else now flows naturally.

"For the meaning of life differs from man to man, from day to day and from hour to hour. What matters, therefore, is not the meaning of life in general but rather the specific meaning of a person's life at a given moment."

Viktor Frankl (1905 - 1997)

---

b) Quote for Evening Contemplation

"All that is great cannot be possessed—and that is one of the most foolish things man goes on doing: man wants to possess." (Osho)

Reflection for Deep Recovery (Sharabi)

Sobriety cannot be possessed; it merely flows through us. That is why we are so free at sharing it. We start from emptiness each morning as we awake and ask God for sobriety that day; we accumulate it through the day, and it gently leaves as we go to sleep at night. Sobriety is a passing. If we become boastful of how many years we have accumulated, we are just displaying our foolishness for we do not own anything. These months—years—of sobriety that I have: do I really think they are mine? If I owned my years of sobriety, I should be allowed to sell some of them, shouldn't I? Make some money on the side?

"If I am what I have and if I lose what I have: who then am I?"

Erich Fromm (1900 - 1980)

"If you have knowledge, let others light their candles in it."

Margaret Fuller (1810 - 1850)

Osho
1931 - 1990

a) Quote for Morning Contemplation

"In love, the other is important; in lust, you are important." (Osho)

Reflection for Deep Recovery (Sharabi)

When I help the newcomer, I try to do it for the sake of the newcomer, not for the sake of my own sobriety or for my ego. If I do it for ego, I will become petty, irritated, and quarrelsome; I will get angry when the newcomer does not do what I am advising. When I am annoyed at the newcomer, my own anger has become the focus; my lack of power and control has become the focus. I have become the important one, not the other. Then it is lust for influencing others and the power to change them—not love of others, not love of service, not love of sobriety. When someone relapses, our natural response must be sadness, not anger. And when someone experiences good fortune or success, our natural reaction must be joy, not jealousy or envy.

"To advise is not to compel."

Anton Chekhov (1860 - 1904)

b) Quote for Evening Contemplation

"A single moment of knowing that you are alone—alone to tread the path, alone to create the path... can penetrate you and society vanishes. You are alone. There is no guru now; there is no one to be followed. There is no leader; there is no guide. You are alone; you are the aloneness. There is no one to adulterate it or contaminate it. It is so pure, innocent and beautiful. This aloneness is the path, this aloneness is meditation." (Osho)

Reflection for Deep Recovery (Sharabi)

The existential awareness of my aloneness drove me to seek company at the bar. But, towards the end, I was intensely lonely in the most miserable way. Now, I have connected with this community of fellows all traveling together but also learning to savor this delicious taste of being alone with myself, even in the midst of a crowded room.

"If you're lonely when you're alone, you're in bad company."

Jean-Paul Sartre (1905 - 1980)

"Loneliness: the pain of being alone. Solitude: the glory of being alone."

Paul Tillich (1886 - 1965)

Osho
1931 - 1990

a) Quote for Morning Contemplation

"When I say be creative, I don't mean that you should all go and become great painters and great poets. I simply mean let your life be a painting; let your life be a poem." (Osho)

Reflection for Deep Recovery (Sharabi)

It is easy to get lost in the seriousness of recovery. At these times, I remind myself that my sober life can be a dance, a poem, a painting. I can be playful and silly, approach life as art. I don't need to be drunk to dance anymore; I can now be drunk with existence itself; I can be high on life!

"Without poets, without artists... There would be no more seasons, no more civilizations, no more thought, no more humanity, no more life even, and impotent darkness would reign forever."

Apollinaire (1880 - 1918)

---

b) Quote for Evening Contemplation

"Everything is simply happy. Trees are happy for no reason; they are not going to become prime ministers or presidents, and they are not going to become rich, and they will never have any bank balance. Look at the flowers—for no reason, it is simply unbelievable how happy flowers are." (Osho)

Reflection for Deep Recovery (Sharabi)

Being happy needs no reason; being unhappy requires reasons. Our natural way—our default state of being—is joy; it is only thinking that make us anxious or unhappy. All it takes to be happy is to stop thinking the thoughts that are responsible for unhappiness—forget tomorrow and forget yesterday—and wake up, be happy today, be joyful right now. A smiling flower is a constant reminder that life is temporary, that happiness, beauty, and joy lie in the moment only, and that is okay—everything is fine. Whatever needs to be done can be done with a smile on our face and joy in our heart while whistling a happy tune.

"Now and then, it's good to pause in our pursuit of happiness and just be happy."

Apollinaire (1880 - 1918)

Osho
1931 - 1990

a) Quote for Morning Contemplation

"There exists no God. What exists is godliness, and that godliness surrounds you. We are all in the same ocean." (Osho)

Reflection for Deep Recovery (Sharabi)

As I look around the meeting room, I realize we are all in the same ocean. I become aware of the godliness we are immersed in. Once we were all struggling in the river of alcoholism and now we have reached safety in the ocean of recovery. My thoughts of God just serve to remind me of the godliness that surrounds me. It is the godliness in this fellowship that inspires me; I allow myself to be touched and moved, to be transformed.

b) Quote for Evening Contemplation

"Love is not a relationship; love is a state of being; it has nothing to do with anybody else. One is not "in love," one is love. And of course when one is love, one is in love—but that is an outcome, a by-product, that is not the source. The source is that one is love." (Osho)

Reflection for Deep Recovery (Sharabi)

Who I am is love. The moment I acknowledge that I am love, loving flows naturally. I need not try to "get" to love or try to figure out whom I love or what loving entails. Love is the source of Being; it is at the center of Being. I am never so at peace as when I am in touch with my natural love, and then love comes pouring out as joy. My love is not a feeling; it is simply being a loving presence —naturally—and has nothing to do with the choices that people make or the conditions I find myself in. If they want to leave, I love them as they go. Yes, I may lose them, but I will find myself—from loving with such generosity.

"Love is not a thing to understand or a thing to feel. Love is not a thing to give and receive. Love is a thing only to become... and eternally be.

Sri Chinmoy (1931 - 2007)

Osho
1931 - 1990

a) Quote for Morning Contemplation

"I had always wanted not to be a master to anybody. But people want a master; they want to be disciples; hence, I played the role. It is time that I should say to you that now many of you are ready to accept me as the friend." (Osho)

Reflection for Deep Recovery (Sharabi)

If I find a sponsor who wants to be my master, I shall bid him or her goodbye. I am not here to find a master; I am here to find a friend and a guide who will help me find myself. Masters want obedience, and guides want me to grow. Masters want to name my destination; guides want me to name my destination and then help me get there.

"Friendship marks a life even more deeply than love. Love risks degenerating into obsession; friendship is never anything but sharing."
Elie Wiesel (1928 - 2016)

---

b) Quote for Evening Contemplation

"My whole love and respect is for the person who accepts himself totally, as he is. He has courage. He has courage to face the whole pressure of the society which is bent upon splitting him into divisions—into good and bad, into saint and sinner. He is really a brave, courageous being who... declares to the skies his reality, whatever it is." (Osho)

Reflection for Deep Recovery (Sharabi)

The antidote to self-hate is not self-love or self-esteem; it is self-acceptance. Acceptance requires no preparation and is available any moment I choose it. It takes courage to move away from "good" and "bad." Acceptance does not mean stagnation; rather, it is the starting point for growth and change. When change is motivated by self-loathing, it feels forced—a struggle. But with self-acceptance, change happens by itself, easily, rather naturally, motivated by moving "towards" rather than "away from."

"Many of us pretend to believe we are sinners. Consequently, all we can do is pretend to believe we have been forgiven. As a result, our whole spiritual life is pseudo repentance and pseudo bliss."
Brennan Manning (1934 -2013)

Osho
1931 - 1990

a) Quote for Morning Contemplation

"This pain is not to make you sad. This pain is just to make you more alert—because people become alert only when the arrow goes deep into their heart and wounds them." (Osho)

Reflection for Deep Recovery (Sharabi)

I have been wounded by the pain of alcoholism. That arrow has penetrated deep into my heart and soul. It is with me always, perhaps as a memory, perhaps as just a vague awareness, but it has made me alert and awake. While many in the world are asleep we alcoholics have been awakened by pain. In recovery, I am learning to live with the pain I have suffered, and it has sanctified me; I am grateful for the experience, grateful that I have been awakened. I thank the pain. Sometimes, a completely happy childhood is the worst preparation for life.

"Lord, bring me difficulties because they carry me closer to you, faster."
John of the Cross (1542 - 1591)

---

b) Quote for Evening Contemplation

"The natural desire of the human mind is to become special. The mind is always ready to go on some ego trip. Unless the desire to be special disappears, you will never be special. Unless you relax into your ordinariness, you will never relax." (Osho)

Reflection for Deep Recovery (Sharabi)

I am a garden-variety alcoholic—just like everyone else. I am not obliged to be more clever, witty, honest, or deep than others. Above all, I do not need to be more humble than others. I can be average; be content, be ordinary. Anonymity is the spiritual antidote to the urge to be special. The messages I received growing up were that I needed to perform, accomplish, excel, and distinguish myself. Perhaps I made this up myself, but it became my habitual way of impressing others. In my adulthood, my need to be special shows up as jealousy when someone else is successful. Here in recovery, I can relax into being ordinary; they accept me. I no longer need to put others down in order to distinguish myself. It is a great relief after all these years of trying to be extraordinary.

Osho
1931 - 1990

a) Quote for Morning Contemplation

"It has been discovered by psychologists that in wartime people are more happy than in peacetime. In wartime, their life has a thrill. In peacetime, they look bored." (Osho)

Reflection for Deep Recovery (Sharabi)

The tumult and chaos of the drinking life were thrilling until circumstances forced me to turn away. In the beginning, the prospect of a life without alcohol or drugs seemed boring, even if it was peaceful. But recovery has brought a purpose and meaning to life. In Deep Recovery, that purpose for me is contemplation, meditation, and spiritual growth. The contemplation of the thoughts in this book is now thrilling in its own right. I never knew that peace could be so exciting!

"People don't notice whether it's winter or summer when they're happy."
Anton Chekhov (1860 - 1904)

---

b) Quote for Evening Contemplation

"A holy scripture that comes through tradition ... to simply imbibe it like a parrot is suicidal. You are poisoning yourself because the more knowledgeable you become, the less is the possibility for you to search, seek, and find ... Unless you attain it by your own effort, it is absolutely useless. A God that is handed over to you is worth nothing ... A word is always empty unless it contains your experience." (Osho)

Reflection for Deep Recovery (Sharabi)

Just memorizing the Big Book will not keep me sober; simply quoting lines from it will not get the job done. It is my efforts to search, seek and find my truth that will illuminate my path. Other people's ideas of God become an obstacle rather than a help. I have a responsibility in recovery, not simply to believe in Him or Her, but to get to know God—my God.

"These people have learned not from books, but in the fields, in the wood, on the river bank. Their teachers have been the birds themselves when they sang to them..."
Anton Checkhov (1860 - 1904)

Osho
1931 - 1990

a) Quote for Morning Contemplation

"Anarchism is basically the transformation of the individual in such a way that the government becomes superfluous. He lives in the light of his consciousness, fully aware of what he is doing ... Making an effort to convert someone to your ideology, is a trespass of that individual's consciousness. Unless he invites you, it is aggression." (Osho)

Reflection for Deep Recovery (Sharabi)

The recovery movement is true anarchy: no "authority" and no "rules." No one decides who can be admitted and who is thrown out. Each is his or her own master, choosing a "Higher Power" of his own understanding and taking on only those precepts that he or she chooses. Recovery is for those who want it, not for those who need it; I cannot make anyone "want" recovery or make them work the Steps when they are unwilling. That would be aggression, an intrusion into their autonomy, and simply ineffective in the long run.

---

b) Quote for Evening Contemplation

"They are chatterboxes, but they can believe they are transferring something to you because they themselves don't have anything other than the word... But a man who knows can never feel that it is possible to transfer truth. He can inspire you to inquire, but he cannot transfer to you the truth itself." (Osho)

Reflection for Deep Recovery (Sharabi)

A sponsor who never stops lecturing is the sponsor from hell. And often, the words he or she is saying are things someone else said to him or her. But the true and committed sponsor is here, not to teach precepts and beliefs, but to inspire me to inquire, to come to my own truth. My truth can only come from personal experience and inquiry, not from hearsay, and my truth can only be mine, not something I get from someone else, not something I can transfer to someone else. Truth is more than mere facts; truth is personal, while facts are impersonal. Powerlessness is deeply personal; it cannot simply be given or transferred to someone.

"It was impossible to get a conversation going; everybody was talking too much."

Yogi Berra (1925 - 2015)

Osho
1931 - 1990

a) Quote for Morning Contemplation

"Freedom from is always from the past. Freedom for is always for the future. Freedom from is ordinary, mundane... Freedom for is creativity. You have a certain vision that you would like to materialize, and you want freedom for it. Freedom from, at the most, can take away your handcuffs. Freedom for is a spiritual dimension." (Osho)

Reflection for Deep Recovery (Sharabi)

Initially, I came to recovery to get freedom from oppression—the oppression of a drinking life. But, in Deep Recovery I continue in the fellowship, not because I am afraid of going back to drinking, but because sobriety offers me "freedom for," not just "freedom from." The question facing me today is: what am I going to do with the freedom that I now have?

"You wanna fly, you got to give up the shit that weighs you down."
Toni Morrison (1931-2019)

---

b) Quote for Evening Contemplation

"Being happy, you create a possibility for others to be happy. And this is real service; this is not sacrifice at all." (Osho)

Reflection for Deep Recovery (Sharabi)

The best way to help another alcoholic is to find my happiness and to show my happiness. This is service work, much more effective than telling others to pray or telling them they ought to be grateful. True gratitude is private and will show itself naturally as joy. This backdrop of joy is always present for the sober individual in recovery and can be accessed even during life's difficulties. Let me display this joy rather than admonishing others to be grateful. It is real service if I can show my authentic joy at meetings.

"Being happy is a matter of personal taste."
Pierre Teilhard de Chardin (1881 - 1955)

Voltaire
1694 - 1779

a) Quote for Morning Contemplation

"God is a circle whose center is everywhere and circumference nowhere." (Voltaire)

(Attributed to Timaeus of Locres, a character in Plato's Dialogues, quoted by Voltaire in his "Philosophical Dictionary.")

Reflection for Deep Recovery (Sharabi)

Wherever I am—the center of God is right there. And the place where God ends and something else begins—the edge of God—is nowhere. It does not exist. Therefore, there should be no difficulty finding God; He is already wherever I am. In fact, God is not to be found, for finding implies He has been lost. God has always been here; He needs merely to be acknowledged. The fish in the ocean cannot "find" water, but it can acknowledge water; so it is with us and God.

---

b) Quote for Evening Contemplation

"Each player must accept the cards life deals him or her, but once they are in hand, he or she alone must decide how to play the cards in order to win the game." (Voltaire)

Reflection for Deep Recovery (Sharabi)

It is fruitless to ask: why am I alcoholic? But the moment I acknowledge powerlessness over alcohol, then I have accepted the particular genetic condition I have rather than stubbornly fighting it. I can begin working out how to play the game of life with the cards I have been dealt. Winning the game of life simply means having a life that is working. Yes, it is possible to have been dealt the card of alcoholism and the cards of every other misfortune that I have encountered and still win the game of life. Recovery teaches me how.

"In the face of an obstacle which is impossible to overcome, stubbornness is stupid."

Simone de Beauvoir (1908 - 1986)

Voltaire
1694 - 1779

a) Quote for Morning Contemplation

"Four thousand volumes of metaphysics will not teach us what the soul is." (Voltaire)

Reflection for Deep Recovery (Sharabi)

Getting to know ourselves in our depth cannot be accomplished by the mere reading of books, by taking on belief systems, or even through intellectual inquiry. I cannot create an intellectual plan to live from the heart or from the soul. The soul is not accessible through thinking. The soul exists in a plane beyond mind and thought. Sobriety exists beyond mere abstinence. Abstinence belongs in the physical plane, but sobriety lies in those vast spiritual heights. Sobriety requires soulfulness and heart, not just metaphysics, intellectualism, positive thinking, or beliefs.

"The constant assertion of beliefs is an indication of fear."
Krishnamurti (1895 - 1986)

b) Quote for Evening Contemplation

"Every man is guilty of all the good he did not do." (Voltaire)

Reflection for Deep Recovery (Sharabi)

There are sins of omission and sins of commission. "Defects of character" refer to the wrongs we have committed, and "shortcomings" refers to the good things we walked away from doing. In recovery, it is insufficient merely to be willing to help others. We must actively seek out alcoholics and befriend them gently, even when they are too shy and restrained to reach out. At every meeting, we must find someone we have not spoken with before; we must not merely hang out in comfort with familiar friends. And we must consciously strive not to turn away from "difficult" newcomers. Perhaps they have been sent here to teach us. After all, if we turn away from them, who will befriend them?

"One's life has value so long as one attributes value to the life of others."
Simone de Beauvoir (1908 - 1986)

"I'd rather be sorry for something I had done than for something I didn't do."
Kris Kristofferson (born 1936)

Voltaire
1694 - 1779

a) Quote for Morning Contemplation

**"Judge a man by his questions rather than by his answers."
(Voltaire)**

Reflection for Deep Recovery (Sharabi)

It is easy for me to stand up at meetings to declare my eager
convictions, my sincere beliefs, and the answers I have settled
on. But it takes courage for me to stand up and to declare the
questions I am still struggling with. It opens up the entire room
to the spirit of inquiry. In recovery, we are not concerned that you
are grappling with questions; we are worried about the answers
you claim to have found. Contemplative spirituality is about
lingering with the deep questions, about keeping heart and mind
open, not accepting canned answers. "Question" comes from
"quest": seeking.

*"One of the things that is wrong with religion is that it teaches us to be
satisfied with answers which are not really answers at all."*

Richard Dawkins (born 1941)

b) Quote for Evening Contemplation

**"Let us read and let us dance; these two amusements will never do
any harm to the world." (Voltaire)**

Reflection for Deep Recovery (Sharabi)

Reading turns us inwards, and dancing turns us outwards. By
balancing these two rather harmless activities—mental and
physical—we can grow while having fun. You are apparently
reading this book; now you need to go out and dance. Dancing
sober is a true victory, especially for those of us who needed
to drink to dance. From times immemorial, dancing has been a
universal expression of joy in every tribe, every culture, and every
nation. Isn't it appropriate to celebrate our newfound sober life
with dance? We can live life itself like a dance, expressing our
freedom and our joy! Dancing is about forgetting self and rejoicing
in the sense of space, freedom, and movement. Let us focus on
the dance itself and not on how others might watch and judge our
dance. Let us not even judge ourselves.

"I would believe only in a God that knows how to dance."

Friedrich Nietzsche (1844 - 1900)

Voltaire
1694 - 1779

a) Quote for Morning Contemplation

"Men will always be mad, and those who think they can cure them are the maddest of all." (Voltaire)

Reflection for Deep Recovery (Sharabi)

There is madness—and arrogance—in thinking that we know exactly how to get another person sober. We must all be humbled by how much we don't know about the madness of this disease, how much we don't know about the madness of the individual in front of us, and, most of all, how unaware we are of our own madness. Thinking that we know why we drank is madness; believing that we know exactly how we got ourselves sober is madness too. We must become available to the mystery of the disease and the mystery of this gift of sobriety, develop a deep reverance for something larger than us which is at work here.

"A tavern is a place where madness is sold by the bottle."

Jonathan Swift (1667 - 1745)

---

b) Quote for Evening Contemplation

"Those who can make you believe absurdities can make you commit atrocities." (Voltaire)

Reflection for Deep Recovery (Sharabi)

Even if I believe that God's will exists, I must be humble in believing that anyone can know God's will. Before I accept any belief or point of view, I must ask myself: "Can this belief harm me? Can this belief harm others?" Numerous atrocities have been committed in the name of God and religion—and self-righteousness. It continues even today.

"Men never do evil so completely and cheerfully as when they do it from religious conviction."

Blaise Pascal (1623 - 1662)

"Religion! How it dominates man's mind, how it humiliates and degrades his soul. God is everything, man is nothing, says religion. But out of that nothing God has created a kingdom so despotic, so tyrannical, so cruel, that... gloom and tears and blood have ruled the world since gods began."

Emma Goldman (1869 - 1940)

Voltaire
1694 - 1779

a) Quote for Morning Contemplation

"Think for yourselves and let others enjoy the privilege to do so too." (Voltaire)

Reflection for Deep Recovery (Sharabi)

I must allow others to do their own thinking, and I must respect them and the conclusions they come to, even if I disagree. They do not live in the same space of consciousness that I inhabit. I try to operate on the notion that nobody is ever wrong. I cannot get frozen into my opinions, which may be valid in my universe, but their opinions are valid in theirs. What may seem obvious to me as the only correct view is—always—just one of many possible views on the subject.

"We cling to our own point of view, as though everything depended on it. Yet, our opinions have no permanence; like autumn and winter, they gradually pass away."

Chuang Tzu (370 - 287 B.C.)

b) Quote for Evening Contemplation

"Every man is a creature of the age in which he lives, and few are able to raise themselves above the ideas of the time." (Voltaire)

Reflection for Deep Recovery (Sharabi)

Our thinking is determined by society and the times we exist in, the communities we belong to, and the culture surrounding us. Weakness and powerlessness are not fashionable in today's culture; society is entranced with the archetypes of the hero and the warrior who never gives up. Yet, it is precisely this "giving up" of our fight with alcohol that allows us to crawl away. Recovery involves principles that rose above the ideas of the time. And recovery spirituality must grow and expand beyond traditional religious principles and the thinking of our present time, even the thinking within these rooms.

"No great idea in its beginning can ever be within the law. How can it be within the law? The law is stationary; the law is fixed. The law is a chariot wheel which binds us all regardless of conditions or place or time."

Emma Goldman (1869 - 1940)

"All great truth begin as blasphemies."

George Bernard Shaw (1856 - 1950)

Voltaire
1694 - 1779

a) Quote for Morning Contemplation

"God is a comedian playing to an audience that is too afraid to laugh." (Voltaire)

Reflection for Deep Recovery (Sharabi)

I must never get so solemn in recovery that I fail to appreciate God's jokes. Many religions bring out only the terrifying aspects of God, but looking around at the world, it is apparent that God is a comedian. The thought of God should bring a smile to my face, not a frown, not anxiety. Spirituality should not be grim; it must include playfulness, joy, laughter, and mischief. In Deep Recovery, I view the world with amusement and appreciate absurdity. I am among people who laugh a lot, don't take life too seriously but take sobriety seriously.

"The reason angels can fly is because they take themselves lightly."
G. K. Chesterton (1874 - 1936)

---

b) Quote for Evening Contemplation

"Opinions have caused more ills than the plague or earthquakes on this little globe of ours." (Voltaire)

Reflection for Deep Recovery (Sharabi)

Facts may exist, but opinions are not facts. There is no "honesty" about an opinion; it is just an opinion. Ultimately, there are no truths—only opinions. I have to be careful of getting riled up while pressing my opinion or arguing against another one's opinion. If I want to experience freedom, I can give up my opinion of others and my opinion of their opinions; simply accept everybody where they are and deal with them as they are. I may have opinions and beliefs, but I am not my opinions or beliefs. Who I am is deeper. If I take my opinions seriously, my opinions will become my prison. Just as A.A. "has no opinion on outside issues," I can try to have fewer opinions on outside matters. I can also see multiple sides to issues; therefore, I don't have to be rigid.

"Nothing is more dangerous than an idea when it's the only one we have."
Emile Chartier (1868 - 1951)

Voltaire
1694 - 1779

a) Quote for Morning Contemplation

"The safest course is to do nothing against one's conscience. With this secret, we can enjoy life and have no fear." (Voltaire)

Reflection for Deep Recovery (Sharabi)

We each have the ability to sense right from wrong. If we just do the next right thing, we will live with a clean conscience and sleep well each night. But if we are trying to justify something to ourselves, then we must suspect that it is probably wrong. If we live with integrity, there should never be a need to justify anything to ourselves or feel guilty. I fooled myself for years with rationalization and self-justification. Now I recognize them.

"Do the right thing. It will gratify some people and astonish the rest."
Mark Twain (1835 - 1910)

"With integrity, you have nothing to fear, since you have nothing to hide. With integrity, you will do the right thing, so you will have no guilt."
Zig Ziglar (1926 - 2012)

b) Quote for Evening Contemplation

"We are rarely proud when we are alone." (Voltaire)

Reflection for Deep Recovery (Sharabi)

Pride and vanity are always the result of imagining how others are judging us. So is "self-esteem"—which sounds rather arrogant, doesn't it? What is needed is not "self-esteem" but avoidance of self-deprecation. When there is no one to judge us, we will be free of pride and vanity—and shame—unless we have internalized these "others" and proceed to judge ourselves. If we can avoid this, there will be no shame or self-esteem—low or high. Humility involves no comparisons. Vanity and pride are always the result of comparing, as are self-deprecation and shame. We do not need to shame ourselves into good behavior, nor are we proud of our talents and goodness. It is all part of just being natural.

"A person with high self-esteem is often one with a narcissistic personality disorder... devoted to hiding his or her secret emptiness."
James Hollis (born 1940)

"Radical humility.: take no credit for your talents, intellectual abilities, aptitudes, or proficiencies. Be in a state of awe and bewilderment."
Wayne Dyer (1940 - 2015)

Voltaire
1694 - 1779

a) Quote for Morning Contemplation

"It is dangerous to be right in matters on which the established authorities are wrong." (Voltaire)

Reflection for Deep Recovery (Sharabi)

Every organization—including the recovery community—will make trouble for the person who challenges the current hierarchical thinking, who goes against commonly accepted thought. But for recovery to evolve, grow, and remain vital, change is needed. How can an organization which preaches that change is essential for the individual in recovery, itself remain frozen and unchanging?

"I cannot help fearing that men may reach a point where they look on every new theory as a danger, every innovation as a toilsome trouble, every social advance as a first step toward revolution, and that they may absolutely refuse to move at all."

Alexis de Tocqueville (1805 - 1859)

---

b) Quote for Evening Contemplation

"One great use of words is to hide our thoughts." (Voltaire)

Reflection for Deep Recovery (Sharabi)

It is possible to repeat cliches and quotes from the Big Book and to avoid revealing any of our own thoughts—indeed, to avoid thinking itself. "Not thinking" may have some limited use in the beginning when we are confused and our "thoughts" reject this program or justify drinking. But in the long haul, avoiding thinking for myself will stunt my growth. It will keep me stagnant, and I will begin to rot. In deep recovery, we are not afraid of people contemplating things and having their own thoughts; we encourage it, and we require it.

"... my face is a mask which, with or without my consent, conceals my real nature from others."

W. H. Auden (1907 - 1973)

a) Quote for Morning Contemplation

"The most important decision you make is to be in a good mood." (Voltaire)

Reflection for Deep Recovery (Sharabi)

The mood I am in is a function of what I am focusing on, what alternative reality I am comparing "now" to, what things I consider myself entitled to, and what expectations I have. Any sober person can put himself or herself in a good mood just by thinking of the drunken life he or she has left behind. Gratitude will always put me in a good mood, and all it takes to be grateful is to remember. Another name for gratitude is appreciation. I can put myself in a good mood by appreciating what is present—what I have available. It is purely a matter of perspective.

"The ultimate reality of the world is neither matter nor spirit; it is no definite thing, but a perspective."
Jose Ortega y Gasset (1883 - 1955)

---

b) Quote for Evening Contemplation

"The secret of being a bore is to tell everything." (Voltaire)

Reflection for Deep Recovery (Sharabi)

My words are usually more interesting to me than to others. I should say what I need to say, then stop. Rambling is irresponsible, selfish, boring, and annoying. I must avoid sharing everything my mind while others are waiting for me to sit down. I should not abuse their politeness and graciousness. I need to distill the essence and offer my words as if each is precious. Recovery happens also in the silence between comments; I should not rush to fill the silence. Excessive speaking is often an attempt to alleviate anxiety. Instead, I can counter internal anxiety by getting interested in others. Then, I will always be engaged and entertained, even excited; I will also be better liked.

"Enjoyment appears at the boundary between boredom and anxiety when the challenges are just balanced with the person's capacity to act."
Mihaly Csikszentmihalyi (born 1934)

Voltaire
1694 - 1779

a) Quote for Morning Contemplation

"Faith consists in believing what reason cannot." (Voltaire)

Reflection for Deep Recovery (Sharabi)

Faith inspires and moves us in ways that reason cannot. The disease of alcoholism may not be amenable to reason, but it can be dislodged by faith. From the depths of depravity that alcohol led me to, recovery looked impossible. But I acquired some faith, and I became open to miracles; I came to believe that I could be restored to sanity even if I could not see exactly how this could happen. Many reasonable men who looked at me, shook their heads, and walked away would be quite surprised to see where I am today: a happy, productive member of the human race.

"Only when you drink from the river of silence shall you indeed sing. And when you have reached the mountain top, then you shall begin to climb. And when the earth shall claim your limbs, then shall you truly dance."

Kahlil Gibran (1883 - 1931)

---

b) Quote for Evening Contemplation

"God gave us the gift of life; it is up to us to give ourselves the gift of living well." (Voltaire)

Reflection for Deep Recovery (Sharabi)

We were put into this world with no guidelines. We were given life but no instruction book. Our parents, teachers, and priests tried to give us advice, but it was made-up, anyway, and often, their advice did not work for us. In recovery, we don't give advice, but we present some principles for people to consider—sobriety, honesty, thoughtfulness, and concern for others. These principles will allow me to give myself a gift—that of living life well. Living well is a daily process. Life comes at us point-blank, stunning in its immediacy. We must be creative and generate ourselves anew each moment. Life is always new, and our stale old perspectives and attitudes may not be what is needed. Today is new; today is to be lived well, starting from scratch.

"Your living is determined not so much by what life brings to you as by the attitude you bring to life; not so much by what happens to you as by the way your mind looks at what happens."

Kahlil Gibran (1883 - 1931)

Voltaire
1694 - 1779

a) Quote for Morning Contemplation

"Regimen is superior to medicine." (Voltaire)

Reflection for Deep Recovery (Sharabi)

A regimen is a disciplined and consistent set of behaviors. In recovery, we are after lasting remedies to the problems of life, not temporary fixes with chemicals and resolutions. Recovery is a regimen that works to restore people to sobriety and sanity. However, we are not doctors, and we have no business telling people to stop taking drugs that their doctors have prescribed. Certain individuals may require pharmaceutical remedies for the treatment of acute conditions, and such support may be necessary to allow them to participate fully in a program of recovery. In the long run, however, there is no shortcut to, or avoidance of, the regimen of work required for recovery.

"Discipline yourself, and others won't need to."

John Wooden (1910 - 2010)

b) Quote for Evening Contemplation

"Life is thickly sown with thorns, and I know no other remedy than to pass quickly through them. The longer we dwell on our misfortunes, the greater is their power to harm us." (Voltaire)

Reflection for Deep Recovery (Sharabi)

We may not have control over the thoughts and feelings that well up in us, but we have some control over how long we dwell on them and how much we focus on them. Obsessing over things we cannot change does not help anything or anyone. In my youth, my parents gave me attention when something was wrong; I got trained to claim that that the sky was falling to get attention. Life will give us problems and misfortunes; none of them is ever a reason to drink, and we should not think that they could be. Today, labeling situations or events as "sobriety-threatening" is creating unnecessary drama. Stop making a fuss.

"If you're going through hell, keep going."

Winston Churchill (1874 - 1965)

"Your thoughts and emotions are the drama that you create in your mind."

Sadhguru (born 1957)

Voltaire
1694 - 1779

a) Quote for Morning Contemplation

"Man is free at the instant he wants to be." (Voltaire)

Reflection for Deep Recovery (Sharabi)

As long as I keep battling this demon—keep trying to control and conquer my drinking—I will never be free. But that freedom from the domination of alcohol is available the moment I accept that I cannot handle that first drink. This program does not take away the freedom to drink; it has, instead, offered me the freedom to be sober. If the value of the sacrifice is measured in how attached I was to it, then I have made a great investment in freedom by sacrificing my attachment to alcohol.

"The person most in control is the person who can give up control."
Fritz Perls (1883 - 1970)

---

b) Quote for Evening Contemplation

"To learn who rules over you, simply find out who you are not allowed to criticize." (Voltaire)

Reflection for Deep Recovery (Sharabi)

In early sobriety, I heard someone criticizing the Big Book. I thought, "Oh, he cannot do that! Surely he is going to drink." But his critique was a thoughtful one, showing that he was engaging with the questions. After all, the Big Book was written a long time ago by drunks who had been sober for just a few years. The founders had many character defects themselves. While there is great wisdom in the Big Book, there probably is some nonsense. As long as I am thoughtful, inquisitive, and respectful, I can contemplate and debate things said in it—and grow from it. In recovery, nobody rules over me; there is nothing and no idea I am not allowed to criticize in a constructive way that furthers my growth and recovery. Nor can I claim immunity from criticism myself for my ideas and interpretations.

"The need to be right is the sign of a vulgar mind."
Albert Camus (1913 - 1960)

Voltaire
1694 - 1779

a) Quote for Morning Contemplation

"Ice-cream is exquisite. What a pity it isn't illegal." (Voltaire)

Reflection for Deep Recovery (Sharabi)

When alcohol is illegal, as it is to young adults, it is precisely the forbidden nature of drink that makes it attractive. It is the soul trying to break free, asserting its individuality, breaking from the demand for obedience and conformity. But today, when most people are drinking, I assert my individuality by staying sober. I get to create my own idea of "goodness" and to live an ethical life based on my own standards, to generate my own morals and style.

"To become a person does not necessarily mean to be well-adjusted, well-adapted, approved of by others. It means to become who we are... not just to fit in. We are here to be different. We are here to be the individual.
James Hollis (born 1940)

"Society in general always seems to honor its living conformists and its dead troublemakers."
Wayne Dyer (1940 - 2015)

b) Quote for Evening Contemplation

"If God did not exist, it would be necessary to invent him." (Voltaire)

Reflection for Deep Recovery (Sharabi)

People have the power to imbue sacredness to any object or image they choose and then to use that as a focus for attention and prayer. Through this, they can access a feeling of sacredness and a sense of the deep—a numinous feeling. This sense of the deep is necessary for sustaining recovery. The acknowledgment of this dimension is what distinguishes 12-step recovery programs from mere psychological or cognitive attempts to get people to stop drinking. It is not that we just invent or conjure up the idea of God, but that the notion of God is a light that illuminates the path of recovery. The word "God"—and even the concept of God—is simply a placeholder for something that allows each of us to access a state of deep awe, reverence, humility, and silence to escape from the noisy hubbub of the material world. Recovery calls on us to develop such a placeholder—a symbolic entity that we each can call our Higher Power—and use that as a resource, not just for staying sober but for inspiration to live a sound, moral life.

Voltaire
1694 - 1779

a) Quote for Morning Contemplation

"Life is a shipwreck, but we must not forget to sing in the lifeboats." (Voltaire)

Reflection for Deep Recovery (Sharabi)

It is inevitable that shipwrecks will occur in life, but when we have been rescued and are sitting in a lifeboat, we must remember to sing. Expressing that joy is the surest way to show gratitude and to offer encouragement to others. Let us not lament the loss of room service on the ship or the half-eaten steak we had to abandon. And thoughts of the still-suffering alcoholic, while legitimate, must not dampen our joy at being rescued or weaken our voice. For it is our song that may ultimately attract him to our boat.

"Tell the truth. Sing with passion. Work with laughter. Love with heart. 'Cause that's all that matters in the end."

Kris Kristofferson (born 1936)

---

b) Quote for Evening Contemplation

"Cherish those who seek the truth but beware of those who find it." (Voltaire)

Reflection for Deep Recovery (Sharabi)

Seeking the truth is a journey, and we all are on it. But when we "find" the truth, the journey has ended. We become boring and predictable, trying to preach our truth to people we can corner. We stop growing and we stop changing; finding the truth makes us lazy. It is in the seeking—and not the finding—that our salvation lies.

"To travel hopefully is a better thing than to arrive."

Robert Louis Stevenson (1850 - 1894)

"Let me keep my distance, always, from those who think they have the answers.
"Let me keep company, always, with those who say, 'Look!' and laugh in astonishment, and bow their heads."

Mary Oliver (born 1935)

Voltaire
1694 - 1779

a) Quote for Morning Contemplation

"Wherever my travels may lead, paradise is where I am." (Voltaire)

Reflection for Deep Recovery (Sharabi)

Faith is not the expectation that, at some point, life will be okay.
Faith is the realization that everything is okay right now. Nothing
is wrong. Heaven is not some utopia in the imagination or in the
distant future. Heaven is what is now. The Kingdom of God is right
here, at hand right now. I need to wake up to what is. I should
not fritter away the gift of consciousness on thoughts about how
things are not the way they "should" be; regrets that things did not
happen differently from the way they did—thoughts that take me
away from the here and now.

"Paradise is not a place; it is a state of consciousness."

Sri Chinmoy (1931 - 2007)

---

b) Quote for Evening Contemplation

"To pray to God is to flatter oneself that with words, one can alter nature." (Voltaire)

Reflection for Deep Recovery (Sharabi)

We do not appeal to God to change the world; we pray to God to
help us change ourselves. In that act of prayer, it is we who are
transformed. We need our prayer; God does not need our prayer.
In my drinking days, my prayers used to be: "God, please let me
get away with it this one time, and I promise never to do it again!"
I fancied myself to be a deal maker who could negotiate his way
out of jams. I thought I could coax God into following my will
and my wishes, flattering myself that with words, I could alter
the course of the world. A part of me still believes in this magic,
for it is comforting. But I am learning, instead, to pray simply for
acceptance.

*"Prayer is not an old woman's idle amusement. Properly understood and
applied, it is the most potent instrument of action."*

Mahatma Gandhi (1869 - 1948)

Voltaire
1694 - 1779

a) Quote for Morning Contemplation

"We are neither pure, nor wise, nor good; we do the best we know." (Voltaire)

Reflection for Deep Recovery (Sharabi)

We don't know why we drank, and we don't know how we stopped. We are not saints, nor do we consider ourselves virtuous or pious. But we get together, shake hands, drink some bad coffee, tell stories, and laugh—and somehow, we keep each other sober. This humble and grateful approach to recovery is apparently sufficient to sustain sobriety for millions of alcoholics.

"No institution can possibly survive if it needs geniuses or supermen to manage it. It must be organized in such a way as to be able to get along under a leadership composed of average human beings."

Peter Drucker (1909 - 2005)

b) Quote for Evening Contemplation

"Optimism is the madness of insisting that all is well when we are miserable." (Voltaire)

Reflection for Deep Recovery (Sharabi)

There seems to be pressure in these recovery rooms to stand up and declare how wonderful life is and how grateful I am. But life has its ups and downs; some days, I just feel miserable. I don't need to pretend that all is wonderful. Don't worry, they tell me; it is normal, and this too shall pass. A good day is when I feel great, and I don't take a drink. A great day is when I feel miserable, and I still don't take a drink. These days harden me, mature me, make me sturdy in sobriety. I do not indulge in foolish and false public optimism; I try to be real. When someone asks me, "How is your life?" I reply, "Good enough! Good enough, right now!"

"Let us learn to appreciate there will be times when the trees will be bare and look forward to the time when we may pick the fruit."

Anton Chekhov (1860 - 1904)

a) Quote for Morning Contemplation

"Hope is patience with the lamp lit." (Tertullian)

Reflection for Deep Recovery (Sharabi)

I spent my drinking life at the bottom of a hole, hoping that someone would pull me out. I would sit in a dark corner of the bar waiting for that special person to walk in, become enamored with me, and rescue me. But I was not actively seeking or searching. I was not working on myself, nor was I trying to get anywhere: I did not have the lamp lit. Today, I have stopped drinking; I keep the lamp lit, and I stay alert. I peer for a visitor to appear in the darkness: a sage, a thought, an inspiration, an insight, a revelation, an awakening...

"The soul should always stand ajar... ready to welcome the ecstatic experience."

Emily Dickinson (1830 - 1886)

---

b) Quote for Evening Contemplation

"The pleasure of those who injure you lies in your pain. Therefore they will suffer if you take away their pleasure by not feeling pain." (Tertullian)

Reflection for Deep Recovery (Sharabi)

Resentment is our way of punishing ourselves for other people's shortcomings. I wish to be the one to determine my mood, not hand that decision over to others. And, specifically, when I am in a "bad" mood, I do not want to blame someone else as the cause of it like I used to do. People act based on self-interest; that is just a human trait. I do not hold on to the notion that wrong has been done to me or that I am a victim of injustice. Praying for someone is a way of proclaiming that I have risen above my resentment. This gesture alone shall reduce my suffering.

"There is no point in hanging someone if he is not averse to the idea."

Mark Twain (1835 - 1910)

"Holding on to anger is like grasping a hot coal with the intent of throwing it at someone else; you are the one who gets burned."

Ancient Buddhist saying from "Visuddhimagga" (5th century)

339

Tertullian
c.160 - c.225 A.D.

a) Quote for Morning Contemplation

"Fear is the foundation of safety." (Tertullian)

Reflection for Deep Recovery (Sharabi)

Fear of alcohol is healthy. It is the foundation of safety in early recovery. It is fear, too, that kept my evolutionary ancestors safe from dangers and allowed them to survive long enough for their lineage to produce me. The quality of fearlessness has been eliminated from our genes by natural selection. I am thankful to God for putting fear as an emotion, but I also ask God for help in dispelling the fear of unreal and imaginary dangers that can keep me paralyzed. Physical safety is primary, but "emotional safety" is a concept to protect the false front—persona or self-image that I am presenting to the universe—from metaphorical threats.

"Being able to feel safe with other people is probably the single most important aspect of mental health; safe connections are fundamental to meaningful and satisfying lives."

Bessel van der Kolk (born 1943)

b) Quote for Evening Contemplation

"Nothing that is God's is obtainable by money." (Tertullian)

Reflection for Deep Recovery (Sharabi)

God's grace cannot be bought with money or with promises of good behavior—or even with good behavior itself. As a drunk, I tried to barter with God. I had thoughts of accumulating so much power and money and of having everything handled that I would not need God anymore. Today I know that I cannot buy sobriety no matter how much money I bring or by checking myself into the most expensive treatment center in the country. In recovery, sobriety is free. However, it calls for the surrender of all I own. I need not take a vow of poverty, but I seek to be satisfied with the money I have so that the pursuit of money does not distract me from the spiritual path.

"What's money? A man is a success if he gets up in the morning and goes to bed at night and in between does what he wants to do."

Bob Dylan (born 1941)

"Money won't make you happy... but everybody wants to find out for themselves."

Zig Ziglar (1926 - 2012)

Tertullian
c.160 - c.225 A.D.

a) Quote for Morning Contemplation

"Truth engenders hatred of truth. As soon as it appears, it is the enemy." (Tertullian)

Reflection for Deep Recovery (Sharabi)

When confronted with the truth about alcohol—or even about myself—my response was hostility towards, and hatred of, the person who spoke that truth. Then it was denial and hatred of the truth itself. It wasn't alcohol that was the enemy; it was the truth about alcohol that had appeared as the enemy. For years I had loved my delusions; they were my friends and reality was the enemy. Today, I try to perceive and accept truth as it is, and my willingness to be humble is the tool that averts distortion. Humility is just a willingness to face the truth, and truth threatens any false front I am trying to keep up. Therefore, humility requires a willingness to not attach myself to any self-image I may have created. The True Self requires no image to shore it up.

---

b) Quote for Evening Contemplation

"The entire fruit is already present in the seed." (Tertullian)

Reflection for Deep Recovery (Sharabi)

The entire drunken evening—that sordid episode that people report was last night—was already contained in that first drink. An entire ruined life is present in the seed of "One drink won't hurt." And the whole fruit of sobriety is contained in that first seed: the willingness to get honest with myself. With each new insight I have in recovery; each time I respond thoughtfully instead of reacting mindlessly, and with each newcomer I embrace and welcome into the fellowship—I have planted a seed for future change.

"Don't judge each day by the harvest you reap but by the seeds that you plant."

Robert Louis Stevenson (1850 - 1894)

Tertullian
c.160 - c.225 A.D.

a) Quote for Morning Contemplation

"You cannot parcel out freedom in pieces because freedom is all or nothing." (Tertullian)

Reflection for Deep Recovery (Sharabi)

I cannot be somewhat sober, just like I cannot be somewhat pregnant or have a "little bit of alcoholism." I cannot surrender progressively; some things in life are just all or nothing. I cannot be somewhat committed to the recovery path. I cannot turn some things over to the care of God while keeping the right to practice some character defects. I have to be entirely ready—not somewhat ready—to have God remove all these defects of character—all of them, not some of them. As the Big Book tells us: it is necessary to let go absolutely. Then you are free.

---

b) Quote for Evening Contemplation

"He who lives only to benefit himself confers on the world a benefit when he dies." (Tertullian)

Reflection for Deep Recovery (Sharabi)

Selfishness, self-centeredness... these characterized me. As a practicing alcoholic, my continued survival was of little benefit to anyone else. The cards I received in rehab felt like they said: "Get well or die... please!" Even in recovery, going around the room with each person talking about his or her self-centeredness is only a further manifestation of self-centeredness. The way out of this vicious circle is to stop focusing on my internal experience and to practice empathy. When I encounter a surly waitress or a rude waiter, I can—rather than going with my instinct to get angry and to denounce poor service—make myself think about the bad day or even bad life that the person is having. The surly ones in the world need my love more than happy ones, for they are the people having a difficult time.

Self-centeredness prayer: "Lord, please help me to learn thoughtfulness and concern for others in addition to my concern for myself."

from DEEP RECOVERY

a) Quote for Morning Contemplation

"It is certain because it is impossible." (Tertullian)

Reflection for Deep Recovery (Sharabi)

Miracles exist only because they are impossible. Faith is necessary precisely because belief in God is irrational. Powerlessness proves that victory over alcohol is impossible, yet it is powerlessness that makes recovery certain. The acceptance of powerlessness over alcohol follows the three stages explained by Schopenhauer below:

"All truth passes through three stages. First, it is ridiculed. Second, it is violently opposed. Third, it is accepted as being self-evident."

Arthur Schopenhauer (1788 - 1860)

b) Quote for Evening Contemplation

"Arguments about Scripture achieve nothing but a stomachache and a headache." (Tertullian)

Reflection for Deep Recovery (Sharabi)

Arguments about the passages in the Big Book and the "correct" interpretation of the words result only in a stomachache and a headache. But it appears that some people come to meetings for a stomachache and a headache; maybe it is an acceptable substitute for a hangover. I hereby accept all interpretations of the Big Book as long as it works for the person—and only he or she gets to decide if it is working or not. Their drinking does not prove that their interpretation is wrong—just like my sobriety does not prove that my interpretation is right.

"I learned long ago, never to wrestle with a pig. You get dirty, and besides, the pig likes it."

George Bernard Shaw (1856 - 1950)

Tertullian
c.160 - c.225 A.D.

a) Quote for Morning Contemplation

"He who flees will fight again." (Tertullian)

Reflection for Deep Recovery (Sharabi)

We must flee our battle with alcohol so we can win our war with alcoholism.

"The reason fat men are good-natured is they can neither fight nor run."
Theodore Roosevelt, (1858-1919)

---

b) Quote for Evening Contemplation

"Man is one name belonging to every nation upon earth. In them all is one soul though many tongues, one spirit though many sounds." (Tertullian)

Reflection for Deep Recovery (Sharabi)

That name "alcoholic" belongs to every nation, every tribe, every profession, every social class—the same sickness of the soul. The recovery movement is international—planet-wide. We may, one day, export the soul of recovery to other star systems, even to life forms who may have no tongues and cannot speak (but can swallow.) Yes, we have unity within this fellowship of recovery, but can we extend it to the commonality we have with all humans on the planet? Any "club" we form—defined by values, principles, belief systems, geographical boundaries, even common goals—tends to exclude others who may not subscribe to this fixed idealogy. Atheists versus believers; religion versus religion; ethnic groups fighting; nations at war with other nations, and "good" people condemning "bad" people. Even opinions different from our own are not tolerated. We reject the person, not just the opinion. Tertullian's vision of unity—one nation of man (and woman)—is monumental, especially expressed in his time.

344

Tertullian
c.160 - c.225 A.D.

a) Quote for Morning Contemplation

**"Truth persuades by teaching, but does not teach by persuading."
(Tertullian)**

Reflection for Deep Recovery (Sharabi)

We do not persuade the newcomer with our words; we let truth
teach him or her. We cannot convince someone that she or he is
alcoholic; she needs to convince herself. We allow his or her own
experience to be the teacher. We help her see that she is powerless
over alcohol once that first drink enters her body. We explain that
a certain percentage of the human race has this condition that
they are unable to stop once they start drinking—at least with any
consistency. And for such people, alcohol constitutes a perennial
threat unless they commit to total abstinence. Even then, it is not
clear, for alcohol is cunning, baffling, and powerful.

*"Experience is not what happens to you; it's what you do with what
happens to you."*
Aldous Huxley (1894 - 1963)

---

b) Quote for Evening Contemplation

"Truth does not blush." (Tertullian)

Reflection for Deep Recovery (Sharabi)

Truth reveals itself with no embarrassment about being seen
fully. It is the "I," seeing the truth who may blush. I blushed
when I first got a glimpse of who I had become. But I covered my
embarrassment with more alcohol. Today I can face the truth of
my alcoholism—and my character defects—without blushing.
It is acceptance of my character defects that ultimately leads to
transcending them. I neither regret the past nor wish to shut the
door on it. At the foundation of my recovery is my commitment
and my willingness to face the truth squarely: the truth about
alcohol and the truth about myself. And it is surprising how
willing Truth is to be naked before me.

*"In order to discover truth, we must be truthful ourselves, and must
welcome those who point out our errors as heartily as those who approve
and confirm our discoveries."*
Max Muller (1823 - 1900)

Tertullian
c.160 - c.225 A.D.

a) Quote for Morning Contemplation

"Out of the frying pan into the fire." (Tertullian)

Reflection for Deep Recovery (Sharabi)

This phrase—invented by Tertullian two thousand years ago—aptly describes my own creative attempts to solve my drinking problems. Every attempt to get out of a jam landed me in a bigger jam. Perhaps you can relate to it? Today we are still going to encounter problems and challenges, but we have the tools and support to cope with them, to survive them, indeed, even to grow from them.

"What matters most is how well you walk through the fire."
Charles Buchowski (1920 - 1994)

b) Quote for Evening Contemplation

"One man's religion neither harms nor helps another man." (Tertullian)

Reflection for Deep Recovery (Sharabi)

Religion is a personal thing in recovery, which can neither harm nor hurt anyone as long as it is kept private and not imposed. It is not something to be shouted from the podium nor preached to the bewildered newcomer under the guise of recovery. As sponsors, we must be careful about pushing our religion down the throats of our sponsees; they may gag and choke, and they may run away forever. Religion can be beaten into people (and children,) but spirituality has to be discovered—from the inside. Then it can grow into religion. Each person must find his or her own truth and his own religion, and the recovery movement strongly supports this self-discovery. The God from your upbringing can be like training wheels on your bicycle while you find your balance—your own Higher Power.

"Don't limit a child to your own learning, for he was born in another time."

Rabindranath Tagore (1861 - 1941)

Tertullian
c.160 - c.225 A.D.

a) Quote for Morning Contemplation

**"We have it in our power to begin the world over again."
(Tertullian)**

Reflection for Deep Recovery (Sharabi)

*"Waking up this morning, I smile,
Twenty-four brand new hours are before me.
I vow to live fully in each moment and to look at all beings with
eyes of compassion."*

Thich Nhat Hanh (born 1926)

This is a wonderful thought with which to begin each day. And, "...
looking at all beings with eyes of compassion" includes myself. I
must forgive myself for all my past foolishness and mistakes, for
today is the first day of the rest of my recovery.

---

b) Quote for Evening Contemplation

**"You can't undo anything you've already done, but you can face up
to it. You can tell the truth. You can seek forgiveness. And then
let God do the rest." (Tertullian)**

Reflection for Deep Recovery (Sharabi)

Tertullian said this almost two thousand years ago, and it
continues to be a framework for living with integrity. These
thoughts have filtered down to form the backbone of the program
of recovery. Facing up to the truth—indeed, becoming willing
to acknowledge the truth—is the key characteristic required for
recovery. We walk the fine line between acknowledging the past
and beating ourselves up about it. When we were drinking, we
used to feel bad about our behavior, and we sought forgiveness;
but then we repeated the behavior. Of what use was that? We
were helpless. Helplessness is about the past, about excuses;
powerlessness opens up the future; it is about honesty.

*"It is astonishing what force, purity, and wisdom it requires for a human
being to keep clear of falsehoods."*

Margaret Fuller (1810 - 1850)

Wittgenstein
1889 - 1951

a) Quote for Morning Contemplation

"For a truly religious man, nothing is tragic." (Wittgenstein)

Reflection for Deep Recovery (Sharabi)

When I truly turn my will and my life over to the care of God, I stop attaching labels of "good" and "bad" to things that happen. When I accept something—anything, even my pain—it ceases to be "tragic." It ceases to be a "problem" and becomes just something to be dealt with. Misfortunes and death are inevitable—though often inconvenient. In the view of the universe, even earthquakes and floods, and tsunamis are just "natural phenomenon." It is we who label things "tragic." For the recovering, alcoholism is not tragic but a blessing. For the ones in Deep Recovery, nothing is tragic.

"All great spirituality is about what we do with our pain. If we do not transform our pain, we will transmit it to those around us."

Richard Rohr (born 1943)

b) Quote for Evening Contemplation

"One of the most misleading representational techniques in our language is the use of the word 'I.' " (Wittgenstein)

Reflection for Deep Recovery (Sharabi)

"Since every other thought can occur only after the rise of the 'I'-thought and since the mind is nothing but a bundle of thoughts, it is only through the inquiry 'Who am I?' that the mind subsides."

Ramana Maharshi (1879 - 1950)

"Who am I?" is the deepest question possible. If I stay with it, knowing that any answer I come up with is insufficient and incorrect, it can become the entire basis for my spiritual growth and my entry into the deep mystery of existence. We are not talking about our body, our face that might appear on a wanted poster, or the identity we have on social media. We are talking about the "I" in the space of consciousness, not the stories about "I" that we are living out of. We might discover at some point that there is no "I;" only Being.

Wittgenstein
1889 - 1951

a) Quote for Morning Contemplation

"When one is frightened of the truth, it is never the whole truth that one has an inkling of." (Wittgenstein)

Reflection for Deep Recovery (Sharabi)

The whole truth can set me free, but the partial truth can terrify and imprison me. If I am fearful of a life without alcohol and the responsibility it entails, I am not seeing the entire truth. If I am frightened at the prospect of having to give up all my character defects, I just haven't glimpsed the freedom of letting go. If I just see the truth of powerlessness and unmanageability without realizing that restoration to sanity is possible, it is not just frightening—it is terrifying.

"The facts are always friendly. Every bit of evidence one can acquire, in any area, leads one that much closer to what is true."

Carl Rogers (1902 - 1987)

b) Quote for Evening Contemplation

"Hell isn't other people. Hell is yourself." (Wittgenstein)

Reflection for Deep Recovery (Sharabi)

"... placing principles before personalities... "

(Tradition Twelve.)

In Tradition Twelve, the personality referred to here is not the personality of the one I am annoyed with. The "personality" is me—the one who is generating the annoyance, the one who is being judgmental and controlling—feeling righteous and superior. When I am agitated and angry, I am to act on recovery principles instead of my urges. That first reaction is my personality; what I do with it is "principles." Once I enter recovery, I cannot let my personality run the show; I must surrender to principles.

"Nobody is ever sent to Hell: he or she insists on going there."

W. H. Auden (1907 - 1973)

Wittgenstein
1889 - 1951

a) Quote for Morning Contemplation

"A confession has to be part of your new life." (Wittgenstein)

Reflection for Deep Recovery (Sharabi)

My transformation begins with an acknowledgment of what is—by the confession of obvious truths that I have been resisting. The most critical quality necessary for successful recovery (according to "How it Works") is the capacity to be honest with myself. The Steps involve some form of confession in the First, Fourth, Fifth, Sixth, Seventh, Eighth, Ninth, and Tenth Steps—indeed, eight of the Twelve Steps! Some are acknowledgments to myself, and some, confession to others. These confessions will lead me to my new life.

---

b) Quote for Evening Contemplation

"You get tragedy where the tree, instead of bending, breaks." (Wittgenstein)

Reflection for Deep Recovery (Sharabi)

In recovery, willfulness, stubbornness, and rigidity are the sickness, while flexibility and willingness to change are the virtues. It is the rigid oak tree that gets broken by the storm, not the blade of grass that blends easily.

"Willingness is a realization that one is already a part of some cosmic process, and it is a commitment to participation in that process... Willfulness is the setting oneself apart from the fundamental essence of life in an attempt to master, direct, control or otherwise manipulate existence."

Gerald May (1940 - 2005)

"Gnosticism has always been difficult to define, largely because it is a system of thought based upon and frequently amended by experiences of nonordinary states of consciousness, and thus it is resistant to theological rigidity."

Stephan Hoeller (born 1931)

Wittgenstein
1889 - 1951

a) Quote for Morning Contemplation

"Philosophy is like trying to open a safe with a combination lock: each little adjustment of the dials seems to achieve nothing, only when everything is in place does the door open." (Wittgenstein)

Reflection for Deep Recovery (Sharabi)

Each of the Twelve Steps is a little adjustment of the dials of a combination lock. Each by itself may seem to achieve little or nothing. But when everything is in place, the door opens to a spiritual awakening. If I do the Steps, I will be surprised at the place I end up at—something I could not have anticipated. There is no prize for reading and understanding the Steps; I must actually do them to get the benefits.

"Knowledge is the reward of action. For it is by doing things that one becomes transformed. Executing a symbolical gesture, actually living through, to the very limit, a particular role, one comes to realize the truth inherent in the role."

Heinrich Zimmer (1890 - 1943)

b) Quote for Evening Contemplation

"The mystical is not how the world is, but that it is." (Wittgenstein)

Reflection for Deep Recovery (Sharabi)

The magic of enlightened consciousness is the fundamental awareness, "I am," and "The world is." And the mystery to contemplate, perhaps, is not just that the world "is," but that my consciousness is able to perceive and to participate in the "is-ness" of the universe. My consciousness could be seen as the universe itself, acquiring self-awareness, for my consciousness is a part of the universe.

"The universe shivers with wonder in the depths of the human..."

Brian Swimme (born 1950)

Wittgenstein
1889 - 1951

a) Quote for Morning Contemplation

"It is much easier patiently—and tolerantly—to avoid the person you have injured than to approach him as a friend. You need courage for that." (Wittgenstein)

Reflection for Deep Recovery (Sharabi)

From afar, the Ninth Step looks terrifying. But the eight Steps prior—particularly the Third Step—will give me the self-acceptance and the courage necessary, so I no longer have to avoid these people that I have harmed. I am free of guilt by this time and have no self-hate: it is not about me. I am at a place where I can apologize and make amends without trying to convince them that I feel "really bad," for that would be about me, not about them. Amends is not about healing me but about facilitating their healing—their mending—from the unjust suffering they had to endure in my hands. This takes courage and generosity; there is nothing I want from them.

---

b) Quote for Evening Contemplation

"Philosophy is not a theory but an activity." (Wittgenstein)

Reflection for Deep Recovery (Sharabi)

Recovery is not a theory but a set of actions—new activity and behavior inspired by a change of attitude. Attitude is seen only through the behavior it generates. My gratitude manifests itself not as a feeling but as actions that show gratefulness. And my love of sobriety is not merely a pleasant thought or a desire; it is a willingness to inconvenience myself for the sake of the newcomer and others in recovery, a willingness to inconvenience myself for myself. When I think about it, I realize the only thing I have control over is which muscles to contract and in what sequence. All actions—breathing, speaking, laughing, traveling, moving my head or my eyeballs, sitting down and getting up from my chair, arguing, eating, pissing, going to meetings, dialing someone on the phone—these are all made up of muscle contractions. My philosophy must lead to the correct muscle contractions.

"For one human being to love another; that is perhaps the most difficult of all our tasks, the ultimate, the last test and proof, the work for which all other work is but preparation."

Rainer Maria Rilke (1875 - 1926)

Wittgenstein
1889 - 1951

a) Quote for Morning Contemplation

"It is one of the chief skills of the philosopher not to occupy himself with questions which do not concern him." (Wittgenstein)

Reflection for Deep Recovery (Sharabi)

The philosophy of recovery is a personal philosophy meant only for me. I must not occupy myself with preaching these principles to others in my life who are not dealing with alcoholism. The way they live and the choices they make are not questions that concern me. I must not take the lazy way out by getting angry or annoyed with them. On the other hand, the way I adjust to their choices and their intrusion in my life are questions that must concern me constantly, and a personal struggle I engage with daily.

"What we observe is not nature itself but nature exposed to our method of questioning. Our scientific work in physics consists in asking questions about nature in the language that we possess and trying to get an answer from experiment by the means that are at our disposal."

Werner Heisenberg (1901-1976)

b) Quote for Evening Contemplation

"If we spoke a different language, we would perceive a somewhat different world." (Wittgenstein)

Reflection for Deep Recovery (Sharabi)

My worldview is determined by the words I use to describe it. The people in my life show up consistent with the way I describe them to myself. If I wish people to change, I simply need to speak differently of them—not just in my words but in my thoughts and in my attitude towards them. I can choose to see them with appreciation and compassion; I can attribute the highest motives to their actions, and I need not feed the condemning thoughts about them that occasionally pop up. Most of all, I must stop seeking validation for my complaints about them, using words to present a convincing case to others and to myself. If I share my complaint, it must be to find an insight, a lever, a perspective that will allow me to drop the complaint. If we spoke a language without the notion of "should," "shouldn't," "if," and "is," we would relate to the world in an entirely different way.

"Whatever you might say the object "is", well it is not."

Alfred Korzybski (1879 - 1950)

Wittgenstein
1889 - 1951

a) Quote for Morning Contemplation

"Wisdom is passionless. But faith is... a passion." (Wittgenstein)

Reflection for Deep Recovery (Sharabi)

Wittgenstein said a religious belief "could only be something like a passionate commitment to a frame of reference." In recovery, we are not satisfied with wisdom about staying sober. We want more. We want passion about this path—this interpretation—about helping other alcoholics, about living according to the principles of recovery. This passion is what brings recovery to life, fully and with awareness.

""The difference between passion and addiction is that between a divine spark and a flame that incinerates."
Gabor Maté (born 1944)

"Destiny unfolds in the pursuit of individual fascinations and interests... The unity of the world rests on the pursuit of passion."
Brian Swimme (born 1950)

---

b) Quote for Evening Contemplation

"At the core of all well-founded belief, lies belief that is unfounded." (Wittgenstein)

Reflection for Deep Recovery (Sharabi)

All beliefs rest on some fundamental assumptions that are taken a priori; in other words, strong edifices of "knowledge" are built on foundations that fall apart when deeply questioned. Underneath all world views lie axioms that can neither be proved nor disproved. Anything presented in language is a mere convenience; it cannot be presented as unshakable "truth." In recovery, I am not so concerned whether these recovery principles are true. I am more interested in showing that they are practical and useful—that they work. We ask the newcomer not just to believe our program but to practice it.

"There lives more faith in honest doubt, believe me, than in half the creeds."
Alfred Lord Tennyson (1809 - 1892)

"Any proposition containing the word "is" creates a linguistic structural confusion which will eventually give birth to serious fallacies."
Alfred Korzybski (1879 - 1950)

Wittgenstein
1889 - 1951

a) Quote for Morning Contemplation

"Never stay up on the barren heights of cleverness, but come down into the green valleys of silliness. If people never did silly things, nothing intelligent would ever get done." (Wittgenstein)

Reflection for Deep Recovery (Sharabi)

Wittgenstein also said that a serious and useful philosophical work could be written consisting entirely of jokes. In recovery, we transmit deep philosophical concepts through humor and wit. There is a playfulness and silliness present in meetings that allow us to joke about deadly serious matters. Silliness is often the foundation of creativity and intelligence; many "silly" cliches form important principles of recovery. That odd, inconsequential, and whimsical thought, pursued further, can lead to buried treasure that provides a significant turn to the course of life.

"There are things that are so serious that you can only joke about them."
Werner Heisenberg (1901-1976)

---

b) Quote for Evening Contemplation

"The limits of my language means the limits of my world." (Wittgenstein)

Reflection for Deep Recovery (Sharabi)

My world is defined, limited, by the language I have available to speak about it. My internal experience is often molded by the words available in my language to describe it. People who speak a different language often have access to new feelings and new states of being that their language has words for. To be spiritual in a way that transcends worldly languages, I must leave the universe of language and rise into silence. If you can speak about it, it is not spiritual. Words are only pointers to deeper things—and they are not even things!

"I sometimes find it half a sin, To put to words the grief I feel, For words like nature, half reveal, and half conceal the soul within."
Alfred Lord Tennyson (1809 - 1892)

"To use words to sense reality is like going with a lamp to search for darkness."
Alfred Korzybski (1879 - 1950)

Wittgenstein
1889 - 1951

a) Quote for Morning Contemplation

"I don't know why we are here, but I'm pretty sure that it is not in order to enjoy ourselves." (Wittgenstein)

Reflection for Deep Recovery (Sharabi)

Enjoying myself is fine, but it cannot become the purpose of living, as it had during my drinking days. The universe does not owe me happiness. And happiness, being transitory, can never be the end-point of any strategy but it can be a by-product of correct living, which can lead to moments of happiness. In recovery, I am striving to find a purpose that is larger than my petty personal concerns. My life has to be about things that are larger than my life.

"This is the true joy in life, the being used for a purpose recognized by yourself as a mighty one, the being thoroughly worn out before you are thrown on the scrap heap; the being a force of Nature instead of a feverish selfish little clod of ailments and grievances, complaining that the world will not devote itself to making you happy."

George Bernard Shaw (1856 - 1950)

b) Quote for Evening Contemplation

"Resting on your laurels is as dangerous as resting when you are walking in the snow. You doze off and die in your sleep." (Wittgenstein)

Reflection for Deep Recovery (Sharabi)

Recovery requires moving constantly. I am living on the down escalator; I need to keep moving just to maintain my place in recovery. Resting on my laurels and getting satisfied with the sober days that I have accumulated is certain disaster. I cannot afford to doze off in recovery. I will drink in my sleep. Perhaps my drinking dreams are my deep unconscious urging me to wake up and to get moving.

"The best moments in our lives are not the passive, receptive, relaxing times... the best moments usually occur when a person's body or mind is stretched to its limit in voluntary effort to accomplish something difficult and worthwhile."

Mihaly Csikszentmihalyi (born 1934)

"To keep a lamp burning, we have to keep putting oil in it."

Mother Teresa (1910 - 1997)

Wittgenstein
1889 - 1951

a) Quote for Morning Contemplation

"The world is independent of my will." (Wittgenstein)

Reflection for Deep Recovery (Sharabi)

When I drank, my drinking was happening independent of my will. Today my sobriety is also happening independent of my will. For if I could will myself into sobriety, there would be no need for this program or, this fellowship: no need for God. Today when I cannot impose my will, when others refuse to obey my rules, and when the world will not let me have my way—that is when my recovery is tested. It is how I behave at these times that determines whether I am a mature individual in recovery or a child on the verge of a tantrum.

"In the world, there are only two tragedies. One is not getting what one wants, and the other is getting it."

Oscar Wilde (1854 - 1900)

---

b) Quote for Evening Contemplation

"If a lion could talk, we could not understand him." (Wittgenstein)

Reflection for Deep Recovery (Sharabi)

If I cannot refer to a shared experience, I have no way of understanding the lion's world or his concerns. So too, ordinary people cannot understand addiction. And newcomers are incapable of "understanding" the process of recovery. I must also be wary of claiming that I "understand" the Steps or the Big Book. My understanding is limited to things I can relate to my prior experience. If I am presented something totally new, something that requires a leap, I do not have the resources to decide on it. "Understanding" or agreeing is, therefore, not a tool with which to approach a transformative awakening or a paradigm shift. A spiritual awakening is a quantum leap. Progressive understanding can get us ready for it, but the moment of epiphany itself is a transcendence.

"The Polhode rolls without slipping on the Herpolhode lying in the Invariable Plane."

A principle in Classical Physics describing the motion of spinning tops.

Wittgenstein
1889 - 1951

a) Quote for Morning Contemplation

**"Whereof one cannot speak, thereof one must be silent."
(Wittgenstein)**

Reflection for Deep Recovery (Sharabi)

Only silence can speak about God, about lofty things; words are not adequate. And the silences at meetings are an essential part of recovery; they touch us in places that words cannot. Even words move us only in the silence that follows them. Silence can be absence of sound but a higher silence is absence of thought. Many of us are addicted to thinking; my first thought leads to a second and then a third... much like drinking. And as long as I am drinking or thinking, I am separated from God, from Being.

"Silence is the ocean; speech is a river."

Rumi (1207 - 1273)

"Silence is often misunderstood but never misquoted."

(Unknown)

b) Quote for Evening Contemplation

"Nothing is so difficult as not deceiving oneself." (Wittgenstein)

Reflection for Deep Recovery (Sharabi)

The biggest challenge to sobriety is the ability of the mind to believe its own lies and distortions. And the most important trait for successful and sustained sobriety—as the Big Book asserts—is the ability to "be honest with themselves." The journey to crack the armor of rationalization, justification, and self-deception that I had covered myself with began with the desire and willingness to be honest with myself about myself. Total honesty with myself may be out of reach, but a willingness to be honest is accessible.

"Contempt prior to examination is an intellectual vice, from which the greatest faculties of mind are not free."

William Paley (1743 - 1805)

"If it is necessary sometimes to lie to others, it is always despicable to lie to oneself."

Somerset Maugham (1874 -1965)

Wittgenstein
1889 - 1951

a) Quote for Morning Contemplation

"I sit astride life like a bad rider on a horse. I only owe it to the horse's good nature that I am not thrown off at this very moment." (Wittgenstein)

Reflection for Deep Recovery (Sharabi)

I spent many years sitting astride the horse, drunk out of my mind. The only reason I attribute to being here today, safe, is the benevolence of the horse, the kindness of the universe, and the Grace of God. And—even working the program rather imperfectly as I am—the only reason I continue to be sober today is the Grace of God and the good nature of the fellowship. I cannot take credit for my sobriety.

"A horse can be so quick that he can leave the rider behind."

(Unknown)

b) Quote for Evening Contemplation

"A man will be imprisoned in a room with a door that's unlocked and opens inwards as long as it does not occur to him to pull rather than push." (Wittgenstein)

Reflection for Deep Recovery (Sharabi)

All those years I spent trying to control my drinking! All I needed was to acknowledge my helplessness and stop struggling. I was like the fly bashing its head fruitlessly against the glass window, only to drop, exhausted onto the window sill and find that the window had been open all along—a crack. Much of our struggle comes from not realizing that we have the capacity to be free and that the people we are struggling against are actually trying to help us. As long as we are fighting our helplessness, we are imprisoned; when we acknowledge our powerlessness, we become free.

Wittgenstein
1889 - 1951

a) Quote for Morning Contemplation

"What can be shown, cannot be said." (Wittgenstein)

Reflection for Deep Recovery (Sharabi)

We cannot tell you how to get sober. We can show you how we got sober.

"Don't tell me the moon is shining; show me the glint of light on broken glass."

Anton Chekhov (1860 - 1904)

---

b) Quote for Evening Contemplation

"Death is not an event in life: we do not live to experience death. If we take eternity to mean not infinite temporal duration but timelessness, then eternal life belongs to those who live in the present." (Wittgenstein)

Reflection for Deep Recovery (Sharabi)

Eternity—as timelessness—is not a property of the future; it is a property of the present moment. Eternal life is available to those who are fully immersed in the present moment. Eternity is not composed of a succession of moments. Eternity is composed of one single moment: NOW. The Kingdom of God is at hand—right NOW. Eternal salvation exists only in this moment. Sobriety exists only today. A certain temporary amnesia about the past and the future is necessary for me to be with God in the present, for me to be in today.

"All of us are creatures of a day; the rememberer and the remembered alike. All is ephemeral—both memory and the object of memory."

Marcus Aurelius (121 - 180 A.D.)

Wittgenstein
1889 - 1951

a) Quote for Morning Contemplation

"One often makes a remark and only later sees how true it is."
(Wittgenstein)

Reflection for Deep Recovery (Sharabi)

Many deep comments are made in meetings, but the true depth contained in them may not be obvious or available even to the speaker. We are still discovering new and deeper meanings of phrases in the Big Book that the writers themselves may not have anticipated. In recovery, we know many things that we do not understand. In recovery, I have learned many things that I am still not consciously aware of, that I cannot explain in words and concepts. But these learnings are playing a role in keeping me sober in ways that I cannot fathom or comprehend.

"I needed to write, to express myself through written language not only so that others might hear me but so that I could hear myself."

Gabor Mate (born 1944)

b) Quote for Evening Contemplation

"The real question of life after death isn't whether or not it exists, but even if it does what problem this really solves."
(Wittgenstein)

Reflection for Deep Recovery (Sharabi)

In recovery, we are clear that what matters is how we live today, not what happens after we die. It is not about how long we live; it is about how we live today. This "one day at a time" is a simple philosophy that contains a deep and profound truth: focusing on the present stops my mind from churning about the past, about tomorrow, about life after death. Denying my wrongs took energy; justifying myself took energy. But when I am willing to admit my wrongs, a load lifts off my shoulders. The sun rises on the present, cleaning away the shadows of the past and dispelling my vague fears about death and darkness. I am good and decent today, not to accumulate brownie points for the future, but because I am committed to living the principles of recovery.

"Always go to other people's funerals. Otherwise they won't come to yours..."

Yogi Berra (1925 - 2015)

Kierkegaard
1813 - 1855

a) Quote for Morning Contemplation

"What I really need is to get clear about what I must do, not what I must know, except insofar as knowledge must precede every act." (Kierkegaard)

Reflection for Deep Recovery (Sharabi)

Recovery is a program of action, not a philosophy, theology or a body of knowledge. Armchair contemplation and brooding will not get me sober. The Steps tell me what to do, not what "not-to-do." They never say things like: "don't drink," or "don't lie;" they advise in positive language: "think of elephants," rather than "don't think of elephants."

"...happiness cannot be pursued; it must ensue... as the unintended side-effect of one's personal dedication to a course greater than oneself."

Mihaly Csikszentmihalyi (born 1934)

---

b) Quote for Evening Contemplation

"Life can only be understood backward, but it must be lived forward." (Kierkegaard)

Reflection for Deep Recovery (Sharabi)

I must take committed action without obtaining guarantees on how things are going to turn out. I have been told to focus on the work and to leave the results up to God. My job is to make the best decisions I can, based on the information I have, grounded in the principles of recovery. I can influence—but I cannot control—the future. This has been a huge relief for me because I used to think I had to control future happenings. Today I am fully behind any decisions I take, and I do not waste time in second-guessing myself after the fact. I do not indulge in fruitless, "perhaps I should have taken the other road..." and "what if"s.

"When you come to a fork in the road, take it."

Yogi Berra (1925 - 2015)

Kierkegaard
1813 - 1855

a) Quote for Morning Contemplation

"What matters is to find a purpose, to see what it really is that God wills that I shall do; the crucial thing is to find a truth which is truth for me, to find the idea for which I am willing to live and die." (Kierkegaard)

Reflection for Deep Recovery (Sharabi)

For every recovering alcoholic, sobriety has become an idea to live and die for. Anything less is insufficient except for this mad and total surrender—to the necessity of avoiding even a sip of that first drink. Later, I devote myself to a life of service so I can be useful to my fellow beings. Service and spiritual growth have become my purpose now—looking for God's will and asking for the power to carry it out—in contrast to my purposeless drinking days.

"Find what you love and let it kill you."

Charles Buchowski (1920 - 1994)

b) Quote for Evening Contemplation

"God creates out of nothing. Wonderful you say. Yes, to be sure, but he does what is still more wonderful: He makes saints out of sinners." (Kierkegaard)

Reflection for Deep Recovery (Sharabi)

I am responsible for bringing a nothingness to God so God can create me. I cannot bring my self-will and ask God to create; I must turn my will and my life completely over to God, as asked of us in the Third Step. When I do that, God can make saints out of sinners and sober, responsible, decent citizens out of drunks.

"The whole world is a cyclone. But once you have found the center, the cyclone disappears. This nothingness is the ultimate peak of consciousness."

Osho (1931 - 1990)

Kierkegaard
1813 - 1855

a) Quote for Morning Contemplation

**"Life is not a problem to be solved, but a reality to be lived."
(Kierkegaard)**

Reflection for Deep Recovery (Sharabi)

Things in life appear as problems only when I say: "It shouldn't have been so!" When I practice total acceptance of everything as God's will—or even just acknowledge that "it is what it is,"—I am no longer experiencing life as problems; my complaints vanish. There still will be things that need to be handled, but not with the heaviness of "problems." Given that life is what it is, my job is just to choose what to do next with a light heart and a broad smile, finding joy and amusement and enjoying the beauty around me.

"The most beautiful thing in the world is, of course, the world itself."

Wallace Stevens (1879 - 1955)

---

b) Quote for Evening Contemplation

"People demand freedom of speech as compensation for the freedom of thought which they seldom use. How absurd men are! They never use the liberties they have; they demand those they do not have." (Kierkegaard)

Reflection for Deep Recovery (Sharabi)

I spent years claiming that I had the liberty to get drunk if I wanted to, and I would sit at the bar brooding over my complaints, fretting about the things I didn't have. Today I am using my liberty to be sober: to be clean in mind, body, and soul, to think freely for myself, and to speak my thoughts. The fellowship guarantees me that freedom, and how wonderful it is to be allowed to think for myself. Even the simple things in life that I used to take for granted are beginning to show up as gifts. I focus on enjoying and using the things I have rather than fretting about what I don't have.

"Give me the liberty to know, to utter, and to argue freely according to conscience, above all liberties."

John Milton (1608 - 1674)

Kierkegaard
1813 - 1855

a) Quote for Morning Contemplation

"Face the facts of being what you are, for that is what changes what you are." (Kierkegaard)

Reflection for Deep Recovery (Sharabi)

Any person who has acknowledged that he or she is alcoholic is already a different person than the one before. The First Step contains the kernel of change: the seed of the future. Continuing to face what and who I am, I do an unbiased assessment: an inventory. Just that simple acknowledgment of who I am is sufficient to set the wheels of change in motion.

"If you want the present to be different from the past, study the past."

Spinoza (1632 - 1677)

b) Quote for Evening Contemplation

"Don't forget to love yourself." (Kierkegaard)

Reflection for Deep Recovery (Sharabi)

Loving myself must not be confused with the narcissistic self-obsession I may have practiced. When I am self-centered and self-focused, others exist only as peripheral figures and cardboard cutouts on the drama set of life; I am the lead role. However, when I love myself, I am very aware of others. Loving myself means merely a refusal to condemn and desecrate this creation of God that is me. Change does not need to be motivated by self-hate. Perhaps the past could not have been any different, given the genes I was born with and the experiences I had to go through. I am now at a place where I do not regret the past nor wish to shut the door on it. I proceed from here on with love and acceptance of who I am today.

"Love yourself. Then forget it.
Then, love the world."

Mary Oliver (born 1935)

Kierkegaard
1813 - 1855

a) Quote for Morning Contemplation

"Boredom is the root of all evil—the despairing refusal to be oneself." (Kierkegaard)

Reflection for Deep Recovery (Sharabi)

Boredom is just hostility to existence but without enthusiasm; an anger at the world and at myself, a demand that the world entertains me; a refusal to engage in the enduring richness of this conscious existence that I have been given. "I drink because I am bored," alcoholics have claimed as if a state of numbness and unconsciousness is better than being alive and present. Also: "I won't stop drinking because sobriety sounds awfully boring." It certainly sounds like the refusal to engage meaningfully with life—as it is. In recovery, we take on the job of creating a life for ourselves and engaging in it.

"Alcohol is the anesthesia by which we endure the operation of life."
George Bernard Shaw (1856 - 1950)

---

b) Quote for Evening Contemplation

"Once you label me, you negate me." (Kierkegaard)

Reflection for Deep Recovery (Sharabi)

Once you label me you define me, you limit me, you deny the huge possibility of all that I am outside of your little label. When you label me you also freeze me; you deny me the possibility of changing. But paradoxically, once I label myself alcoholic, I wake up. You labeling me as an alcoholic is a condemnation and a sentence; me labeling myself "alcoholic" is a liberation and a wake-up call. All kinds of change and possibility open up; support and resources become available, and doors open for me to walk through. The Steps become available as a personal resource, not as some intellectual list of possible actions. Accepting this label has freed me and allowed me to create myself anew. This is a disease where self-diagnosis is the only useful one, not a diagnosis by others.

"A name is a label, and as soon as there is a label, the ideas disappear and out comes label-worship and label-bashing, and instead of living by a theme of ideas, people begin dying for labels."

Richard Bach (born 1936)

Kierkegaard
1813 - 1855

a) Quote for Morning Contemplation

The function of prayer is not to influence God, but rather to change the nature of the one who prays." (Kierkegaard)

Reflection for Deep Recovery (Sharabi)

God does not need my prayer, I do. Prayer is not to change God or influence God, but to change me. My willingness to pray, to kneel and surrender, changes my nature and attitude—changes me. The refusal to pray is an unwillingness to subordinate myself. It is the same trait that prevented me from acknowledging the dominance of alcohol in my life, that trait of mad, stubborn, self-will run riot. Prayer represents a posture rather than a plea. Recovery in this program calls for me to acknowledge that I am not Master of everything, that I cannot just instantaneously transform myself into who I wish to be. I need God's help to change.

I hear and behold God in every object, yet understand God not in the least.

Walt Whitman (1819 - 1892)

---

b) Quote for Evening Contemplation

"Patience is necessary, and one cannot reap immediately where one has sown." (Kierkegaard)

Reflection for Deep Recovery (Sharabi)

Nowhere is patience as necessary as in the area of changing my personality and mending broken relationships. I cannot expect people to jump up and embrace me just because I have acknowledged wrongdoing or made (what I thought) were amends. Healing takes time. I must allow people the time and space to resolve their issues with me in their own way and in their own time. Whatever attitude they have towards me., I must show them that I am not crushed, that it is okay with me, and that I accept them with their attitude. Their feelings and stance towards me are their business, not mine. I can only work on my stance towards them, and I have to give time, time.

"Patience is the ability to idle your motor when you feel like stripping your gears."

Barbara Johnson (1927 - 2007)

Kierkegaard
1813 - 1855

a) Quote for Morning Contemplation

"If I am capable of grasping God objectively, I do not believe, but precisely because I cannot do this, I must believe." (Kierkegaard)

Reflection for Deep Recovery (Sharabi)

A "God of my understanding" is merely a placeholder to serve as a focus for my prayer while I develop awe for the immensity of God and the notion that God is beyond anything I am capable of understanding. Indeed the word "God" and even the concept of "God" can only be placeholders for God. It is precisely because the notion of God can be so preposterous to the "objective" mind that faith is necessary.

"Awareness of the divine begins with wonder. When wonder ripens into a full awareness of God, it turns to awe."

Heschel (1907 - 1972)

---

b) Quote for Evening Contemplation

"Anxiety is the dizziness of freedom." (Kierkegaard)

Reflection for Deep Recovery (Sharabi)

The freedom that sobriety represents carries with it the end of avoidance, the willingness to face life, and the terrifying idea of personal responsibility. That is why many turn away from this path. The anxiety in early recovery is because freedom can be dizzying to the prisoner who has been locked in his cell for years, submerged in the stupor of drunkenness. That is why a Higher Power to lean on—and the support of people in the fellowship—will steady my gait as I stumble out into this strange new world. I understand that if I make my choices humbly and allow God into the process, I can relinquish attempting to control happenings. As long as I accept what happens, I can never claim to have made a bad choice or a wrong choice. Whichever way it turns out is God's will for me.

"Freeing yourself was one thing; claiming ownership of that freed self was another."

Toni Morrison (1931-2019)

Kierkegaard
1813 - 1855

a) Quote for Morning Contemplation

"There is nothing with which every man is so afraid as getting to know how enormously much he is capable of doing and... becoming." (Kierkegaard)

Reflection for Deep Recovery (Sharabi)

It is conventional in the rooms of recovery and in religious circles to studiously avoid taking personal credit for sobriety, or indeed, any success, attributing these entirely to God's grace. But the recovering alcoholic has had a role in the matter. He or she is capable of living a disciplined and responsible life, fulfilling obligations to family and society, settint goals, making plans, and completing projects. Glorious accomplishments become possible that could barely be imagined during those chaotic drinking days. Recovery has taught us patience, persistence, and commitment.

"People often overestimate what they can accomplish in one year. But they greatly underestimate what they could accomplish in five years."
Peter Drucker (1909 - 2005)

b) Quote for Evening Contemplation

"Listen to the cry of a woman in labor at the hour of giving birth; look at the dying man's struggle at his last extremity, and then tell me whether something that begins and ends thus could be intended for enjoyment." (Kierkegaard)

Reflection for Deep Recovery (Sharabi)

My feeble search for enjoyment, my fear of missing out on exciting things, my fear of the suffering and pain that life may hold—these drove me to despair, to seek comfort in alcohol. When I gave up this obsession with "enjoying" life, I was able to tune in to a meaningful, rich, and purposeful existence, one that provides deep and lasting contentment. Instead of asking what others could do for me, I began to ask: what can I do for others? This was my spiritual awakening. It gave me the strength to bear pain, to accept my solitude as a soulful place.

"In the country of pain we are each alone."

May Sarton (1912 - 1995)

"When there is pain, there are no words. All pain is the same."
Toni Morrison (1931-2019)

Kierkegaard
1813 - 1855

a) Quote for Morning Contemplation

"Most men pursue pleasure with such breathless haste that they hurry past it." (Kierkegaard)

Reflection for Deep Recovery (Sharabi)

One of the greatest gifts of sobriety is that it has taught me to slow down. I can stop drinking now, but I can enter sobriety only slowly, very slowly. There is no point in being in a hurry to get to some place called serenity. There is plenty of time and plenty of moments to enjoy along the way. If you cannot allow yourself to linger, to savor the joy of wandering, then you are already lost.

"Rivers know this: there is no hurry. We shall get there someday."
A. A. Milne (1882 - 1956)

"When you are in a hurry to do something, just hold back a few seconds. That is all it takes to switch from compulsiveness to consciousness."
Sadhguru (born 1957)

---

b) Quote for Evening Contemplation

"Since my earliest childhood, a barb of sorrow has lodged in my heart. As long as it stays, I am ironic; if it is pulled out, I shall die." (Kierkegaard)

Reflection for Deep Recovery (Sharabi)

Each one of us (alcoholics) carries a barb of sorrow embedded in us, some pain from a childhood event, some wounding from our past. This pain defines us and gives us character. My task is not to get rid of this pain but to learn to carry it with dignity, wit, and a sense of humor. This irony leads me to acceptance rather than bitterness. If I accept this pain as mine and mine alone, it can give me a backbone for navigating life. It can teach me compassion, allow me to relate to others in pain, make me soulful, deep, and gentle. But if I deny this pain, I spend my life simply lashing out at others; it will destroy me.

"I tell you this
to break your heart, by which I mean only
that it break open and never close again
to the rest of the world."

Mary Oliver (born 1935)

Kierkegaard
1813 - 1855

a) Quote for Morning Contemplation

"I have just now come from a party where I was its life and soul; witticisms streamed from my lips, everyone laughed and admired me, but I went away ——————— yes, the dash should be as long as the radius of the earth's orbit—and wanted to shoot myself." (Kierkegaard)

Reflection for Deep Recovery (Sharabi)

We alcoholics can surely understand Kierkegaard's sentiment. We have been so desperately eager to impress; we have often tried to be the life of the party, and yet, we have returned home to an emptiness and an inner bankruptcy. Our pathetic striving for admiration and acceptance can only be resolved when we see that God accepts us. Then, we can accept ourselves. This is the point of the Fifth Step.

b) Quote for Evening Contemplation

"Far from idleness being the root of all evil, it is rather the only true good." (Kierkegaard)

Reflection for Deep Recovery (Sharabi)

Idle people are generally not dangerous; they have not done much harm to humanity. On the other hand, busy, motivated, greedy, and driven people have rained ruin and sorrow on the multitudes. Just look at history. In recovery, I have learned to slow down and practice a special idleness. I have stopped my feverish attempts to change the world and to change others. The only one I am working on is myself, and there is no hurry as long as I am making progress. Oh... and when the urge hits me to walk to the bar or to the fridge for a beer, my idleness can help to keep me sitting in the rocking chair on the porch. And I can use that space to indulge in contemplation.

"It is in our idleness, in our dreams, that the submerged truth sometimes comes to the top."

Virginia Woolf (1882 - 1941)

Kierkegaard
1813 - 1855

a) Quote for Morning Contemplation

"One can advise comfortably from a safe port." (Kierkegaard)

Reflection for Deep Recovery (Sharabi)

Most advice is useless and superior. I must offer the newcomer love until he himself or herself becomes open to advice. I must offer to pick him/her up and drive to a meeting, rather than just telling him to go to meetings. Giving advice is the lazy way of "trying" to "help" the newcomer. It is safe, it requires no investment, and poses no risk. Advice-giving does not necessarily help—it merely creates the illusion of helping and is often done to help the advice-giver feel better. Unsolicited advice equals criticism. Advice-giving creates a superior-inferior relationship, while "support" comes from equals. We support people in their efforts to get sober, not just "advise" them to do things.

"We are advised and led along by second-rate moralists who only know how to work themselves into a delirium and pass their illness onto others."

Emile Chartier (1868 - 1951)

b) Quote for Evening Contemplation

"Never cease loving a person, and never give up hope for him, for even the prodigal son who had fallen most low, could still be saved." (Kierkegaard)

Reflection for Deep Recovery (Sharabi)

"When do I give up hope on an alcoholic?" someone asked. "About two minutes after he has taken his last breath," was the answer. Even that may be questioned, given modern methods of resuscitation. It is necessary for me to keep this in mind because alcoholics and addicts can try my patience and that of even the most devoted, loving, and compassionate family members. Alas, no one can make an alcoholic want to get sober. We have to learn to love from a distance and be ready to help when the occasion is right. I have an understanding now that my impatience comes from an unwillingness to let God's will unfold, an attempt to impose my own will and my timetable. The alcoholic coming in is welcomed with the same love and celebration extended to the prodigal son returning home.

"It ain't over till it's over."

Yogi Berra (1925 - 2015)

Kierkegaard
1813 - 1855

a) Quote for Morning Contemplation

"Trouble is the common denominator of living. It is the great equalizer." (Kierkegaard)

Reflection for Deep Recovery (Sharabi)

Recovery is the one place where the high-powered business executive and the grandmother who has never held a paid job are considered equal, joke with each other, and help each other. Their common denominator—and the great equalizer—has been the trouble that alcohol has created in his or her life. It is amazing how much the educated academic and the sophisticated philosopher can learn about living and about life from the simple person in these rooms. And this learning can continue decades into recovery. We keep coming to meetings not just to share our wisdom, but also to continue our own education.

"There is no sun without shadow, and it is essential to know the night."
Albert Camus (1913 - 1960)

---

b) Quote for Evening Contemplation

"If I were to wish for anything, I should not wish for wealth and power, but for the passionate sense of potential—for the eye which, ever young and ardent, sees the possible. Pleasure disappoints; possibility never." (Kierkegaard)

Reflection for Deep Recovery (Sharabi)

What is life? In one word: possibility. For the drunk, entering recovery is merely the act of becoming present to the possibility of life—of sobriety, of restoration to sanity. This is a huge jump, from the empty dreams of pleasure entertained by the drunk to the ardent and passionate possibility for the sober individual. With recovery, everything is possible, and possibility is everything.

"We discover that as human beings we can live in a possibility instead of in what we have inherited, that instead of just being a human being because we were born that way, we can declare the possibility of being for human beings."

Werner Erhard (born 1935)

Kierkegaard
1813 - 1855

a) Quote for Morning Contemplation

"Faith is the highest passion in a human being. Many in every generation may not come that far, but none comes further." (Kierkegaard)

Reflection for Deep Recovery (Sharabi)

Faith is different from belief. Belief is often driven by fear and avoidance of fearful things, by mindless acceptance and repetition of what we have been told. Beliefs are also stories we make up to comfort ourselves in our despair. But faith becomes possible when we rise beyond despair into the realm of the sublime. Faith is not motivated by the avoidance of unpleasantness but by the drive to be reunited with God. That is the highest passion in a human being. My alcoholism was a perversion of that passion, and in recovery, I returned to the original aim. True faith is surrendering to God without hoping for any particular outcome.

---

b) Quote for Evening Contemplation

"A man who, as a physical being, is always turned toward the outside, thinking that his happiness lies outside him, finally turns inward and discovers that the source is within him." (Kierkegaard)

Reflection for Deep Recovery (Sharabi)

I sought people, places, and things to make me happy. Failing in this, I turned to drink. Curiously, drinking turned me inwards and provided some temporary comfort, but it ended up creating more problems. In recovery, I have learned that the true source of happiness lies inside me. I fill my inside with spirit rather than with distilled spirits. I find the capacity to be happy no matter what the external circumstance.

"If you turn your vision inwards, the whole world will be full of spirit."
Ramana Maharshi (1879 - 1950)

374

Kierkegaard
1813 - 1855

a) Quote for Morning Contemplation

"People understand me so little that they do not even understand when I complain of being misunderstood." (Kierkegaard)

Reflection for Deep Recovery (Sharabi)

Misunderstandings are inevitable; can you survive? We are each going to be misunderstood, misjudged, and treated unfairly at times. Ultimately it is our relationship with God that allows us to survive misunderstandings and continue to "trudge the road of happy destiny." Once you yourself understand and accept this, you will stop feeling forlorn when you are not understood.

"In this place, I am a barbarian because men do not understand me."
Ovid (43 B.C. - 17A.D.)

"There are men too superior to be seen except by the few, as there are notes too high for the scale of most ears."
Emerson (1803 - 1882)

---

b) Quote for Evening Contemplation

"In order to learn true humility, it is good for a person to withdraw from the turmoil of the world, for in life either the depressing or the elevating impression is too dominant for a true balance to come about." (Kierkegaard)

Reflection for Deep Recovery (Sharabi)

Recovery is about learning humility. We withdraw from the turmoil of the world; we turn our will and our life over to the care of God. That is a necessary step for true humility to take hold. In humility, the self and its hankerings get out of the picture, and we can truly see things the way they are, without injecting our own hopes, wants, and beliefs into the picture. We give up our "shoulds" and "shouldn't," both for the world and for people. We approach life with equanimity, and a true balance comes about. Such balance is long-lasting in contrast to the temporary elevations of joy and hollows of depression. We have declared a truce: we will not be everything that others might want us to be, and they do not have to be anything or any way for us to approve of them.

"A person does what he does because he sees the world as he sees it."
Alfred Korzybski (1879 - 1950)

375

Thomas Merton
1915 - 1968

a) Quote for Morning Contemplation

"The beginning of love is the will to let those we love be perfectly themselves, the resolution not to twist them to fit our own image." (Thomas Merton)

Reflection for Deep Recovery (Sharabi)

We think we love, but often, we are in love with our internal image of that person. Then, we will get angry when they do their own thing. When I love a person truly and cleanly, I am just watching them unfold. I support them as they explore this life. It is impossible to be disappointed by them, for I shall not be requiring them to be any particular way. I must love the newcomer like this: offer him or her what I have—what we have—but not get mad at them if they don't want it. People come to recovery and progress through it in their own time, not on mine.

"Love and work are the cornerstones of our humanness."
Sigmund Freud (1856 - 1939)

---

b) Quote for Evening Contemplation

"My Lord God, I have no idea where I am going. I do not see the road ahead of me. I cannot know for certain where it will end. Nor do I really know myself, and the fact that I think that I am following your will does not mean that I am actually doing so. But I believe that the desire to please you does, in fact, please you. And I hope I have that desire in all that I am doing. I hope that I will never do anything apart from that desire. And I know that if I do this, you will lead me by the right road though I may know nothing about it. Therefore will I trust you always though I may seem to be lost and in the shadow of death. I will not fear, for you are ever with me, and you will never leave me to face my perils alone."

"Prayer of Abandonment." by Thomas Merton

Reflection for Deep Recovery (Sharabi)

My desire to please God is the most I can genuinely offer. It is its own end and reward. We don't please God in order to... anything!

"Believe that none of the effort you put into coming closer to God is ever wasted—even if in the end, you don't achieve what you are striving for."
Nachman (1772 - 1810)

Thomas Merton
1915 - 1968

a) Quote for Morning Contemplation

"To be grateful is to recognize the Love of God in everything He has given us—and He has given us everything. Every breath we draw is a gift of His love, every moment of existence is a grace, for it brings with it immense graces from Him." (Thomas Merton)

Reflection for Deep Recovery (Sharabi)

My gratitude is for existence itself—for every breath I take and for every conscious moment I experience. My existence itself is proof that I have been touched by God. My gratitude is not just for the "good" things or achievements; my gratitude is for consciousness itself. Every moment of existence—and consciousness of existence manifested by consciousness of breath—is a manifestation of grace. Gratitude is simply awareness of grace.

"I would rather be able to appreciate things I cannot have than to have things I am not able to appreciate."

Elbert Hubbard (1856 - 1915)

---

b) Quote for Evening Contemplation

"Gratitude, therefore, takes nothing for granted, is never unresponsive, is constantly awakening to new wonder and to praise of the goodness of God. For the grateful person knows that God is good, not by hearsay but by experience. And that is what makes all the difference." (Thomas Merton)

Reflection for Deep Recovery (Sharabi)

I can be grateful for a day when nothing has happened precisely because nothing has happened that day. I can be grateful that my house did not burn down; I do not take that for granted. I can be grateful that I did not contract smallpox. In even the smallest thing—or non-thing—I am able to find wonder; I experience the goodness of God. To truly experience this goodness, I must let go of my petty judgments of good and bad and my bondage to my likes and my dislikes. By letting in the goodness of God, I experience the wonder of God. And when I am standing in that space, the desire for drink simply does not exist.

"The hardest arithmetic to master is that which enables us to count our blessings."

Eric Hoffer (1898 - 1983)

Thomas Merton
1915 - 1968

a) Quote for Morning Contemplation

**"Our job is to love others without stopping to inquire whether or not they are worthy. That is not our business and, in fact, it is nobody's business. What we are asked to do is to love, and this love itself will render both ourselves and our neighbors worthy."
(Thomas Merton)**

Reflection for Deep Recovery (Sharabi)

The entire notion of judging someone as being "worthy" of my love seems haughty when I consider that God loves and accepts each of us unconditionally. Behavior is either love-giving or love-seeking. If their behavior doesn't appear as love-giving, then it must be love-seeking. If I am annoyed with the behavior of others, it means I have failed to see it as an attempt to seek love and acceptance. This way, I do not condemn the behavior of unhappy people. The "jerks" of this world need my love more than the happy and "good" people; these are probably attracting plenty of love already.

---

b) Quote for Evening Contemplation

"The more you try to avoid suffering, the more you suffer because smaller and more insignificant things begin to torture you in proportion to your fear of being hurt." (Thomas Merton)

Reflection for Deep Recovery (Sharabi)

Fear of suffering—itself—is the greatest suffering. It is called anxiety. People disturb themselves immensely with concern about how to avoid pain and hurt—in the present and in the future. We avoid things, and the burden of those tasks we have kept procrastinating ends up crushing our capacity for joy. However, the willingness to accept and endure difficulties in life is itself, the doorway to serenity. Buddha preached: living is suffering, and life includes distress. The moment I accept that, I have begun to live in the real world—not in my utopian fantasy. The acceptance of difficulties brings me the freedom to do what is needed without drowning in my own complaints.

"The dominant characteristic of an authentic spiritual life is the gratitude that flows from trust—not only for all the gifts that I receive from God but gratitude for all the suffering. Because in that purifying experience, suffering has often been the shortest path to intimacy with God."

Brennan Manning (1934 -2013)

Thomas Merton
1915 - 1968

a) Quote for Morning Contemplation

"Solitude is a way to defend the spirit against the murderous din of our materialism." (Thomas Merton)

Reflection for Deep Recovery (Sharabi)

Solitude is a withdrawal, a cessation of engagement with the mad cacophony of material obsessions, financial success, and public opinion. Solitude is quietness: a silence of the mind. We let go of ideas of doing and having; we banish thoughts of what we are missing. We cannot be alone when our thoughts are raising a murderous din drowning out God's presence. I can be with God only in solitude.

"Tell me to what you pay attention, and I will tell you who you are."
Jose Ortega y Gasset (1883 - 1955)

b) Quote for Evening Contemplation

"Do not depend on the hope of results. You may have to face the fact that your work will be apparently worthless and even achieve no result at all, if not perhaps results opposite to what you expect. As you get used to this idea, you start more and more to concentrate not on the results, but on the value, the rightness, the truth of the work itself." (Thomas Merton)

Reflection for Deep Recovery (Sharabi)

The work in recovery is the sacred engagement with the present and wrestling with the day's challenges. The struggle with the immediacy of existence is what keeps me moving towards a spiritual awakening. Abstract hope and desire can distract me from being fully present to what is, from the activity that is the work itself. In recovery, I must focus on the Steps, not on the Promises. I work the Steps, and sobriety and spiritual growth happen as a by-product—perhaps. That is not my direct concern at the moment. My job is just to chop wood, carry water. This is a deep understanding of the spiritual thrust of recovery.

"Happiness is not a goal...it's a by-product of a life well-lived."
Eleanor Roosevelt (1884 - 1962)

379

Thomas Merton
1915 - 1968

a) Quote for Morning Contemplation

**"Our idea of God tells us more about ourselves than about Him."
(Thomas Merton)**

Reflection for Deep Recovery (Sharabi)

Ideas are constructs of the human mind and, therefore, do not contain God. My ideas of God merely speak to the limitations of the human mind, not to the limitless nature of God. God cannot just be an idea in my mind; God's existence does not rest on my capacity for imagination.

"I want God, not my idea of God."

C. S. Lewis (1898 - 1963)

"The problems of language here are really serious. We wish to speak in some way about the structure of the atoms. But we cannot speak about atoms in ordinary language."

Werner Heisenberg (1901-1976)

---

b) Quote for Evening Contemplation

**"Finally, I am coming to the conclusion that my highest ambition is to be what I already am. That I will never fulfill my obligation to surpass myself unless I first accept myself, and if I accept myself fully in the right way, I will already have surpassed myself."
(Thomas Merton)**

Reflection for Deep Recovery (Sharabi)

I accept myself, and I also accept the present as it is. And in so acknowledging the present as all there is, I lose my notion of "self." For "self" is a postulated entity continuing from the past through present to the future. In the pure awareness of the present, "self" disappears, time disappears, my ego disappears, and with it, the distinction of subject-object evaporates as a fog vanishes with the arrival of sunlight. Acceptance transcends notions of self and brings us to a spiritually awakened state where "is-ness" is all that exists—a sense of union with God. I will have surpassed myself and my notions of self; all is God.

"Genuine self-acceptance is not derived from the power of positive thinking, mind games, or pop psychology. It is an act of faith in the grace of God."

Brennan Manning (1934 -2013)

Thomas Merton
1915 - 1968

a) Quote for Morning Contemplation

"But there is greater comfort in the substance of silence than in the answer to a question." (Thomas Merton)

Reflection for Deep Recovery (Sharabi)

The answers to questions reverberate for a few moments and dissipate. Then the next question pops up. But silence is timeless. In silence, there are no questions, no past or future, no "understanding," no resentment, no regrets, no worry. A spiritual awakening does not happen with the finding of answers; it happens with the disappearing of questions, of thought.

"Have you not noticed that love is silence? It may be while holding the hand of another or looking lovingly at a child or taking in the beauty of an evening. Love has no past or future, and so it is with this extraordinary state of silence."
Krishnamurti (1895 - 1986)

"Computers are useless. They can only give you answers."
Pablo Picasso (1881 - 1973)

b) Quote for Evening Contemplation

"To allow oneself to be carried away by a multitude of conflicting concerns, to surrender to too many demands, to commit oneself to too many projects, to want to help everyone in everything, is to succumb to the violence of our times." (Thomas Merton)

Reflection for Deep Recovery (Sharabi)

It is not necessary for all the wrongs in the world to be righted; the peaceful draw clear boundaries, simply withdrawing from mad, contentious involvement with everything. They carefully pick an individual flower to hold and appreciate instead of getting overwhelmed by all the weeds present everywhere or even, all the flowers. In recovery, if you are expecting to improve everything in your life all at once, you are committing violence on your own soul. Sponsors who feverishly surround themselves with an entourage of "sponsees" have succumbed to a want to help everyone in everything. Finally, if you are hell-bent on improving the whole world, you end up committing violence on everyone—and on yourself.

"Adapt yourself to the life you have been given and truly love the people with whom destiny has surrounded you."
Marcus Aurelius (121 - 180 A.D.)

Thomas Merton
1915 - 1968

a) Quote for Morning Contemplation

**"If you write for God, you will reach many men and bring them joy. If you write for men—you may make some money, and you may give someone a little joy, and you may make a noise in the world, for a little while. If you write for yourself, you can read what you yourself have written, and after ten minutes you will be so disgusted that you will wish that you were dead."
(Thomas Merton)**

Reflection for Deep Recovery (Sharabi)

You can write to please yourself or to please others. But you can also write humbly as a way to serve God and to carry out His will for you. If you decide to write for God, God will write for you.

"You don't write because you want to say something; you write because you have something to say. "

F. Scott Fitzgerald (1896 - 1940)

---

b) Quote for Evening Contemplation

"Reason is, in fact, the path to faith, and faith takes over when reason can say no more." (Thomas Merton)

Reflection for Deep Recovery (Sharabi)

Reason is the trusted horse that can carry me, not into heaven, but right to the stairway to heaven. In that last phase, reason cannot accompany me; only faith gives my legs the strength to climb. Reason can bring you to recovery, but your journey from then on is powered by faith.

"The first gulp from the glass of natural sciences will turn you into an atheist, but at the bottom of the glass, God is waiting for you."

Werner Heisenberg (1901-1976)

"Faith is taking the first step, even when you don't see the whole staircase."

Martin Luther King Jr. (1929 - 1968)

Thomas Merton
1915 - 1968

a) Quote for Morning Contemplation

"The logic of worldly success rests on a fallacy: the strange error that our perfection depends on the thoughts and opinions and applause of other men!" (Thomas Merton)

Reflection for Deep Recovery (Sharabi)

From early childhood, people have manipulated us using approval and disapproval. Many of us never recover; our whole life becomes about seeking regard and respect and avoiding ridicule. My task as an adult is to rise above this need to be applauded by others, to realize that "success" does not depend on how others judge me. My only failure can be a deviation from my truth. Perfection lies in being true to myself; then there is no failure.

"To thine own self be true."

Shakespeare (1564 - 1616) (Polonius, in 'Hamlet.')

b) Quote for Evening Contemplation

"The greatest need of our time is to clean out the enormous mass of mental and emotional rubbish that clutters our minds." (Thomas Merton)

Reflection for Deep Recovery (Sharabi)

I cannot clean my mind out with more thinking; I need to stand outside the mind—in silence—to sweep clean the mind. That is the function of meditation. The mind judges criticizes and condemns; it delivers opinions, declares its likes and dislikes, announces its wishes, complains, and asks why it isn't some other way. It is so tiresome! When I point my accusatory finger at someone, three fingers are pointing back at me. At the same time, my thumb points up at God, reminding me that the person in front of me, as well as I, are God's creation. It allows me to access awe, humility, and reverence and reminds me of the presence of God.

"Whenever you are about to find fault with someone, ask yourself the following question: What fault of mine most nearly resembles the one I am about to criticize?"

Marcus Aurelius (121 - 180 A.D.)

Thomas Merton
1915 - 1968

a) Quote for Morning Contemplation

"When you expect the world to end at any moment, you know there is no need to hurry. You take your time; you do your work well." (Thomas Merton)

Reflection for Deep Recovery (Sharabi)

When I occupy the present fully, time expands, and there is no hurry. I take my time and do each step well. I engage fully with each task in life. Just do the next right thing; don't take shortcuts and do it right. Remember, the world may end at any moment, and knowing this, I have the luxury of living each day as if I will live forever.

"The day you stop racing is the day you win the race."

Bob Marley (1845 - 1981)

b) Quote for Evening Contemplation

"The man who fears to be alone will never be anything but lonely, no matter how much he may surround himself with people. But the man who learns, in solitude and recollection, to be at peace with his own loneliness, and to prefer its reality to the illusion of merely natural companionship, comes to know the invisible companionship of God." (Thomas Merton)

Reflection for Deep Recovery (Sharabi)

I went to the bars because of my tremendous discomfort with sitting alone in my apartment. Surrounded by loud people, I forgot my loneliness. Later, as they abandoned me, my own drunken thoughts kept me company. These thoughts created a fantasy world where I was the center of everything. But today, I consider being alone a sweet luxury, and I do not automatically turn on the television or go seek conversations at the bar. I am alert and awake—to the present and to God's presence.

"I, however, cannot force myself to use drugs to cheat on my loneliness... my loneliness is all that I have."

Franz Kafka (1883 - 1924)

Thomas Merton
1915 - 1968

a) Quote for Morning Contemplation

"Ask me not where I live or what I like to eat. Ask me what I am living for and what I think is keeping me from living fully that." (Thomas Merton)

Reflection for Deep Recovery (Sharabi)

Today my life is not occupied with finding a bigger house to live in, fancy cars, more clothes, or the best restaurant in town. Instead, I am looking for something that will consume me, take over my life—give me purpose—so the petty concerns of ordinary living seem trivial. By giving myself over to recovery—to the pursuit of spiritual advancement—I am marching to the beat of a different drum, swaying to a higher music. The only question I have to examine is: what is keeping me from living fully that?

"We make a living by what we get, but we make a life by what we give."
Winston Churchill (1874 - 1965)

---

b) Quote for Evening Contemplation

"Despair is the absolute extreme of self-love. It is reached when a person deliberately turns his back on all help from anyone else in order to taste the rotten luxury of knowing himself to be lost." (Thomas Merton)

Reflection for Deep Recovery (Sharabi)

My despair in the last days of my drinking came from self-centeredness. It came from a self-inflicted isolation, indulgence in self-pity, and glorification of myself as a helpless victim—of people, events, places, and circumstances. I pushed away any help that was offered because it did not come on my terms. I considered to be romantic—in some perverse way—the despair, isolation, brooding rage, and self-pity that I wallowed in. Today in recovery, I still feel periods of despair, but I have stopped romanticizing it and glorifying it. I know I just have to choose courage, trust God, get off my ass and reach out to people, take the focus off my own feelings and thoughts, and become active.

"We have to go into the despair and go beyond it, by working and doing for somebody else, by using it for something else."
Elie Wiesel (1928 - 2016)

Thomas Merton
1915 - 1968

a) Quote for Morning Contemplation

"The solution of the problem of life is life itself. Life is not attained by reason and analysis but first of all by living." (Thomas Merton)

Reflection for Deep Recovery (Sharabi)

I cannot think my way out of the problem of life. I cannot reason my way out of the challenges of living. I cannot drink to avoid life, nor is it useful to come up with psychological explanations for my procrastination. I cannot sit in my armchair, awaiting motivation. I must attain life by getting sober... now... today. Life must be attacked head-on: by living, and for me—as an alcoholic—living means working a program of recovery.

"We cannot put off living until we are ready. The most salient characteristic of life is its coerciveness: it is always urgent, "here and now" without any possible postponement. Life is fired at us point-blank."

Jose Ortega y Gasset (1883 - 1955)

b) Quote for Evening Contemplation

"But the man who is not afraid to admit everything that he sees to be wrong with himself, and yet recognizes that he may be the object of God's love precisely because of his shortcomings, can begin to be sincere." (Thomas Merton)

Reflection for Deep Recovery (Sharabi)

The thing that gives me the strength to freely admit my wrongs is the knowledge that God accepts me and loves me all as I am—with our defects and shortcomings. In recovery—as in many religions—we learn that God's love is unconditional. Without this knowledge, it is difficult to do a sincere review of who I have become. If I am still bracing myself against judgment and condemnation, and if I am concerned about how I will be seen, I will be tempted to hide things and provide excuses; I will try to appear better than I really am. I will be hiding, even from myself. That is why the Fourth Step inventory comes after the Third Step. I must be careful about attempting the inventory before developing acceptance, love, and compassion for myself. I do not need to fix myself to deserve God's love. It is only after I turn things over that I will be able to look at myself honestly without wincing.

Thomas Merton
1915 - 1968

a) Quote for Morning Contemplation

"We do not want to be beginners. But let us be convinced of the fact that we will never be anything but beginners, all our life!" (Thomas Merton)

Reflection for Deep Recovery (Sharabi)

I went to this meeting, and there was a separate meeting—a subsection of this meeting—called Back to Basics: Beginner's Meeting. "We should never have to go back to basics because we should never have left the basics," I told myself, "... and heck! We are all beginners here." Each day is a new opportunity to lose sobriety; each morning is a beginning of a new day of staying sober. This is what keeps recovery fresh and exciting.

"There are no classes in life for beginners; right away, you are always asked to deal with what is most difficult."

Rainer Maria Rilke (1875 - 1926)

b) Quote for Evening Contemplation

"We stumble and fall constantly even when we are most enlightened. But when we are in true spiritual darkness, we do not even know that we have fallen." (Thomas Merton)

Reflection for Deep Recovery (Sharabi)

Sometimes, even in recovery, I am embarrassed at the way I have behaved, the things I have said, and even the emotions that arose in me. Being successful in recovery does not mean having no defects; instead, recovery gives us the ability to notice them quickly. When I was drinking I either justified my behavior or had no memory of it the next morning—but I was never wrong. Today, I can look upon myself with compassion; I know I am human. So while I am searching for self-acceptance, I can see that there is no point in beating myself up about beating myself up.

"Your problem is you are... too busy holding onto your unworthiness."
Baba Ram Dass (1931 - 2019)

"The most difficult times for many of us are the ones we give ourselves."
Pema Chödrön (born 1936)

387

Thomas Merton
1915 - 1968

a) Quote for Morning Contemplation

"We are not at peace with others because we are not at peace with ourselves, and we are not at peace with ourselves because we are not at peace with God." (Thomas Merton)

Reflection for Deep Recovery (Sharabi)

As long as I am trying to prove my own worth, my goodness, and my lovability, I will be judging others too, and be disappointed in them. But once I accept myself, I will no longer be looking for approval or adulation from others, and my judging of others will disappear; I will accept them as they are. And the key to accepting myself is seeing that God accepts me as I am. If I am at peace with God, all else follows effortlessly.

"Joy is the infallible sign of the presence of God."

Pierre Teilhard de Chardin (1881 - 1955)

---

b) Quote for Evening Contemplation

"In the last analysis, the individual person is responsible for living his own life and for 'finding himself.' If he persists in shifting his responsibility to somebody else, he fails to find out the meaning of his own existence." (Thomas Merton)

Reflection for Deep Recovery (Sharabi)

The central purpose of recovery is to find myself. I get there by becoming responsible for myself, by making my choices boldly and with full commitment. As long as I keep looking to somebody else, even a sponsor, to make my choices for me, as long as I keep looking over my shoulder for validation, I will fail to find out the meaning of my own existence. It is entirely appropriate, in the beginning, to check with others, but I have a responsibility to walk my life true to myself. When I have found myself, I will no longer be explaining myself, apologizing for who I am, second-guessing myself, or justifying myself. I will also not be telling others what to do; I will have compassion for their efforts to find themselves.

"Every person, all the events of your life are there because you have drawn them there. What you choose to do with them is up to you."

Richard Bach (born 1936)

Thomas Merton
1915 - 1968

a) Quote for Morning Contemplation

"The first step toward finding God, Who is Truth, is to discover the truth about myself: and if I have been in error, this first step to truth is the discovery of my error." (Thomas Merton)

Reflection for Deep Recovery (Sharabi)

Trying to be authentic—is fake. "Trying" to be sincere is fake. "Trying" to be humble is fake. I can only know that "persona" that I have created for the world, that mask I always wear, the way I wish to be seen. Even though I might be willing to look at myself, I lie hidden from myself; I cannot even see that I have a mask on. To be authentic, I have to know myself, and to know myself, I have to become authentic. How to solve this riddle? Simple. The first step to authenticity begins with admitting my inability to be authentic.

"It's not what you look at that matters; it's what you see."
Thoreau (1817 - 1862)

---

b) Quote for Evening Contemplation

"Pride makes us artificial, and humility makes us real." (Thomas Merton)

Reflection for Deep Recovery (Sharabi)

The world condemns "false pride," as if "real pride" is okay. But all pride is suspect. It is gloating over how I am going to be seen, about how people will whisper their admiration of my accomplishment. Pride is based on taking credit personally, not realizing that others—that God—must have had a hand in this. I will realize at some point that I cannot accomplish anything or achieve anything without the support of others and without the help of God. This is the doorway to humility. With humility, I am real because I have no need to hold up something artificial and false, something manufactured.

"Humility is not thinking less of yourself; it is thinking of yourself less."
C. S. Lewis (1898 - 1963)

Alan Watts
1915 - 1973

a) Quote for Morning Contemplation

**"Trying to define yourself is like trying to bite your own teeth."
(Alan Watts)**

Reflection for Deep Recovery (Sharabi)

I need not define myself as a particular kind of person. And anyway, who am I defining myself for? If I decide that I am a good person, who will I carry that news to? If I decide I am a liar, a cheat, and a thief, who am I interested in convincing? Why does it matter what I, or others, decide about the "kind of person" I am? I can refuse to be labeled by anyone, even by myself. I avoid the notion of "who I really am." This is freedom of the highest order, for I am free each moment to be who I chose to be, based on the needs of the moment. There is no point defining myself in a static way or as a fixed entity. I do not need to refer to my definition of myself to decide how to act; I will intuitively know how to act, and through my actions I will be creating myself anew, unfolding as a fresh new person each moment. Existence becomes novel and exciting.

---

b) Quote for Evening Contemplation

"Man suffers only because he takes seriously what the gods made for fun." (Alan Watts)

Reflection for Deep Recovery (Sharabi)

The biggest joke God has played on me is made me alcoholic. I have to stop drinking and come to meetings to get the joke. Here, we laugh at our foolishness and insanity, and we raise a toast to the life we have today. Another joke that God has played on me is: He has given me life—which means I am going to die! And He is laughing as I run around in circles trying to figure out life—scared and confused, complaining to everyone, taking offense, building resentments, offending people and getting crushed by their criticism, being proud and ashamed alternately, beating up on myself, getting in a frenzy about my silly plans and goals, struggling, fighting, kicking and clawing, getting disappointed and getting elated... Whew! The watching Gods must be laughing.

"We're all going to die, all of us, what a circus! That alone should make us love each other, but it doesn't. We are terrorized and flattened by trivialities; we are eaten up by nothing."

Charles Buchowski (1920 - 1994)

Alan Watts
1915 - 1973

a) Quote for Morning Contemplation

"This is the real secret of life—to be completely engaged with what you are doing in the here and now. And instead of calling it work, realize it is play." (Alan Watts)

Reflection for Deep Recovery (Sharabi)

Recovery is not a journey with a destination. The end-point of recovery is today. Its destination is where I am right now; it is who I am right now. There is nothing greater available in life than to be fully engaged and occupied with what is in front of me; that is all I must deal with. And when something needs doing, it does not matter whether it is easy or difficult, for it just has to get done. When I am completely engaged with it, it is not a chore; it is play. The way to "presence" is to get playful with what is, right now.

"A pure and cheerful life is impossible without work... Only entropy comes easy."

Anton Chekhov (1860 - 1904)

---

b) Quote for Evening Contemplation

"The meaning of life is just to be alive. It is so plain and so obvious and so simple. And yet, everybody rushes around in a great panic as if it were necessary to achieve something beyond themselves." (Alan Watts)

Reflection for Deep Recovery (Sharabi)

To be fully alive and present to the moment—to the hour, to the day—that is the meaning of recovery. Let not my dreams, aspirations, and plans occupy me so much that I am spending my time in the illusory world of the future. Or my regrets may be uppermost, so that I am re-dreaming the dream of the past. As they say, most of us are standing with one foot in the past and one foot in the future. Then, all we can do is urinate and defecate on the now. What a waste! Because "now" is where life is happening. There is nothing to achieve in recovery except to be alive—NOW.

"Life's but a walking shadow, a poor player, that struts and frets his hour upon the stage, and then is heard no more. It is a tale told by an idiot, full of sound and fury, signifying nothing."

Shakespeare (1564 - 1616) (Macbeth)

Alan Watts
1915 - 1973

a) Quote for Morning Contemplation

"The only way to make sense out of change is to plunge into it, move with it, and join the dance." (Alan Watts)

Reflection for Deep Recovery (Sharabi)

The terror of change comes because we resist change; we cannot see where it will take us. But we think too much, trying to imagine where we will land if we jump now and how it will be there. I remember how long I resisted giving up drinking, terrified of life without alcohol. Now, I am dressed up and dancing, participating with my full being. I extend my hand out to the newcomer hanging around the outside, waiting to be invited, and I pull them into the dance circle, to plunge into the fellowship without concern about how long the song is, how long recovery will take, or where it will lead.

"There is no such thing as a long piece of work, except one that you dare not start."

Charles Baudelaire (1821 - 1867)

---

b) Quote for Evening Contemplation

"The art of living... is neither careless drifting on the one hand nor fearful clinging to the past on the other. It consists of being sensitive to each moment, in regarding it as utterly new and unique, in having the mind open and wholly receptive." (Alan Watts)

Reflection for Deep Recovery (Sharabi)

I do not focus on change; "change" requires two made-up stories: the story of who I used to be in the past and the story of who I am as I enter the present. Instead, I try and live fully in the now, allowing myself to emerge fresh in the moment, like a chick constantly hatching. I wish to be sensitive to each moment as new and unique and to live each moment with aliveness, authenticity, wonder, and compassion. In this space, I cannot remember any resentment; I cannot think of anyone who has wronged me. Everyone I encounter is also totally new, not the person I knew yesterday, and this generous welcome of mine and my acceptance allows them too to generate themselves anew. How exciting!

"Men, for the sake of getting a living, forget to live."

Margaret Fuller (1810 - 1850)

Alan Watts
1915 - 1973

a) Quote for Morning Contemplation

"Things are as they are. Looking out into the universe at night, we make no comparisons between right and wrong stars, nor between well and badly arranged constellations." (Alan Watts)

Reflection for Deep Recovery (Sharabi)

This can refer to people too, and events happening in the world. We do not have to label people and events: decide who is right and who is wrong, what should be and what shouldn't; who is going to stay sober and who is going to drink, etc. We accept people and events as they are, and we learn to be fully present to everyone and everything we encounter—with appreciation, respect, acceptance, and delight. Nobody is right; nothing is wrong. Everyone and everything is as they are—perfect.

"Out beyond ideas of wrong-doing and right-doing, there is a field. I will meet you there."

Rumi

---

b) Quote for Evening Contemplation

"Tomorrow and plans for tomorrow can have no significance at all unless you are in full contact with the reality of the present since it is in the present and only in the present that you live." (Alan Watts)

Reflection for Deep Recovery (Sharabi)

One day at a time does not mean tomorrow will be better. If it is raining today, I do not try to think that tomorrow the sun will shine. Instead, I go out in the rain, listen to the pitter-patter of the raindrops on the puddles, and marvel at how happy the earth and plants are to receive this life-giving nourishment. Acceptance in recovery means acceptance of whatever is: an embracing of life as it is and conditions as they are. Only such acceptance brings me in full contact with—and immersion in—the reality of the present.

"Therefore, do not be anxious about tomorrow, for tomorrow will be anxious for itself. Sufficient for the day is its own trouble."

Matthew 6:34 (Bible)

"The sun is new each day."

Heraclitus (circa 500 B.C.)

Alan Watts
1915 - 1973

a) Quote for Morning Contemplation

"Zen does not confuse spirituality with thinking about God while one is peeling potatoes. Zen spirituality is just to peel the potatoes." (Alan Watts)

Reflection for Deep Recovery (Sharabi)

Spirituality is not something to aim for in the future and not something to think about or struggle for. Zen spirituality lies in Being, not in thinking. God is not my thought about God or my concept of God. Spirituality is fully engaging in whatever activity is present in front of me right now. I am not told to "not drink" for the rest of my life or to fantasize about a spiritual awakening. I am just to live today—sober—and engage fully in the tasks before me today, like peeling potatoes, carrying water, or chopping wood. Oh, and doing the next right thing.

"Success is simple. Do what is right, the right way, at the right time."
Arnold Glasow (1905 - 1998)

---

b) Quote for Evening Contemplation

"When we attempt to exercise power or control over someone else, we cannot avoid giving that person the very same power or control over us." (Alan Watts)

Reflection for Deep Recovery (Sharabi)

Whatever I am trying to control is controlling me. Whoever I am trying to change has power over me. By not changing, he or she has the power to frustrate me, to disturb me, to occupy my mind, and to live there rent-free—indefinitely—until I stop trying to change them. I must accept people the way they are if I am to have serenity. Nowhere is this as important as in my own family and in my intimate relationships. People have power over me when I want something from them, even if it is just wanting them to be different. We must stop trying to change people; in fact, we cannot change anyone. They must change on their own, if they wish, and not for us. If we connect with our sense of relatedness, we will have no wish to change others.

"Change occurs when one becomes what one is, not when one tries to become what one is not."
Paradoxical Theory of Change in Gestalt Psychology

Alan Watts
1915 - 1973

a) Quote for Morning Contemplation

"One is a great deal less anxious if one feels perfectly free to be anxious, and the same may be said of guilt." (Alan Watts)

Reflection for Deep Recovery (Sharabi)

Once I become perfectly free to acknowledge the domination of alcohol—that I am powerless over alcohol—I will escape the domination of alcohol. The freedom of sobriety comes from knowing that I am perfectly free to drink; no one can stop me. Once I realize I am entirely free to be an ass and a jerk, I can choose to be kind and loving—naturally—without anyone telling me I should. And once I become perfectly free of guilt, I will be eager to make amends, naturally. Also, if I am telling myself not to be anxious, I will naturally become anxious, just like if I tell myself not to think of pink elephants, I will think of pink elephants.

"God may forgive your sins, but your nervous system won't."
Alfred Korzybski (1879 - 1950)

b) Quote for Evening Contemplation

"Running away from fear is fear; fighting pain is pain; trying to be brave is being scared. If the mind is in pain, the mind is pain. The thinker has no other form than his thought. There is no escape." (Alan Watts)

Reflection for Deep Recovery (Sharabi)

It is foolish to talk about mental illness, for the mind itself is the illness. Our thoughts and concepts have become our prison; our mind is our torture. We cannot transcend the problems created by mind through the mind. Thoughts are clouds obscuring the open sky, and as long as we live in our thoughts, we live underneath the clouds. Society defines mental health as the absence of specific mental illnesses cataloged in a large book called DSM-5. True, some of the problems of the physical world can be solved through analysis and thinking, but problems of the mind itself—like the anxiety about death, the irreversibility of the past, the temporariness of life and the unpredictability of the future—cannot be solved by mind. The thinker has no escape from thought because he thinks he is thought. But spiritual awakening takes us to a plane beyond thoughts and thinking.

Alan Watts
1915 - 1973

a) Quote for Morning Contemplation

"A priest once quoted to me the Roman saying that a religion is dead when the priests laugh at each other across the altar. I always laugh at the altar, be it Christian, Hindu, or Buddhist, because real religion is the transformation of anxiety into laughter." (Alan Watts)

Reflection for Deep Recovery (Sharabi)

Perhaps religion and religious ceremonies can be somber and humorless, but spirituality—never. Sometimes, recovery meetings seem somber and humorless because people have become afraid of God's wrath and have lost touch with God's humor, God's playfulness, and God's compassion. The fear of alcohol disappears when we admit powerlessness and turn our will and our life over to the care of God. Now we can laugh and enjoy life. And you know, we do: just listen to the laughter coming from these rooms.

---

b) Quote for Evening Contemplation

"To put it still more plainly: the desire for security and the feeling of insecurity are the same thing. To hold your breath is to lose your breath. A society based on the quest for security is nothing but a breath-retention contest in which everyone is as taut as a drum and as purple as a beet." (Alan Watts)

Reflection for Deep Recovery (Sharabi)

If I want surety and certainty that I will never drink again, I will be rushing to meetings, taut as a drum, purple in the face, looking for advice from everyone on how to stay sober, calling my sponsor all the time, and shrieking at everyone about what they need to be doing. Relax, they tell me, Easy Does It. Understand that after the Third Step, there is no need for security or any assurances. Anything can happen: God may show up one day and ask me to drink so he can make of me an example to other alcoholics. What do I do then? Turn it over. I wear sobriety as a loose garment; I don't want to make it a straight-jacket.

"Men are convinced of your arguments, your sincerity, and the seriousness of your efforts only by your death.

Albert Camus (1913 - 1960)

Alan Watts
1915 - 1973

a) Quote for Morning Contemplation

"When we make music, we don't do it in order to reach a certain point, such as the end of the composition... Also, when we are dancing, we are not aiming to arrive at a particular place on the floor as in a journey. When we dance, the journey itself is the point, as when we play music, the playing itself is the point." (Alan Watts)

Reflection for Deep Recovery (Sharabi)

Sobriety can only end in relapse or death. I must not hurry through sobriety. I must enjoy the dance in the moment, in today. In recovery, I am not promised life after death; the Promises are offered for life before death. I don't want to miss life while waiting for something else. Life is here now—no waiting.

"The philosopher proves that the philosopher exists. The poet merely enjoys existence."

Wallace Stevens (1879 - 1955)

b) Quote for Evening Contemplation

"Consciousness is radar that is scanning the environment to look out for trouble, in the same way that a ship's radar is looking for rocks or other ships. The radar does not notice the vast amount of space where there are no rocks and other ships. By and large, we scan things over, but we pay attention only to what our set of values tells us we should pay attention to." (Alan Watts)

Reflection for Deep Recovery (Sharabi)

We have trained ourselves to pay attention to what is wrong. When everything is alright, we get nervous, jumpy. There is nothing to attend to except consciousness itself. Simply being present to consciousness can be nerve-racking because it is about being present to emptiness. Most people cannot sit in silence even for two minutes; they start thinking; they fill their consciousness with thoughts and things. And when their mind is chattering, they are missing the vast silence—the emptiness the universe is mostly made of.

"Regular matter comprises a mere 5% of the universe. The remaining 95%: we are not sure what it is, except we cannot see it."

(Cosmology as of 2021)

Alan Watts
1915 - 1973

a) Quote for Morning Contemplation

**"We love to see a child lost in the dance and not performing for an audience. To be happy and know that you are happy is really the overflowing cup of life. To dance as if there was no audience."
(Alan Watts)**

Reflection for Deep Recovery (Sharabi)

Must I grade myself and apply a label to my condition as "happy?" Can I just be happy, or do I also have to make a note that I am happy? A child lost in the dance is not aware that it is happy. The audience may look and say, "Oh, the child is so happy!" but the child is just dancing, enjoying. Can I be happy without an audience? Can I avoid even being my own audience and just dance? Happy people are not concerned about happiness; they are just dancing. Is it okay to be happy without realizing that I am happy? Can I just engage in life without passing a commentary on whether I am unhappy or happy? Can I enjoy a vacation without telling everyone that I had a great vacation?

---

b) Quote for Evening Contemplation

**"There are, then, two ways of understanding an experience. The first is to compare it with the memories of other experiences, and so to name and define it. This is to interpret it in accordance with the dead and the past. The second is to be aware of it as it is, as when, in the intensity of joy, we forget past and future, let the present be all, and then do not even stop to think 'I am happy.' "
(Alan Watts)**

Reflection for Deep Recovery (Sharabi)

Gratitude and regret both require imagining that the present could have been different from how it is. But that is just hypothetical; there is no other "now," and no reason to think it could have been different. Gratitude is necessary only to talk myself out of my complaints about what is, and to counter any regrets. Gratitude is training wheels prior to a spiritual awakening, prior to finding my balance, my state of joy. With true acceptance of the present, there is merely joy: no gratitude, no regret, and no complaint. I don't feel sorry about the things I don't have, and I am not "grateful" for what I have. I just enjoy and appreciate. I am immersed in what I have: the now and everything in it. This is awakening.

Alan Watts
1915 - 1973

a) Quote for Morning Contemplation

"There is nothing at all that can be talked about adequately, and the whole art of poetry is to say what can't be said." (Alan Watts)

Reflection for Deep Recovery (Sharabi)

The words spoken at meetings can only point to the silence that is the poetry of sobriety. That is why incessant prayer and appeal, continuous self-examination, and reading the Big Book without the silence of meditation will drive anyone crazy. We must not ask for things to turn out a certain way nor try to pin down the exact meaning of things. We ask, instead, for the courage to accept whatever is—without understanding it—because whatever is, is the poetry of life, and poetry is not to be understood: just felt, just experienced.

"Perhaps the truth depends upon a walk around the lake "

Wallace Stevens (1879 - 1955)

---

b) Quote for Evening Contemplation

"The word 'person' comes from the Latin word 'persona,' which referred to the masks worn by actors in which sound would come through. The 'person' is the mask—the role you're playing. And all of your friends and relations and teachers are busy telling you who you are and what your role in life is." (Alan Watts)

Reflection for Deep Recovery (Sharabi)

It is not possible to know myself. I can only know the labels and the stories I have created about myself. And once I have settled on a label, the label possesses me, for I have been defined. The liberated person is constantly generating themselves anew in the moment about to be. That is the edge of living. The present is frozen, fixed, gone. I cannot "live" in the present, but I am constantly toppling into the moment about to be, uncertain, excited, and undefined. I refuse to be defined—by others, by my past, or even by myself! I am free in the moment.

"No man ever steps in the same river twice, for it's not the same river, and he's not the same man."

Heraclitus (circa 500 B.C.)

Cicero
106 BC - 46 BC

a) Quote for Morning Contemplation

"Just as the soul fills the body, so God fills the world. Just as the soul bears the body, so God endures the world. Just as the soul sees but is not seen, so God sees but is not seen." (Cicero)

Reflection for Deep Recovery (Sharabi)

My soul did not fill my body. It had left this little dark hole, an emptiness that I tried to fill with alcohol every evening in a feeble attempt to become whole. Today, God fills that hole in my soul, and I have no need to drink anymore. Indeed, God fills my whole body; God fills my whole world. Indeed my entire awareness is a direct gift from God.

"There is a God-shaped vacuum in the heart of every man which cannot be filled by any created thing, but only by God."

Blaise Pascal (1623 - 1662)

---

b) Quote for Evening Contemplation

"Any man can make mistakes, but only an idiot persists in his error." (Cicero)

Reflection for Deep Recovery (Sharabi)

The first time I got drunk and made a spectacle of myself, they thought it was funny: "Oh, he drank too much. Any man can make an error." But when I drank too much and made a fool of myself for the seven hundred and fifty-ninth time, they were not willing to call it my seven hundred and fifty-ninth mistake. Instead, they called me an idiot. I was an idiot for keeping thinking that I was going to stop after a couple of drinks. All of us have been idiots, not because we have this disease, but because of the ways we have tried to deal with it. That is why we are here.

"I might scatter the southern clouds, drain the sea,
or cure someone hopelessly ill.
But to change the mind of a fool
Is beyond me."

Lal Ded/Lalleshwari (1320 - 1392)

Cicero
106 BC - 46 BC

a) Quote for Morning Contemplation

"Gratitude is not only the greatest of virtues but the parent of all the others." (Cicero)

Reflection for Deep Recovery (Sharabi)

Without gratitude, all other virtues appear contrived; they can be tainted with bitterness, resentment, and egotism. But with gratitude, even the ordinary things in life begin to shine. Never say or think, "I am too busy for gratitude." Set aside time for contemplating it; your whole life will begin to glow, and a look of delight will spread across your consciousness.

"When it comes to life, the critical thing is whether you take things for granted or take them with gratitude."
G. K. Chesterton (1874 - 1936)

"Happy is the person who knows what to remember of the past, what to enjoy in the present, and what to plan for in the future."
Arnold Glasow (1905-1998)

---

b) Quote for Evening Contemplation

"Six mistakes mankind keeps making century after century:
- **— Believing that personal gain is made by crushing others;**
- **— Worrying about things that cannot be changed or corrected;**
- **— Insisting that a thing is impossible because we cannot accomplish it;**
- **— Refusing to set aside trivial preferences;**
- **— Neglecting development and refinement of the mind;**
- **— Attempting to compel others to believe and live as we do."**
(Cicero)

Reflection for Deep Recovery (Sharabi)

Mankind has persisted in the same mistakes, century after century. When we enter recovery, we become aware that there may be undiscovered errors we have been living by. It is worth carefully examining the six mistakes Cicero lists here (around 100 B.C.!). Self-examination happens when we acknowledge uncertainty about things we thought we were sure of. We stop defending ourselves, justifying, and explaining. Change begins.

"We learn from history that we do not learn from history."
Hegel (1770 - 1831)

Cicero
106 BC - 46 BC

a) Quote for Morning Contemplation

"In a republic, this rule ought to be observed: that the majority should not have the predominant power." (Cicero)

Reflection for Deep Recovery (Sharabi)

It is always dissatisfying at a group conscience meeting when the majority votes down the minority. It is important that the little voices are heard, not just the loudest; we must invite the quiet to speak. We do not want oppression by the majority through smothering of the minority under the excuse of "unity." In recovery, each alcoholic is important, is honored, and is entirely free to be themselves. We must seek consensus, a solution that everyone can live with, not just one that the majority likes.

"The worst government is often the most moral... when fanatics are on top, there is no limit to oppression."

H. L. Mencken (1880 - 1956)

---

b) Quote for Evening Contemplation

"The enemy is within the gates; it is with our own luxury, our own folly, our own criminality that we have to contend." (Cicero)

Reflection for Deep Recovery (Sharabi)

My enemy is not the alcohol out there; my enemy is the disease inside me that causes me to reach for that alcohol. It is the distorted perspective, the devious rationalization, and the desperate justification that well up inside me. My enemy is my insecurity that makes disagreement and criticism intolerable. It is my demand that others follow my rules, that my judgments and my opinions are more correct than that of others, that my perspective, alone, is the truth, and that the world has been unfair to me. My enemy is selfishness and self-centeredness, the evaluation of happenings mostly on how they affect me and my inability to be gracious when I cannot have my way. These tendencies—common to all of humanity—are particularly poisonous to me; it takes extraordinary effort to recognize them.

"The range of what we think and do is limited by what we fail to notice. And because we fail to notice that we fail to notice, there is little we can do to change."

R. D. Laing (1927 - 1989)

Cicero
106 BC - 46 BC

a) Quote for Morning Contemplation

"Justice consists in doing no injury to men; decency in giving them no offense." (Cicero)

Reflection for Deep Recovery (Sharabi)

As we grow in recovery, we stop injuring the ones who come close to us—as we did in our drinking days. But we also stop offending people, and we stop getting offended by people: that is how growth shows itself. There is no such thing as getting offended "on principle," for nowhere does any principle support this. There is always a way to stay loyal to my values and to myself without getting indignant, fanatic, injuring others, or causing them offense. To learn this, I must hold back, pause, be thoughtful. Each time I behave differently from my habitual pattern, I am creating new neural pathways in my brain.

"A fanatic is one who can't change his mind and won't change the subject."
Winston Churchill (1874 - 1965)

---

b) Quote for Evening Contemplation

"Let us not listen to those who think we ought to be angry with our enemies and who believe this to be great and manly. Nothing is so praiseworthy, nothing so clearly shows a great and noble soul, as clemency and readiness to forgive." (Cicero)

Reflection for Deep Recovery (Sharabi)

Whatever has happened, it is how I label that experience and store the memory that determines if I stay bitter and resentful. As long as I maintain that I have been wronged, I remain a victim, and I will suffer. Forgiveness occurs when I finally realize there is nothing to forgive. People were just being people, and they didn't follow my rules of conduct or my moral and ethical standards. If I do not pass judgment on others, there will be nothing to forgive. My work is to accept what happened without bitterness—bear my fate without complaining.

"Here is the rule to remember in the future when anything tempts you to be bitter: not, 'This is a misfortune,' but 'To bear this worthily is good fortune.' "

Marcus Aurelius (121 - 180 A.D.)

Cicero
106 BC - 46 BC

a) Quote for Morning Contemplation

"The authority of those who teach is often an obstacle to those who want to learn." (Cicero)

Reflection for Deep Recovery (Sharabi)

A humble sponsor speaking softly may have more to offer and may teach more effectively than the fiery sponsor from Hell who never misses an opportunity to lecture and expound on his or her opinions. Such authorities themselves become the obstacle to the newcomer who wants to learn. Learning is a process of discovery, and some of us learn through inquiry, debate, argument, and contemplation. Let us who are sponsors be grateful to the newcomers who disagree with us; they have been sent to us to help us grow. They are here teaching us how to deal elegantly and effectively with opposition, objection, and alternate viewpoints.

"Whatever you do in life, surround yourself with smart people who'll argue with you."

John Wooden (1910 - 2010)

b) Quote for Evening Contemplation

"In so far as the mind is stronger than the body, so are the ills contracted by the mind more severe than those contracted by the body. In a disordered mind, as in a disordered body, soundness of health is impossible." (Cicero)

Reflection for Deep Recovery (Sharabi)

The healing from the physical effects of alcohol can occur quickly in sobriety in many—though not all—cases. But the mental, emotional, and spiritual healing will take much longer. The sick body has a natural tendency to heal itself, but the sick mind has no such inclination; it persists in justifying itself. Unless I focus on healing these aspects of my disordered mind, my sobriety is tenuous and precarious, and soundness of health is impossible. Recovery from alcoholism is like recovery from brain damage. It takes a long time for new neural pathways to develop and for learning and change to grow roots. Sometimes the problems are so severe that the best we can do is manage them. We must be modest in our expectations of returning to a "normal" life, for we will ever remain alcoholics. That is why we continue to attend meetings.

Cicero
106 BC - 46 BC

a) Quote for Morning Contemplation

"It is foolish to tear one's hair in grief, as though sorrow would be made less by baldness." (Cicero)

Reflection for Deep Recovery (Sharabi)

It is equally foolish to tear one's hair in rage or frustration. Resentments are not lessened by baldness either, and the object of my resentment does not feel the pain of my hair being pulled. Often, I am angry or sad that people—and the universe—are not behaving the way I want. A brief sadness over a loss is understandable, but a dogged, persistent, and self-justifying grief is a resentment. Am I not entitled to the universe unfolding according to my desires, especially if I pray? Persistent grief and despair are secret forms of resentment that, at its center, things in the universe are beyond my control.

"Resentment is like drinking poison and waiting for the other person to die."

Saint Augustine (354 - 430 A.D.)

---

b) Quote for Evening Contemplation

"He does not seem to me to be a free man who does not sometimes do nothing." (Cicero)

Reflection for Deep Recovery (Sharabi)

Modern Western society is action-oriented—doing-oriented: "Don't just sit there... do something!" But ancient Eastern traditions are different; they would say, instead: "Don't just do something... sit there!" There is nothing so good to calm the mind as simply sitting, doing nothing, thinking of nothing. It is a meditation that should be practiced daily. It cleanses the soul. And why even give it a name like "meditation," as if you are doing something? Just sit. This is not just a program of action; it is also a program of inaction when confronted with bad ideas and "brainstorms"—impulses that will get us into trouble. People who are unable to just sit still for ten minutes doing nothing are in their own prison. They are not free.

"One of the lessons of history is that nothing is often a good thing to do and always a clever thing to say."

Will Durant (1885 - 1991)

Cicero
106 BC - 46 BC

a) Quote for Morning Contemplation

"To know the laws is not to memorize their letter but to grasp their full force and meaning." (Cicero)

Reflection for Deep Recovery (Sharabi)

It is useless to memorize the Steps without working. The ability to quote from the Big Book will not keep me sober, nor will knowing the Steps. In order to be a learned man or woman in recovery, I have to study them, work them, practice them, and integrate them into my life. It is necessary to absorb the spirit of the Steps, not just memorize the letter of the Steps.

"A man is not learned because he talks much; he who is patient, free from hatred and fear, he is called learned."

Max Muller (1823 - 1900)

---

b) Quote for Evening Contemplation

"When you are aspiring to the highest place, it is honorable to reach the second or even the third rank." (Cicero)

Reflection for Deep Recovery (Sharabi)

I set out to do a searching and fearless moral inventory. At the halfway point, I was dissatisfied with its thoroughness and sought to postpone my Fifth Step. Do not go this route. Make an appointment for the Fifth Step before completing your Fourth Step inventory. Keep the appointment bringing with you as best an inventory as you can. You may not win a gold medal, but a silver or bronze medal inventory is excellent—even no medal. It will do the job for now. A poor inventory is better than none at all. There will be plenty of time to do more thorough inventories; maybe one day, you will even have the best inventory in the whole world. Unfortunately, it will not be something you want to publish; it will bring infamy, not fame and admiration. "Looking good" or providing believable explanations is not the purpose of an inventory. Don't seek a medal.

"You can't eat applause for breakfast. You can't sleep with it."

Bob Dylan (born 1941)

Cicero
106 BC - 46 BC

a) Quote for Morning Contemplation

"There is nothing so absurd that some philosopher has not already said it." (Cicero)

Reflection for Deep Recovery (Sharabi)

Most thoughts we have today have probably occurred to others before. But the one profound thought I had never heard earlier that was presented to me when I came to recovery was this: "If you don't take that first drink, you will never be drunk!" Initially, I thought: "Don't even take one drink? How absurd! They are asking me to abandon the car just because I got a flat tire?" But today I see the simple wisdom contained in it.

"We are still living in a wonderful new world where man thinks himself astonishingly new and "modern." This is unmistakable proof of the youthfulness of human consciousness, which has not yet grown aware of its historical antecedents."

Carl Jung ((1875 - 1961)

b) Quote for Evening Contemplation

"The pursuit, even of the best things, ought to be calm and tranquil." (Cicero)

Reflection for Deep Recovery (Sharabi)

Let us not rush to sobriety in a frenzy of impatience. There are no rewards for doing the Steps quickly, but there are rewards for doing them thoroughly. Let us be calm and tranquil in recovery. It is a simple program, and we have all of our life. I say: don't drink, and don't make a big drama about it! Don't make a drama out of your agitation, restlessness, worries, regrets, resentments, or complaints. Don't create drama just to get attention, and don't try to ensnare others in your drama. Focus on something that makes you calm and tranquil—an image of a chair on a beach or of a cottage adjoining a meadow. Take a deep breath as you picture the image and learn to return to this image whenever necessary to calm yourself.

"Nature does not hurry; yet, everything is accomplished."

Lao-Tzu (6th century B.C.)

Cicero
106 BC - 46 BC

a) Quote for Morning Contemplation

"It is the peculiar quality of a fool to perceive the faults of others and to forget his own." (Cicero)

Reflection for Deep Recovery (Sharabi)

In recovery, we acknowledge that we are all fools. I was asked to consider that when I was pointing my finger at someone, three fingers were pointing back at me. They also said, "If you can spot it, you got it!" Wherever I look, I see aspects of myself. I get enraged at angry people; I want to punish unforgiving people; I will not tolerate intolerant people; I will fault others for being too critical. We perceive the faults of others, oblivious to our own. Yes, I am a fool, and we are all fools. That is the nature of human beings.

"Remember... no matter where you go—there you are."

Buckaroo Banzai (1984)

---

b) Quote for Evening Contemplation

"Silence is one of the great arts of conversation." (Cicero)

Reflection for Deep Recovery (Sharabi)

For those of us used to holding court in the bars, being silent at meetings is difficult. Sometimes the barrage of words that accost us at recovery meetings—noises emanating from faces—needs to be countered by internal quietness. There is often no time given to absorb and digest a comment, so eager others are to jump in with their thoughts. Merely being present in a room full of recovering alcoholics is a sacred event. I do not need to embellish the experience with noise. Recovery is happening even in the emptiness between comments and the silence between words, just as music is contained in the pauses between notes. And consider this: people get to say things only because everyone else is silent.

"Beware of those who seek constant crowds; they are nothing alone."

Charles Buchowski (1920 - 1994)

"Our view of man will remain superficial so long as we fail to go back to that origin [of silence], so long as we fail to find, beneath the chatter of words, the primordial silence."

Maurice Merleau-Ponty (1908 - 1961)

Cicero
106 BC - 46 BC

a) Quote for Morning Contemplation

"Hatred is congealed anger." (Cicero)

Reflection for Deep Recovery (Sharabi)

Anger propped up with justification is resentment. A resentment that is retained congeals into hatred. Hatred ruts the psyche and destroys the soul. In fact, whatever we hate becomes our "Higher Power." I may not be able to avoid anger, but if I refuse to justify it, the anger will dissipate in its normal course. All I may have to do is count to ten. But if I justify it, anger will turn into resentment, and any time I remember my justification, my anger will regenerate itself. The place to interrupt this cycle is to avoid justifying my anger, avoid "being right" about my complaint. This is the way to the lightness of being.

"Hate the sin; love the sinner."

Mahatma Gandhi (1869 - 1948)

---

b) Quote for Evening Contemplation

"If we are not ashamed to think it, we should not be ashamed to say it." (Cicero)

Reflection for Deep Recovery (Sharabi)

Being authentic means willingness to reveal what is going on inside without defending it or justifying it: merely a desire to live in the open. Shame is generated by thinking I have to hide my thoughts and feelings. If I reveal my thoughts, we can all laugh at them together, and there is no shame. However, I have to be careful revealing my critical thoughts: do I really want them to deal with my judgment and condemnation of them? In revealing my judgments, I expose myself, not them. There is no "authenticity" in my judgments.

"Authenticity is a survival need... If you want to stay alive, stay authentic."

Gabor Maté (born 1944)

"Authenticity is a collection of choices that we have to make every day. It's about the choice to show up and be real. The choice to be honest. The choice to let our true selves be seen."

Brené Brown (born 1965)

Cicero
106 BC - 46 BC

a) Quote for Morning Contemplation

"If you have a garden and a library, you have everything you need." (Cicero)

Reflection for Deep Recovery (Sharabi)

Today we have public parks and public libraries, so if I have access to these, I have everything I need. Okay, Cicero did not know about the internet. So, if I have access to a garden, a library, and a cell phone or a computer with an internet connection, I should not be complaining about life. (Come to think of it, libraries today have free access to the internet; Cicero might have been anticipating this!) So in recovery, we open up to the joy of simple things.

"Know how to live without wants, suffer without complaint, die singing."
Alexis de Tocqueville (1805 - 1859)

"The world is so full of a number of things,
I'm sure we should all be as happy as kings.."
Robert Louis Stevenson (1850 - 1894)

---

b) Quote for Evening Contemplation

"We should not be so taken up in the search for truth as to neglect the needful duties of active life; for it is only action that gives a truth value and commendation to virtue." (Cicero)

Reflection for Deep Recovery (Sharabi)

It is not uncommon for people in early recovery to get so addicted to meetings and service work that they neglect their normal obligations and duties to family and to society. Perhaps this can be excused for a period of time. But soon, our loved ones, our employer, and society at large should benefit from the fact that we are in recovery, not suffer from our commitment to this path. There is never really any conflict between recovery work and life, but we can make such conflict appear by denying our responsibility to others—who have to depend on us—under the excuse that sobriety is the most important thing for us (which it is.) We can be committed to recovery without being selfish and self-centered about it. Managing conflicting demands and creating some balance in our life is undoubtedly a key requirement for successful recovery. We go to extremes in our willingness for sobriety, and paradoxically, this leads to balance in life.

NOTES

NOTES

NOTES

NOTES

NOTES

WIT AND WISDOM

ⓞF

ANONYMOUS ALCOHOLICS

Lessons on Living
from 25 years in the
Halls of Recovery

SHARABI

Humor, psychology and spirituality come together in this entertaining and extensive collection of 3300+ anecdotes and insights into life from more than a thousand recovering alcoholics. Compiled over 25 years, this book shows diverse viewpoints, both reverential and rebellious, and provides an intimate view into the rooms of modern sobriety.

80 illustrations; 648 pages.

ISBN 978-0-9816054-5-6
640 pp 80 illustr. Cloth bound (hardcover)
sewn binding $29.95

"I thoroughly enjoyed reading it. The book is an amazing compilation of the thinking, attitudes, emotions and behaviors of alcoholics and addicts everywhere. The "addictive insanity" of the disease is clearly portrayed in the sardonic humor that is so characteristic of recovering A.A. members. The insights gained in the struggle for recovery are precious gems that only those who have been there can share so very well. This is a book of wisdom and guidance for the human condition, not just for recovery from alcoholism. It is worth reading and studying if one is to know and understand real humanity.

I really am impressed with (this) marvelous collection. Bravo!"

Dr. Gregory B. Collins, MD,
Section Head, Alcohol and Drug recovery Center,
The Cleveland Clinic.

... the author attempts to enlarge the frame of recovery for believers and nonbelievers. He integrates the best of both the Eastern and Western views of spirituality... It is not a ponderous tome but a readable, wise and humorous look into the lives of the real people who daily live the life and sanctify the struggle.

Gloria Hanson,
MSW, CAC (Certified Alcoholism Counselor) (retired)

"This book captures the pithy and insightful snippets from recovering people that one comes across in today's A.A. meetings. It is possible to really "get" the issues and understand the experience of recovery from reading this book. It also highlights the humor, self-examination and self-deprecation that is part of the recovery process.

"I enjoyed this book and heartily recommend it to people in recovery as well as to therapists dealing with substance abuse issues in their clients."

Les Wyman,Ph.D.,
LISW, Gestalt Therapist

"At first, the book overwhelmed me. I thought, "What? Just words from meetings? I could have done that!" But then, I began to open it to a page here or a page there and I found such incredible wisdom and, yes, wit, that I couldn't stop reading... All in all, I found this book to be a wonderful addition to my collection! I use it during morning meditations to inspire my thoughts, and find myself opening it up randomly during the day or if I am looking for a shot of wisdom to carry me through to the next level of sanity!"

Beverly A. Buncher, MA, PCC, CTPC, ICCF Certified Life Coach.

"People pick up Wit and Wisdom, read a passage or two, and are ready to purchase it. It's a great gift for old timers, because when you've been around many twenty four hours, it's easy to think you've heard it all! So, it's refreshing to read something new that rings true and often brings a laugh. If the $29.95 price tag is too much for them in the moment, they come back another time or mutter, "I'll ask my sponsor to buy it for me." This book sells itself. I sell a case every month or two!"

Jan Smoots, Owner, Happy Joyous and Free (12 Step Bookstore)
116 B West Broad St., Falls Church, VA 22046.

From Amazon Reviews (Rating 4 stars out of 5)

(1) As a person in recovery I regularly read several pages to supplement my meeting schedule and as a basis for meditation - and often for a good laugh - working through the book and then going back and starting over. Of additional great value and interest are the numerous appendices which include the developmental stages of the Twelve Steps and Traditions; excellent discussions of anger and resentment in recovery, the "God " issue in A.A. and suggestions for getting an alcoholic sober; and influences on Bill Wilson by Carl Jung and John D. Rockefeller, Jr.

(2) I liked this book so much I bought it for a friend of mine. She also loves it. You can open it anywhere and just read a few lines to get some insight or understanding. I think this book is more than a book for members of A.A. I do not belong to A.A. and I still can relate to the oneliners and wisdom in this book. I have it sitting next to my bed to read a bit every night and on occasion I will take it with me so when I need to stop I can read for a short time and have something to think about.

(3) The book is also useful because it contains so many different perspectives on A.A. Anyone can pick it up and find something they totally identify with, something they completely disagree with, and something that may shift their whole perspective. I would highly recommend this book.

From Barnes and Noble Reviews (Rating 5 stars out of 5)

This book is definitely a great compilation of A.A. wit and wisdom. If someone has difficulty with the "God" or "higher power" concept, this book will help you. Don't reject A.A.'s help because you're an agnostic or atheist. There is room for you! Serious, entertaining, amazingly thorough and organized.

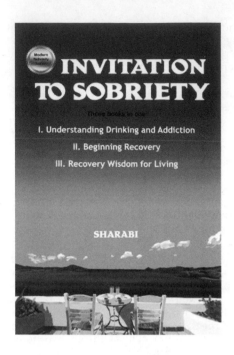

INVITATION
TO SOBRIETY

Three books in one

I. Understanding Drinking and Addiction

II. Beginning Recovery

III. Recovery Wisdom for Living

SHARABI

"For the tenuous newcomer or anyone with reservations about abstinence or the culture and structure of A.A., it provides a wellspring of clear explanation and calming practical advice. Reading your book(s) has simply dissolved my points of resistance with the program. You have curated and generated much beauty and wisdom about recovery, but more importantly, about life."

Robert W.

"I found it full of ideas, experiences, and simple honesty that I could reuse in discussions, meetings, and as topics to counter the stale cliches often heard there."

Campbell P.

"Sharabi's latest work is chock-full of useful information for the undecided, the beginner, the family, and the long-timer alike.

Jeff Y.

ISBN 978-0-9816054-3-2
576 pp, Sewn Paperback $23.95

10% of people are born with a curious "allergy" to alcohol. One could consider this to be a "birth-defect" or congenital disability. Their bodies are attracted to alcohol, yet they are missing a factor that tells them when to stop. The author has coined the term "Alcohol Positive" to label people born with this unusual susceptibility to alcohol. Just as there is a condition called "HIV Positive," which can turn into full-blown AIDS, one can diagnose oneself as "Alcohol Positive" and understand that he or she is at risk for developing full-blown alcoholism.

"I heartily recommend Invitation to Sobriety for anyone beginning to ask the question: Do I have a problem with alcohol, and what can I do to get help? The format of the book is inviting, in that it simply helps readers to explore their relationship with something that may be causing problems in their lives, without accusation or judgment, but rather by normalizing the pain, fear and guilt which always accompany any outreach for information or help with addictive behaviors.

"Through its comprehensive treatment of the natural human love-hate relationship with alcohol and other drugs, this book is exceedingly effective in the wise and sensitive way it addresses the phenomenon of addiction, the solution, and the various struggles encountered on the road of recovery and how those struggles can be resolved."

William C. Hale, Ph.D., LICDC-CS-R
Psychologist

Invitation to Sobriety
Selected Topics from the Table of Contents

Chapter 10: After a few meetings.

248: Why do I need to go to meetings?
251: Frankly, I'm sick of you A.A.s and your damn "program."
253: A.A. is for weak people
256: There is too much mindless dogma in A.A.

Chapter 11: Committing to sobriety.

285: What if my problem is other drugs, not alcohol?
287: I'm not that bad that I have to come to A.A.
294: Why can't I simply stop drinking on my own?
303 An alcohol and drug-free life seems bleak and boring.

Chapter 12: The First Three Steps.

310: I just can't see myself as powerless.
312: How is "surrendering" going to help me?
317: The Serenity Prayer

Chapter 13: Working on getting better.

320: I want to quit smoking too.
321: The role of diet and exercise in recovery.
335: Childhood wounds and parental issues.

Chapter 14: Typical problems in early recovery.

338: Loneliness and romantic love in early sobriety.
350: My problem is anxiety.
353: People won't let me talk about my drug problem.
371: Everything in A.A. and in the Steps... is so negative.

Chapter 15: Dealing with relapse.

393: I relapsed: what went wrong?
396: Does relapse occur suddenly?
399: What can I do to not relapse?

Chapter 16 - 18: Recovery Wisdom for Living.

Chapter 16 explains 107 phrases and sayings useful in early recovery;
Chapter 17 discusses 95 phrases and sayings on advanced or "deep" recovery.
Chapter 18 discusses the Five Pillars of Recovery: Kindness, Generosity, Authenticity, Integrity and Celebration, and, "Why do I need spiritual principles in life?"

APPENDICES

APPENDIX I: The Twelve Steps of Alcoholics Anonymous
APPENDIX II: The Twelve Traditions of Alcoholics Anonymous.
APPENDIX III: To the alcoholic who has trouble praying.
APPENDIX IV: Wrong answers to life.
APPENDIX V: A guide to the Fourth Step.
APPENDIX VI: Anger, rage, and resentment in recovery.
APPENDIX VII: Humanization.
APPENDIX VIII: The deeper Self.
APPENDIX IX: Spiritual paths towards an awakening.
APPENDIX X: What is a spiritual awakening?
APPENDIX XI: Enrolling the subconscious in recovery.

"The Appendices alone are worth the price of the book!"   Ray M.

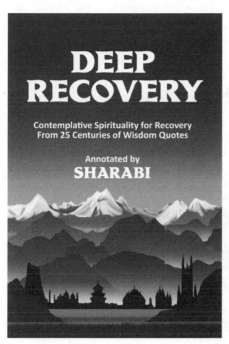

DEEP RECOVERY

Contemplative Spirituality for Recovery
From 25 Centuries of Wisdom Quotes

Annotated by

SHARABI

ISBN 978-0-9816054-1-8
480 pp, Sewn Paperback $19.95

Dipping into sources of perennial wisdom, the author carves a broad arc through the area of contemplative spirituality to provide a resource for recovering alcoholics and addicts. This collection could be read, just for the original words of priceless wisdom, or supplemented with the thoughts of the author provided beneath each quote, that relates the idea directly to concepts of modern day recovery.

"A very impressive book! These quotations and accompanying commentaries extend the wisdom of the 12-Step recovery programs into deep and fertile areas that have been explored by many great thinkers, both ancient and modern. This book does not hand you perspectives on a platter; it is simple but not simplistic, deep but not overwhelming. It is not for people who want to be told what to do, but for those who wish to engage in contemplation, and who take responsibility for their path in recovery and in life.

Lawrence J. Nichta Jr., Ph.D.,
Clinical psychologist

"This is a significant book for the recovery community. A.A. introduced alcoholics to the essential numinous power of spiritual experience in their struggle to overcome addiction. Here, the ageless voices of sages, poets and mystics are invoked to help deepen the seeker's journey into wholeness. I found important things in this book about aspects of the unconscious that I hadn't thought about in my many years as a Jungian Analyst."

Vocata George, Ph.D Jungian Analyst.

LAO TZU (6th CENTURY B.C.)	FREIDRICH NIETZSCHE (1844-1900)
PLATO (424 B.C.-348 B.C.)	SIMONE WEIL (1909-1943)
CICERO (106 B.C.-46 B.C.)	GURDJIEFF (1866-1949)
EPECTITUS (55-135)	LUDWIG WITTGENSTEIN (1889-1951)
TERTULLIAN (c 160-225)	CARL JUNG (1875-1961)
NAGARJUNA (c 150-240)	MARTIN BUBER (1978-1965)
RUMI (1207-1275)	THOMAS MERTON (1915-1968)
MEISTER ECKHART (1268-1327)	VIRGINIA SATIR (1916-1988)
KABIR (1440-1518)	OSHO (1931-1990)
MICHEL de MONTAIGNE (1533-1592)	NISARGADATTA MAHARAJ (1897-1991)
VOLTAIRE (1694-1779)	ELISABETH KUBLER-ROSS (1926–2004)
SOREN KIERKEGAARD (1813-1855)	MAYA ANJELOU (1928-2014)
RALPH WALDO EMERSON (1803-1882)	ALAN WATTS (1915 - 1973)

VISITING GOD

WITH MEISTER ECKHART

*Reflections on a Higher Power,
and the 3rd and 11th Steps
in Recovery*

Sharabi

Eckhart's vision of God avoids belief systems and speaks directly to the heart, inviting complete surrender, contemplation and love of God. His writings can provide inspiration, clarity, guidance and liberation for recovering alcoholics today struggling to come up with their own concept of God and a Higher Power. Even some people calling themselves atheists and agnostics have been drawn to Eckhart's vision, finding it a refreshing alternative to traditional religious beliefs and theological ideas about God.

This book expands the section on Meister Eckhart contained in DEEP RECOVERY.

Being prepared for publication in 2022

ISBN 978-0-9816054-0-1
96 pp, PAPERBACk $8.95

Meister Eckhart (c 1260 – c.1328) was a German theologian, philosopher and mystic. Eckharts' teachings were radical, pure and powerful, so much so that he was accused of heresy and investigated by the Pope. He died before his appeal has decided upon, and he has been spared total condemnation by the Church. His voice represents the mystical side of Christianity, transcending specific religious beliefs and having similarities to Sufi and Eastern spiritual perspectives as well as Jewish Cabblistic teachings.

> *"Spirituality is not to be learned by flight from the world, or by running away from things, or by turning solitary and going apart from the world. Rather, we must learn an inner solitude wherever or with whomsoever we may be. We must learn to penetrate things and find God there."* (Eckhart)

> *"For you to ask me: Who is God? What is God? I reply: Is-ness. Is-ness is God."* (Eckhart)

> *"If I had a God that I could understand, I would not regard him as God. If you understand anything about him, then he is not in it."* (Eckhart)

DEEP RECOVERY: Detailed Index by Item Number

25a: even when God has left, He is close by
25b: gratitude is sufficient prayer
26a: make a Fifth Step appointment before Fourth Step is done
26b: eternity is just one moment, and you are in it right now
27a: to be full of things is to be empty of God
27b: mastering books is useless; master life itself
28a: you have to unlearn before you can learn
28b: if you live a contemplative life, the right actions will follow
29a: the more you have, the less you own
29b: you are not your likes and dislikes, your opinions, or reactions
30a: be a beginner every morning
30b: an inner solitude is available even amidst people
31a: trust the magic at the beginning of a sober life
31b: God appears in silence and stillness
32a: do everything you do with delight
32b: do not love God for the good things He brings you
33a: focus on Being, not on Doing
33b: your surroundings cannot disturb you
34a: I saw God enjoying a good joke
34b: do you really need to offer God suggestions?
35a: theologians argue, but mystics do not
35b: even your consciousness is owned by God
36a: the first outburst needs to be compassion
36b: God is in everything, even in small things
37a: sobriety is the inmost truth for the alcoholic
37b: God has no boundary; therefore God is indefinable
38a: a God of my beyond understanding
38b: flowing along effortlessly, carried by God's will
39a: God does not need you; you need God
39b: God, do with me whatever you will
40a: the most important hour for staying sober is the present hour
40b: a wholeness beyond contradiction is available to you
41a: spirituality is not about attending church, temple or mosque
41b: God is not a concept
42a: with acceptance, you can see God everywhere
42b: be at peace if your path is different from others
43a: to the quiet mind, all things are possible
43b: there are no rewards in life
44a: you are not a sport critic reporting on God's performance
44b: declaring your love of God will not keep you sober
45a: God is the is-ness of existence
45b: in the presence of God, past and future disappear
46a: the ultimate aim in sobriety is beyond time and place
46b: what is the use of trying to be humble?
47a: your penances and external devotions are ego-driven
47b: be silent; do not chatter about God
48a: any concept of God is not God, but an intermediary
48b: surrender and become still; God will remove the compulsion

Kabir   **(1440 - 1518)**   **49**

49a: God is the innermost essence of being
49b: you do not have to go looking for God
50a: if the mirror makes you sad, it does not know you

50b: do not die pursuing a futile dream
51a: you are not just in the fellowship, you are the fellowship now
51b: the truth is a sound because words are too limiting
52a: if you want love, give love
52b: are you running around trying to find the right meeting?
53a: wherever you are is the entry point
53b: love is just a name for a feel of God
54a: love of sobriety has to be beyond reason
54b: God with form or God without form
55a: the truth cannot be put into words
55b: recovery is a return to your original self
56a: the sponsor can retire when the ego is transcended
56b: the enlightened space is all around you
57a: you already have everything you need
57b: the same river is flowing in each of us
58a: no one, not even you, has ever been guilty
58b: God cannot come in if you are still talking
59a: the deepest Self is the same as God
59b: your truth can resist attack
60a: we are all the same, seeking the same
60b: we are all slaves of the spirit of the quest
61a: the seed of recovery is already inside you
61b: many do not go the full distance in recovery
62a: once you gain knowledge, you can put away the books
62b: be gentle how you handle the gift of sobriety
63a: do not quote from the books unless you see
63b: the noise can coexist peacefully with the silence
64a: getting to know yourself as an embodied self
64b: if you have not lived through it, it is not true for you
65a: loving and accepting everything as it is right now
65b: you, God, and I: what is the puzzle?
66a: all you want is on this side of the river
66b: God is simply the love in your heart
67a: do not try to be less thirsty; direct it towards contact with God
67b: there is no boatmen, no boat, and no river
68a: here your meat and your bones are of no use
68b: the daily sense of failure goes away

Nagarjuna   (c 150 - 250A.D.)   69

69a: all philosophies are mental fabrications
69b: there is nothing to be denied or affirmed
70a: in emptiness, all becomes possible
70b: your notion of the real me is a fabrication
71a: let go of desires, even the desire to let go
71b: a supreme pleasure awaits
72a: truth as opposed to facts
72b: a teacher teaches differently based on the pupil
73a: it is no use memorizing the Steps
73b: you are not alive just because you take breath
74a: what is the point of singing God's praises if your heart is not clean?
74b: working with one alcoholic is no less than speaking to a hundred
75a: the knowledge taught here is more than how to earn a living
75b: you possess much that could be abandoned

76a: there is no place for haughtiness in recovery
76b: peace can be yours if you can accept contradictions
77a: your feelings do not imply failure or success
77b: resentment arises when others don't accept my shoulds
78a: parting and separation are inevitable
78b: as long as you keep walking in the right direction?
79a: sobriety, like anthills, is built grain by grain
79b: it is inevitable that you will miss many things
80a: beware of postponing the remedy
80b: however high you rise, be not proud
81a: what is the point of being attractive, wealthy and happy?
81b: if you want to be lazy, find an easy sponsor
82a: you are a web of interconnections
82b: sobriety is okay but transcending the self is the ultimate

Kübler-Ross   (1926 - 2004)   83

83a: there are no mistakes, no coincidences; only blessings
83b: you cannot live to conform to people's expectations
84a: no one can tell you what your lessons are
84b: unconditional love begins with yourself
85a: the truth does not need to be defended
85b: serenity is not about ending but accepting your struggles
86a: dying sober is a graduation from the program
86b: living each day as if you will live forever
87a: your responsibility is to live life, not to live death
87b: service can take a million forms
88a: you are solely responsible for where you are
88b: anger, when justified fossilizes into resentment
89a: we are the ones who have known defeat
89b: my judgment of other is my burden to bear
90a: true beauty is revealed when there is a light from within
90b: the blows of His chisel are what form us
91a: there is no joy without hardship, no pleasure without pain
91b: your journey as an alcoholic mirrors the stages of dying
92a: if only good people recovered, most of us would be doomed
92b: life is half working, half dancing

Lao-Tzu   (6th century B.C.)   93

93a: a thousand days of sobriety begin with the first step
93b: simplicity, patience and compassion are the treasures
94a: there is no endpoint of sobriety
94b: resisting change only creates sorrow
95a: those who know do not speak
95b: there is no need to overtake anyone
96a: let go of notions of who you are to be who you can be
96b: you can always make time for what is valuable
97a: caring about what people think makes me their prisoner
97b: accepting myself is possible at any moment
98a: every life is full; nothing is missing
98b: stop thinking and end your problems
99a: do not be in a hurry to act
99b: recovery calls for conscious, deliberate, moral effort
100a: depression is living in the past; anxiety is living in the future

100b: you have no entitlement to any particular result
101a: if you don't change, you'll go where you are heading
101b: your job is simply to make the best decisions you can
102a: as a sponsor, do you get angry when disobeyed or ignored?
102b: it is the rigid oak that breaks, not the supple blade of grass
103a: the end for the caterpillar is the beginning for the butterfly
103b: every goal is possible from where you are now
104a: the wise man knows what he does not know
104b: stop searching, and you will see
105a: manage yourself, not others
105b: if you correct your thinking, all else will follow
106a: thoughts simply appear in your head; laugh at them
106b: do not insist that everyone walks your path
107a: perfection is the willingness to be imperfect
107b: not seeing the self as self
108a: wisdom is knowing others; enlightenment is knowing yourself
108b: your actions should depend on you, not on others
109a: the sage does not hard
109b: sobriety is based on perseverance
110a: if you are seeking wealth, be generous with your money
110b: it is the emptiness of the pot that gives it value
111a: the more you know, the less teachable you are
111b: sobriety is neither earned nor possessed

Nietzsche   (1844 - 1900)   112

112a: God is dead, or at least, rendered lifeless
112b: alcoholism has made me stronger
113a: is there a correct interpretation?
113b: no price is too high to own yourself
114a: finding meaning in suffering
114b: acceptance removes the need for faith
115a: hope prolongs the torments of man
115b: become comfortable among people who disagree with you
116a: love your enemies but also hate your friends
116b: love is not just blind; it is blindness
117a: faith: not wanting to know the truth
117b: experiencing the lightness of being
118a: do not expect to fly into recovery
118b: religiousness is a disease
119a: every complaint already contains revenge
119b: facts do not cease to exist because they are ignored
120a: in heaven, all the interesting people are missing
120b: the abyss will gaze back at you
121a: there are no facts; only interpretations
121b: art is necessary so you are not killed by truth
122a: lying to yourself is the most common lie
122b: the demand to be loved is so arrogant
123a: does God really need to be praised all the time?
123b: turning difficulties into advantage
124a: listen to the message, not the messenger
124b: he who gets angry has already lost the argument
125a: I am always followed by a dog named ego
125b: fear is the mother of morality

126a: God could be one of man's blunders
126b: sharing suffering and sharing joy
127a: do not be vain about your virtues
127b: forgetting your purpose makes you stupid
128a: people's convictions make them dangerous
128b: the body knows better than the mind
129a: talking as a way of hiding
129b: religion can be a drug
130a: is there virtue in demeaning yourself?
130b: loving actions are beyond good and evil
131a: the truth cannot be contained in words
131b: extremism begets extremism
132a: praise or blame? Both are madness
132b: kindness is sparing people their shame
133a: shared experiences make understanding possible
133b: is the truth alright or do you prefer your illusions?
134a: do not be afraid of work and effort
134b: what is great in you exists only when you are reaching out
135a: the birthing process is chaotic
135b: don't become monstrous to fight a monster

Nisargadatta   (1897 - 1981)   136

136a: anticipation and hope make you insecure
136b: how about not offering resistance to trouble?
137a: even the desire for truth is a desire
137b: the idea of cause is an 1
138a: by helping yourself you help everybody
138b: it is always the false that makes you suffer
139a: when you demand nothing, expect nothing, awakening happens
139b: you cannot transcend what you do not know
140a: past and future are creations of the mind
140b: the unblemished serenity of a simple mind
141a: the journey itself is the destination of recovery
141b: the urge to drink is not wrong, but the act of drinking is
142a: only the deepest and truest thing can make you happy
142b: begin for now, by clearing up misunderstanding
143a: nothing is ever wrong; everything is just what it is
143b: if you can quieten the mind, everything will follow naturally
144a: do deal with alcohol, you must know and understand alcohol
144b: your spiritual awakening has already happened
145a: absolute perfection is exactly what is
145b: happiness is the booby prize
146a: sobriety is not a reward for being good
146b: all you need, you already have
147a: you are nothing, and you are everything
147b: faith is not propped up by events or explanations
148a: the spirit can cross the barriers the mind creates
148b: a quiet mind is all you need
149a: why spend all that energy building a prison for yourself?
149b: the river never flows into the rocks
150a: what you think important is not
150b: happiness is not about circumstances or situations
151a: the only thing that can trouble you is your imagination

151b: love is an overflowing
152a: meditation is stopping of words, of commentary
152b: to be yourself, you have to stop seeking
153a: every day contain all of life in it; it is complete
153b: there is no way to not drink
154a: if you attend meetings, are you in recovery?
154b: you are getting perturbed by your own imaginings
155a: as long as you think you exist, you will have fear
155b: there is nothing to do; just be
156a: there is no sugar; only sweetness exists
156b: don't be fooled; survival is only temporary

Epictetus   (55 - 135 A.D)   157

157a: insanity is worrying about things you cannot change
157b: philosophy is not to be explained, but lived
158a: the less you want, the richer you become
158b: do you think you have to be faultless to survive?
159a: everything is possible if you will do what it takes
159b: don't just read the book; use the reading
160a: problems are not the problem; anxiety is the problem
160b: your concern about looking good is keeping you from improving
161a: people who make you feel bad are not useful
161b: life is not the cards you are dealt; life is how you play them
162a: no one can make you angry
162b: you can keep postponing growth and one day you die
163a: learn to laugh at yourself and you will never be bored
163b: two ears, one mouth: what does that tell you?
164a: everyone must find his or her own path to heaven
164b: difficulties reveal who you are
165a: when you have spoken, stop and sit down; don't go on and on
165b: when you are seeking your path, don't look for approval
166a: do not grieve for what is not; appreciate an enjoy what is
166b: criticism: either accept it or laugh it off
167a: wish for things to be whichever way they are
167b: events arrive by appointment
168a: do not try to appear wise? or humble
168b: life presents difficulties so you can grow
169a: you are not responsible for things working out
169b: understand where you end, and someone else begins
170a: philosophers take responsibility; vulgar people blame others
170b: getting rid of your personality

Montaigne   (1533 - 1592)   171

171a: wisdom leads to cheerfulness
171b: fear of suffering is worse than suffering itself
172a: self-esteem is based on what you think others think of you
172b: you are not one thing; you are made of multitudes
173a: books banish the clouds from your mind
173b: you can learn from others but you have to get to wisdom yourself
174a: obsession can be either madness or genius
174b: wrestling a thought down is like wrestling a porcupine
175a: education teaches us to rationalize anything
175b: if you become honest yourself, you will be able to trust others

176a: longing requires no effort; striving requires effort
176b: when you let go, things turn out
177a: surrender is the doorway to freedom
177b: every person contains the entire human condition
178a: what is the point of speaking nonsense solemnly?
178b: knowledge of how to live well is hard to acquire
179a: if you have no destination, you are never lost
179b: most of the things you worry about will never happen
180a: you should not have to shout to make your point
180b: you cannot manage the world; it is easier to manage yourself
181a: don't discuss yourself; it is a losing proposition
181b: spiritually evolved souls have no need for rigidity
182a: there are no angels or saints in recovery
182b: it is easy to slip into lethargy in recovery
183a: do not do anything that is not good and kind
183b: it is not the length of sobriety but the depth
184a: sobriety is the walk, not the destination
184b: do you need people who disagree with you to stumble and fall?
185a: don't just agree; disagree or add something
185b: age adds wrinkles to your opinions

Maya Angelou   (1928 - 2014)   186

186a: you have some choice on how down you get
186b: people are beautiful because of all they have been through
187a: the need for change will make itself apparent
187b: even the people you resent are God's creation
188a: words need to be spoken to infuse them with meaning
188b: potential is simply ability that is not realized
189a: self-acceptance is the most valuable thing to teach your children
189b: recovery cannot be just dry; it has to have passion
190a: nature does not shirk from punishing stupidity and stubbornness
190b: as long as you know how to love, you will survive
191a: what were the consequences in childhood, of making a mistake?
191b: self-pity feels comforting until it sets and hardens
192a: facts can obscure truth
192b: your personal tragedy could become boring to others
193a: do not get greedy about enjoyment
193b: we are children inside, innocent and shy as magnolias
194a: stop complaining to people who cannot change it, whatever it is
194b: are you trembling in anticipation of discovering the real you?

Virginia Satir   (1916 - 1988)   195

195a: you must not be defined by how others see you
195b: life is whatever it is; it is how you deal with it that counts
196a: approaching others from healthy, mature boundaries
196b: discard what doesn't fit and invent something new in its place
197a: problems are deeper than how they appear
197b: treat your body gently, with honor, and with love
198a: you can go far beyond where you are right now
198b: finding yourself means giving up your shoulds
199a: taste everything but swallow only what fits
199b: the Chinese symbol for crisis also means opportunity
200a: people will do anything to avoid uncertainty and ambiguity

200b: the biggest problem is thinking we know when we don't
201a: if you hang out only with people like you, you'll never grow
201b: meaning does not exist; it is created by the human mind
202a: you need twelve hugs a day
202b: unity in recovery means tolerating differences
203a: see, hear, understand, and touch another person
203b: you cannot live so as not to hurt or disappoint anyone
204a: we are all children pretending to be adults
204b: we are not concerned about your problems, but your solutions
205a: let life unfold at its own pace

Emerson   (1803 - 1882)   205

205b: glory is not in never failing but in rising up every time you fail
206a: every comment and every speaker has impacted my recovery
206b: the glory of friendship is in having someone who believes in you
207a: what you see out there is a reflection of what exists inside you
207b: what lies behind/before us are tiny vs.what lies inside us
208a: being yourself in a world that is constantly trying to change you
208b: go where there is no path but leave a trail
209a: you can never again not know what has been revealed
209b: gather the nectar from many flowers; make your own bible
210a: what you do drowns out your claims of who you are
210b: there will always be people to tell you: you are wrong
211a: life must be lived to be understood
211b: the purpose of life is not happiness
212a: it is not the length of life, but the depth
212b: you should be grateful for everything, good and bad
213a: do not postpone kind deeds
213b: the newcomer will inspire you to be what you can be
214a: you must go beyond what you have already mastered
214b: there is creative reading, not just creative writing
215a: the longer you persist in not drinking, the easier it becomes
215b: for everything you miss, you gain something else
216a: consistency can be foolish
216b: most ideas and thoughts have been expressed before
217a: do not forget to marvel at things you see every day
217b: you can find solitude in the middle of a crowd
218a: a sponsor's job is to elicit promises and hold you accountable
218b: don't waste life in doubts and fears
219a: seek perfection in order to make progress
219b: sorrow looks back; worry looks around; faith looks up
220a: you cannot help someone without helping yourself
220b: comfort, smiles, rainbows, laughter: our collective wish for you

Simone Weil   (1909 - 1943)   221

221a: struggling against anguish only produces more anguish
221b: if you are seeking love, learn to give love
222a: humility is attentive patience
222b: an atheist may simply be focusing on impersonal aspects of God
223a: suppressing doubts is a form of tyranny
223b: the highest ecstasy is full attention
224a: you are responsible for helping when you have the chance
224b: sins are attempts to fly from emptiness

225a: do not be proud of your large cell in the prison
225b: reality can only be attained by someone who is detached
226a: love is best characterized by interest and listening
226b: most unhappy people have not received the attention they need
227a: the job of a sponsor is to make himself or herself redundant
227b: it is only the impossible that is possible for God
228a: the future is made of the same stuff as the present
228b: a mind enclosed in language is in prison
229a: what is real is going to be hard and rough
229b: contemplation is superior to agreeing or disagreeing
230a: do not allow mysteries to degenerate into beliefs
230b: life need not mutilate itself in order to be pure
231a: everything is a privilege, not a right
231b: your disappointment with the newcomer must not turn to anger
232a: recovery is not a self-help program
232b: when you are parched and thirsty, a glass of water is heaven
233a: your attention to others is the purest form of generosity
233b: you always possess in you what you report as desire
234a: to be rooted is the most important need of the soul
234b: persistent effort will, one day, suddenly produce results
235a: God's love for you is the reason to love yourself
235b: compassion directed at yourself is true humility
236a: grace can only enter where there is emptiness
236b: imagining something out there has to change is a path to misery
237a: God crosses the universe and comes to you
237b: joy, as well as suffering, must inspire your gratitude
238a: the only way to truth is by destroying the ego
238b: your troubles will not disappear but they will be transformed

Carl Jung   (1875 - 1961)   239

239a: knowing God is different from believing in God
239b: it is stupid to prove or to disprove God
240a: develop a healthy ego and then let go of it
240b: things are not as they are but as how you look at them
241a: God is the name for everything that changes your path
241b: finding meaning makes a great many things endurable
242a: the impulses in my soul are more real than things outside of me
242b: we do not invent myth; it shows up by itself
243a: every addiction is bad: alcohol, narcotics or idealism
243b: the attainment of wholeness requires complete surrender
244a: spiritual awakening is the fruit of an inward journey
244b: inner experience is as valid as outer reality
245a: you cannot change anything until you accept it
245b: know your own darkness
246a: difficulties are necessary to wake you up
246b: a tree can tell you more than you can find in a book
247a: beware of a sponsor who has the same advice for everybody
247b: you cannot love anyone if you hate yourself
248a: enlightenment is making the darkness conscious
248b: your pride is compensation for low self-esteem
249a: learning from grandiosity and inflation is impossible
249b: true self-acceptance can be terrifying
250a: the fundamental problems of life cannot be solved, only outgrown

250b: your parents dumped their unfilled ambitions on you
251a: even your imagined illnesses can kill you
251b: loneliness comes from not being understood
252a: every emotion you experience declares that you are human
252b: you are not what happened to you, but who you choose to become
253a: just because you got sober does not mean troubles will go away
253b: there can be no love where there is power
254a: what you wish to change in others is to be changed in yourself
254b: neither worship joy nor be terrified of sadness
255a: wholeness is achieved by integration of the contraries
255b: do not content yourself with inadequate or superficial answers
256a: existence is a darkness until illuminated by a spiritual awakening
256b: all growth is accompanied by loss

Gurdjieff   (1866 - 1949)   256

257a: emotional faith is slavery and mechanical faith is foolishness
257b: most people are unwilling to give up suffering and victimhood
258a: recovery is a long, engrossing journey fueled by perseverance
258b: who you are is different each moment
259a: infinite are the stupidity of man and the mercy of God
259b: your internal and external struggles must come together
260a: common aim is stronger than blood
260b: do not believe in things that you cannot verify for yourself
261a: thank everyone who gives you an opportunity to struggle
261b: great knowledge can come to you from studying yourself
262a: gratitude without action is mere fantasy
262b: most people on the planet are asleep
263a: if you recognize something is wrong, you also know what is right
263b: deciding to be honest with yourself elevates you from humanity
264a: we all talk a good deal too much
264b: not necessary to have faith in God but to trust the process
265a: you must awake in order to die
265b: recovery is the process of dying and being reborn
266a: man is a machine; his reactions are mindless and predictable
266b: your reaction to people depends of the story you have about them
267a: your awe when you gaze on something majestic is from God
267b: in recovery, we are all trying to be remarkable men and women
268a: if you want to lose your faith, make friends with a priest
268b: each day you must take off your mask, little by little
269a: only help those who are willing to work
269b: being is not passive; it comes from a spiritual awakening
270a: by teaching others you will learn yourself
270b: you must leave every meeting different from the one who came in

Martin Buber   (1878 - 1965)   271

271a: journeys have secret destinations of which the traveler is unaware
271b: when people really meet, God is the electricity between them
272a: the atheist is nearer to God than the believer with false images
272b: everyone comes out of their exile of drinking in their own way
273a: recovery requires doing with your whole being
273b: your meetings with people and conversations define who you are
274a: you cannot comprehend people, but you can embrace them
274b: solitude is where you purify yourself

275a: thinking about self-absorption is still self-absorption
275b: allow who you are to emerge fresh each moment
276a: if someone comes to you for help, do not tell them to go, pray
276b: the desire to help others can come from generosity or from ego
277a: the goal of recovery is to be human, not a God
277b: say what you mean and do what you say
278a: spiritual awakening can lead to awe and trembling, but not always
278b: something special occurs when one alcoholic works with another
279a: a sponsor must reveal his or her own humanity
279b: correction does much but encouragement does more
280a: give up the drive for fame, recognition and self-affirmation
280b: it is impossible to avoid the word God but it can mean anything
281a: no matter how old you are, you can always begin
281b: you are constantly giving birth to yourself
282a: you cannot confine yourself to books; you must see faces
282b: the real struggle is between education and propaganda

Plato   (c. 424 B.C. - 348 B.C.)   283

283a: willingness is not enough; you must do
283b: be kind, for everyone you meet is fighting a hard battle
284a: we transmit our wisdom through stories and storytelling
284b: the beginning is the most important part of recovery
285a: the tragedy of life is when men and women are afraid of the light
285b: even slow progress is encouraging
286a: a rat from the sewers is confused and afraid of daylight
286b: do not confuse having a thought of drinking for actual thinking
287a: I know one thing and that is that I know nothing
287b: courage is knowing what not to fear
288a: everyone can find willing partners to sing the song of sobriety
288b: character is simply habit long continued
289a: connecting with the inherent goodness in you, you need no books
289b: learn to desire the right things
290a: if you can change it or if you cannot—don't get angry
290b: avoid people who are threatened by your change and growth
291a: truth is more important than honor
291b: if you have nothing to say, don't take five minutes to prove it
292a: long proclamations of humility, gratitude, devotion are cover-ups
292b: help each newcomer to unveil his own talents and genius
293a: in deep recovery we live in this world but are not of it
293b: the wealthiest people are the ones who are content with little
294a: forced exercise can do you good, but not forced knowledge
294b: the meaning of things lie not in the speaker but in the listener
295a: humility is the greatest achievement possible but is invisible
295b: man is a being in search of meaning
296a: it took a wise man to invent God
296b: serenity cannot be based on things being any particular way
297a: reverence for sobriety and recovery is the greatest asset
297b: the unexamined life is not worth living
298a: no need to take an oath of abstinence; it does not work anyway
298b: if you have found the real truth, you will not be seeking validation

299a: in sobriety, you are accepting immense responsibility
299b: recovery is a rebellion against your own darkness
300a: do not become a blind follower of a spiritual guide or sponsor
300b: meditation is noticing that you are not your thoughts
301a: meditation needs the presence of other meditators
301b: the one you are looking for is you; find yourself
302a: you cannot surrender little by little; it is all or nothing
302b: your job is simply to become a witness to your process
303a: your roots of sadness allow your tree of happiness to grow
303b: nobody can make you angry; nobody can make you happy
304a: if you love a flower, don't pick it up
304b: are you willing to be happy without knowing that you are happy?
305a: be realistic; plan for a miracle
305b: in deep recovery, there are no footprints to follow
306a: truth is different from facts
306b: self-consciousness is really a lack of consciousness
307a: you need to silence your own chatter to listen to God
307b: nobody can do two steps at a time in recovery
308a: you can be restored to sanity if you simply cooperate
308b: you can live as if today is your last day; you can live as if forever
309a: meditate fifteen minutes daily—but half an hour if you are busy
309b: freedom is moving from rules to no rules and back again
310a: meditation is simply the gap between words
310b: you can turn your life over to God as you understand her
311a: the moment powerlessness was born, a Higher Power was born
311b: jump into the program; we will teach you to desire sobriety
312a: your petty complaints will disappear when you find purpose
312b: pursuit of Truth and pursuit of Love both lead to the same peak
313a: your existence is a penetration of eternity into the here and now
313b: you can celebrate your existence without laying down conditions
314a: you will find meaning only if you create it
314b: nothing that is great can be possessed or owned
315a: in love the other is important; in lust you are important
315b: loneliness is the pain, solitude the glory, of being alone
316a: what rules stop you from dancing, painting, from making poetry?
316b: trees and flowers are happy for no reason at all; so can you be
317a: what exists is not God but Godliness
317b: love is not a feeling, but a state of being; who you are is love
318a: a sponsor is not a master but a friend
318b: the ultimate goal in recovery is enlightened self-acceptance
319a: wounds and difficulties make you alert; bring you close to God
319b: you are unique just like everyone else; do not try to be special
320a: the tumult and chaos of drinking was exciting to you
320b: simply absorbing and repeating clichés will not keep you sober
321a: recovery is a true anarchy with no authorities
321b: a sponsor can inspire you to inquire, cannot give you the truth
322a: freedom from is different from freedom to
322b: recovery is about opening others up to possibility

323a: God is a circle whose center is everywhere
323b: playing the game of life with the cards you have been dealt
324a: the soul is not accessible through thoughts or thinking
324b: at every meeting, you should seek out someone new to you
325a: announce your questions rather than your answers
325b: read to turn inwards; dance to turn outwards
326a: it is madness to think you know how to get anyone sober
326b: if someone claims to know God's will for you, be very careful
327a: you cannot get frozen by the ideas and opinions you have today
327b: you must raise yourself above the thinking that surrounds you
328a: God is a comedian, but the audience is afraid to laugh
328b: the most dangerous thing in the world is opinions
329a: if you are justifying something to yourself, you are already lying
329b: you are never proud when you are alone
330a: can A.A. preach individual change while itself refusing change?
330b: one use of words is to hide your thoughts
331a: decide to be in a good mood: an important decision you can make
331b: rambling at meetings is irresponsible, selfish and boring
332a: faith can inspire and move us to get sober; reason often cannot
332b: there is a big difference between having life and being alive
333a: there is no shortcut to the regimen of work required in recovery
333b: the longer you dwell misfortunes, the more they can harm you
334a: you can be free of the power of alcohol the instant you want to be
334b: since there are no authorities, you can criticize anything
335a: when something is made illegal, it acquires a mystique and charm
335b: you can invent and invoke sacredness and a sense of the deep
336a: if the ship is wrecked, you should sing in the lifeboats
336b: it is in the seeking and not in the finding that your purpose lies
337a: no matter where you go, there you are
337b: do not pray to God to change the world; pray to change you
338a: we get together, shake hands, drink bad coffee, tell stories, laugh
338b: do not indulge in foolish and false optimism; practice acceptance

Tertullian   **(c. 160 - 225 A.D.)**   **339**

339a: hope is patience while keeping the lamp lit
339b: no point in hanging someone if he is not averse to the idea
340a: you wouldn't exist if your ancestors were fearless
340b: nothing that is God's can be bought with money
341a: truth is often the enemy, and it is hated
341b: the seed of a thought can contain an entire ruined life
342a: you cannot turn just some things over to God
342b: is your continued survival of benefit to anyone else?
343a: faith is necessary because belief in God is irrational
343b: arguments about the Book achieve stomachaches and headaches
344a: flee from the battle with alcohol to win the war with alcoholism
344b: alcoholism is the same soul-sickness no matter what language
345a: we do not persuade the newcomer; we let the truth teach
345b: truth has no embarrassment about being fully seen
346a: out of the frying pan into the fire
346b: you should not preach your religion under the guise of recovery
347a: you have it in your power to begin the world over again
347b: you cannot undo your wrongs, but you can make amends

Wittgenstein   (1889 - 1951)   348

348a: for a truly religious man, nothing is tragic
348b: through the inquiry, who am I? the mind subsides
349a: the whole truth can set you free but partial truth can terrify you
349b: "principles before personalities," refers to your personality
350a: all transformation begins with confession about what is
350b: the rigid oak that gets broken by the storm, not the blade of grass
351a: each Step is a little adjustment of the dial until the safe opens up
351b: the mystical starts with the perception of is-ness of the universe
352a: self-acceptance will give you the courage to make amends
352b: philosophy is not a theory but an activity
353a: choices of others do not concern you, your own reactions should
353b: your view of the world is determined by the language you use
354a: wisdom is passionless but faith is a passion
354b: all beliefs are structures built on foundations that are made up
355a: deep philosophical concepts can be conveyed through humor
355b: spirituality must break out from the limits imposed by language
356a: enjoying yourself cannot become the purpose of living
356b: on the down escalator, keep moving just to retain your place
357a: if you could will yourself to sobriety, you wouldn't need A.A.
357b: if a lion could talk we could not understand him
358a: only silence can speak about God; words are inadequate
358b: honesty with yourself may be out of reach, willingness to be so, is
359a: do not take full credit for your sobriety; you owe it to the horse
359b: much of your struggles come from not realizing that you are free
360a: you cannot tell someone how to get sober; you must show them
360b: eternal life is available to those fully immersed in the now
361a: the speaker makes comments that even he does not understand
361b: even if life exists after death, what does that solve?

Kierkegaard   (1813 - 1855)   362

362a: sobriety is a by-product of action towards spiritual growth
362b: focus on the work; do not second-guess yourself
363a: you must find an idea to live and die for
363b: bring your emptiness to God
364a: let go of the idea of problems
364b: are you using the freedom of thought?
365a: facing the fact about who you are
365b: remember to love yourself
366a: boredom is the refusal to be yourself
366b: by labeling me you freeze me
367a: pray to change yourself, not to influence God
367b: mending broken relationships may take time
368a: it is impossible to grasp God objectively
368b: responsibility is a terrifying idea
369a: it is your own enormity that frightens you
369b: surely, the purpose of life is not enjoyment
370a: slow down to savor pleasure
370b: your wounds gives you character
371a: your eagerness to impress others is a search for acceptance
371b: idleness contains goodness; don't be in a frenzy
372a: giving advice is the lazy way of helping
372b: when do you give up on someone?

373a: trouble is our common denominator
373b: possibility is everything
374a: faith as the highest passion in the human
374b: the ultimate source of happiness is within you
375a: misunderstanding is inevitable; so whát?
375b: to learn humility, withdraw from the turmoil

Merton   (1915 - 1968)   376

376a: with true love it is impossible to be disappointed
376b: the prayer of abandonment
377a: experience gratitude for existence itself
377b: let in the goodness of God
378a: love those who are worthy and those who are not
378b: you can overcome your fear of suffering
379a: solitude is defense against materialism
379b: focus on the Steps, not the Promises
380a: your idea of God reflects your own limitation
380b: self-acceptance is the highest ambition
381a: there is more comfort in silence than in answers
381b: attempting too much is a form of violence on self
382a: if you decide to write for God, God will write for you
382b: reason is a path leading to faith
383a: it is an error to be concerned about how others judge you
383b: clean out the rubbish in your mind with silence
384a: freedom comes from knowing that it may all end any moment
384b: be at peace with loneliness
385a: live fully for something
385b: connection is an antidote for despair
386a: living cannot be postponed
386b: God's love frees you to see your defects
387a: you are always beginning
387b: stop beating yourself up for beating yourself up
388a: peace with God is the source of all peace
388b: you are responsible for finding yourself and living your life
389a: authenticity is the doorway to God
389b: false pride is bad, but real pride is just as bad

Alan Watts   (1915 - 1973)   390

390a: it is useless trying to define yourself
390b: are you taking life too seriously?
391a: be completely engaged with what is in front of you
391b: life is about being fully alive now
392a: plunge into the dance of change
392b: in the now, there is no concept of change
393a: nothing is wrong; nobody is wrong
393b: tomorrow need not be better
394a: peeling potatoes is more important than thinking about God
394b: whoever you are trying to control is controlling you
395a: feel free to be anxious
395b: there is no escape
396a: laughter in the presence of God is sacred
396b: wanting security is what's making you insecure
397a: you are missing life, waiting for something

397b: consciousness is nerve-racking
398a: dance as if there is no audience
398b: no regret, no gratitude, no complaint
399a: poetry: saying what cannot be said
399b: everyone is telling you what your role is

Cicero   (106 B.C. - 46 B.C.)   400

400a: God sees but is not seen
400b: only an idiot persists in his error
401a: gratitude makes ordinary things glow
401b: mistakes that have lasted two thousand years
402a: little voices also need to be heard
402b: the enemy is not alcohol
403a: not going with your first impulse
403b: forgiveness is seeing there is nothing to forgive
404a: authorities are barriers to learning
404b: it takes time for new neural pathways to form
405a: is sorrow reduced by baldness?
405b: the importance of sometimes doing nothing
406a: knowing the Steps will not keep you sober
406b: even a poor inventory is better than none
407a: the wisdom of absurdity
407b: don't drink and don't make a big fuss about it
408a: not tolerating intolerance
408b: the silence between comments
409a: justified anger is resentment
409b: authenticity needs no justification
410a: enjoying life for free
410b: in recovery, we cannot neglect obligations

INDEX by Subject

creation, 363b
crisis, 199b
criticism, 161a, 191a, 195a, 210b, 267b, 334a
crowd-funding, 89a
dance, 117b, 325b, 392a, 398a
darkness, 55b, 90a
death, 9b, 50b, 56a, 86a, 87a, 103a, 177a, 265b, 360b
debate, 124b
decision(s), 80a; 97b; 101b, 105a, 141b, 157a, 169a, 169b, 186a, 272b, 311b, 331a, 362b
deep structure, 124a, 196b, 197a, 218b
deeper knowing, 62a
default reaction, see default setting
default setting, 36a, 99a, 105b, 162a, 165b, 267b, 316b
defecation, 182a
defects, see character defects
defining myself, 390a
demands, 122b
denial, 91b
dent your drinking, 209a
denying pain, 370b
dependence, 300a
depression, see grief, loss, sadness, loneliness, acceptance, etc.
depth, 212a
deserving love, 122b
desire(s), 12a, 71b, 75b, 137a, 139a, 141b, 151a, 158a, 233b
despair, 55b, 90a, 191b, 385b
destination, 179a
destinations, 271a
destiny,147b, 312a
detachment, see attachment
diamond, 59b
differences, 202b
difficulties, 3b, 21b, 71b, 84a, 89a, 90b, 91a, 112b, 123b, 161b, 168b, 186a, 232b, 246a, 323b, 373a; see also pain, suffering, troubles, misfortune
disagreement, 184b, 404a
disciple, 318a
discipline, 28b, 99a, 188b, 277b, 283a, 333a, 369a
discomfort, 197a, 200a
discovery, 361a
disillusionment, 133b
disorder, 15b
disordered mind, 404b

dissatisfaction, 232b
disturbance prayer, 152a
diversity, 106b, 115b, 164a, 201a, 202b, 247a, 269a, 312b, 344b
divine, 65a
do the next right thing, 32a, 218b
doctrine, 69a
dog, 125a
dogma, 181b
doing nothing, 405b
doing see also actions, 283a
doing too much, 381b
domination, 253b, 334a, 394b
doubt, 126a, 218b, 223a,
dreams, 50b, 66b, 93a, 139a, 154b, 156a, 198a, 229a, 244a, 304b, 391b
drinking dreams, 356b
drinking thoughts, 106a
dying, see death
easy does it, 390b, 396b
ecstasy, 17b, 63b, 223b, 301b
education, 75a, 81b, 180a, 200a, 280a, 286b, 289b
efficiency vs. thoroughness, 307b
effort, 99a, 112b, 176a
effort and result, 100b, 169a, 362b
ego, 40b, 47a, 107b, 124a, 125a, 139b, 232a, 240a, 249a, 276b, 280a, 295a, 302a,
Eighth Step, see Step 8
Elevent Step, see Step 11
embarrassment, 345b
embodied self, 64a; see also body
embrace, 274a
emerging self, 172b, 258b, 275b
emotional safety, 340a
empathy, 177b, 231b
emptiness, 27a, 56b, 67b, 70a, 110b, 111a, 139a, 147a, 152b, 224b, 236a, 363b
encouragement, 59b, 161a, 206b, 210b, 231b, 279b, 283b, 285a
enemies, 116a
enemy within, 402b
enjoyment, 29a, 94a, 141a, 184a, 193a, 308b, 356a, 369b
enlightenment, 56b, 70b, 72b, 137a, 144b, 148b, 155a, 155b, 248a, 351b
enthusiasm, 44b
entitlement, 100b, 122b, 225b; see also rights
entry point, 53a
envy, see jealousy
equanimity, 254b, 375b

152a,
randomness, 241a
rationalization, 85a, 108a, 110a, 149a,
358b, 402b; see also justification
reaction, 165b, 166b, see first thought
reactiveness, 61b, 203b
reading, 159b, 173a, 206a, 214b, 325b
reality, 69b, 117a, 129b, 140a, 225b,
229a, 240a, 327a, 331a, 341a,
393b364a
reason and faith, 382b
reasons, see why
reasonable, 54a, 148a
rebellion, 203b, 299b
rebirth, 9b, 103a, 177a, 103a, 265b,
299b
recollection, 286b
recovery after stopping drinking, 118a
regimen, 333a
regrets, 98b, 122b, 136a, 140a, 151a,
174b, 219b, 345b, 398b
relapse, 2a, 2b, 16a, 159b
relatedness, 66b, 224b, 271b, 394b;
278b; see also, connection
relationship, 105a, 169b, 280a, 317b,
376a, 393a
religion, 1a, 64b, 106b, 118b, 129b,
164a, 181b, 223a, 244b, 262a, 326b,
328a, 346b
- and humor, 396a
remembering, 201b
renunciation, 40b, 75b
resentment, 77b, 88b, 119a, 136b,
169b, 187b, 221b, 259a, 339b, 392b,
403b, 405a, 409a
- avoiding resentment, 19a, 28a, 77b,
119a, 169b, 187b, 277b, 407b, 409a
resignation, 6b, 73b
responding, 108b, 186a, 403a
responding vs. reacting, 165b, 195b,
252b
responsibility, 88a, 115a, 157a, 169a,
169b, 170a, 180b, 224a, 236b, 299a,
303b, 368b, 388b
resting, 356b
restlessness, 140b
restraint, 267b
results, 39b, 100b, 234b, 379b; see
also effort
resurrection, 9b; see also rebirth
returning, 301b
revealed, 294b
revenge, 77b, 88a, 119a, 221b
reward, 32a, 32b, 43b, 92a, 146a, 234b

reverence, 33a, 146b, 199b, 225a,
297a
riches, 14b, 29a
right way, 113a, 263a
righteousness, 11a, 125a, 162a, 349b;
see also justification
rights, 231a; see also entitlement
rigidity, 76b, 102b, 106b, 163b, 181b,
327a, 350b
risk-taking, 198b
river, 57b, 66a, 67b, 149b
roots, 234a, 303a
rules, 181b, 298a, 309a, 321a
running away, 395b
sacred books, 64b
sacredness, 335b
sadness, 50a, 190b, 254b, 303a
safety, 180a
sanctimoniousness, 118b, 130a
sanity, 2b, 114b, 195a, 308a; see also
insanity
scratch, 71b
scripture, 22a, 63a, 320b, 343b
second-guessing, 362b, 388b
Second Step, see Step 2
second thought prayer, 165b
seed, 341b
seeking, 7a, 9a, 10b, 23a, 23b, 25a,
237a, 336b
seeking God, see seeking, paths to
God, looking for God
self, 82b
- as sacred, 230b
Self (as in Higher Self), 50a, 70b, 142a,
144b, 240a, 244b, 301b
self-absorption, 275a, see also, self-
centeredness
self-acceptance, 18a, 84b, 97b, 107a,
170a, 170b, 172a, 197b, 249b, 270a,
279b, 318b, 371a, 380b, 388a
self-actualization, see indivduation
self-awareness, 108b, 143b
self-centeredness, 12a, 26b, 275a,
342b, 402b; see also narcissism,
selfishness,
self-centeredness prayer, 342b
self-condemnation, 97b, 105b, 146b,
174b, 181a, 230b, 249b; see also
self-deprecation, beating myself up,
feeling bad, self-love
self-consciousness, 306b, 398a
self-deception, 358b
self-deprecation, 50a, 158b, 163a,
174b, 230b, 251a, see also self-love

To use this book for daily contemplation,
select the page number for today, and go to that page.

Date	Jan	Feb	Mar	Apr	May	Jun	Jul	Aug	Sep	Oct	Nov	Dec
1	41	192	100	280	234	193	60	203	103	373	329	59
2	56	107	54	332	341	188	318	321	284	378	367	355
3	166	35	122	384	161	402	351	352	260	10	264	172
4	305	344	361	350	198	149	246	230	51	20	301	24
5	62	185	338	393	386	169	226	13	195	272	328	259
6	295	23	222	187	262	133	8	71	397	311	224	97
7	371	19	370	6	359	81	281	52	218	34	44	140
8	11	37	275	53	43	190	85	104	183	73	236	112
9	363	65	199	238	26	300	233	125	331	31	366	3
10	285	186	134	196	68	403	95	99	55	158	299	216
11	113	127	375	82	138	181	167	42	253	383	105	261
12	287	25	30	390	368	283	76	50	252	156	353	143
13	369	263	220	342	119	207	47	116	387	286	129	148
14	70	92	131	254	89	266	358	48	395	87	400	72
15	200	408	146	45	225	404	135	382	244	270	269	214
16	221	184	405	257	175	282	372	9	376	124	80	159
17	380	401	14	111	77	7	157	152	171	304	250	365
18	302	339	46	209	154	406	202	79	265	33	255	36
19	15	201	276	277	16	27	337	223	407	128	139	320
20	162	388	160	110	86	268	309	69	306	4	182	396
21	176	114	153	102	289	197	392	297	155	391	245	232
22	205	179	364	22	241	315	381	235	115	66	356	174
23	173	243	410	170	12	239	345	271	191	340	130	94
24	32	141	88	237	96	399	357	28	314	217	290	346
25	177	303	63	120	298	279	335	17	147	137	132	83
26	330	38	150	108	324	291	208	313	231	308	242	64
27	258	385	98	67	240	327	123	296	307	180	267	58
28	213	168	325	194	21	74	142	118	90	40	343	409
29	106	312	163	210	204	61	334	288	326	212	93	228
30	2		211	84	336	151	379	189	348	164	278	248
31	101		349		121		274	251		273		310

This book contains 410 pages of quotes but there are 365
or 366 days in a year. So 366 pages have been included
randomly in the table above.

The remaining 44 pages not listed in the daily readings
table are:
    1,   5,   18,   29,   39,   49,   57,   75,   78,   91, 109,
117, 136, 144, 145, 165, 178, 206, 215, 219, 227, 229,
247, 249, 256, 292, 293, 294, 316, 317, 319, 322, 323,
333, 347, 354, 360, 362, 374, 377, 389, 394, 398, 401.

Please visit these also; they may contain gems for you.